The Irish Legal Sy

The Irish Legal System

By

Allison Kenneally
BCL, BA, LLM, PgCert,

John Tully
LLB, LLM, Barrister (Middle Temple), PGCE, PG Cert

CLARUS PRESS

Published by
Clarus Press Ltd,
Griffith Campus,
South Circular Road,
Dublin 8.

Typeset by
Deanta Global Publishing Services

Printed by
Sprint Print,
Dublin

ISBN
978-1-905536-58-0

All rights reserved. No part of this publication may be reproduced, or transmitted in any form or by any means, including recording and photocopying, without the written permission of the copyright holder, application for which should be addressed to the publisher. Written permission should also be obtained before any part of the publication is stored in a retrieval system of any nature.

Disclaimer

Whilst every effort has been made to ensure that the contents of this book are accurate, neither the publisher or authors can accept responsibility for any errors or omissions or loss occasioned to any person acting or refraining from acting as result of any material in this publication.

© Allison Kenneally & John Tully 2013

To my parents, David and Susan, and my sister, Claire
Allison Kenneally

To my wife, Valerie, and sons, Joe and Liam
John Tully

Preface

The aim of this book is to provide a comprehensive and accessible account of the nature, structures and functions of the Irish legal system. It seeks to use straightforward and uncomplicated language to explain what can be challenging concepts. Diagrams and summaries are utilised to reinforce the information in the body of the text. Tables and flowcharts are also used which, we hope, will provide a convenient and helpful summary of key points, especially where an overview of a particular topic is sought. These can also provide a quick visual guide to the subject and can be useful for revision purposes.

The content of the book is intended to be wide-ranging and its layout designed to assist the reader to more easily navigate the material. It is an essential textbook for undergraduate students and indeed all people with an interest in the Irish legal system. The book seeks to give the reader a solid grounding in the features, architecture and role of the Irish legal system by providing a comprehensible and coherent account of the constitutional principles and institutional structures which form its building blocks, together with references to, and explanations of, important areas of substantive law.

Each chapter examines key legal principles and seeks to put each area of law into context. This should provide the reader with the means to acquire a sound understanding of the relevant issues.

The book is intended to act as a broad introduction to the Irish legal system which will allow readers to establish firm foundations on which to build greater and deeper knowledge. The book is up-to-date and includes recent legislative and constitutional changes and amendments to EU law. It also includes international treaties between EU Member States to which Ireland has recently become a party. We have attempted to state the law as at 24 July 2013. Any errors or omissions are our own.

Allison Kenneally
John Tully
9th September 2013

Acknowledgments

We would like to thank our colleagues and friends at the Institute of Technology Carlow, in particular Ivan Sheeran, Margaret Crowley and Pauline McHugh. Thanks also to Cathy Fitzgerald, Gary Fitzgerald BL and Kieron Wood BL. We would particularly like to express our appreciation to David McCartney of Clarus Press for his assistance, patience and support throughout the writing of this book. Finally, we would like to thank our families for their constant encouragement and support which made this book possible.

Contents

Preface vii
Acknowledgments ix
Table of Cases xiii
Table of Legislation xxi

Section A — Introduction to the Irish Legal System
1. The Nature and Purpose of Law 3
2. Types and Features of Legal Systems 11
3. Classification of Laws 19

Section B — The Development of the Irish Legal System
4. The Development of the Irish Legal System 35

Section C — Sources of Law
5. The 1937 Constitution 47
6. Legislation 79
7. Common Law and Precedent 113
8. EU Law 127
9. International Law Including the European Convention
   of Human Rights 163
10. Other Sources of Law 187

Section D — Personnel of the Law
11. Personnel of the Law 195

Section E — The Administration of Justice in Ireland
12. The Administration of Justice in Ireland: An Introduction 233
13. Structure of the Irish Court System 239
14. Civil Courts: Jurisdiction and Procedure 247
15. Criminal Courts: Jurisdiction and Procedure 273
16. Procedural Matters and Evidence 295
17. Decisions of the Courts: Remedies and Enforcement 307
18. Reform of the Court System 323
19. Access to Justice 327

Section F — Alternative Dispute Resolution
20. Alternative Dispute Resolution 337

Section G — Law Reform
21. Law Reform..369

Index 377

Table of Cases

Abrahamson and Others v Law Society of Ireland and the Attorney
General [1996] 2 IR 406..218
ACT Shipping (Pte) Ltd v Minister for the Marine [1995] 3 IR 406..............170
Airey v Ireland [1979] 2 EHRR...331
Anton Piller KG v Manufacturing Process Ltd [1976] Ch. 55; [1976] 2 WLR
162; [1976] 1 All ER 779)..311
Antonio Munoz Cia SA v Frumar Ltd [2002] ECR I-7289
(Case C-253/00)...154
AP v DPP [2011] IESC 2..284
Applications for Orders in Relation to Costs in Intended Proceedings:
Coffey & ors, Re [2013] IESC 11..331
Article 26 and Section 5 and 10 of the Illegal Immigrants (Trafficking)
Bill 1999, Re [2000] 2 IR 360..329
Associated Provincial Picture Houses v Wednesbury Corporation
[1948] 1 KB 223..321
Attorney General v Paperlink Ltd [1984] ILRM 343 70
Attorney General v Ryan's Car Hire Ltd [1965] IR 642...............................125
Attorney General v X [1992] 1 IR 1..227
Azienda Agricola Monte Arcosu v Regione Autonoma della
Sardegna [2001] ECR I-103 (Case C-403/98)...154

Bloomer and Ors v Incorporated Law Society of Ireland [1995] 3 IR..........218
Brasserie du Pecheur SA v Germany [1996] ECR I-1029, [1996]
1 CMLR 889 (Case C- 46)...157
Broekmeulen v Huisarts Registratie Commissie (Case 246/80)
[1981] ECR 2311..262
Bromley London Borough Council v Greater London Council
[1982] 2 WLR 62 321
Browne v Bank of Ireland Finance Ltd [1991] 1 IR 431................................245

Cahill v Sutton [1980] IR 269..299
Campus Oil v Minister for Energy & Others [1983] IR 88...........................264
Campus Oil Ltd. v Minister for Industry & Energy (No 2) [1983] IR 88......310
Canada v Employment Appeals Tribunal [1992] 2 IR 484..................171, 172
Carroll v Dublin Bus [2006] ELR 149...190

Chambers v An Bord Pleanála and Sandoz [1992] ILRM 296 299
City View Press Ltd v An Comhaire Oiliúna (AnCo) [1980] IR 381...............92
CM v TM (No. 2) [1991] ILRM 268 71
CILFIT Srl v Ministero della Sanita (Case 283/81) [1982] ECR 3515,
    [1983] 1 CMLR 472) 145, 264
Cole v Webb Caravans Ltd [1983] ILRM 595..24, 25
Collier v Hicks (1831) 2 B & Ad 663...330
Conroy v Attorney General [1965] IR 411..276
Costa v ENEL (Case 6/64) [1964] ECR 585 [1964] CMLR 425......145, 152, 263
County Cork Council v Whillock [1993] 1 IR 231..107
Crilly v Farrington [2001] 3 IR...110
Croke v Waterford Crystal [2005] 1 ILRM 321)...268
Curust v Loewe GmbH [1993] ILRM 723; [1994] 1 IR 450) 310
CW Shipping Co Ltd v Limerick Harbour Commissioners
    [1989] ILRM 416..109

Da Costa en Schaake NV v Nederlandse-Belastingadministratie
    (Cases 28-30/62) [1963] ECR 31; [1963] CMLR 224 ....263, 264
Defrenne v Sabena [1976] ECR 455, [1976] 2 CMLR 98 (Case 43/75)........154
Devonald v Rosser & Sons [1906] 2 KB 728 190
Dillane v Ireland [1980] ILRM 167...333
Director of Corporate Enforcement v Bailey [2007] IEHC 365;
    [2008] 2 ILRM 13..304
Doe v Armour Pharmaceutical Co Inc [1994] 1 ILRM 416............................184
Donegan v Dublin City Council [2012] IESC 18...181
Donoghue v Stevenson [1932] AC 432..14
Doris Saltzmann (Case C-178/99) [2001] ECR I–4421...................................262
Doughty v Rolls-Royce [1992] 1 CMLR 1045...155
Dowling v Ireland [1991] 2 IR 379..106
DPP v Farrell [1978] IR 13..109
DPP v O'Shea [1982] IR 384..72, 73
DPP v O'Sullivan [2007] IEHC 248..123
DPP (Ivers) v Murphy [1999] 1 IR 98..102
DS v Judges of the Cork Circuit Court [2008] 4 IR 379 284
Dublin City Council v Fennell [2005] 1 IR 604 ....180, 181
Dublin Wellwoman Centre Ltd v Ireland [1995] 1 ILRM..............................202
Dudgeon v United Kingdom (1981) 4 EHRR 149...173
Duggan v An Taoiseach [1989] ILRM 710..64
Dunphy (a Minor) v DPP [2005] 3 IR 585; [2005] IESC 75)..........................291

East Donegal Livestock Mart v Attorney General [1970] IR 317 106
Eccles v Ireland [1985] IR 545 279
E(G) v DPP [2008] IESC 61 226
Ellis v O'Dea (No 1) [1989] IR 530 51
Eviston v DPP [2002] 3 IR 260; [2002] 1 ILRM 134 (HC); [2003]
    1 ILRM 178... 226

*Factortame (R v Secretary of State for Transport ex parte Factortame
    Ltd)* [1990] ECR 2433 (Case C-213/89)... 153
Farrell (Dublin City Coroner) v The Attorney General [1998] 1 IR 203 362
Foster v British Gas [1990] ECR I-3313 (Case C-188/89) 155
Foy v An t-Ard Chláraitheoir [2007] IEHC 470 181
Fratelli Constanzo v Milano [1989] ECR 1839 (Case 103/88).................... 155
Francovich and Bonifaci v Italy (Francovich) [1991]
    ECR I-5537 (C-6/90 & 9/90).. 156, 157

G v An Bord Uchtála [1980] IR 32 .... 68, 70
Gilligan v Ireland [2001] 1 ILRM 473... 279
Gilligan and Zappone v Revenue Commissioners [2008] 2 IR 417 74
Grimes v Owners of SS Bangor Bay [1948] IR 350... 275

Hamilton v Hamilton [1982] IR 266.. 108, 126
Hanley v Newsgroup Newspapers Ltd [2004] 1 IR 471 266
Hanrahan v Merck Sharp & Dohme Ltd [1988] ILRM 629 245
Hay v O'Grady [1992] 1 IR 210... 245
Hegarty v O'Loughran [1990] 1 IR 148.. 300
Holohan v Donohoe [1986] IR 45... 242
Horgan v Ireland [2003] 2 IR 468... 171
Howard v Commissioner of Public Works [1994] 1 IR 101 99
Hynes-O'Sullivan v O'Driscoll [1989] ILRM 349... 126

In the Matter of NIB (No 2) [1999] 2 ILRM 443... 284
In Re Ó Laighléis [1960] IR 93... 172
In Re the Offences against the State (Amendment) Bill 1940
    [1940] IR 470 172
Internationale Handelsgesselschaft (Case 11/70)... 152
Inspector of Taxes v Kiernan [1981] 1 IR 117... 108
Irish Times Ltd v Ireland [1998] 1 IR 359 237
Irish Trust Bank Ltd v Central Bank of Ireland [1976-7] ILRM 50................ 126

JM and GM v An Bord Uchtála [1988] ILRM 203 245
Johnston v Chief Constable of the RUC [1986] ECR 1651 (Case 222/84).....155

Kavanagh v Government of Ireland [1996] 1 IR 321 279
Kearns v Manresa Estates Ltd (Unreported, High Court,
　25 July 1975) 126
Kennedy v Ireland [1987] IR 587 71
Kenny v Trinity College [2008] 2 IR 40..203
Kiely v Minister for Social Welfare [1977] IR 267...109
Kobler v Austria (Case C-224/01) [2003] ECR I-10239.................................157
Kruse v Johnson [1898] 2 QB 91 of 9 92
Kupferberg [1982] ECR 3641 (Case 104/81) 155

Laurentiu v Minister for Justice [1999] 4 IR 26 93
Lawe v Irish Country Meats Ltd [1998 CC] ELR 266).....................................190
Lelimo v Minister for Justice, Equality and Law Reform [2004] 2 IR 178......180
Lyckeskog, Criminal Proceedings [2002] ECR I-4839 (Case C-99/00) 263

M v M [1979] ILRM 160 245
Macauley v Minister for Post and Telegraphs [1966] IR 345...................70, 329
*Marshall v Southampton and Southwest Hampshire Area Health
　Authority* [1986] ECR 723 155
*Marleasing SA v La Comercial Internacionale de Alimentacion
　SA* [1990] ECR I-4135 (Case C-106/89)..156
Mareva Compania Naviera v International Bulk Carriers
　[1980] 1 All ER 213..311
Mason v Levy [1952] IR 40 at 47..97
McCann v Judge of Monaghan District Court [2009] IEHC 276...........313, 314
McCrystal v Minister for Children & Youth Affairs [2012] IESC 53...............77
McDonald v Bord na gCon [1965] IR 217 ....65, 235
McDonnell v Byrne Engineering Co Ltd, The Irish Times,
　3 October 1978..123
McElhinney v Williams [1995] 3 IR 382 ....171, 172
McGee v Attorney General [1974] IR 284 ....70, 74
McGlinchey v Governor of Portlaoise Prison [1988] IR 671 279
McGonagle v McGonagle [1951] IR 123 109
McGrath v McDermott [1988] IR 258..94, 99
McKee v Culligan [1992] 1 IR 233 108
McKenna v An Taoiseach (No 2) [1985] 2 IR 10...76

McKenzie v McKenzie [1971] P 33; [1970] 3 WLR 472;
 [1970] 3 All ER 1034..330
McIlwraith v Fawsitt [1990] 1 IR 343 204
McNamara v ESB [1975] IR 1 125
McSorley v Governor of Mountjoy Prison [1996] 2 ILRM 331......................332
Meagher v Minister for Agriculture and Food [1994] 1 IR 329 153
Melling v O Mathghamhna [1962] IR 1 276
Minister for Industry and Commerce v Hales [1971] IR 30............................96
*Minister for Industry and Commerce v Hammond Lane Metal
 Company Ltd* [1947] Ir Jur Rep 59..100
Minister for Industry and Commerce v Pim Brothers Ltd [1996] IR 154......100
Mogul of Ireland Ltd v Tipperary North Riding County Council
 [1976] IR 260 126
Murphy v Bord Telecom Éireann [1989] ILRM 53 106
Murphy v Minister for Justice [2001] 2 ILRM 144; 1 IR 95..........................332
Murphy v Stewart [1973] IR 97...70
Murray v Attorney General [1985] IR 352..71
Murren v Brennan [1942] IR 466..256

Nester v Murphy [1979] IR 326...101, 311
Norris v Attorney General [1984] IR 36...173, 226, 245
Northern Bank Finance Corporation Ltd v Charlton [1979] IR 149 245

O'Brien v Keogh [1972] IR 144..330
O'Callaghan v Sullivan [1925] 1 IR 90 ....23, 25, 190
O'Donoghue v Legal Aid Board [2004] IEHC 413..331
O'Domhnaill v Merrick [1984] IR 151 301
O'Keefe v An Bord Pleanála [1993] 1 IR 39)...321
O'Mahony v Horgan [1996] 1 ILRM 161 311
O'T v B [1998] 2 IR 321..71

Pepper v Hart [1993] AC 593 103
Pringle v Ireland (C-370/12) [2013] 158

R v R [1984] IR 296...253, 255, 256
R v Secretary of State for Transport ex parte Factortame Ltd
 (Factortame) (No 2)..153
*R v Secretary of State for Transport ex parte Factortame Ltd and
 Others* (C-48/93)..157
R v Stanley [1920] 2 KB 235..22

Rahill v Brady [1971] IR 69 95
Ratti (Case 148/78) 155
RD v McGuiness [1999] 2 IR 411 331
Re Adoption (No. 2) Bill 1987 [1989] IR 656 71
Re Applications for Orders in Relation to Costs in Intended Proceedings:
Coffey & ors [2013] IESC 11 331
Re-Article 26 and the Housing (Private Rented Dwellings)
Bill 1981 [1983] IR 181 258
Re-Article 26 and the Regulation of Information (Services outside the State
for Termination of Pregnancies) Bill 1995 [1995] 1 IR 1 258
Re Article 26 and Section 5 and 10 of the Illegal Immigrants (Trafficking)
Bill 1999 [2000] 2 IR 360 329
Re: DG (an Infant) [1991] 1 IR 491 245
Re Haughey [1971] IR 217 70
Re JH [1985] IR 375 106
Re O Laighleis [1960] IR 93 .... 172, 173
Re McKerr [2004] UKHL 12, [2004] 1 WLR 807 180
Re R Ltd [1989] ILRM 759 236
Re Solicitors Act 1954 [1960] IR 239 65
Re The Criminal Law (Jurisdiction) Bill 1975 [1977] IR 129 279
Reddy v Bates [1983] IR 141 118
Roache v News Group Newspapers Limited and Others
[1998] EMLR 161 269
Robinson v Harman [1848] 1 Exch 850) 309
Roe v Blood Transfusion Service Board [1996] 1 ILRM 555 237
Ryan v Attorney General [1965] IR 294 .... 69, 70, 75
Ryan v Minister for Justice [2000] IESC 33 118

Shannon v McGuinness [1999 HC] 3 IR 274 298
Shannon Realties v St Michael (Ville de) [1924] AC 185 96
Simmenthal (Case 106/77) [1978] ECR 629 .... 152, 153
Sinnott v Minister for Education [2001] 2 IR 505 68
SPUC v Coogan and Others [1989] ITLR (SC) 299
State (C) v Frawley [1976] IR 365 70
State (Healy) v Donohue [1976] IR 325 .... 70, 332
State (Keegan) v Minister for Justice [1954] IR 207 235
State (Keegan) v Stardust Victims' Compensation Tribunal [1986] IR 642 ... 321
State (Lynch) v Cooney [1982] IR 337 298
State (M) v Attorney General [1979] IR 73 70

State (McCormack) v Curran [1987] ILRM 225 291
State (O'Callaghan) v O hUadhaigh [1977] IR 42 .... 226, 291
State (Quinn) v Ryan [1965] IR 70 329
State (Walsh) v Murphy [1981] 1 IR 275 202

TD v Minister for Education [2001] 4 IR 259 71
Texaco (Ireland) Ltd v Murphy [1991] 2 IR 449 99
The Electoral (Amendment) Bill 1983 [1984] IR 268 259
The People (Attorney General) v Byrne [1974] IR 1 301
The People (Attorney General) v McGlynn [1967] IR 232 96
The People (Attorney General) v Moore [1964] Ir Jur Rep 6 126
The People (Attorney General) v O'Neill [1964] Ir Jur Rep 1 126
The People (DPP) v Farrell [1978] IR 13 108
The People (DPP) v Best [2000] 2 IR 17 22
Toal v Duignan [1991] ILRM 135 301
Todd v Murphy [1999] 2 IR 1 277
Tormey v Ireland [1985] IR 289 .... 73, 255, 256
Touhy v Courtney [1994] 3 IR 1 329

Van Gend en Loos (Case 26/62) [1963] ECR 1 .... 145, 151, 153, 155
Variola (Case 34/73) 148
Von Colson (Case 14/83) 156

Wall v Hegarty [1980] ILRM 124 309
Wavin Pipes Ltd v Hepworth Iron Co Ltd [1982] 8 FSR 32 110
White v Dublin City Council [2004] 1 IR 545 329

Table of Legislation

Constitutional Provisions

Constitution 1922	41, 42, 43, 49, 83, 235, 242
Art 64	235, 275
Art 65	235
Art 66	235
Art 67	235
Art 68	235
Art 69	235
Art 70	235
Art 71	235
Art 72	235
Art 73	235
Bunreacht na hÉireann 1937	14, 23, 27, 30, 42, 43, 49, 50, 51, 52, 74, 76, 77, 78, 83, 86, 159, 171, 181, 182, 189, 235, 242, 257, 290, 299, 350
Art 2	44, 50, 51
Art 3	44, 50, 51
Art 5	52
Art 6	50, 52, 63
Art 7	52
Art 8	52
Art 12	52, 53, 265
Art 12.1	53
Art 12.2.1	49
Art 12.3.1	56, 258
Art 12.9	53
Art 12.10	56
Art 13	52, 53
Art 13.1	54
Art 13.2	54
Art 13.2.3	54
Art 13.3	55
Art 13.4	55
Art 13.9	53
Art 14	52, 53, 56

Art 15 .... 52, 57
    Art 15.2 .... 90, 92, 150
        Art 15.2.1 .... 57, 63, 64, 82
    Art 15.5 9
        Art 15.5.1 .... 105, 108
    Art 15.9 .... 59, 60
    Art 15.12 58
    Art 15.13 58
Art 16 .... 52, 57, 58
    Art 16.1 58
Art 17 .... 52, 57, 58
Art 18 .... 52, 57, 59
Art 19 .... 52, 57, 59
Art 20 .... 52, 57, 84
Art 21 .... 52, 57, 84
Art 22 .... 52, 57, 84
Art 23 .... 52, 57, 60, 84
Art 24 .... 52, 57, 84, 258
Art 25 .... 52, 55, 57, 84
Art 26 .... 52, 55, 56, 57, 64, 84, 87, 124, 125, 258, 265
    Art 26.1 201
        Art 26.1.2 258
Art 27 .... 52, 57, 60, 75, 84
Art 28 .... 52, 61
    Art 28.1 61
    Art 28.2 .... 61, 63, 64
    Art 28.4 .... 61, 62
        Art 28.5.1 62
        Art 28.6.2 63
        Art 28.6.3 63
Art 29 44
    Art 29.3 .... 170, 171, 172
    Art 29.4 .... 150, 151
        Art 29.4.3 43
    Art 29.6 .... 170, 172
Art 30 .... 52, 225, 226
    Art 30.2 227
    Art 30.3 .... 225, 227
Art 31 .... 52, 56

Art 32	52
Art 33	52
Art 34	52, 198, 227, 235, 241
Art 34.1	63, 65, 198, 235, 237
Art 34.2	241
Art 34.3	241
Art 34.3.1	73, 241, 242, 253, 254, 255, 256, 278
Art 34.3.2	241, 252, 255
Art 34.3.3	252
Art 34.3.4	242, 243, 250, 275, 276
Art 34.4	241
Art 34.4.1	241, 255
Art 34.4.3	72, 241, 243, 261
Art 34.4.4	241, 260
Art 34.5.1	202
Art 35	52, 198, 235, 241
Art 35.1	200
Art 35.2	202
Art 35.3	202
Art 35.4.1	205
Art 35.4.2	205
Art 35.4.3	205
Art 35.5	203
Art 36	52, 198, 235, 241, 243
Art 37	52, 235, 241
Art 37.1	65, 236, 340
Art 38	241, 288
Art 38.1	284
Art 38.2	275, 276
Art 38.3	287
Art 38.3.1	278
Art 38.3.2	279
Art 38.5	207, 277, 278
Art 39	278, 287
Art 40	50, 66, 67, 71
s 3(1)	70
Art 40.1	67
Art 40.3	67, 69, 329
Art 40.3.1	69

Art 40.3.3 67
Art 40.4 ....67, 173, 292
Art 40.5 67
   Art 40.6.1 66
      (i) 67
      (ii) 67
      (iii) 67
Art 41 ....50, 66, 67, 68
  Art 41.1 68
  Art 41.2 68
  Art 41.3 68
Art 42 ....50, 66, 67, 68, 69
  Art 42.1 ....68, 106
  Art 42.2 68
Art 43 ....50, 66, 67, 69
Art 44 ....50, 66, 67, 69
  Art 44.1 50
  Art 44.2 50
Art 45 51
Art 47 75
  Art 47.2 75

Primary Legislation

Act of Union 1800 40
Adoption Act 2010 185
Anti-Discrimination (Pay) Act 1976 106
Arbitration Act 2010 ....341, 343, 344, 345, 347, 349

Bail Act 1997 ....292, 293
Bankruptcy Act 1988 256

Central Bank and Financial Service Authority of Ireland Act 2003
  s 35
    Schedule 1 289
Central Bank and Financial Services Authority, Ireland Act 2004 357
Chancery (Ireland) Act 1865
  s 155 312
Child Care Act 1991 266
  s 25 330

s 26...330
Children Act 1997
   s 11..330
   s 28..302
Children Act 2001
   s 75..277
Civil Law (Miscellaneous Provisions) Act 2008
   s 9..332
Civil Legal Aid Act 1995 333
Civil Liability and Courts Act 2004
   s 7..300
   s 25..267
Companies Act 1963 256
   s 205..237
Companies Act 1990 256
Competition Act 2002
   s 6..278, 287
   s 7..278, 287
Constitution Act 1972
   Third Amendment 150
Constitution (Judges' Remuneration) Act 2011
   Twenty-Ninth Amendment..203
Consumer Credit Act 1995...251, 254
   s 14..289
Contractual Obligations (Applicable Law) Act 1991 185
Courts Act 1971
   s 13..282
Courts Acts 1981
   s 5..253
   s 22..310
   s 31..73, 255
Courts Acts 1991
   s 2..255
   s 4..250
   s 4(c) 251
Courts (No 2) Act 1986 313
   s 4..252
Courts (Establishment and Constitution) Act 1961...........235, 242, 275
   s 6..205

Courts of Justice Act 1924 ....41, 42, 43, 198, 235, 243
   s 77..250
Courts of Justice Act 1928
   s 18..280
Courts of Justice Act 1936
   s 58..280
Court and Courts Officers Act 1985
   s 53..253
Court and Courts Officers Act 1995
   s 13..200
   s 32..277
   s 49..214
Court and Courts Officers (Amendment) Act 2007 243
Court and Courts Officers Act 2002 201
Courts and Civil Law (Miscellaneous Provisions) Act 2013....243, 250, 325
   s 23..207
   Part 3 250
Court Orders (Amendment) Act 2009...314
Courts (Supplemental Provisions) Act 1961 ....235, 243, 257, 282
   s 7..282
   s 8..282
   s 9(4) 257
   s 21..282
   s 22..252
   s 25(2) 278
   s 33..250
   s 45(1) 237
   s 52(2) 281
   Third Schedule...252
Courts Service Act 1998
   Second Schedule...332
Conspiracy and Protection of Property Act 1875
   s 7..287
Copyright and Related Rights Act 2000
   s 11(1) 289
Coroners Act 1962...362, 363, 364
Coroner's (Amendment) Act 2005...362, 364
Courts Service Act 1998...230, 271

Criminal Damage Act 1991 287
Criminal Evidence Act 1992
   s 5 302
   s 27 302
Criminal Justice Act 1951 .... 276, 292, 318
   s 7 300
   Schedule 1 292
Criminal Justice Act 1984
   s 21 305
   s 22 305
Criminal Justice Act 1993 318
   s 2 .... 283, 286
   s 5 315
   s 6 297
Criminal Justice Act 1994 319
Criminal Justice Act 2002
   s 167 16
Criminal Justice Act 2003 284
Criminal Justice Act 2006 358
   s 21 283
   s 22 283
   s 100 315
Criminal Justice Act 2007 358
   s 59 283
Criminal Justice (Administration) Act 1924 293
Criminal Justice (Community Service) Act 1983 318
Criminal Justice (Legal Aid) Act 1962 .... 332, 333
Criminal Justice (Miscellaneous Provisions) Act 1997
   s 6(1) 102
Criminal Justice (Public Order) Act 1994
   s 6 21
Criminal Justice (Safety of United Nations Workers) Act 2000
   s 2 287
Criminal Justice (United Nations Convention against
   Torture) Act 2000 .... 278, 319
Criminal Justice (Safety of United Nations Workers) Act 2000
   s 2 278
Criminal Law Act 1997

s 2(1) 289
s 3(1) 289
Criminal Law Amendment Act 1935
　s 17 74
Criminal Law (Rape) Acts 1981-1990 294
Criminal Law (Rape) (Amendment) Act 1990 ....277, 278, 287
Criminal Law (Sexual Offences) Act 1993 173
Criminal Procedure Act 1967
　s 6 292
　s 34 ....278, 286
Criminal Procedure Act 1993 283
　s 2 286
　s 2(1)(b) 283
　s 3 282
　s 9 283
　s 11 73
Criminal Procedure Act 2010 ....283, 284, 285, 286, 315

Defence Act 1954 55
Disability Act 2005 355
Domestic Violence Act 1996 266

Electoral Act 1992
　s 132 257
Electronic Commerce Act 2000
　s 6(1) 289
Enforcement of Court Orders Act 1926 ....312, 313, 314
Enforcement of Court Orders Act 1940 ....313, 314
Environmental Protection Agency Act 1992
　s 11 289
European Communities Act 1972
　s 2 150
European Convention on Human
　Rights Act 2003 ....44, 172, 173, 174, 179, 181
　s 1(1) 180
　s 2 179
　s 3(1) 180
　s 3(2) 180
　s 4 180

    s 5 181
    s 6(1) 181
Equal Status Act 2000
    s 44 289
Explosive Substances Act 1883 287

Family Law Act 1995 314
Family Law (Divorce) Act 1996
    s 38 253
Family Home Protection Act 1976
    s 3(1) 101, 102
    s 9 251
Fines Act 2010 316
    s 3 316
    s 4 316
    s 5 316
    s 6 316
    s 7 316
    s 8 316
    s 9 317
    s 10 317
    s 15 317
    s 16 317
Firearms Acts 1925 to 1990 287
Forfeiture Act 1870 289

Garda Síochána Act 2005 358
    s 8 290
Geneva Conventions Act 1962 .... 278, 287
Genocide Act 1973 .... 278, 287
Greyhound Industry Act 1958
    s 47 235
Guardianship of Infants Act 1964 266
    s 3 106
    s 28 330
Government of Ireland Act 41

Health (Amendment) Act 1986
    2(1) 110

Health (Fluoridation of Water Supplies) Act 1960 69
Hotel Proprietors Act 1963 .... 251, 254
Housing Act 1966
    s 62(3) 181

Income Tax Act 1967
    s 78 98
    s 128 298
International Criminal Court Act 2006 319
International War Crimes Tribunals Act 1998 202
Interpretation Act 1937 91
Interpretation Act 2005 .... 97, 98
    s 5 .... 96, 97
    s 6 .... 97, 107
    s 18 97
Interpretation (Amendment) Act 1997 290
Irish European Communities Act 1972 160

Judicial Separation and Family Law Reform Act 1989 253
Juries Act 1976 209

Land Law (Ireland) Act 1881 40
Law Reform Commission Act 1975 .... 373, 374
Legal Aid Act 1995 .... 331, 332
Legal Services Ombudsman Act 2009 .... 222, 358
Licensing Acts 1833 to 2004 253
Licensing of Indoor Events Act 2003
    s 16 289
Local Elections (Petitions and Disqualifications) Act 1974 254
Local Government (Water Pollution) Acts 1977 .... 251, 253
Local Government (Water Pollution) Acts 1990 .... 251, 253
Lunacy Regulation (Ireland) Act 1871 257

Malicious Injuries Acts 1981 254
Malicious Injuries Act 1986 254
Malicious Injuries (Amendment) Act 1986 255
Mineral Development Act 1999
    s 4 289
Ministers and Secretaries Act 1924
    s 2 (1) 329

National Beef Assurance Scheme Act 2000
    s 26 289
Non-fatal offences against a Person Act 1997 5
    s 3 5
    s 4 5

Oaths Act 1888 302
Offences against the Person Act 1861 173
Offences against the State Act 1939
    s 6 ....278, 287
    s 7 ....278, 287
    s 8 ....278, 287
    s 30 108
    s 36 287
    s 39 279
    s 39(1) 279
    s 43 279
    Part V 279, 280
Offences against the State Acts 1939 to 1998 280
Offences against the State (Amendment) Act 1998 287
Ombudsman Act 1980 355
Ombudsman (Amendment) Act 1984 355
Ombudsman (Amendment) Act 2012 ....355, 356
Ombudsman for Children Act 2002 357
Ombudsman (Defence Forces) Act 2004 358

Pensions Act 1990
    Part XI 358
Pensions (Amendment) Act 2002 358
Personal Injuries Assessment Board Act 2003 ....309, 310, 359, 360
Personal Injuries Assessment (Amendment) Act 2007 ....310, 359, 361
Petty Sessions (Ireland) Act 1851 243
    s 29 129
Poynings' Law 1494-5 38
Planning and Development Act 2000
    s 50 (4)(b) 299
Probation of Offenders Act 1907 318
Prosecutions of Offences Act 1974 228
    s 2 225

Protection of Children (Hague Convention) Act 2000 185

Referendum Act 1994
   s 132 257
Referendum Ac t 1998 76
Referendum Act 2001 76
Republic of Ireland Act 1948 .... 43, 51
Road Traffic Act 2010
   s 4 25
Roman Catholic Relief Act 1793 40

Safety, Health and Welfare at Work Act 2005 318
Sea Pollution Act 1991 185
Sex Offenders Act 2001
   Part 6 294
Single European Act 1986 .... 133, 134, 136
Solicitors (Ireland) Act 1898 216
Solicitors Act 1954
   s 59 220
Solicitors Acts 1954 – 2008 .... 216, 220
Spouses and Children Act 1976 266
Statute of Limitations Acts 1957 to 2000 299
Statute of Limitations 1957 .... 299, 300, 329
   s 49(2)(a)(ii) 330
Statute of Limitations (amendment) Act 1991
   s 3 300
   s 3(1) 300
Status of Children Act 1987 266
Statutory Instrument Act 1947 91
Summary Jurisdiction Act 1857 243
Supreme Court of Judicature Act 1873 40
Supreme Court of Judicature (Ireland) Act 1877 .... 29, 40, 243

Taxes Consolidation Act 1997
   s 987 298
Treason Act 1939
   s 2 .... 278, 287
   s 3 .... 278, 287
Tribunals of Inquiry (Evidence) Acts 1921 to 2004 352

Twenty-eighth Amendment of the Constitution
  (Treaty of Lisbon) Act 2009 150

Unclaimed Life Assurance Policies Act 2003
  s 5(4) 289

War Crimes Tribunal Act 1998 319

Secondary Legislation

Circuit Court Rules 2001 269
Circuit Court (Fees) Order 2013 (SI No 240 of 2013) 332
District Court (Fees) Order 2013 (SI No 241 of 2013) 332
District Court Rules 1997 269
  Ord 53A 251
Local Government (Planning and Development)
  Regulation (SI No 89 of 1990) 83
Rules of the Superior Courts (Commercial Proceedings)
  2004 (SI No 2 of 2004) 256, 271
Rules of the Superior Courts 1986 (SI No 15 of 1986) 92
  Ord 28, r 2 267
  Ord 21, r 1 268
  Ord 22 269
  Ord 23, r 1 268
  Ord 19, r 29 312
  Ord 31, r 12 268
  Ord 63A, r 14 (1) 256
  Ord 84, r 20(4) 299
  Ord 84 , r 24(1) 321, 322
  Ord 125, r 1 267
Rules of the Superior Courts (No 6) (Disclosure of Reports and
  Statements) 1998 (SI No 391 of 1998) 305
Sheriff's Fees and Expenses Order (SI No 644 of 2005) 312
Solicitors (Advertising) Regulations 2004 (SI No 518 of 2002)
  s 9(a) 220
Supreme Court And High Court (Fees) Order 2013
  (SI No 239 of 2013) 332

International Treaties And Conventions

Anglo Irish Treaty 1921 (The Treaty between Great Britain and Ireland
  signed at London on the 6th day of December, 1921) 41, 42
Budgetary Treaty 146
Convention Relating to the Status of Refugees 168
Convention on the Rights of the Child 168
EEC Treaty 132, 133, 135, 151
  Art 2 133
  Art 119 154
European Convention on Human Rights 44
  Art 5 173,
  Art 6 173
  Art 8 .... 173, 181
European Convention for the Protection of Human Rights and
  Fundamental Freedoms 168
Good Friday Agreement 43
Maastricht Treaty (Treaty on European Union) 1992 133
Merger Treaty 1965 .... 130, 133, 134
North Atlantic Treaty Organisation (NATO), ... 130
Rome Statute of the International Criminal Court 168
Statute of the International Court of Justice 167
  Art 38(1) 168, 169
  Art 38(2) 167
  Art 59 .... 167, 169
Treaty of Amsterdam 1997 .... 133, 135, 136
Treaty on European Union 1992 134
Treaty on European Union (TEU) 130, 146
  Art 6 137
  Art 19 149
  Art 47 150
  Art 48 147
  Art 49 .... 137, 160
  Art 50 .... 136, 160
Treaty on the Functioning of the European Union (TFEU) 130, 136
  Part Three 147
  Art 4 156
  Art 267 .... 262, 263, 264
    (3) 263

Art 288..148, 149, 154
Art 290..143
Art 291..144
Treaty of Lisbon 2007 ('The Reform Treaty')............................130, 133, 136
Treaty of Nice 2000 ....130, 133, 135, 136
Treaty of Paris..130, 131, 132
Treaty of Rome 43, 136
UN CHARTER..168, 175, 176
    Art 1..166, 174
    Art 2..174
Vienna Convention on the Law of Treaties
    Art 54..183
    Art 56..183
    Art 60..183
    Art 61(1)...183
    Art 62..183

EU Directives, Framework Decisions and Regulations

Council Regulation 44/2001 (Brussels II Regulation)..............................185
Equal Treatment Directive (Council Directive (76/207/EEC))...............155

Other

UK
Civil Evidence Act 1995
    s 1...304
Civil Procedure Act 1997 (UK)..271
Human Rights Act 1998 ....180, 181
    s 6(1)...180
Legal Services Act 2007 224

Bills

Legal Recognition of Gender Bill 2013...181
Legal Services Regulation Bill..223
Lisbon Treaty (Twenty-eight Amendment of the Constitution)
    Bill 2008 76
Mediation and Conciliation Bill 2010...349
Thirty second Amendment of the Constitution
    (abolition of Seanad Éireann) Bill 2013...61

Thirty-third Amendment of the Constitution
   (Court of Appeal Bill 2013) 325
Coroner's Bill 2007 364
Treaty of Nice (Twenty-fourth Amendment of the Constitution)
   Bill 2001 76
Tribunals of Inquiry Bill 2005 354

Section A

Introduction to the Irish Legal System

CHAPTER ONE

THE NATURE AND PURPOSE OF LAW

A. What is Law? 5
B. Characteristics of Law 5
C. Functions of Law 6
D. Law and Morality 6
E. Legal Theories 6
    Legal Positivism 6
    Natural Law Theory 8
F. Legal Personality 8
G. The Rule of Law 9

Learning Outcomes

Upon completion of this chapter, the student should be able to:

- Describe what is meant by *Law*;
- Explain the characteristics of law and its purpose in society;
- Discuss and contrast the theories of legal positivism and natural law;
- Explain the concept of 'legal personality' and differentiate between natural legal personality and legal personality attributed to artificial entities;
- Identify the key principles of the *Rule of Law*.

A. What is Law?
"Law is the formal glue that holds fundamentally disorganized societies together."

Thomas Hobbes, *Leviathan* (1651)

Many definitions of law have been offered through the centuries by various legal scholars, philosophers and professors. Law is often defined as a system *of legal principles, rules and procedures which aim to regulate the behaviour of individuals in society.*

A legal principle is the idea or moral behind the law. An example of a legal principle is that it is wrong to cause physical harm to another person. Legal rules are the actual laws which give effect to that principle or moral. For example, in Ireland, the Non-Fatal Offences against the Person Act 1997 sets out a number of criminal offences, including assault causing harm under s 3 and assault causing serious harm under s 4. These are the laws which give effect to the principle that it is wrong to cause harm to another. Finally, legal procedures are the laws or rules relating to court procedure and evidence. In the example used here, the rules of criminal procedure and evidence are essential in order to secure a prosecution against a person who has harmed another, thus giving effect to the legal principle and rule.

The geographical area in which these or laws rules apply is known as the jurisdiction. For example, if the Oireachtas (Irish Parliament) passes a written law, it will generally have effect or jurisdiction in the Republic of Ireland. If the European Union (EU) passes a regulation, it will have jurisdiction in the Member States of the EU.

B. Characteristics of Law
Joseph Raz in *The Concept of a Legal System* (Oxford University Press, 1980) sets out the three key characteristics of law:

1. It is normative — "it serves, and is meant to serve as a guide for human behaviour."
2. It is institutionalised — "its application and modification are to a large extent performed or regulated by institutions."
3. It is coercive — "obedience to it, and its application, are internally guaranteed, ultimately, by the use of force."

When this theory is applied to the Irish legal system, it is evident that our laws are normative — they establish what behaviour is acceptable in our society and what is not. Our laws are institutionalised — the Oireachtas is the main institution responsible for creating and amending laws in Ireland — and, finally, our laws are coercive — An Garda Síochána and ultimately the courts, guarantee obedience to our laws.

C. Functions of Law

When examining what law is, it is necessary to look at what law does, i.e. what is its purpose or functions. Law:

1. Establishes a code for human behaviour by setting out rules on what behaviours are acceptable in society and what are not;
2. Acts as a deterrent to crime;
3. Punishes wrongdoers who have committed criminal offences;
4. Allows an individual/company who has suffered loss due to the actions of another to take action to redress that loss through compensation, usually in the form of damages. Having such a mechanism available through the courts stops people from taking the law into their own hands;
5. Provides a means for enforcing legal rights and obligations.

D. Law and Morality

There is a clear connection between law, which establishes a code of human behaviour, and morality, which has a similar objective. In that sense, both are normative.

The main difference between law and morals is that law is authoritative or coercive. Law is enforced ultimately by the courts, either by punishment or the re-adjustment of rights and liabilities. The rules of morality, on the other hand, depend upon our good conscience and societal pressures for obedience.

Max Weber, a leading German sociologist, acknowledged the need for coercion when he stated that law exists "if it is externally guaranteed by the probability of coercion to bring about conformity or avenge violation, and is applied by a staff of people holding themselves specially ready for that purpose."

E. Legal Theories

The study of the philosophy of law legal theory is known as *jurisprudence*. This involves the study of what law is and what law does. There are two leading theories of law which are described below.

Legal Positivism

This theory of law is supported by a number of eminent legal philosophers and jurists such as Jeremy Bentham, John Austin, Professor HLA Hart and Joseph Raz. Legal positivism focuses on what the law actually is, rather than what it should be.

John Austin in *Province of Jurisprudence Determined* (1832) stated that law is "[a] body of rules fixed and enforced by a sovereign political authority." Professor HLA Hart in *The Concept of Law* (Oxford University Press, 1961) identified five elements which he argued all legal systems must include:

1. Rules forbidding certain behaviour with some form of penalty or sanction for non-compliance (e.g. criminal law);
2. Rules that make people compensate other people that they have wronged for the damage caused by the wrong (e.g. tort law);
3. Rules that regulate the conduct of, and that enforce, agreements, arrangements and relationships between individuals (e.g. contracts or wills);
4. A system of courts in which to enforce all of the above rights and obligations;
5. A legislature of some form to make new laws to fit new situations and also to amend or repeal outdated laws (e.g. a Parliament).

Hart called the rules which regulate conduct the "primary rules". He also recognised that, on their own, these rules are insufficient for a system of law to operate effectively. There must also be "secondary rules". He classified the secondary rules as follows:

1. *Rules of recognition*: these would be the separate branches of law — for example, crime, tort, contract, succession, matrimonial, company law. Each individual body of rules must have a character allowing it to be distinguished from any other body of rules.
2. *Rules of change*: there is a need for a legislature (in Ireland, the Oireachtas), to change the law and ensure it is relevant. There must therefore be superior systems of conduct which will authorise alteration of the rules to accommodate social and economic changes in society, but which themselves operate according to law.
3. *Rules of adjudication*: courts are the place where disputes are heard but they also must have rules regulating the methods by which those disputes are resolved, otherwise the law would be administered in an arbitrary manner and may be seen as unfair.

Hart states that the secondary rules are equally important and the presence of both types of rules is what separates a legal system from a more primitive code of behaviour — or, for that matter, dictatorship.

Legal positivism contends that the only legitimate sources of law are those written rules, regulations and principles that have been expressly enacted, adopted or recognised by a governmental entity or political institution, including administrative, executive, legislative and judicial bodies.

If a behavioural or societal norm is pronounced by anyone or anything other than a duly authorised body or institution, it will not qualify as law in the minds of legal positivists.

Natural Law Theory
Natural law theorists believe that law is not just the rules which our institutions create, but that there is a *higher law* which constrains us all. This higher law is a system of justice held to be common to all humans and derived from nature, rather than from the rules of society or positive law. This natural law is superior to all law or rules enacted by man.

Natural law also refers to the use of reason to analyse human nature and deduce binding rules of moral behaviour from it. Classical Greek philosophers such as Plato and Aristotle and the medieval philosopher St Thomas Aquinas were exponents of natural law theory.

Aristotle stated that law is "an embodiment of reason", whether in the individual or the community. He argued that what was "just by nature" was not always the same as what was "just by law," but that there was a natural justice which was valid everywhere. This is essentially the moral dimension to the law.

St Thomas Aquinas refers to law as being "[n]othing else than an ordinance of reason for the common good, made by him who has care of the community, and promulgated" (*Summa Theologiae (Summary of Theology)* Question 90, Art 4).

Natural law is often contrasted with the positive law of a given political community, society or state and thus serves as a standard by which to criticise the positive law rules.

F. Legal Personality
All human beings as natural, living persons have a legal personality. This means that they have certain legal rights i.e. can sue and be sued, own and inherit property, enter into contracts and incur debt in their own name. This also means that a natural person can be subject to certain legal obligations under the law, such the obligation to pay tax.

However, artificial entities can also have legal personality. Legal personality is where a non-living entity (such as a company) is regarded as having the character of being a person attributed to it.

For example, a company can buy and own property, enter into contracts, sue and be sued, although it is not capable of entering into certain types of contract, e.g., a contract of marriage. Companies are also not entitled to claim for breach of the fundamental rights enshrined under our Constitution.

In the case of companies, this legal personality allows the company to be considered separately at law from its individual members or shareholders and may shield its shareholders from personal liability. However, this separate legal personality assigned to companies can in certain circumstances be removed by the courts, which can hold the shareholders and directors of a company liable for the debts or wrongs of the company. This is known as 'lifting the corporate veil' and may happen in cases of fraud or illegality, for example.

G. The Rule of Law

The *Rule of Law* sometimes known as the principle of legality, is a key principle of most democratic legal systems. Central to the rule of law is the notion that the power of government must be limited to legal rules which have been published in advance and with fair notice. Nobody is above the law, which reigns supreme.

Power is distributed between the different institutions of the State, with no one institution reigning supreme. This *Rule of Law* has a number of practical consequences for our legal system.

First, it requires that laws conferring rights and imposing obligations must be produced in the correct legal manner and form and must only be amended using the procedure permitted by law.

Secondly, an individual is entitled to fair notice of the laws which govern his/her conduct. Therefore retrospective laws (applying new laws to past events) are prohibited. This rule is reflected by the Latin maxims *nullen crimen sine lege* (no crime without law) and *nullum poena sine lege* (no punishment without law). This rule against retrospective criminal law is also reflected in Article 15.5 of the 1937 Constitution which states that:

> the Oireachtas shall not declare acts to be infringements of the law which were not so at the date of their commission.

Fair notice also requires that the law be announced to those who are bound by it and that the laws should be relatively easy to find. In Ireland, *An Iris Oifigúil*, the official state gazette, publishes announcement notices for all new legislation. The courts read out and record their judgments for public record. Legislation is accessible from the Stationery Office and online at www.irishstatutebook.ie. Law reports and judicial decisions have also become easier to locate in recent years. Traditionally these were only available in printed series of reports, but most of these have now become available online. All of the recent decisions of the Irish superior courts are now available to the public on www.courts.ie, the website of the Courts Service of Ireland.

However, locating the laws and understanding them are different tasks entirely. Laws should not only be accessible, but must also be clear and intelligible. Unfortunately, much of our legislation may be difficult for a lay person to comprehend. It is the product of different draughtsmen and uses what is termed *legalese* — a specialist and complex language used by the legal profession. Judicial decisions can also be difficult for the ordinary citizen to interpret. The extent to which our laws are intelligible is certainly worthy of reflection.

CHAPTER TWO

Types and Features of Legal Systems

A. Introduction 13
B. **The Common Law System** 13
    Advantages 15
    Disadvantages 15
C. **Civil Law Systems** 15
    Advantages 15
    Disadvantages 16
D. **Pluralist Systems** 16
E. **Adversarial and Inquisitorial Systems** 16
    Adversarial Systems 16
    Inquisitorial Systems 17

Learning Outcomes

Upon completion of this chapter, the student should be able to:

- Classify and distinguish between the two main types of legal systems giving examples of each;
- Discuss the advantages and disadvantages of each system;
- Recognise other types of pluralist legal systems;
- Differentiate between adversarial and inquisitorial approaches to justice.

A. Introduction

There are two main types of legal systems in operation throughout the western world. Common law and civil law:

Figure 2.1

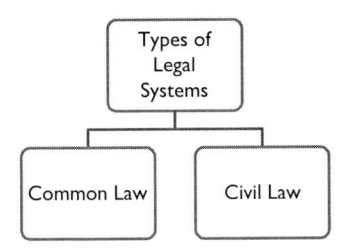

```
        ┌──────────┐
        │ Types of │
        │  Legal   │
        │ Systems  │
        └────┬─────┘
      ┌──────┴──────┐
┌───────────┐  ┌──────────┐
│Common Law │  │ Civil Law│
└───────────┘  └──────────┘
```

Ireland has a common law system.

B. The Common Law System

The common law system was established in England by the Normans after the conquest of 1066. It became known as 'common law' as the old unwritten laws of England were made common to England and Wales after the Norman conquest in the 11th century. Ireland was the next country colonised by Normans after England and they brought with them the common law system which they had adopted in England.

Common law systems have subsequently been introduced into the majority of countries which were colonised by the British and consequently they generally operate in the English-speaking world. Forty nine states of the United States of America (with the exception of Louisiana, as it was colonised by the French), Canada (with the exception of Quebec for the same reason), Australia, New Zealand, India, Barbados, Singapore and Uganda are all examples of common law countries.

Common law is based on a body of judge-made law and has grown out of nine centuries of judicial decision-making. When a judge makes a decision, that decision is binding and must be followed by other judges according to the rule of precedent or *stare decisis* —' let the decision stand'. Judicial decisions reached even centuries ago still apply unless they have been replaced or altered. Over time, these decisions grew into a coherent body of law.

Common law systems usually involve both written law (such as legislation) and unwritten rules which are based on centuries of judges' decisions. In common law legal systems, judges not only interpret and apply the written law, but can, in the absence of appropriate written law, create their own rules. For example, there is no written law in Ireland or the UK setting out the legal right to claim for negligence. However, the courts through a series of judicial decisions starting with *Donoghue v Stevenson* [1932] AC 432, have established the legal basis upon which modern negligence actions can be taken. In the absence of written rules, judges have created their own legal principles to provide a remedy where justice demands.

The Irish common law system consists of both written and unwritten rules. The written laws come from:

- Our Constitution, Bunreacht na hÉireann 1937;
- Legislation — written law consisting of Acts of the Oireachtas and statutory instruments;
- EU law in the form of treaties, directives, regulations and decisions;
- International treaties and conventions.

There is also a substantial body of common law or case law, where the law is based on a series of legal principles established by judges over the course of our legal history. These judgments are recorded in law reports and are a crucial part of understanding many legal subjects.

Figure 2.2

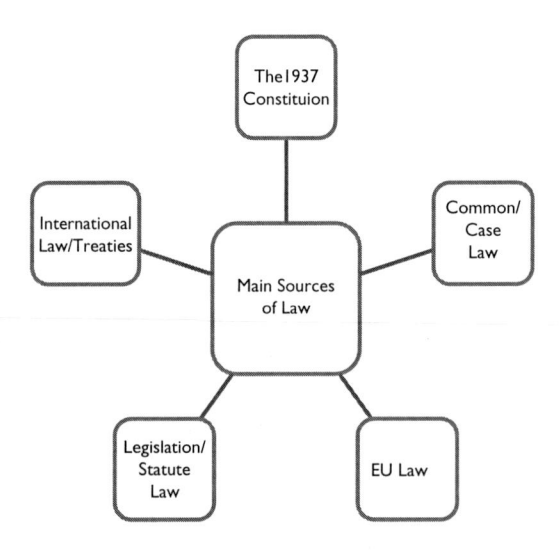

```
                    The 1937
                    Constituion
                         |
  International    ┌─────────────┐    Common/
  Law/Treaties ────│ Main Sources│──── Case
                   │   of Law    │     Law
                   └─────────────┘
                    /         \
           Legislation/        EU Law
           Statute
           Law
```

Each of these sources of law will be discussed in more detail in section C of this text.

Advantages

The common law system is thought to be flexible and adaptable. Judges can create legal principles to cover a wide range of areas, even those not specifically provided for in the written law. Judges can also adapt these principles to suit the circumstances of different cases and keep pace with changes in society.

Disadvantages

As not all of the legal rules are written down, or codified, it can make the law less clear and certain than it otherwise might be. The task of finding and clarifying legal principles can be quite difficult as, instead of going directly to written law, it is sometimes necessary to trace legal principles through a vast number of judicial decisions. Also, due to the greater level of discretion given to judges in common law countries, the decisions made by those judges may at times appear to be inconsistent.

C. Civil Law Systems

The other main types of legal systems are known as civil law systems. Civil systems are the most common type of legal system in Europe and operate mainly in continental European countries and their former colonies. Civil law systems derive from the Roman Empire and, more particularly, the *Corpus Juris Civilis* from AD 529. This brought together the various laws throughout the Byzantine Empire into codified documents. More recently, many civil law systems were influenced by the Napoleonic Code. Civil law is also influenced by religious laws such as the law of the Catholic Church (known as canon law) and Islamic law (sharia law). France, Germany, Spain, Portugal, Brazil, Japan and China are all examples of civil law countries. Not all civil law systems operate in the same way. The German system, for example, is more adversarial and more similar to the systems in England and Ireland than those in France and Italy.

In civil systems, the law is contained in comprehensive codes, often known as penal codes. These written codes are enacted by legislators who attempt to respond to every possible future legal contingency. Only the laws passed by legislators are binding. The role of judges is simply to interpret and apply the written law. Their decisions are not considered to form part of the law. Judges in civil law systems have less discretion than those in common law systems and, in the absence of written rules, do not have the power to create new legal principles to do justice in a particular case.

Advantages

As the laws in civil law systems are codified, they tend to be clearer and more accessible. Having a comprehensive system of written laws helps avoid the uncertainty which can creep into common law systems and ensures a greater degree of consistency in judicial decision-making.

Disadvantages
Civil law systems tend to be more rigid. In the absence of written rules covering a particular scenario, judges generally cannot create new legal principles to provide a legal remedy in a situation where one might be merited. This inflexibility can lead to unfairness.

In recent years, a significant effort has gone into producing a comprehensive criminal law code for Ireland. The Criminal Law Codification Advisory Committee was established by s 167 of the Criminal Justice Act 2002 to oversee the development of a programme for the codification of the criminal law. The code, though not yet complete, aims to make the criminal law easier to find and understand, and to eliminate obscurity, inefficiencies and lack of clarity.

D. Pluralist Systems

The legal system of each country is shaped by its unique history and so may have variations on the systems described above. Some countries have what can be described as pluralist systems.

These pluralist systems can consist of a mixture of common and civil law, such as the South African system, which is a mixture of English common law, Roman-Dutch civil law and customary law.

Other systems are a mixture of civil/common law rules heavily influenced by religious law. An example of this would be Morocco, where the law is based on Islamic law and the French and Spanish civil law system.

E. Adversarial and Inquisitorial Systems

An additional feature of most common law systems is that they are adversarial in nature, while most civil law systems are said to be inquisitorial.

Adversarial Systems
These systems are found in common law countries. An adversarial system is one where the adjudication of a dispute is seen as a contest between the two (or more) sides to a dispute. The contest is fought out in front of a neutral adjudicator — the judge and/or jury. The judge does not become an investigator but rather ensures that both sides are obeying the procedural and evidential rules while presenting their case. It is up to the parties in the case, not the judge, to gather their evidence, call whichever witnesses they require and cross

examine witnesses presented by the other party to the dispute. This is often done in a combative style.

The adversarial system also relies heavily on oral evidence and there is still an assumption that providing oral evidence directly to the court is the best way of determining the facts of a case.

Inquisitorial Systems

In inquisitorial systems, which are used mainly in civil law countries, the judge becomes the investigator of the dispute between the parties. The judge is given the power to gather evidence and examine witnesses. It is up to the parties in the dispute to control the process and ensure that the relevant procedural and evidential rules are followed.

CHAPTER THREE

CLASSIFICATION OF LAWS

A. **Criminal and Civil Law** 21
    Criminal Law 21
    Civil Law 22
    Key Differences between Criminal and Civil Law 24
B. **Substantive and Procedural Law** 25
    Substantive Law 26
    Procedural Law 26
C. **Public and Private Law** 27
    Public Law 27
    Private Law 28
    Other Areas of Law 29
D. **Common Law and Equity** 29
E. **Specific Legal Areas/Subjects** 29

Learning Outcomes

Upon completion of this chapter, the student should be able to:

- Classify and compare civil and criminal laws in Ireland;
- Differentiate between substantive and procedural laws and illustrate an understanding of the interrelationship between them;
- Distinguish between public and private laws;
- Explain the historical division between common law and equity;
- Describe specific legal areas/subjects commonly studied in the Irish legal system.

A. Criminal and Civil Law

Two main types of legal cases are brought before the Irish courts: criminal law cases and civil law cases (not to be confused with civil law legal systems).

Criminal Law

Criminal law defines conduct which is prohibited by the State by creating offences which are punishable by a range of sanctions, including fines, prison sentences, community service or binding to the peace. Criminal law aims to protect society by both prohibiting and punishing wrongdoers who commit a crime. In this way, it acts as a deterrent to crime.

Criminal acts usually involve deliberate intention — this is known as the *mens rea* or guilty mind of the accused and is necessary to secure a conviction in most criminal cases. Criminal offences can include, for example, offences against the person, offences against property and offences against the State.

In Ireland, criminal offences may classified as

1. Summary (or minor) offences; or
2. Indictable (or serious) offences.

Figure 3.1

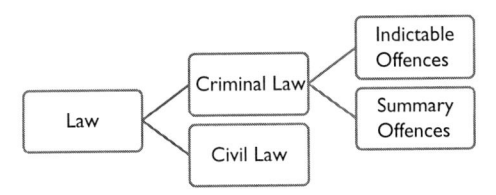

Summary offences are minor in nature and are prosecuted by the State in the District Court. These cases are heard by one judge only and the maximum sentence is usually 12 months' imprisonment.

An example of a summary offence is s 6 of the Criminal Justice (Public Order) Act of 1994 which makes it an offence to use threatening, abusive or insulting words or behaviour in a public place with the intention of causing a breach of the peace. The penalties available to a judge where a person is found guilty of this offence are a class D fine or a term of imprisonment of up to three months or both.

Indictable offences are more serious in nature and are prosecuted by the DPP (Director of Public Prosecutions) on behalf of the Irish people. Indictable offences are tried in the Circuit Criminal Court, Central Criminal Court or Special Criminal Court, depending on the offence. Indictable offences are tried by a judge and jury of 12 people, with the exception of cases which are heard in the Special Criminal Court, which are tried by three judges only. A person found guilty of an indictable criminal offence has a right of appeal to the Court of Criminal Appeal and finally the Supreme Court on a point of law of exceptional public importance. Examples of indictable offences include murder, rape, piracy, manslaughter, aggravated sexual assault and assault causing serious harm.

In criminal cases, the presumption of innocence applies and the accused person is presumed to be innocent until the contrary is proven by the prosecutor. Thus the burden of proof is on the State/DPP to prove the guilt of the defendant. The standard or level of proof required in criminal cases is very high and the prosecutor must prove beyond a reasonable doubt that the accused is guilty of the crime in question. This is taken to mean that, if there is a real doubt, based upon reason and common sense after careful and impartial consideration of all the evidence, or lack of evidence, then that level of proof has not been met.

This high level of proof can make it difficult to secure convictions in criminal cases but is clearly justifiable when one thinks of the potentially serious repercussions of an accused being found guilty — the deprivation of his/her constitutional right to liberty.

When studying law, students can easily identify criminal cases as they will be cited as follows: *The People (Director of Public Prosecutions) v Best* [2000] 2 IR 17. In speech these cases are referred to as "The People against Best". It is generally acceptable to use the abbreviation DPP when citing criminal cases. In England and Wales, most criminal cases are prosecuted in the name of the Crown. Cases are cited as *R v Stanley* [1920] 2 KB 235 and are referred to in speech as "the Crown against Stanley."

The *R* used stands for *Rex* (King) or *Regina* (Queen), depending on the gender of the reigning monarch.

Civil Law

Civil law aims to regulate relations and resolve disputes which may arise between private individuals/entities. Civil law allows a private individual/entity who has suffered loss due to the behaviour of another to seek compensation for that loss. Many civil law cases involve claims for damages to compensate for loss, commonly arising under the tort of negligence.

Civil law also provides a mechanism for enforcing rights or obligations a person may have under the 1937 Constitution or under a contract, for example.

Civil law cases are taken by a plaintiff and are brought against a defendant. In order to take a civil case, the plaintiff must have *locus standi* or standing. This means that the plaintiff must have a legitimate interest in the outcome of the case. He/she must be able to show sufficient connection to and harm from the law or action challenged to take a case. If the court is not satisfied that this is so, it can rule that the plaintiff lacks standing and cannot bring an action.

Civil cases are heard in the District Court, Circuit Court or High Court, depending on the type of claim and the remedy sought. Civil claims are generally heard by one judge only and there is no jury (although there are some exceptions).

The burden of proof in a civil case is usually placed on the plaintiff and the standard of proof required is on the balance of probability. This is frequently referred to in judgments as "more likely than not". This is clearly a lower evidential burden than that paced on the prosecutor in criminal cases. However, the same constitutional considerations about the right to liberty do not apply.

A plaintiff who successfully takes a civil case will most commonly be awarded damages to compensate for loss suffered (which can include loss suffered to date and future loss). Injunctions may be awarded to prevent potential wrongful actions or orders for specific performance granted to enforce rights or obligations under a contract. A plaintiff may also seek a declaration (for example that a law is unconstitutional), or may look for rectification or rescission of a contract. No civil case can result directly in the imprisonment of the defendant, nor any other criminal sanction.

It is also possible for civil cases to be resolved outside of the formal court setting, and many civil disputes may be negotiated and settled at pre-trial stage. Other disputes may be referred to arbitration or mediation for resolution. There are also a number of rights tribunals (e.g. Employment Appeals Tribunal) and Ombudsmen who can investigate and resolve civil disputes.

When studying law, students can easily identify civil cases, as they will be cited using the name of the plaintiff and defendant. The DPP will normally not be involved in the action. In the case of individuals, the surnames of the parties are usually used, for example, *O'Callaghan v Sullivan* [1925] 1 IR 90. When a party to a civil case is a company, the name is given in full and includes "Ltd" or "plc" as the case may be, for example, *Cole v Webb Caravans Ltd* [1983] ILRM 595.

Key Differences between Criminal and Civil Law

Table on the key characteristics and differences between criminal and civil law.

	Criminal Law	Civil Law
Aims	Deter crime Punish wrongdoers	Compensate for loss Enforce rights and obligations
Parties	DPP (Director of Public Prosecutions) prosecutes serious (indictable) crimes on behalf of the People The State – prosecutes summary offences Accused	Plaintiff/Applicant (person instituting proceedings — must have *locus standi*) Defendant/Respondent (person against whom proceedings are issued)
Standard of Proof	Beyond a reasonable doubt	On the balance of probability
Court(s)	District Court Circuit Criminal Court Central Criminal Court Special Criminal Court Court of Criminal Appeal Supreme Court	District Court Circuit Court High Court Supreme Court
Alternative to Court(s)	None	Quasi-judicial tribunals Arbitration Mediation Injuries Board Ombudsmen

Penalties/ remedies	Fine and/or imprisonment	Damages
		Injunctions
		Declarations
		Rescission
		Rectification
		Specific performance
Example of Citation	*The People (DPP) v Best* [2000] 2 IR 17	*Cole v Webb Caravans Ltd* [1983] ILRM 595
	R v Stanley [1920] 2 KB 235	*O'Callaghan v Sullivan* [1925] 1 IR 90

> It is important to note that one action could possibly give rise to both criminal and civil claims. For example, if a person is driving a car under the influence of alcohol and crashes into other people, causing them personal injuries and damaging their car, the following actions could potentially arise:
>
> - Criminal Law
>
> The person may be prosecuted by the State in the District Court under s 4 of the Road Traffic Act 2010 for driving a mechanically propelled vehicle in a public place while under the influence of an intoxicant to such an extent as to be incapable of having proper control of the vehicle. The person might also be charged with an offence under the Non-Fatal Offences against the Person Act and perhaps also with causing property damage.
>
> - Civil Law
>
> The individual who suffered personal injuries and damage to his/her vehicle could take a civil action under the tort of negligence to seek an award of damages to compensate for the loss suffered.

B. Substantive and Procedural Law

Another key distinction in the law is the difference between substantive and procedural law.

As mentioned above, HLA Hart in *The Concept of Law*, 1961, argued that law can be classified into primary and secondary rules. Primary rules are those which set out rights, duties and obligations. They are essentially rules which govern conduct. Secondary rules determine how primary rules are to be recognised, interpreted and applied. They are the procedural methods by which primary rules are enforced. These definitions neatly explain the distinction between substantive and procedural law.

Substantive Law

Substantive laws are the primary rules which Hart refers to. They are the laws which confer rights, powers, duties, obligations or liabilities. These substantive laws cover the main legal subjects which students will study over the course of their legal education and include, for example, criminal law, the law of tort, land law and contract law. Substantive laws can be further divided into *public* law and *private* law.

Procedural Law

Procedural laws, on the other hand, are the secondary rules referred to by Hart. These laws are concerned with the implementation of the substantive rules and govern the procedures by which primary rules are enforced. Procedural laws in Ireland consist of the laws of civil procedure, the laws of criminal procedure and the law of evidence.

Figure 3.2

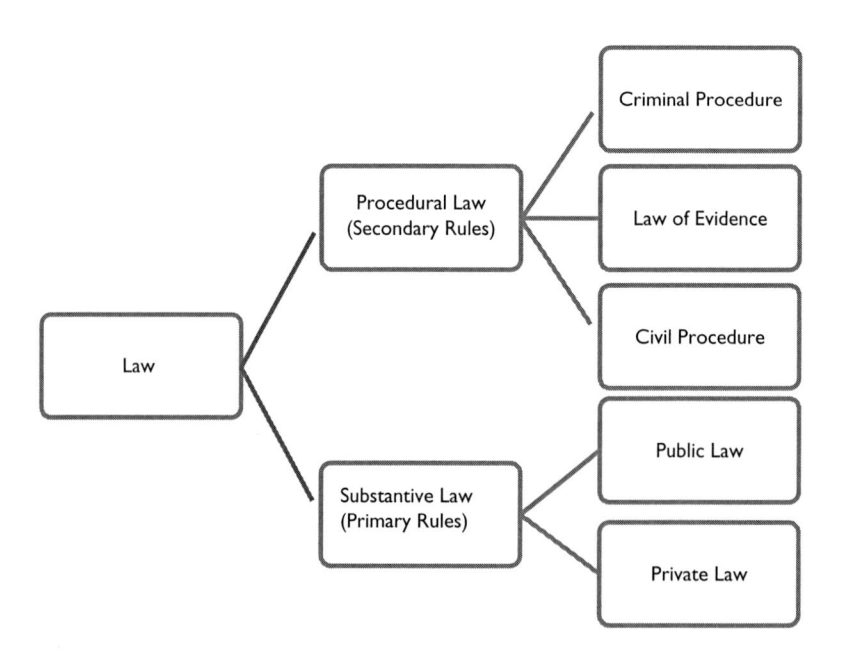

> Substantive and procedural rules are inter-dependent. One does not work without the other. Take the example used earlier, of the person driving a car under the influence of alcohol, who crashes into another person, causing them personal injuries and damaging their car. Both substantive and procedural law would apply:
>
> - Substantive Law
>
> The substantive laws of criminal law and the law of tort would apply. These would set out the criminal and civil liability of the wrongdoer, the power of the State to initiate a prosecution and the right of the injured person to seek damages for injuries and loss.
>
> - Procedural law
>
> Procedural rules would also apply. In order to prosecute the wrongdoer, the State would need to follow both the rules of criminal procedure and the laws of evidence when taking the prosecution. The rules of civil procedure would also be applied if the injured person were to initiate a civil claim for damages.

C. Public and Private Law

Both public and private law form part of the substantive law, establishing rights, powers, duties, obligations and liabilities.

Public Law

Public law is the law which applies to the Irish State and State agencies, or which is concerned with the public good or public interest. It usually involves disputes between the State and individuals. It includes the following:

- Criminal law — As we saw above, this establishes conduct which is prohibited by the State by creating criminal offences which are punishable by fines and/or imprisonment.
- Constitutional law — This is the body of law which has grown out of the interpretation of the 1937 Constitution and involves the laws which create and govern the organs of the Irish State and which establish the fundamental rights of Irish citizens.
- Administrative law — This is the law which governs the administration of the Irish State and the operation, powers and duties of public authorities.

Private Law

Private laws deal with disputes between citizens/private entities where there is no significant public interest. Traditionally, there are three core private law subjects:

- The law of torts — One of the most commonly litigated areas of law, this deals with private or civil wrongs where the act or omission of one party has caused loss or damage to another.
- Contract law — This deals with laws governing legally-binding agreements which are entered into voluntarily between two or more parties.
- Land law — This is the body of law which governs the ownership of property in Ireland.

It should be noted that public bodies are also subject to private law. For example, you can sue a public body for breach of contract or for negligence.

Figure 3.3

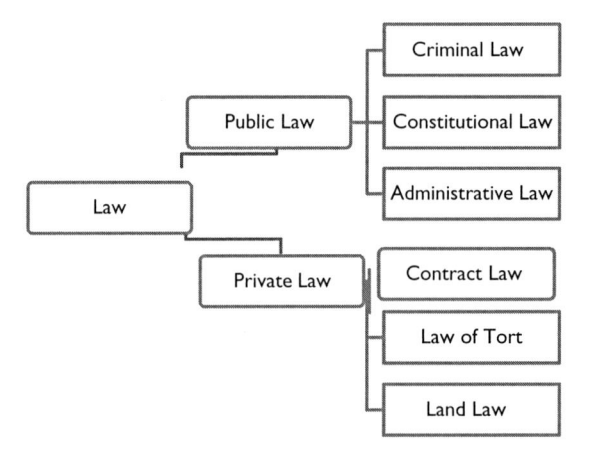

```
                          ┌── Criminal Law
             ┌── Public Law ──┼── Constitutional Law
             │                └── Administrative Law
    Law ─────┤
             │                 ┌── Contract Law
             └── Private Law ──┼── Law of Tort
                               └── Land Law
```

One action could possibly give rise to both public and private law cases. Coming back to the example of a person driving a car under the influence of alcohol that crashes into another person, causing that person injuries and damaging their car, the following actions could potentially arise:

- Public Law

The person may be prosecuted by the State/DPP in a criminal law case.

- Private Law

The individual who suffered personal injuries and damage to his/her vehicle could take a private action under the tort of negligence to seek an award of damages to compensate for the loss suffered.

Other Areas of Law
Over time, other areas of law have developed which have now become distinct bodies of law in their own right. These may be composed of elements of private law, such as tort, contract and land law, as well as some public law elements, and do not fit neatly into the categorisation above. Such subjects include family law, employment law and company law.

Family law, for example, contains elements of criminal law (domestic violence), constitutional law (rights of families and children), contract law (separation agreements) and land law (ownership of the family home), amongst others.

D. Common Law and Equity

Although no longer separate, at one stage during our legal history two branches or divisions of the law — known as *common law* and *equity* — developed.

Common law involved the application of legal principles and rules which had developed over the centuries to resolve disputes. However, if no common law rule is breached or if the application of a common law rule would lead to an injustice, the body of law known as *equity* could be invoked. Equity, which means fairness, was designed to provide justice by righting wrongs and providing remedies where the common law did not. Courts of Chancery or Courts of Equity emerged which allowed plaintiffs to seek relief in circumstances where no common law rule was breached. They also issued remedies which were appropriate to the circumstances of the case, such as injunctions or rectification, rather than the traditional common law remedy of damages. If there was a conflict between the common law and equity, equity would prevail.

Although the two branches of the law merged under the Supreme Court of Judicature Act 1877, many equitable principles and remedies still form part of the law today.

E. Specific Legal Areas/Subjects

The table below provides a brief explanation of the main legal subjects which will be encountered by law students. These subjects are often a mixture of civil and criminal rules, with public and private law aspects (e.g. company law, family law).

Legal Subject	Description
Administrative Law	This is the law which governs the administration of the Irish State and the operation, powers and duties of public authorities.
Arbitration Law	This is the body of law regulating arbitrations — where the parties to a civil dispute agree to refer disputes between them for resolution to an independent third party known as the arbitrator.
Banking Law	This is a body of law which regulates the Irish banking sector including licensing and supervision arrangements, consumer credit and payment methods.
Contract Law	This deals with laws governing legally-binding agreements which are entered into voluntarily between two or more parties.
Canon Law	This is the law of the Catholic Church. It exists separately from the law of the State and does not enjoy force of law.
Commercial Law	This is the law governing commercial entities in Ireland and usually involves the study of consumer protection law, competition law, alternative dispute resolution, intellectual property law, corporate finance law, etc.
Competition Law	This body of law, based primarily on EU rules, is designed to encourage or maintain market competition by regulating anti-competitive conduct by companies.
Comparative Law	This involves the study of the similarities and differences between the legal systems and laws of different countries.
Company Law	This is the body of law which applies to corporate entities, dealing with all aspects of their governance from incorporation to dissolution.
Constitutional Law	This is the body of law which has grown out of the interpretation of the 1937 Constitution and involves the laws which establish and govern the institutions of the Irish State and the fundamental rights given to Irish citizens.
Criminal Law	Criminal law establishes conduct which is prohibited by the State by creating criminal offences which are punishable by fines and/or imprisonment.
Equity and Trusts Law	This is the body of law which grew out of the doctrine of equity and involves the application of equitable principles by the courts.

EU Law	This is a body of treaties — and legislation made by the EU institutions — which have primacy over the laws of EU Member States.
Employment Law	This is the law governing the relationship between an employer and employee.
Evidence (The Law of)	This establishes the rules and legal principles governing the admissibility of evidence and the proof of facts in legal proceedings.
Environmental and Planning Law	This body of law regulates the interaction of humans with the natural environment and regulates the planning process in Ireland.
Family Law	This body of law governs legal relationships between members of a family and their children, if any.
Human Rights Law	This is a body of international and domestic law which seeks to promote and protect human rights.
Intellectual Property Law	This is the law dealing with ownership of the property of the mind or intellectual property. It includes copyright, patents, trade-marks and passing off.
International Law	This consists of laws which are internationally accepted as binding in relations between states and other nations.
Jurisprudence	This is the study of the theory and philosophy of law. It is sometimes referred to as legal science.
Land Law	This is the body of law which governs the ownership of property in Ireland.
Medical Law	This body of law governs the rights and responsibilities of medical practitioners and patients in Ireland.
Media Law	This body of law regulates the behaviour of the organs of the media in Ireland.
Succession Law	Succession law deals with the inheritance of property or goods upon the death of another.
Tort Law (The Law of Torts)	One of the most commonly litigated laws, this deals with private or civil wrongs where the act or omission of one party has caused loss or damage to another.

Section B

The Development of the Irish Legal System

CHAPTER FOUR

THE DEVELOPMENT OF THE IRISH LEGAL SYSTEM

A. Introduction 37
B. From Brehon to Common Law: 5th to 17th Century 37
    Brehon Law 37
    Journey Towards a Common Law System 37
    Equity 38
    Statute Law 38
C. The Penal Laws — 16th and 17th Century 39
D. The 18th and 19th Century — Rebellion and Reform 39
    Rebellion and the Act of Union 39
    Reform of the Court System 40
    Land Law Reform 40
E. Development of Modern Irish Law: 20th Century to Present 40
    Fight for Independence and Anglo Irish Treaty 41
    The 1922 Constitution of the Irish Free State 41
    A New Irish Court System 41
    The 1937 Constitution 42
    Membership of the European Union 43
    The Belfast Agreement 43
    The European Convention on Human Rights 44

Learning Outcomes

Upon completion of this chapter, students should be able to:

- Outline the development of the current common law system from the Brehon laws to the present day;
- Explain the aims of the penal laws and give examples;
- Understand the origins of the Irish court system;
- Describe the main events of legal significance in modern Irish legal history.

A. Introduction

The Irish legal system developed in parallel with the political history Ireland. It is important to gain an insight into the key legal developments over the course of Irish history as they have given the current legal system its unique structure and characteristics and will enable the student to make essential connections between or laws and legal structures, past and present.

B. From Brehon to Common Law: 5th to 17th Century

Brehon Law

The earliest known form of law in Ireland is known as *Brehon law*.

Developed in the 5th century, Brehon law was a native system of law, based primarily on custom. It focused on compensating or making amends to the victim of a wrongful act, rather than punishing the wrongdoer. Judges known as Brehons travelled around the country adjudicating upon disputes. The parties to a dispute were required to agree in advance to abide by their decisions, although there was no formal method of enforcing the decisions of Brehons. In this manner, they acted more like arbitrators than judges, as their decisions were not enforceable.

Journey Towards a Common Law System

The common law system was first brought to Ireland by the Normans in the 12th century. Following the Anglo-Norman invasion in 1169, King Henry declared that the English common law was to be "by all freely received and confirmed."

The common law was based on the old unwritten laws of England. It became known as the common law as it was made common to England and Wales after the Norman conquest there in the 11th century.

The adoption of the common law system in Ireland was a slow and gradual process due to a number of factors:

1. The English common law system was not fully developed, so the Irish common law system developed in conjunction with the English. The development of the Irish common law courts also closely followed the development of the English court system.
2. It took the English over 500 years to conquer all of Ireland. During this period, the Brehon law system and the common law system existed side by side in Ireland. Consequently, each system interacted with and influenced the other.

It was not until the Tudor conquest of the 17th century that the English common law system fully took hold and Brehon law was finally abolished.

Equity

While the common law was taking hold in Ireland, another branch of law known as equity emerged.

The common law involved the application of legal principles and rules which had developed over the centuries to resolve disputes. However, if no common law rule was breached or if the application of a common law rule would lead to an injustice, equity could be invoked.

Equity (which means fairness or justice) was designed to provide justice by righting wrongs and providing remedies where the common law did not. Courts of Chancery or Courts of Equity emerged which allowed plaintiffs to seek relief in circumstances where no common law rule was breached. They also issued remedies which were appropriate to the circumstances of the case, such as injunctions or rectification, rather than the traditional common law remedy of damages. If there was a conflict between the common law and equity, equity would prevail.

Many principles and remedies established by these courts still form part of the law today.

Statute Law

From the first endeavour to introduce the common law system into Ireland in 1171, many attempts were made to introduce the statute law (legislation) of England into Ireland, which at that time had a parliament of its own.

In 1494-5, *Poynings' Law* was passed. It declared that:

- All statutes previously passed in England should have full effect in Ireland; and
- All proposed legislation must be sent to England for the sanction of the Crown and the English Privy Council before it could be put before the Irish Parliament for consideration.

This legislative procedure remained in force for hundreds of years. To ensure legal uniformity, the Irish Parliament enacted many statutes which had previously been enacted in England. An example of a statute passed under this procedure which is still in force today is the Statute of Frauds, passed by the English parliament in 1677 and by the Irish Parliament in 1695.

Given our shared legal history, it is unsurprising that, to this day, the legislation passed in Ireland is often very similar to the equivalent English statute.

C. The Penal Laws — 16th and 17th Century

Irish 16th and 17th century legal history is defined by the penal laws. The penal laws consisted of a variety of written laws passed between the 16th and 18th centuries. These laws were a reflection of England's determination finally to settle Ireland, abolish the Brehon law system and convert Irish Catholics to Protestantism. The laws were established to penalise Irish people who chose to remain Catholic.

For example, the penal laws prohibited Catholics from:

- Owning land on a lease for more than 31 years;
- Making a profit of more than one third of their rent;
- Voting or serving in Parliament;
- Holding public office;
- Practising law;
- Inheriting land from Protestants;
- Owning arms or a horse worth more than £5;
- Teaching their children or sending them abroad for education.

Additionally, property held by a Catholic was to be inherited equally by his sons unless one was a Protestant, in which case he received all. A Catholic could not inherit property if there was any Protestant heir. The hierarchy of the Catholic Church was banished or suppressed. Cases against Catholics were tried without juries and bounties were given to informers against them. There was also a ban on converting from Protestantism to Catholicism. When allowed, new Catholic churches were to be built from wood, not stone, and away from main roads.

Many of these penal laws were repealed at the end of the 18th century. However, it was not until 1829 that the remaining penal laws were finally abolished and Catholics were allowed to serve in Parliament.

D. The 18th and 19th Century — Rebellion and Reform

Rebellion and the Act of Union

In 1717, the English Parliament declared that it had the right to legislate for Ireland in a statute known as the *Sixth of George I*. It also declared that the English House of Lords, rather than the Irish, was to be the final court of appeal.

The Irish Volunteers and Henry Grattan campaigned for the return of legislative independence for Ireland. This campaign succeeded and, for a short period of time from 1792 until 1800, the legislative independence of the Irish Parliament was restored. This parliament became known as *Grattan's Parliament* and it strove to improve the situation of Catholics through the enactment of the Roman Catholic Relief Act 1793. This Act conferred a limited right to vote and admission to practise at the Bar.

However, the independence of the Irish Parliament was short-lived. Following the War of Independence in 1798, the Act of Union was passed in 1800. This brought about total legal union of Ireland and England, effectively creating a new country from 1 January 1801: the United Kingdom of Great Britain and Ireland.

Reform of the Court System
Major reform of the common law court system was introduced by the Supreme Court of Judicature Act 1873 and its Irish counterpart in 1877.

These Acts merged the administration of common law and equity to create a unified court system. Before this Act, the common law and equity remained separate systems of law, with separate procedures, courts and remedies. This Act unified the two, allowing people to avail of both equitable and common law remedies in one court. This Act also established the Supreme Court of Judicature. The Judicial Committee of the House of Lords remained the final court of appeal for Ireland.

The various courts which had developed over the centuries (such as the Court of Exchequer and the Court of Probate) were subsumed into separate divisions of the High Court, which sat in Dublin.

In addition to these superior courts, there were a number of inferior courts including the Court of Assize which dealt with the most important civil and criminal matters. Justices of the Peace dealt with less serious criminal matters and, on the civil side, the County Court dealt with less serious matters than the assizes.

Land Law Reform
Following the Irish Famine (1845-1850), the campaign for land law reform intensified. Eventually, the Land Law (Ireland) Act 1881 was passed, establishing the Irish Land Commission and granting Irish tenant farmers "the three Fs" — fair rent, freedom of sale and fixity of tenure. Despite the reforms, however, calls for home rule and the repeal of the Act of Union intensified.

E. Development of Modern Irish Law: 20th Century to Present

From 1918 to 1922, a number of significant legal events occurred in Irish history.

Fight for Independence and Anglo Irish Treaty
After the general election of December 1918, the elected Sinn Féin members constituted themselves as a revolutionary parliament, *Dáil Éireann* and drew up the *Constitution of Dáil Éireann*. In January 1919, at its first meeting, Dáil Éireann adopted the Irish Declaration of Independence.

British attempts to stop this quest for independence were met with armed resistance and resulted in the War of Independence, which began in 1919.

In 1920, the British passed the Government of Ireland Act, which partitioned the island into Southern and Northern Ireland with separate parliaments, both of which would be subject to the United Kingdom Parliament and would be required to send some members to sit in Westminster.

Following the War of Independence, the Anglo Irish Treaty between Great Britain and Ireland was signed in London on 6 December 1921.

Southern Ireland was to become the 'Irish Free State' (Saorstát Éireann) and was to have dominion status within the British Empire. The British monarch remained Head of State, represented by a Governor General. Members of the Oireachtas were required to swear an oath of allegiance to the Crown.

The 1922 Constitution of the Irish Free State
The Constitution of the Irish Free State (Saorstát Éireann) Act 1922 was enacted by Dáil Éireann in October 1922, and the Irish Free State came into effect on 6 December 1922.

This written constitution represented a significant break from the English tradition. It established the institutions of the Irish Free State and system of government, and set out the fundamental rights of Irish citizens. It was a judicially enforceable constitution, which meant that the courts were charged with ensuring that no law was passed which would conflict with the Constitution.

Laws which were in force in Ireland immediately prior to the coming into operation of the 1922 Constitution continued to have legal effect, unless they were inconsistent with any provisions of the Constitution, or were repealed by the Oireachtas.

A New Irish Court System
The Courts of Justice Act 1924 substantially reformed the Irish court system, which remains generally the same to this date. It created a District Court to replace the Court of Petty Sessions and the Justices of the Peace, giving jurisdiction

to District Court justices in minor civil and criminal matters. The Circuit Court replaced the former County Court and was granted jurisdiction over more serious civil matters. On the criminal side, it adopted the former jurisdiction of the Court of Assize, dealing with more serious criminal matters. It also had appellate jurisdiction over cases from the District Court.

A High Court was established to hear the most serious criminal offences, such as murder and rape, and a Court of Criminal Appeal was established to hear appeals from the Circuit Court and High Court. A further right of appeal to the Supreme Court on a point of law of exceptional public importance was created. The Supreme Court was established as the final court of appeal, to be presided over by the Chief Justice.

Figure 4.1 Court System established by Courts of Justice Act 1924

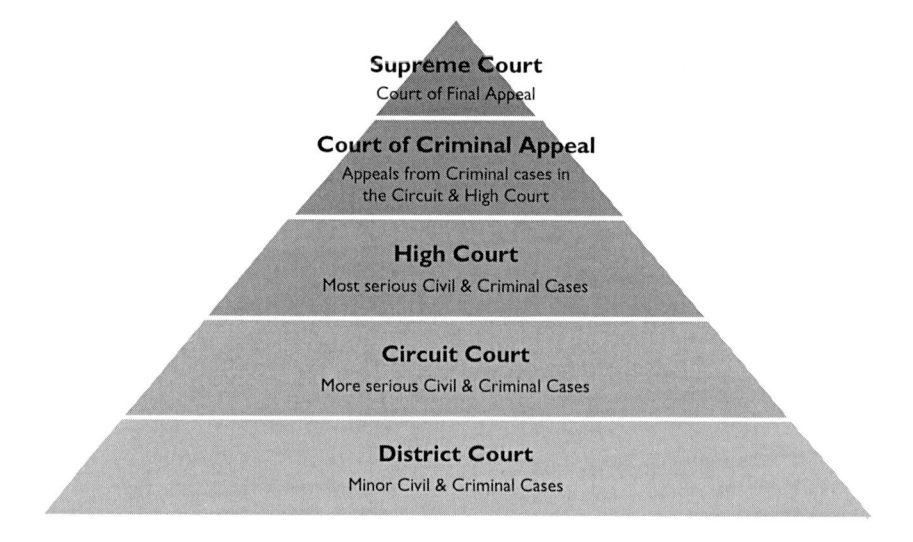

Supreme Court
Court of Final Appeal

Court of Criminal Appeal
Appeals from Criminal cases in the Circuit & High Court

High Court
Most serious Civil & Criminal Cases

Circuit Court
More serious Civil & Criminal Cases

District Court
Minor Civil & Criminal Cases

The 1937 Constitution

The Anglo Irish Treaty and the 1922 Constitution were never fully accepted politically and led to the Irish Civil War.

The 1922 Constitution was continually amended up to 1936. All references to the Crown had been erased, along with the requirement to take the oath of allegiance. When King Edward VIII abdicated in 1936, Ireland passed the External Relations Act, almost completely removing the Crown from constitutional affairs. This paved the way for the 1937 Constitution, Bunreacht na hÉireann, which to this day remains in force as the most important source of Irish law.

The 1937 Constitution was adopted on 1 July 1937 by the Irish people in a plebiscite and came into effect on 29 December 1937.

While broadly similar in many respects to the 1922 Constitution, it distinguished itself as follows:

- It had a more overtly republican ethos;
- It renamed the Irish Free State *Éire* or *Ireland*;
- It established the office of the President as Head of State;
- It replicated the Courts of Justice Act 1924, giving constitutional status to those courts.

It provided that laws which were in force in the Irish Free State immediately prior to the coming into operation of the new Constitution continued in force, unless they were inconsistent with any provisions of the new Constitution.

Relations with the British Crown were finally dissolved, and power in relation to external affairs was repatriated in the Republic of Ireland Act 1948. That Act withdrew the Irish State from the Commonwealth and declared that Ireland shall be known as the 'Republic of Ireland'.

Membership of the European Union

In January 1973, Ireland joined the European Economic Community, which was established by the Treaty of Rome in 1957.

An amendment to the Constitution was necessary so that laws enacted outside the State could have application within the State. This amendment was put to the Irish people in May 1972 and 83% of the population voted in favour of the amendment and Ireland's membership of the European Communities.

This involved the cession of a degree of sovereignty and the subordination of national law to European law. Article 29.4.3° of the Constitution now allows for this.

The sometimes complex relationship between Irish law and EU law will be examined at a later stage.

The Belfast Agreement

The Belfast Agreement, or "Good Friday Agreement", was signed by the Irish and British Governments in Belfast on 10 April 1998. The agreement is made up of two inter-dependent agreements:

1. A multi-party agreement by most of Northern Ireland's political parties (with the exception of the Democratic Unionist Party (DUP));
2. An international agreement between the British and Irish governments.

The Agreement is comprised of three key strands:

- Strand 1 — the status and system of government of Northern Ireland within the United Kingdom;
- Strand 2 — the relationship between Northern Ireland and the Republic of Ireland;
- Strand 3 — the relationship between the Republic of Ireland and the United Kingdom.

The agreement was approved by voters across the island of Ireland and it came into force on 2 December 1999. While the Agreement is primarily concerned with issues such as civil rights, decommissioning of weapons, justice and policing in Northern Ireland, it is constitutionally significant in the Republic of Ireland.

The Agreement resulted in Articles 2 and 3 of the Constitution 1937, which made a territorial claim to the entire island of Ireland, being replaced with new Articles, which declared the desire of the Irish people to unite the entire island of Ireland, but only by the consent of a majority expressed in both jurisdictions on the island.

Article 29 of the Constitution was also amended to allow Ireland to be bound by the Belfast Agreement and to recognise that the jurisdiction of certain institutions formed under that Agreement may be binding on the entire island of Ireland. Both of these changes were agreed by the people in two referendums held on 23 May 1998.

The European Convention on Human Rights

The European Convention on Human Rights, commonly referred to as the *ECHR*, was drafted by the post-World War II Council of Europe in 1950 and was ratified by Ireland in 1953. This international treaty seeks to protect human rights and fundamental freedoms in Europe.

Ireland gave domestic legal effect to the Convention by enacting the European Convention on Human Rights Act 2003. This Act requires the Irish courts to interpret Irish laws in a manner that gives effect to our obligations under the ECHR. Organs of the Irish State must also now act in compliance with the ECHR.

Section C

Sources of Law

CHAPTER FIVE

The 1937 Constitution

A. Introduction — Functions and Features of the Constitution 49
    Introduction 49
    Main Functions 49
    Distinguishing Features 50
B. The Irish State and its Institutions 51
    The Nation 51
    The State 51
    The Institutions of the State 52
        The President, Presidential Commission & Council of State 53
        The National Parliament (Oireachtas) 57
        The Government 61
C. Separation of Powers Doctrine 63
D. Constitutional Rights 66
    Numerated Rights 66
    Unenumerated Rights 69
E. The Interpretation of the Constitution 72
F. Amending the Constitution 75
G. Reviewing the Constitution 77

Learning Outcomes

Upon completion of this chapter, the student should be able to:

- Describe the main features and functions of the Irish Constitution;
- Identify the institutions of the State and explain their functions;
- Discuss the Separation of Powers doctrine and analyse its effectiveness;
- Identify the main fundamental rights enjoyed under the Constitution;
- Explain how the Constitution is interpreted by the courts;
- Describe the process involved in reviewing and amending the Constitution.

A. Introduction – Functions and Features of the Constitution

Introduction

A constitution is typically the supreme source of law for a nation, setting out the institutions of the State and the fundamental rights of its citizens.

Bunreacht na hÉireann 1937, otherwise known as the Irish Constitution 1937, is a primary source of Irish law and is the most important legal document for any student of Irish law. It takes precedence over all domestic legislation and common law rules. No law can be enacted by the Oireachtas which would conflict with the Constitution. While the Constitution is supreme over all domestic law, EU law takes precedence. This relationship will be examined further in the text.

The Constitution was enacted by the Irish people on 1 July 1937 after a plebiscite (public vote) in which 685,105 people voted in favour of the new Constitution, and 526,945 against. Passed by a majority of 158,160 votes, it was designed to replace the 1922 Constitution of the Irish Free State, which had never gained broad acceptance.

Written in both Irish and English, the 1937 Constitution consists of a Preamble, which sets the political, social and religious context for the document, and 50 Articles which establish the Irish State, its institutions and the fundamental rights of its citizens.

The Articles of the Constitution are drafted broadly, and the precise meaning and effect of the Articles of the Constitution have been fleshed out by superior courts since 1937. This is the body of law known as constitutional law.

The 50 Articles of the Constitution are further divided into sections and subsections. For example, Article 12.2.1° of the Constitution, which states that "The President shall be elected by direct vote of the people", is referred to in speech as "Article 12, Section 2, Subsection 1".

Main Functions

The Irish Constitution has two main functions:

1. It establishes the Irish State and its institutions. These include the President, the Parliament, the Courts, Government and local government.
2. It sets out the fundamental rights to be enjoyed under Irish law:

Articles 40 to 44 establish those rights which include personal, family, property, religious, education and children's rights.

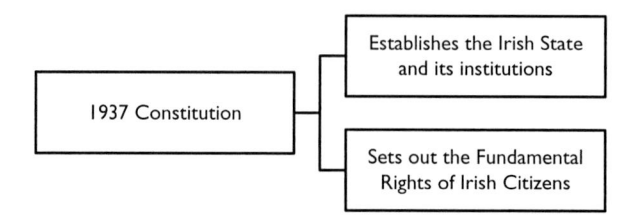

```
                          ┌─── Establishes the Irish State
                          │     and its institutions
    1937 Constitution ────┤
                          │
                          └─── Sets out the Fundamental
                                Rights of Irish Citizens
```

Distinguishing Features of the Irish Constitution

In addition to being one of the oldest written constitutions in Europe and being written in both Irish and English, the Constitution has a number of additional distinguishing features.

It Establishes Ireland as a Democratic State

The 1937 Constitution falls into the democratic tradition, asserting that all powers exercised by the institutions of the State are to be done on behalf of the Irish people (Article 6). It also establishes different institutions to exercise legislative, judicial and executive powers, an arrangement which is found in most other democratic states.

It Reflects a Strong Catholic Ethos

The 1937 Constitution was largely drafted by barrister John Hearne on the instructions of Eamon de Valera. This followed the report of the Constitution Review Committee which was established in 1934 by de Valera. The influence of the Catholic Church on the Constitution is evident. For example the preamble states "In the name of the Most Holy Trinity, from Whom is all authority…" and "We, the people of Eire, humbly acknowledging all our obligations to our Divine Lord, Jesus Christ…" Article 44.2 of the Constitution originally acknowledged the "special position" of the Catholic Church in Ireland as "the guardian of the Faith professed by the great majority of the citizens." This Article was removed by a referendum in 1972. While the influence of the Church has diminished in Irish society, its influence on the Constitution is still clear. The preamble has remained unchanged and Article 44.1 still acknowledges that the "homage of public worship is due to Almighty God".

It Exhibits a Political Aspiration to Unite the Island of Ireland

Former Articles 2 and 3 (which were removed following a referendum after the Good Friday Agreement in 1998) made a territorial claim to Northern Ireland, stating that "the national territory consists of the whole island of Ireland, its islands and the territorial seas" (Article 2). These were replaced with new Articles 2 and 3, which now express the entitlement and birthright of every person born in the island of Ireland, which includes its islands and seas, to be part of the Irish nation (Article 2) and the desire of the Irish nation, in harmony and friendship, to unite all the people who share the territory of the island of Ireland by peaceful means with the consent of a majority of the people, democratically expressed, in both jurisdictions in the island (Article 3). The preamble also makes reference to the "heroic and unremitting struggle" of our fathers "to regain the rightful independence of our nation".

It is Judicially Enforceable

This is a key feature of the Constitution, which means that the Irish courts are charged with upholding (with the exception of Article 45) the provisions of the Constitution. The courts must ensure that all of the institutions of the State act within their powers (*intra vires*), that no laws are passed which would conflict with the Constitution and that the fundamental rights of Irish citizens are protected. Other countries which have enforceable constitutions include Germany, Italy, Spain, Portugal and the USA. Not all constitutions are judicially enforceable. In the UK, for example, the validity of Acts of Parliament is not reviewable by the courts.

B. The Irish State and Its Institutions

The first section of the Constitution (Articles 1 to 39) focuses on establishing the Irish State and the institutions of the State.

The Nation

The Irish nation is established by Articles 1 to 3. Article 1 asserts the independence and sovereignty of the Irish nation, expressing the right of the Irish people to choose their own government and determine the nation's relations with other nations. Article 2 expresses the entitlement and birthright of every person born in the island of Ireland, which includes its islands and seas, to be part of the Irish nation. Article 3 expresses the desire of the Irish nation, in harmony and friendship, to unite all the people who share the territory of the island of Ireland by peaceful means with the consent of a majority of the people, democratically expressed, in both jurisdictions in the island.

The State

The Irish State is established by Articles 4 to 11. Article 4 names the State *Éire*, or *Ireland* in the English language. The Republic of Ireland Act 1948, however, declares that the State shall be described as "The Republic of Ireland." The Supreme Court in *Ellis v O'Dea (No 1)* [1989] IR 530 held that this Act does not change the name of the State, nor could it do so, as legislative provisions cannot override the Constitution. In order to change the name of the State, a referendum would be required.

Article 5 declares that Ireland is a sovereign, independent, democratic state. Article 6 establishes that the powers of government, legislative, executive and judicial, derive from the people. Article 7 establishes the national flag as the tricolour of green, white and orange. Article 8 recognises Irish as the national and first official language of the State, with English being recognised as a second language. If there is a conflict between the texts of the Constitution, the text in Irish, the national language, is to prevail.

The Institutions of the State

The Constitution establishes a number of institutions of the State. Each institution is given specific powers and privileges and is charged with discharging a particular function under the Constitution.

The main institutions/offices established by the Constitution include:

Institution/Office of the State	Articles of the Constitution
The President	Articles 12 to 14
	Article 26
The National Parliament (The Oireachtas)	Articles 15 to 27
Dáil Éireann	Articles 16 and 17
Seanad Éireann	Articles 18 and 19
Government and Local Government	Article 28
The Courts	Articles 34 to 37
The Attorney General	Article 30
The Council of State	Articles 31 to 32
The Comptroller and Auditor General	Article 33

The following institutions of the State are introduced below:

1. The President
2. The National Parliament (the Oireachtas)
   - Dáil Éireann
   - Seanad Éireann
3. The Government

The President, the Presidential Commission and the Council of State

The President

Articles 12 to 14 of the Constitution establish the office of President. The President is the title given to the Irish head of State who, according to Article 12.1 of the Constitution, "shall take precedence over all other persons in the State and who shall exercise and perform the powers and functions conferred on the President by this Constitution."

- Election and Term of Office

The President is elected directly by the people of Ireland in a Presidential election. Voting is by secret ballot on the system of proportional representation by means of the single transferable vote.

The candidates for election must be Irish citizens, have reached the age of 35 years and must be nominated as President by at least 20 members of the Oireachtas or by at least four local authorities. A former or retiring President may nominate him/herself.

The term of office is seven years and a President may not serve more than two terms. The President may, of course, resign from office before the seven-year term comes to an end. A presidential election must take place at least 60 days before the current President's term expires or 60 days after the President departs office.

A new or returning President enters office by publicly making an oath in the presence of members of both Houses of the Oireachtas, the judges of the Supreme Court and the High Court and other public persons, promising to *maintain the Constitution of Ireland and uphold its laws, and to fulfil the duties of the office in accordance with the Constitution and the law.*

- Functions of the President

The main powers or functions of the President are established in Article 13 of the Constitution. Although the President is the Constitutional Head of State, he or she plays mainly a ceremonial role in State affairs.

All of the powers given to the President under the Constitution are only exercisable on the advice of the Government, unless the Constitution specifically states otherwise (Article 13.9). The Government is required to approve all Presidential messages or addresses, both to the Oireachtas and to the public. Article 12.9 dictates that the President cannot leave the State without the consent of Government. The President is also prohibited from exercising some of his/her constitutional powers without first consulting the Council of State. The main powers assigned to the President in the Constitution are explained below:

```
                    ┌─────────────┐
                    │  Appoints   │
                    │ members of  │
                    │    the      │
                    │ Government, │
                    │Judges & Other│
                    │  Officials  │
                    └─────────────┘
┌──────────┐                              ┌──────────┐
│Signs Bills│                             │Can convene│
│into Law & │                             │a meeting of│
│can refer  │                             │   the    │
│them to the│        ┌───────────┐        │Oireachtas│
│  Supreme  │────────│ Powers of │────────└──────────┘
│   Court   │        │    the    │
└──────────┘         │ President │
                     └───────────┘
┌──────────┐                              ┌──────────┐
│Represents│                              │ Summons  │
│ the Irish│                              │& Dissolve│
│  People  │                              │ the Dáil │
└──────────┘                              └──────────┘
                    ┌─────────────┐
                    │   Supreme   │
                    │ Commander   │
                    │   of the    │
                    │   Defence   │
                    │   Forces    │
                    └─────────────┘
```

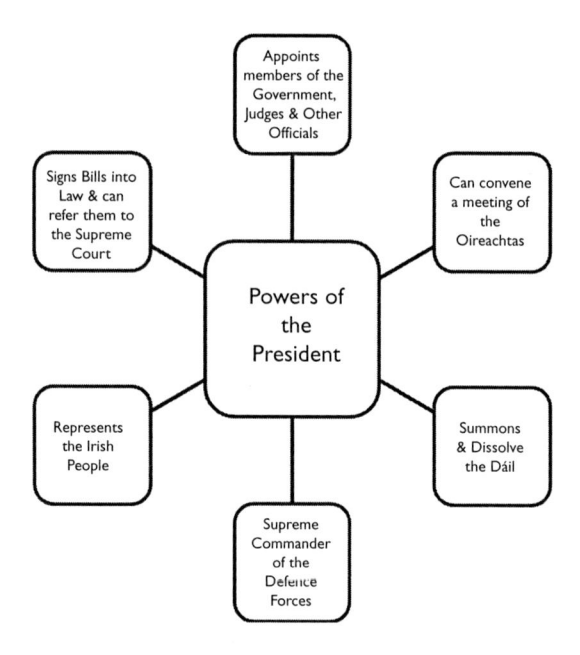

i. Appoints Members of the Government, Judges and other Officials (Article 13.1)
The President appoints:

- the Taoiseach upon nomination of Dáil Éireann;
- the Tánaiste and Government Ministers upon nomination by the Taoiseach;
- the Attorney General, upon nomination by the Taoiseach;
- the Comptroller and Auditor General, upon nomination by Dáil Éireann;
- Judges, upon nomination by the Government.

The President also accepts the resignation or terminates the appointment of any member of the Government on the advice of the Taoiseach.

ii. Summons and Dissolves Dáil Éireann (Article 13.2)
After a general election, the President summons a meeting of the Dáil, on the advice of the Taoiseach. The President also has the power to dissolve or end the Dáil on the advice of the Taoiseach and must do so if a majority of the members of the Dáil agree.

iii. Convenes the Oireachtas (Article 13.2.3°)
The President may, at any time, convene a meeting of either or both Houses of the Oireachtas. The President must first consult the Council of State. The President's power to convene a meeting of either or both Houses of the Oireachtas has never been used.

iv. Signs Bills into Law and Refers Bills to the Supreme Court (Articles 13.3, 25 & 26)

Legislation in Ireland starts life as a Bill, which is passed by both Houses of the Oireachtas. Bills must be signed by the President before they can become law. When a Bill has been presented to the President, he or she has the power to refer it to the Supreme Court within seven days and may do so if he/she doubts the constitutionality of the Bill or any part of it. The President must first consult the Council of State but the decision to refer the Bill is the President's alone. This is undoubtedly the President's most significant constitutional power. If a Bill is referred to the Supreme Court, the Court must decide whether or not the Bill conflicts with the Constitution. If the Supreme Court holds that the Bill is unconstitutional, the President cannot sign it. If the Court upholds the constitutionality of the Bill, the President must sign it into law as soon as possible and the constitutionality of that piece of legislation can never be challenged before the Irish courts.

The President has two additional powers in relation to legislation that have never been exercised:

- He or she may refuse to sign a Bill if a majority of the members of the Seanad and at least one-third of the members of the Dáil petition him or her not to sign the Bill. The President must consult the Council of State before deciding within six days whether or not to sign the Bill. If he or she refuses to sign it, it must be put before the people in an ordinary referendum;
- The President also has a power in relation to money Bills (Bills detailing government spending or taxation). If a conflict arises between the Dáil and the Seanad as to whether or not a particular Bill is a money Bill, the Seanad may ask the President to refer the question to a Committee of Privileges. The President must consult the Council of State before he or she decides whether or not to refer it.

v. Represents the Irish People
The President as the head of State represents Ireland, both at home and abroad, making and receiving State visits.

vi. Supreme Commander of the Defence Forces (Article 13.4)
The President is Supreme Commander of the Irish Defence Forces (Article 13.4). However, under the Defence Act 1954, it is the Minister for Defence who manages and controls the forces.

■ Removal of a President from Office
There are two situations when a President may be removed from office:

- Permanent Incapacitation (Article 12.3.1°)
  If five or more judges of the Supreme Court decide that a President has become permanently incapacitated, the President's term of office will come to an end.
- Impeachment (Article 12.10)
  The President may also be impeached by either House of the Oireachtas for "stated misbehaviour". What stated misbehaviour might be is not specified in the Constitution.

  The procedure is detailed in the Constitution but, simply put, in order to remove the President, two-thirds of the total membership of both Houses of the Oireachtas must vote in favour of impeachment.

The Presidential Commission

If the President is absent, becomes incapacitated, dies, resigns, is removed from office or fails to perform his or her functions, the Presidential Commission acts to perform the functions of the President. The Presidential Commission, established under Article 14 of the Constitution, acts instead of the President while he or she is abroad — for example, by signing Bills into law.

The Presidential Commission is composed of the following:

Member of Presidential Commission	Alternative Member
The Chief Justice of the Supreme Court	President of the High Court if Chief Justice is unavailable
The Ceann Comhairle of the Dáil	Leas (Deputy) Ceann Comhairle if the Ceann Comhairle is unavailable
The Cathaoirleach of the Seanad	Leas (Deputy) Cathaoirleach if the Cathaoirleach is unavailable

Any two of the members of the Presidential Commission can act to perform the functions of the President.

The Council of State

The Council of State is established by Article 31 of the Constitution. It acts as an advisory body to the President. Before the President can exercise some of his or her functions (for example the referral of a Bill to the Supreme Court under Article 26), he or she must consult the Council of State.

There are three categories of members of the Council of State:

Category of Membership of the Council of State	Members of the Council of State
Ex-officio Members (Members by virtue of their office)	The Taoiseach The Tánaiste The Chief Justice The President of the High Court The Ceann Comhairle of the Dáil The Cathaoirleach of the Seanad The Attorney General
Former office holders	Every former President, Taoiseach and Chief Justice who is able and willing to act
Members appointed by the President	Up to seven members are appointed by the President. Their term on the Council lasts only as long as the President is in office.

The National Parliament (The Oireachtas)

The Irish National Parliament, known as the Oireachtas, is established by Articles 15 to 27 of the Constitution. The Oireachtas consists of the President and two Houses, known as Dáil Éireann (a house of directly-elected representatives) and Seanad Éireann (a Senate).

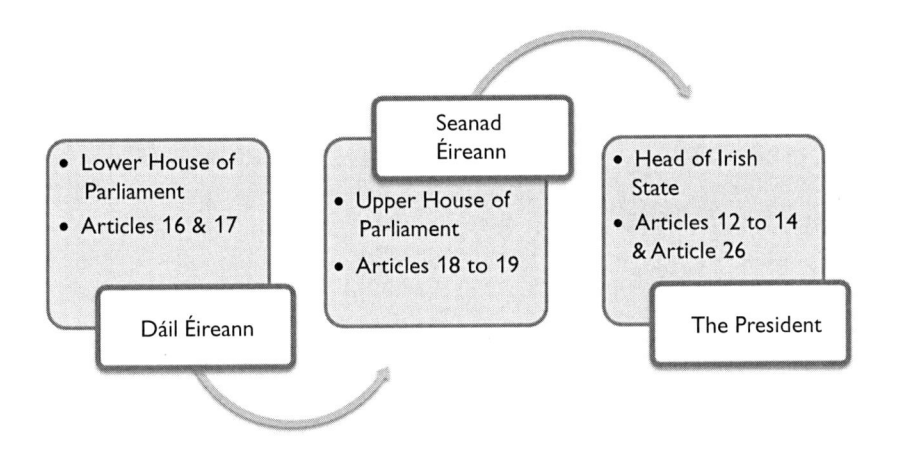

Dáil Éireann
- Lower House of Parliament
- Articles 16 & 17

Seanad Éireann
- Upper House of Parliament
- Articles 18 to 19

The President
- Head of Irish State
- Articles 12 to 14 & Article 26

Article 15.2.1° of the Constitution vests the sole and exclusive power of making laws for the State in the Oireachtas. Therefore, it is the main law making body in Ireland. However, it cannot enact any laws which would be repugnant to the Constitution. The Constitution prescribes that all sittings of both houses of the Oireachtas must be in public, save in cases of emergency.

Members of both houses of the Oireachtas enjoy certain constitutional privileges.

Article 15.12 provides that all official reports and publications of the Oireachtas or utterances made in either House are privileged. This means that members of the Oireachtas may not be sued for defamation for any speech or statement made or question asked in either House and at Committee hearings.

Under Article 15.13, members of the Oireachtas may not be arrested when going to or returning from, or being within the precincts of, either House, except in the case of treason, felony or breach of the peace.

These privileges are granted to ensure freedom of debate, to protect the official documents of the Houses and to protect its members against interference, molestation or attempted corruption. If a member of either House acts in a manner that seems to abuse these privileges, the Oireachtas Committee on Procedures and Privileges may recommend disciplining the member.

- Dáil Éireann

Articles 16 and 17 of the Constitution establish Dáil Éireann, which is the first or primary House of the Oireachtas. Members of the Dáil are known as "TDs" — Teachtaí Dála.

i. Election and Composition

TDs are elected directly to the Dáil in a general election or, on occasion, in a by-election, if a seat becomes vacant during the term of the Dáil. The country is divided into a number of constituencies and, as far as possible, the ratio of population to TD must be equal in each constituency. The number of TDs cannot be more than one for every 20,000 of the population and cannot be less than one for every 30,000. Each constituency elects at least three members and the constituencies must be reviewed every 12 years to take account of changes in our population and its distribution. There are currently 166 TDs.

Eligibility for election to Dáil Éireann is restricted to Irish citizens 21 years of age or over and not disqualified from election to the Dáil (Article 16.1). Certain persons, such as undischarged bankrupts, may be disqualified. Voting in general elections is based on the system of proportional representation by means of the single transferable vote.

Under legislation, the maximum life of the Dáil is five years, although the Constitution does permit a longer lifetime (seven years). There is no minimum period for the duration of the Dáil. If the Taoiseach has the support of the majority of the members of the Dáil, and advises the President to dissolve the Dáil, the President must do so. A general election must be held within 30 days of the dissolution of the previous Dáil.

The 1937 Constitution

ii. Functions of TDs

Members of the Dáil generally divide into political parties or technical groups. In Dáil Éireann, TDs work on various parliamentary committees. They carry out research, prepare speeches and examine proposals for new legislation. Most importantly, they vote on motions before the House. TDs also work in their own constituencies, holding clinics to provide advice to constituents and making representations to ministers or Government departments on their behalf.

iii. The Ceann Comhairle – Chairperson of the Dáil (Article 15.9)

Immediately after a general election, a Ceann Comhairle (Chairperson) is elected from the TDs.

The Ceann Comhairle is the Chairperson of the Dáil. He or she calls upon members to speak, puts motions before the House to be voted upon, keeps proceedings in the House under control, supervises Dáil procedure and has a casting vote should there be a tie in a motion before the House. He/she can also adjourn or suspend proceedings in the Dáil and recommend that TDs be disciplined, if necessary. The outgoing Ceann Comhairle is deemed to be automatically re-elected in the next general election.

- Seanad Éireann (Articles 18 and 19)

Seanad Éireann is the second house of the Oireachtas. It is sometimes referred to as the "Upper House". Its composition is set out below:

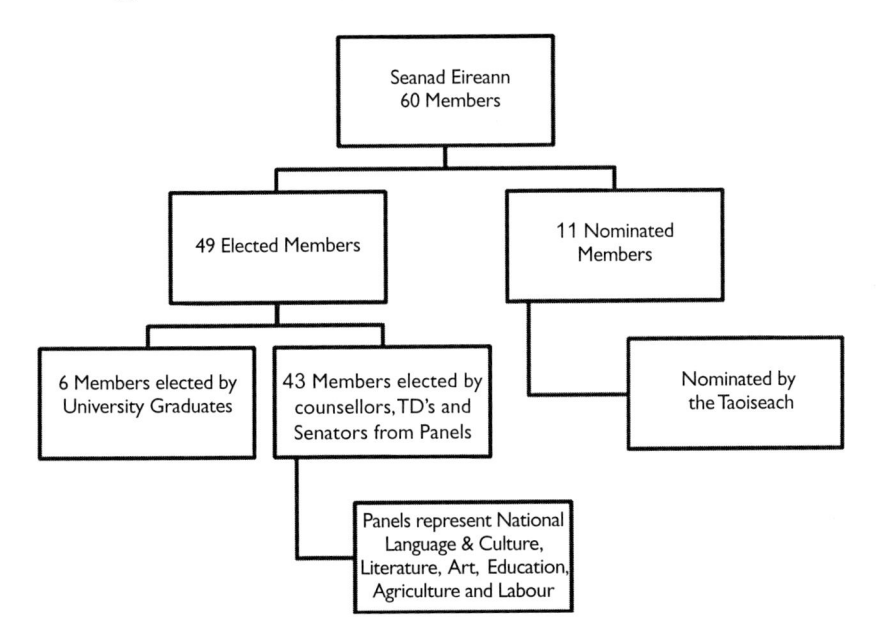

```
                    Seanad Eireann
                     60 Members
                    /            \
          49 Elected Members    11 Nominated Members
           /            \              |
  6 Members elected    43 Members elected by    Nominated by
  by University        counsellors, TD's and    the Taoiseach
  Graduates            Senators from Panels
                              |
                    Panels represent National
                    Language & Culture,
                    Literature, Art, Education,
                    Agriculture and Labour
```

Only Irish citizens who are 21 years of age or over are eligible for election to the Seanad. A new Dáil must be in place before Seanad elections take place.

After the election, a Cathaoirleach, (Chairperson) of the Seanad is appointed to chair proceedings in the House (Article 15.9). The Cathaoirleach has similar functions to the Chairperson of the Dail. While Senators do not officially separate into political parties, they usually divide into groups supporting and opposing the Government when voting. In practice, it is usual for the Government to have the support of the majority of the votes in the Seanad.

■ Functions of the Seanad
i. Voting on and Proposing Legislation
The main function of the Seanad is in relation to legislation. A new proposal for legislation, (a "Bill") may start life in either the Dáil or the Seanad. The majority of Bills originate from the Dáil where they are passed by Government votes. They are then sent to the Seanad for debate and consideration. The Seanad has an important role to play in scrutinising legislation and proposing amendments.

The Seanad generally has 90 days to propose amendments, reject or pass a Bill. However, even if the Seanad rejects the Bill, the Dáil has the power under Article 23 of the Constitution to over-ride the Seanad's rejection and deem the Bill passed by both Houses. If this occurs, Article 27 of the Constitution allows a majority of the members of the Seanad along with at least one third of the members of the Dáil to petition the President not to sign the Bill on the basis that it is of such national importance that is should be referred to the people to ascertain their will.

The power of the Seanad in relation to Money Bills (Bills detailing government spending or taxation) is very restricted. These Bills cannot be initiated in the Seanad, and the Seanad has only 21 days to consider a Money Bill and cannot make amendments to it or reject it.

The Seanad may also propose legislation. A Bill which is proposed in the Seanad is known as a "private members Bill". Such Bills must then pass to the Dáil for consideration, and if rejected by the Dail, will go no further.

ii. Other Functions
The Seanad also has a number of other functions, which it shares with the Dáil, such as:

- Impeachment of the President or a judge;
- Declaring a state of emergency;
- Annulling statutory instruments.

Senators also work on Joint Parliamentary Committees which involve both Seanad and Dáil members sitting and voting together on particular issues.

- Abolition of the Seanad?

While recent debate has focused on the proposed abolition of Seanad Éireann, it still continues as the second House of the Oireachtas, discharging important constitutional functions. However, the 32nd amendment of the Constitution (Abolition of Seanad Éireann) Bill 2013 has been passed by both Houses of the Oireachtas and is due to be presented to the Irish people in a referendum in October 2013. If passed, the Seanad will be abolished and the Oireachtas will consist of the President and Dáil Éireann, who will be vested with legislative power. All references to the Seanad in the Constitution would be removed. Many argue that the Seanad needs reform, rather than abolition.

Arguments for Abolition of the Seanad	Arguments Against Abolition of the Seanad
It will save money (approximately €20,000,000 per year).	There would be no limit on the power of the Dáil, without a second House to keep it in check.
It has very limited functions.	The Seanad represents a more diverse range of views and expertise than the Dáil and these views would not be heard if there were a single chamber.
The legislative process would be simpler and there would be clearer lines of accountability.	The parliamentary committee system might not function effectively without senators to populate it.
The Seanad is undemocratic, as its members are not elected by the public.	

The Government

Article 28 of the Constitution establishes the Government. The Government is often referred to as "the executive" or "the cabinet". Article 28.1 provides that the Government must have at least seven and a maximum of 15 members. These members consist of the senior government ministers responsible for the executive power of the State (Article 28.2), which is the power to implement the law, control public spending and enter into international agreements on behalf of the State.

Article 28.4 provides that the members of the Government are collectively responsible to Dáil Éireann. The Government, therefore, holds office only for as long as it keeps the support of the majority of the members of Dáil Éireann. Additionally, all Government ministers are expected publicly to support policy decisions made by the cabinet.

Article 28.4 also provides for cabinet confidentiality. The confidentiality of Government discussions is assured, subject to disclosure being required in the interests of the administration of justice, by a court, or by virtue of overriding public interest expressed by a tribunal investigating a matter of public importance.

Composition of the Government

The Taoiseach is the Head of the Government. He or she is nominated by the Dáil and formally appointed by the President. Usually, the leader of the largest (or only) party in Government will become Taoiseach. The Taoiseach then nominates the other members of the Government to serve in different State departments. The nominees must be approved by the Dáil and appointed by the President.

The Taoiseach nominates the Attorney General, the legal advisor to the Government who, although not a member of cabinet, usually attends cabinet meetings. The Taoiseach also nominates Ministers of State (junior ministers) who are not members of the Government but assist senior ministers in their work.

The Taoiseach, Tánaiste and the Minister for Finance must be members of the Dáil. It is also possible for up to two members of the Seanad to be appointed to the Government, although this would be highly unusual in practice.

The Taoiseach

Article 28.5.1° provides that the head of the Government, or Prime Minister, shall be called the Taoiseach. The Taoiseach is appointed by the President upon nomination of the Dáil after a general election. The Taoiseach has a number of functions including:

- Nominating the Tánaiste, Government ministers and the Attorney General;
- Keeping the President generally informed on matters of domestic and international policy and presenting Bills to the President for signature;
- Being spokesperson for the Government on major policy issues;
- Chairing meetings of cabinet;
- Representing Ireland abroad, particularly in a European context.

If the Taoiseach loses majority support in the Dáil, he or she must either resign or advise the President to dissolve the Dáil. A general election would then be called. The Taoiseach may also, of course, resign voluntarily. If this happens, then a nomination (or nominations) for a new Taoiseach will be put before the Dáil and the Dáil will approve a new Taoiseach. The new Taoiseach will then appoint new Government ministers.

The Tánaiste

The Tánaiste, who must be a member of Dáil Éireann, is nominated by the Taoiseach. The Tánaiste, who also holds a ministerial portfolio, acts in place of the Taoiseach if:

- The Taoiseach is temporarily absent, for example if he/she is abroad or ill (Article 28.6.3°); or
- The Taoiseach becomes permanently incapacitated, until a new Taoiseach is appointed (Article 28.6.2°).

C. The Separation of Powers

Article 6 of the Irish Constitution declares that the powers given to the institutions of the State under the Constitution are to be exercised by those institutions on behalf of the Irish people, giving effect to the democratic principles upon which the Republic is based.

Article 6 declares that there are three main types of power — legislative power, executive power and judicial power and, under our Constitution, different institutions are charged with exercising the different powers.

The separation of powers is based on the notion that all government functions may be divided into three distinct classes — judicial, executive and legislative — and that each of these functions should be carried out by a different body. If the exclusive power to govern a State is given to one person/body alone, then it is possible that that person/body, and therefore State, could become tyrannical. If, on the other hand, power is divided between different institutions, no one institution can gain absolute control and become tyrannical. The separation of powers doctrine has its foundations in 17th century French political philosophy.

In Ireland, the power to govern the State is theoretically separated as follows:

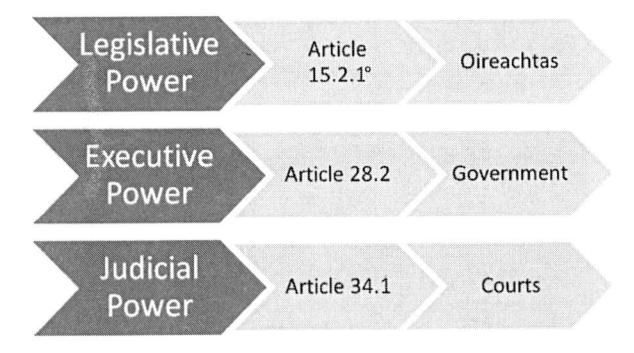

Legislative Power	Article 15.2.1°	Oireachtas
Executive Power	Article 28.2	Government
Judicial Power	Article 34.1	Courts

Legislative Power

Article 15.2.1° states that the sole and exclusive power of making laws for the State is vested in the Oireachtas. Bills must be passed by a majority of votes in both Houses of the Oireachtas and signed by the President before they can become law. The Oireachtas can delegate legislative power, but only to the extent that the delegated power fills in details to implement the principles and policies of the parent statute.

Executive Power

Article 28.2 states that the "executive power of the State is vested in the Government." Executive power is the power to implement the law, to control public spending and to enter into international agreements on behalf of the State.

This power is particularly important in relation to foreign affairs. The Government can enter into international treaties, agreements etc, on behalf of the State and it does not need the prior permission of the Oireachtas to do this, except in certain circumstances. If an agreement involves spending public funds or is intended to become part of Irish law, then Dáil approval is necessary. However, if the agreement is of a technical or administrative character, Dáil approval is not necessary.

In relation to domestic affairs, the Government can use its executive power only to confer benefits on people. It can spend money for the benefit of citizens, once it has parliamentary approval. The Government cannot rely on its executive power to apply restrictions on people or prejudicially to affect people's rights. Such action must be supported by legislation.

Although the Government has no independent legislative power under the Constitution (*Duggan v An Taoiseach* [1989] ILRM 710), it often controls the majority of votes in the Dáil and usually has the majority of votes in the Seanad. Generally, legislation proposed by the Government in the Dáil will be passed unless its own party members vote against it, which is unlikely to happen, as it could have serious consequences for the members in question. Even if a Bill is rejected by the Seanad, the Dáil can deem it passed. Therefore in practice, unless the Bill is deemed to be unconstitutional by the Supreme Court after a referral under Article 26 by the President or a challenge brought by a citizen, the Government effectively controls the legislative process through the party system. Therefore it is fair to say that the legislative and executive powers are intertwined.

The separation of the judicial power is therefore critical, as it is the courts that will ultimately check that the Government is acting within its power and that no unconstitutional legislation is passed into law or remains in force.

Judicial Power

In *Re Solicitors Act* [1954], the Court held that a judicial power is one which could profoundly affect the life, liberty, fortune or reputation of a person.

In *McDonald v Bord na gCon* [1965] IR 217, the Court held that a power is judicial in nature if it involves:

1. A dispute or controversy as to the existence of legal rights or a violation of the law;
2. The determination or ascertainment of the rights of parties or the imposition of liabilities or the infliction of a penalty;
3. The final determination (subject to appeal) of legal rights or liabilities or the imposition of penalties;
4. The enforcement of those rights or liabilities or the imposition of a penalty by the court or by the executive power of the State which is called in by the court to enforce its judgment;
5. The making of an order by the court, which as a matter of history is an order characteristic of courts in this country.

Under Article 34.1, judicial power must be exercised by the courts, which are granted exclusive judicial power regarding criminal matters. Only the courts established by law can try, convict and sentence a person for a criminal wrong. The administration of justice in civil matters is also an exclusive function of the courts. However, under Article 37.1, some limited judicial functions and powers in civil matters may be conferred upon persons who are not judges, or bodies which are not courts — for example, arbitrators or tribunals of inquiry.

Effectiveness of the Doctrine

The separation of the legislative and executive power under the Irish Constitution is not entirely effective, with the two powers being somewhat intertwined in practice.

The real significance of the doctrine lies in the separation of judicial power from the executive power of the Government. The courts check that the Government is acting *intra vires* (i.e. within its powers) and that the Oireachtas does not pass any legislation which is unconstitutional. The Oireachtas, in turn, "checks" the courts. If the courts create any unwritten law of which the Oireachtas does not approve, it may pass written law on the area in question. For this reason, emphasis must be placed in the Irish legal system on independence of the judiciary from the Government.

D. Constitutional Rights

The second key function of the Irish Constitution is to establish the fundamental or constitutional rights of citizens.

Articles 40 to 44 establish the fundamental rights to be enjoyed under Irish law. Since the enactment of the Constitution in 1937, the nature and scope of these rights have been tested before the courts. Irish citizens have sought the assistance of the courts to protect their constitutional rights. The courts have duly upheld the constitutional rights of citizens, confirming that these fundamental rights are legally enforceable and cannot be breached or violated by the State or any other body or person.

There are no "absolute" constitutional rights. All of the rights given to citizens under the Constitution are limited to a certain extent, and the exercise of these rights may be subject to public order, morality or the common good. For example, Article 40.6.1° guarantees the right of citizens to express freely their convictions and opinions, "subject to public order and morality."

The courts have held that all constitutional rights are equal — they have the same status and value — and that it is impossible elevate one right above the others. However, this can cause difficulty if two competing constitutional rights are at issue. In such a case, the court must weigh up the merits of each right, and protect the more important right. For example, in the X case, (*Attorney General v X* [1992] 1 IR 1) two competing rights to life were at the centre of the dispute: the right to life of the mother and the right to life of the unborn. In that case, the Court held that, where there is a real and substantial risk to the life of the mother, and thus a real conflict, the right to life of an expectant mother takes precedence over the life of an unborn child.

All fundamental rights are available to Irish citizens. Non-citizens are only entitled to some limited fundamental rights, such as the right to fair procedures in decision-making and the right to personal liberty. Constitutional rights of citizens are not available to recognised legal entities, such as companies, local authorities and statutory bodies.

Sources of Constitutional Rights
1. Rights expressed in the Constitution — "Numerated Rights";
2. Unenumerated/Unspecified Constitutional Rights

Numerated Rights
These rights are expressly stated in the Constitution and include the following:

- Personal Rights (Article 40)
- Family Rights (Article 41)
- Rights to Education & Children's Rights (Article 42)
- Property Rights (Article 43)
- Religious Rights (Article 44)

■ Personal Rights (Article 40)

Personal Right	Article	Explanation
Right to Equality	Article 40.1	All citizens must, as human persons, be held equal before the law. However, the State may have regard to differences in capacity and social function.
Right to Life, Person, Good Name & Property	Article 40.3.	The State guarantees to respect, defend and vindicate the personal rights of citizens and protect from unjust attack the life, person, good name and property rights of every citizen.
Right to Life of Unborn	Article 40.3.3°	The State acknowledges the right to life of the unborn and guarantees, with due regard to the equal right of life of the mother, to respect and, as far as practicable, defend and vindicate that right.
Right to Liberty	Article 40.4	No citizen shall be deprived of his/her personal liberty, save in accordance with the law.
Right to Inviolability of Dwelling	Article 40.5	The dwelling of every citizen is inviolable and may not be entered forcibly, save in accordance with the law.
Right to Freedom of Expression	Article 40.6.1°(i)	This guarantees the liberty to express freely one's convictions and opinions, subject to public order and morality. It also prohibits the use of the organs of the media to undermine public order or morality or the authority of the State and prohibits the publication of blasphemous, seditious or indecent matter.
Right to Freedom of Assembly	Article 40.6.1°(ii)	This guarantees the right to assemble peacefully and without arms, subject to public order and morality. The law may prevent or control meetings designed to cause a breach of the peace or cause a danger or nuisance to the public. It can also control meetings in the vicinity of either House of the Oireachtas.
Right to Freedom of Association	Article 40.6.1°(iii)	This guarantees the right to form associations and unions, subject to public order and morality.

- Family Rights (Article 41)

Article 41.1 recognises the family as the fundamental unit of society, as a moral institution which possesses "inalienable and imprescriptible rights, antecedent and superior to all positive law." The State guarantees to protect the family as "the basis of authority and social order" and as "indispensable to the welfare of the Nation and State". Article 41.3 pledges to guard with special care the institution of marriage, upon which the family is founded, and to protect it against unjust attack.

The family referred to in the Irish Constitution is based on marriage. In *G v An Bord Úchtála* [1980] IR 32, the Court held that, "as a constitutional unit, the family remains grounded on marriage." A cohabiting couple and their children are not regarded as a family under the Irish Constitution and do not benefit from the constitutional rights conferred upon families.

Article 41.2 recognises the contribution a woman makes to the common good of the State by her "life within the home" and obliges the State to endeavour to ensure that women shall not be obliged by economic necessity to engage in labour to the neglect of their duties in the home.

- Right to Education and Children's Rights (Article 42)

In Article 42.1, the State acknowledges that the primary and natural educator of the child is the family, and guarantees to respect the inalienable right and duty of parents to provide, according to their means, for the religious and moral, intellectual, physical and social education of their children. By virtue of this right, parents can educate their children at home, or in private schools or in schools recognised or established by the State.

Article 42.2 requires the state to provide for free primary education for all children, including those with disabilities. However, in *Sinnott v Minister for Education* [2001] 2 IR 505, the Supreme Court held that the State's obligation does not continue past the age of 18, even if the person would continue to benefit from such education.

Following the enactment of the Thirty First Amendment to the Constitution Bill after a referendum in 2012, Article 42 now recognises and affirms the natural and imprescriptible rights of all children and requires the State to protect and vindicate those rights. These rights are not specified in the Constitution and it will be up to the Irish courts to declare exactly what these natural and imprescriptible rights are.

Article 42 also allows the State to endeavour by proportionate means to supply the place of parents, where the parents, regardless of their marital status, fail in their duty towards their children to such an extent that the safety or welfare of any of their children is likely to be prejudicially affected. It also affirms the right of a child to have his/her own views heard in any proceedings which may be taken by the State under Article 42.

- Property Rights (Article 43)

This Article declares that man has the natural right to the private ownership of property and the State guarantees to pass no law providing for dissolution of the right to own, transfer, bequeath or inherit property. This guarantee is subject to the principles of social justice and the common good.

This allows the law to place restrictions on the uses to which property may be put. Zoning and planning laws and orders for the compulsory acquisition of land by the State are permissible, for example, as they are deemed to be for the common good.

- Religious Rights (Article 44)

Freedom of conscience and the free practice of religion are guaranteed, subject to public order and morality (Article 44). Additionally, the State guarantees not to endow any particular religion and not to discriminate on the grounds of religious belief. It also gives the right to every religious denomination to manage its own affairs.

Unenumerated/Unspecified Constitutional Rights

Unenumerated or unspecified rights are not specified in the Constitution, but have nonetheless been interpreted by the Irish courts as being part of the Constitution.

Article 40.3.1 of the Constitution requires the State to respect, defend and vindicate the personal rights of citizens, and protect from unjust attack the life, person, good name and property rights of every citizen. This Article has been interpreted by the courts as giving rise to various unenumerated (or unspecified) personal rights.

The concept of unenumerated rights first emerged in *Ryan v Attorney General* [1965] IR 294. That case concerned an application by the plaintiff, Mrs Ryan, challenging the constitutionality of the Health (Fluoridation of Water Supplies) Act 1960, which required local authorities to fluoridate the public water supplies in Ireland. She argued that the Act infringed her constitutional rights, including her right to bodily integrity, which she contended is the right to be free from any process imposed by the State which might be harmful to her life or health. Although no right to bodily integrity is specified in any of the Articles in the Constitution, Mrs Ryan argued that the right was implicit in Article 40.3.

Both the High Court, and Supreme Court on appeal, accepted this argument. Kenny J in the High Court held that the general guarantee of personal rights in s 3 (1) of Article 40 extends to rights not specified in the Constitution. He stated that "there are many personal rights of the citizens which follow from the Christian and democratic nature of the State which are not mentioned in the Constitution." He held that a right to bodily integrity was among the personal rights guaranteed by the Constitution.

Despite the fact that the court accepted there was an unspecified right to bodily integrity, the Court held it had not been established that the fluoridation of the public water supply was in fact dangerous and, even if it was, she could filter her own water supply to remove the sodium fluoride without incurring significant expense. Mrs Ryan's challenge, although making legal history, was ultimately unsuccessful on the substantive question.

Following that key decision, a number of other cases have established unenumerated constitutional rights. These unenumerated rights are not absolute and are limited to the extent that they do not infringe upon the common good, public order, morality and social justice. The main unenumerated rights declared by the Irish courts are as follows:

Unenumerated Right	Case Establishing that Right
Right to bodily integrity	*Ryan v Attorney General* [1965] IR 294
Right to travel within the State	*Ryan v Attorney General* [1965] IR 294
Right to marry	*Ryan v Attorney General* [1965] IR 294
Right of access to the courts	*Macauley v Minister for Post and Telegraphs* [1966] IR 345
Right to fair procedures	*Re Haughey* [1971] IR 217
Right to earn a livelihood	*Murphy v Stewart* [1973] IR 97
Right to marital privacy	*McGee v Attorney General* [1974] IR 284
Right to legal representation	*The State (Healy) v Donoghue* [1976] IR 325
Right not to be tortured or ill-treated	*The State (C) v Frawley* [1976] IR 365
Right to travel outside the State	*The State (M) v Attorney General* [1979] IR 73
Rights of an unmarried mother concerning her child	*G v An Bord Úchtála* [1980] IR 32
Right to communicate	*Attorney General v Paperlink Ltd* [1984] ILRM 343

(Continued)

Unenumerated Right	Case Establishing that Right
Right to procreate	*Murray v Attorney General* [1985] IR 532
Right to individual privacy	*Kennedy v Ireland* [1987] IR 587
Rights of a child	*Re the Adoption (No 2) Bill 1987* [1989] IR 656
Right to maintenance and domicile	*CM v TM (No 2)* [1991] ILRM 268
Right to know the identity of one's natural mother	*O'T v B* [1998] 2 IR 321

It remains open to the Irish courts to continue to identify new unenumerated rights, although the practice has diminished in recent years. In *IO'T v B* [1998] 2 IR 321, Keane CJ reiterated the need for judicial restraint in identifying new rights of this nature "save where such an unenumerated right has been unequivocally established by precedent."

In *TD v Minister for Education* [2001] 4 IR 259, Keane CJ again expressed his concern, stating that he had "the gravest doubts as to whether the courts at any stage should assume the function of declaring what are today frequently described as 'socio-economic rights' to be unenumerated rights guaranteed by Article 40."

He also identified two issues concerning unenumerated rights which required further consideration.

1. The criteria by which the unenumerated rights are to be identified.
2. Whether the duty of declaring the unenumerated rights, assuming them to exist, should be the function of the courts, rather than the Oireachtas.

It appears that these calls for restraint have been given due regard by the Irish courts in recent years.

Remedies for Breach of Constitutional Rights

If a citizen's constitutional rights are breached or are about to be breached, the following remedies are available from the courts:

1. An award of damages;
2. An injunction to prevent a potential breach of a person's rights or to stop a continuing breach of constitutional rights;
3. A declaration that a law is unconstitutional and therefore invalid. The law in question becomes null and void and cannot be enforced;
4. An individual may be released from detention because the law under which he/she is being detained is unconstitutional.

E. The Interpretation of the Constitution

The Articles of the Constitution are broadly stated and their precise meaning has been fleshed out by the Superior Courts, which have adopted a number of approaches to interpreting the Constitution. The two main approaches used are the literal approach, which gives the words their literal and ordinary meaning, and the purposive/harmonious approach, which focuses on interpreting a provision in such a manner that it becomes integrated into, and harmonious with, the Constitution as a whole. Two other approaches, known as the historical and natural law approaches are also used.

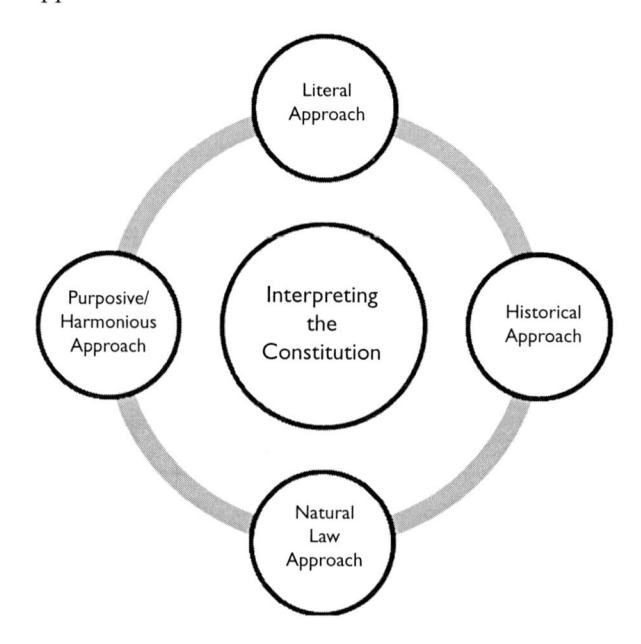

The Literal Approach

This is sometimes referred to as the grammatical approach and it requires the court to give the words their ordinary, literal meaning. It is generally applied in the absence of ambiguity or absurdity in the text.

In *DPP v O'Shea* [1982] IR 384, the Supreme Court considered whether or not Article 34.4.3° of the Constitution, which provided a right of appeal to the Supreme Court from all decisions of the High Court and from other courts as may be prescribed by law, included a right to appeal against acquittals in the Central Criminal Court (the High Court hearing criminal cases).

The majority of the Court (3:2) held, using the literal approach to interpretation, that there was a right of appeal from an acquittal in the Central Criminal Court to the Supreme Court. A literal examination and interpretation of the words would support this decision. However, the two minority judges heavily criticised the literal approach taken in the case and argued that the decision failed to have regard to the historical rule of double jeopardy, which prevents a person being tried for the same crime twice, and *autrefois acquit*, which regarded an acquittal as a final verdict. The minority judges also felt that the Article in question should have been interpreted in light of the Constitution as a whole, and that no such right of appeal existed. This right was subsequently removed by s 11 of the Criminal Procedure Act 1993.

The Purposive/Harmonious Approach

This approach can be summarised by the majority in *DPP v O'Shea* [1982] IR 384, where O Higgins CJ stated:

> ... the Constitution must be looked at as a whole and not merely in parts and, where doubt or ambiguity exists, regard may be had to the other provisions of the Constitution and to the situation which obtained and the laws which were in force when it was enacted.

The purposive or harmonious approach requires the courts to interpret the Constitution in a way which is consistent with the overall scheme or purpose of the Constitution. This may require the words to be given an altered or modified meaning, in light of the spirit or purpose of the Constitution.

The Supreme Court adopted this purposive approach in *Tormey v Ireland* [1985] IR 289. In this case, the plaintiff challenged the constitutionality of s 31 of the Courts Act 1981, which removed the right of an accused to elect to be tried in the Central Criminal Court, rather than the Circuit Criminal Court. The plaintiff argued that this was inconsistent with Article 34.3.1 of the Constitution which vests the High Court with full original jurisdiction in, and power to determine, all matters and questions, whether of fact or law, civil or criminal.

The Supreme Court held that a literal interpretation of Article 34.3.1° would result in an absurdity and would bring Article 34.3.1° into conflict with other provisions of the Constitution. If taken literally, the jurisdiction given to the High Court would be overlapping with other courts and would be unworkable. Instead, the court took a harmonious approach.

Henchy J stated that:

> the literal rule of interpretation...must here give way to the more fundamental rule of constitutional interpretation that the Constitution must be read as a whole and that its several provisions must not be looked at in isolation, but be treated as interlocking parts of the general constitutional scheme.

He held that, despite the apparent unambiguity of a provision, if there were two interpretations which could be attributed to it, the court should:

> adopt the construction which will achieve the smooth and harmonious operation of the Constitution. A judicial attitude of strict construction should be avoided when it would allow the imperfection or inadequacy of the words used to defeat or pervert any of the fundamental purposes of the Constitution.

The Supreme Court subsequently rejected the plaintiff's claim.

The Historical Approach

Sometimes referred to as 'original understanding', this approach requires the court to look at the laws and the political and societal conditions from 1937, when the Constitution was enacted, to derive the original understanding or meaning of the Articles.

This historical approach, however, has a number of difficulties:

- Language may have developed new meanings;
- Political or societal change may have overtaken the original understanding;
- New common law or legislative principles may have emerged which alter the understanding of the Article.

In *Gilligan and Zappone v Revenue Commissioners* [2008] 2 IR 417, the court held that the intention of the drafters of the Constitution and of the Irish people in 1937 was that marriage was between one man and one woman. The court held that society had not changed to such an extent that there was now a consensus to change that historical meaning to include same sex marriage.

In *McGee v Attorney General* [1974] IR 284, the High Court rejected the plaintiff's claim that s 17 of the Criminal Law Amendment Act 1935, which prohibited the importation of contraceptives, violated her right to marital privacy. The High Court held that those who had enacted the 1937 Constitution would not have voted to create a right of marital privacy and repeal s 17 of the Act. However, on appeal, the Supreme Court rejected this contention, with Walsh J stating that no interpretation of the Constitution is intended to be final and for all time, but must change in light of prevailing ideas and concepts.

The Natural Law Approach

Natural law theory involves the belief that law is not just the rules which our institutions create, but that there is a higher law which constrains us all and which is based a system of justice held to be common to all humans, derived from nature. Natural law is therefore superior to all positive law (rules enacted by man).

The natural law approach to interpreting the Constitution focuses on the belief that there are some fundamental human rights (such as the right to life and the right to equality) which are superior to all positive law, including the Constitution. These rights cannot be taken away by any man-made law and they exist independently of the Constitution. In *Ryan v Attorney General* [1965] IR 294, the Court acknowledged these natural rights, which flow from the Christian and democratic nature of our State. Although not specifically mentioned in the Constitution, the court nonetheless upheld these unenumerated, or unspecified rights.

F. Amending the Constitution

The process for a holding a referendum, which is a public vote, is established by Article 47 of the Constitution.

The Constitution allows for two types of referendum:

1. Ordinary referendum;
2. Constitutional referendum.

Ordinary Referendum

This is not a referendum as such, in that it does not relate to amending the Constitution.

However, under Article 27 of the Constitution, an ordinary referendum can take place if the President receives a joint petition from the majority of the members of the Seanad and at least one-third of the members of the Dáil, proposing that a Bill was of such national importance that the will of the people should be ascertained before it is signed by the President into law. The President must consult the Council of State upon receipt of such a petition.

If the President agrees that the Bill contains a proposal of such national importance that the will of the people of Ireland should be ascertained, he or she will refuse to sign the Bill until an ordinary referendum has been held (maximum of 18 months after President's refusal to sign).

Such a proposal will be deemed to have been rejected by the Irish people and cannot be signed into law by the President if the majority of the votes cast is against the Bill and those votes make up at least one-third of the electors on the register of electors (Article 47.2).

To date, an ordinary referendum has not been held in Ireland.

Constitutional Referendum

Because the Government cannot introduce legislation in Ireland that conflicts with the Constitution, it is on occasion necessary to change or amend the Constitution. Referendums have been held on various issues throughout the years, such as Ireland's membership and position within the EU, abortion, divorce and children's rights.

In order to change the Constitution, the Government must hold a referendum. A Bill to amend the Constitution must be proposed in the Dáil and must not contain any other proposal. It must be passed by the Dáil and the Seanad and must be put before the Irish people, who vote for or against the proposed change to the Constitution. The referendum will be passed if a majority of the votes cast is in favour of the proposed change.

If no petition challenging the result is brought to the High Court within seven days of the publication of the provisional certificate of the overall voting result, the certificate becomes final. If it shows that the majority of the votes cast was in favour of the proposal to amend the Constitution, the Bill is signed by the President and the Constitution is then amended.

Unusually, both the Treaty of Nice (Twenty-fourth Amendment of the Constitution Bill 2001) and the Lisbon Treaty (Twenty-eighth Amendment of the Constitution Bill 2008) were rejected in referendums by Irish voters, but each was accepted when a second referendum was held.

The Referendum Commission

In *McKenna v An Taoiseach (No 2)* [1995] 2 IR 10, which was brought following the divorce referendum in 1995, the Supreme Court ruled that it was unconstitutional for the Government to use State monies for the promotion of a particular result or to influence voters in a referendum. However, the court did not overturn the result of the referendum.

Subsequent to this, the Referendum Commission was established in Ireland by the Referendum Act 1998, as amended by the Referendum Act 2001.

Under this legislation, a Referendum Commission is established in Ireland for each new referendum that takes place. Prior to 2001, the Commission was given the task of setting out proposals for and against the referendum. This is no longer the case. The main function of the Referendum Commission is now to prepare and provide independent and unbiased information about the referendum to the public.

The commission publishes and distributes information leaflets and advertisements about the referendum and stimulates debate and discussion about the proposal.

In *McCrystal v Minister for Children and Youth Affairs* [2012] IESC 53, the plaintiff sought an injunction to restrain the Government from continuing to use material prepared by the Referendum Commission for the children's referendum. The Supreme Court ruled that the Government had acted wrongfully by expending public funds to publish and distribute information including a website, booklet and advertisement concerning the referendum that were "not fair, equal or impartial". It stated that the spending of public funds to advocate one side to the detriment of the other would distort the democratic process. Nonetheless, the referendum went ahead two days later and the Thirty-first Amendment to the Constitution Bill concerning children's rights was passed by the people on 10 November 2012 with 58% of the voters voting in favour.

G. Reviewing the Constitution

Over the years, many different bodies have been established to review the relevance and suitability of the Constitution. The political situation in Northern Ireland, Ireland's membership of the EU and developments in human rights all necessitated review of the document. The outcomes of these reviews suggest that the Constitution is still fit for purpose and commands the respect of the Irish people.

Some of the recent review groups include the following:

Constitution Review Group

This group was established by the Government in 1995 to assist the All-Party Oireachtas Group on the Constitution by conducting a review of the Constitution and make recommendations for change. The review group's report was published in 1996, and was one of the most comprehensive analyses of the Constitution ever made.

All-Party Oireachtas Group on the Constitution

This is an informal all-party Oireachtas committee which has been active since 1996. There have been three All-Party Oireachtas Groups on the Constitution, each of which has been given the task of focusing on the place and relevance of the Constitution in Irish society and establishing those areas where Constitutional change may be desirable or necessary:

1. All-Party Oireachtas Group on the Constitution 1996-1997;
2. All-Party Oireachtas Group on the Constitution 1997-2002;
3. All-Party Oireachtas Group on the Constitution 2002-present.

These committees have published a number of progress reports, including the following reports:

Progress Report	Review Topic	Year
Second	Seanad Éireann	1997
Third	The President	1998
Fourth	The Courts and the judiciary	1999
Fifth	Abortion	2000
Sixth	The Referendum	2001
Seventh	Parliament	2002
Eighth	Government	2003
Ninth	Private property	2004
Tenth	The family	2006

The Constitutional Convention

A new body, known as a "Constitutional Convention", was established in July 2012, tasked with considering the suitability of particular aspects of the Irish Constitution for 21st century Ireland and making recommendations to the Oireachtas. The following areas are under consideration by the Convention:

- Reduction of the Presidential term of office to five years;
- Alignment of the presidential election with local and European elections;
- Reduction of the voting age to 17;
- Review of the Dáil electoral system;
- Irish citizens' right to vote at Irish embassies in Presidential elections;
- Provisions for same-sex marriage;
- Amendment to the clause on the role of women in the home and encouraging greater participation of women in public life;
- Increasing the participation of women in politics; and
- Removal of the offence of blasphemy from the Constitution.

The Convention consists of 100 people — 66 citizens, randomly selected and broadly representative of Irish society, 33 members of the Oireachtas and an independent chairman.

CHAPTER SIX

LEGISLATION

A. Introduction 82
    Primary Legislation 82
    Secondary Legislation 82
B. Finding and Understanding Legislation 83
    Finding Legislation 83
    Structure of Legislation 83
        Primary Legislation — Acts of the Oireachtas 83
        Secondary Legislation — Statutory Instruments 83
C. The Legislative Process 84
    Bills 84
    The Legislative Process 85
        Ordinary Legislation 85
        Private Bills 87
        Money/Taxation Bills 87
        Bills to Amend the Constitution 88
        Abridged Time Bills 88
        Private Members' Bills 89
        Consolidation Bills 89
D. Delegated/Secondary Legislation 89
    Introduction 89
    Rationale 90
    Types of Statutory Instrument 91
    Control of Statutory Instruments 92
        Control by the Courts 92
        Control by the Oireachtas 93
E. The Interpretation of Legislation 94
    Introduction 94
    Traditional Rules of Interpretation 95
    The Literal Rule 95
    The Golden Rule 95
    The Mischief Rule 96
    Principal Approaches to Interpretation 96
    The Literal Approach 98
    The Schematic or Teleological Approach 100

F. **Aids to Interpretation**..104
   Intrinsic/Internal Aids 104
      The Statute Itself 104
      Presumptions & Rules of Language...104
      Rules of Language 109
   Extrinsic/External Aids..110
      Historical Setting/Legislative History 110
      Previous Statutes..110
      Reports and Publications of the Law Reform Commission or
         Other Similar Bodies 110
      Parliamentary Materials 110
      Dictionaries and Textbooks..111
      International/EU Treaties and Legislation.............................111
      Previous Practice/Use of the Words.......................................111

Learning Outcomes

Upon completion of this chapter, the student should be able to:

- Define and differentiate between the different types of legislation;
- Locate and identify Acts of the Oireachtas and Statutory Instruments;
- Describe in detail the process for making legislation in Ireland;
- Explain the concept of delegated/ subordinate legislation and discuss how it operates in Ireland;
- Analyse the various approaches to interpretation of legislation in Ireland;
- Identify the various internal and external aids to the interpretation of legislation.

A. Introduction

Legislation, also known as *statute law* is a primary source of Irish law. It consists of written laws which are enacted by the Oireachtas in the manner stipulated by the Irish Constitution. Apart from the European Union, the Oireachtas is the only institution in Ireland with power to make laws for the State (Article 15.2.1° Constitution). There are two main types of legislation: primary and secondary.

Primary Legislation

Primary Legislation consists of *Acts of the Oireachtas*, also known as statutes.

There are three types of primary legislation:

1. Acts to amend the Constitution;
2. Public General Acts — these Acts create law for the public at large;
3. Private Acts — these Acts create law for particular individuals or groups of individuals, such as companies or local authorities.

Secondary Legislation

Secondary legislation is sometimes referred to as subordinate or delegated legislation and consists of laws enacted by a person or body to whom the Oireachtas has delegated legislative authority. These laws are enacted in the form of *statutory instruments*. In general delegated legislation establishes detailed rules while the parent Act under which it is made contains general principles.

Figure 6.1 Types of Legislation in Ireland

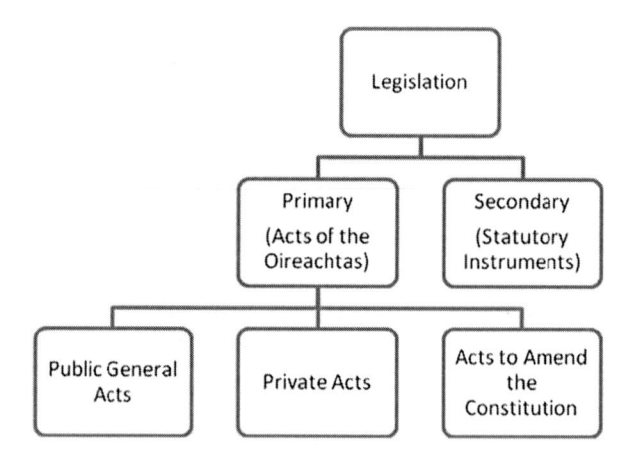

B. Finding and Understanding Legislation

Finding Legislation

Acts of the Oireachtas and statutory instruments are printed by the Government Publications Office and are the official record of the law. They can be found in law libraries and are bound by year.

Legislation is also now available online at the Electronic Irish Statute Book website (known as the eISB — http://www.irishstatutebook.ie). All Acts of the Oireachtas and statutory instruments from 1922 to present may be located there, as well as Bunreacht na hÉireann, 1937.

Structure of Legislation

Primary Legislation — Acts of the Oireachtas

Each Act of the Oireachtas has a long title and a short title. The short title, which is the title used in practice, is the title and year of the Act and is found at the beginning of the Act. The long title is recited at the beginning of the Act in capital letters. The long title usually sets out the purpose of the Act.

Section 1 of each Act is usually an interpretation section, which defines the words used in the Act.

Statutes are divided into sections, sub-sections, paragraphs and sub-paragraphs. Sections can be abbreviated to "s" or "s." and are denoted by numbers. Sub-paragraphs are usually denoted by Roman numerals and may be abbreviated to "subs" and paragraph to "para" For example, a reference to s 6(1)(b)(ii) means section 6, sub-section 1, paragraph b, sub-paragraph (ii).

Many longer statutes are also divided into parts. Some Acts have schedules at the end which may, for example, list earlier statutes being amended or repealed by the present one. The final section of an Act may also provide for a collective citation. This occurs where a later statute supplements or amends an earlier one.

Secondary Legislation — Statutory Instruments

These are generally cited as: SI No XXX of year), for example: Local Government (Planning and Development) Regulation (SI No 89 of 1990).

Some pre-1948 statutory instruments are referred to as Statutory Rules or Orders and are cited as follows SR & O No XXX of year, for example: Aliens Order (SR & O No 395 of 1946).

A statutory instrument is divided in a similar way to an Act, with a short explanatory note indicating its purpose at the end.

C. The Legislative Process

The process by which Acts of the Oireachtas are enacted is governed by Articles 20 to 27 of the Constitution. This constitutional process, which involves Dáil Éireann, Seanad Éireann and the President, is supplemented by a number of informal procedures.

Bills

A new law in Ireland starts life as a *Bill*, which is a proposal for a new piece of legislation. These Bills usually relate to a policy objective of the government, arising from a commitment made in a Programme for government, strategy document, Oireachtas debates or elsewhere. The Government may also publish a Green Paper in which it sets out its ideas for new legislation and invites comment and views from individuals and relevant organisations.

When a decision is made to legislate, the relevant government department will undertake research and draft Heads of the Bill. The Heads of Bill are the key objectives and areas covered by the legislation and are circulated to other Departments for comment. The Heads of Bill are then brought to the cabinet for approval. If approved by cabinet, the process moves to the next stage. After consultation with relevant stakeholders, Department officials then instruct the parliamentary counsel (based in the Office of the Attorney General) who drafts the full text of the Bill and the explanatory memorandum. When the draft Bill is finalised, it begins its passage through the Houses of the Oireachtas.

There are a number of different types of Bills, which are described below.

Type of Bill	Description
Public Bills	Proposals to create law for the public at large.
Private Bills	Proposals to create law for particular individuals or groups of individuals, such as companies or local authorities.
Money/Taxation Bills	Bills which relate to taxation or public spending.
Bills to Amend the Constitution	Proposals to amend the Irish Constitution.
Abridged Time Bills	Bills which are immediately and urgently necessary for the preservation of public peace and security or by reason of national or international emergency.
Private Members' Bills	Bills proposed by a member of the Oireachtas other than a Government minister.
Consolidation Bills	Bills which bring together or 'consolidate' in one Act all of the legislation on a particular topic.

A Bill may be commenced in either the Dáil or the Seanad, but it must be passed by both Houses to become law. Bills are usually initiated by the Government and are commenced in Dáil Éireann. They are then passed to the Seanad for consideration and, if approved there, the Bill is presented to the President, who signs it into law.

However, there are some exceptions to this general rule and the legislative process varies, depending on the type of Bill involved.

The Legislative Process
Ordinary Legislation

The vast majority of Bills are Public Bills. They go through a five-stage process in the Houses of the Oireachtas in which they are proposed (usually the Dáil unless it is a Private Bill). Once passed by the first House of the Oireachtas, the Bill must then go to the second House for approval before being signed into law by the President.

Figure 6.2

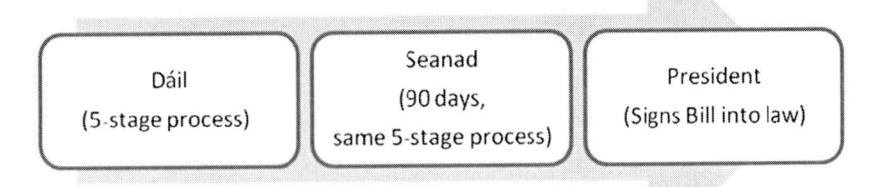

Dáil (5-stage process) → Seanad (90 days, same 5-stage process) → President (Signs Bill into law)

Five Stage Process

Bills usually commence in the Dáil and go through a five-stage process before being sent to the Seanad for consideration. The five-stage process is outlined below:

1. Publication and introduction
   The Bill is published and introduced to the House, usually by a member of the Government. The House then votes to decide whether or not to proceed with the Bill.

2. General debate
   There is a general debate in the house about the principle(s) of the Bill. This involves the relevant minister making a speech outlining the key aspects of the legislation and the merits and objectives of the Bill and contributions from other members of the House.

3. Committee Stage
   The Bill is then sent to select committees to be examined and, if necessary, amended, section by section.

4. Report Stage
   The committee reports back to the House, which then debates the contents of the Bill. Minor amendments can be made at this stage.

5. Final Stage-Vote
   The members of the House vote on the Bill. Members vote by pressing a button at their seat to indicate if they are for or against the proposed legislation. If passed by one House, it goes to the other for consideration and approval.

Seanad Approval

If initiated and approved in the Dáil, the Bill will then be sent to the Seanad to go through the process of debate and committee examination again. The Seanad has 90 days (or any longer period agreed by both Houses) to consider the Bill and do one of the following:

- Pass the Bill without any amendment; or
- Reject the Bill completely; or
- Return the Bill to the Dáil with amendments.

If the Seanad rejects the Bill or returns it to the Dáil with amendments that the Dáil does not accept, the Bill will lapse after 180 days. The Dáil may, within those 180 days, pass a resolution declaring that the Bill is deemed to have been passed by both Houses. This provision means that the Seanad cannot generally stop the Dáil from introducing legislation. However, if the Seanad rejects a Bill which is later deemed to have been passed by the Dáil, a majority of the Seanad together with at least one-third of the members of the Dáil may petition the President not to sign such a Bill on the ground that it contains proposals of such national importance that the view of the people ought to be ascertained. Should the President, after consulting the Council of State, accept the petition, the Bill must either be approved by the people in a referendum or by a resolution of a new Dáil within 18 months. In this respect, the Constitution confers primacy on the Dáil, as the directly-elected House of the Oireachtas.

President's Role in Legislation

Once the Bill has been passed by both Houses of the Oireachtas, the Taoiseach presents a copy of the Bill to the President for signature. Every Bill must be signed by the President before it can become law. Once the President has signed the Bill, it becomes an *Act* and has legal force.

A Bill must be signed on the 5th, 6th or 7th day after it has been presented to the President. However, if the Seanad agrees, the Government may request that the Bill be signed sooner. The Bill becomes law from the day it is signed by the President, unless a contrary intention appears from the Bill or an enactment order is required to be signed by the relevant minister. Once a Bill has been signed, the President must then publish a notice in *Iris Oifigúil* (the official State gazette) stating that the Bill has become law.

Article 26 Reference

When a Bill has been presented to the President, he or she has the power, under Article 26 of the Constitution, to refer it to the Supreme Court within seven days where he/she is in doubt as to whether the Bill is constitutional. The President must first consult the Council of State, but the decision to refer the Bill is the President's alone. If a Bill is referred to the Supreme Court, the Court must decide whether or not the Bill conflicts with the Constitution. If the Supreme Court holds that the Bill is unconstitutional, the President cannot sign it. If the Supreme Court upholds the validity of the Bill, then its constitutionality can never be challenged again and the President must sign the Bill as soon as possible.

Private Bills

These Bills must commence in Seanad Éireann. If passed there, the Bill will progress to the Dáil for approval and finally be presented to the President for signature.

Figure 6.3

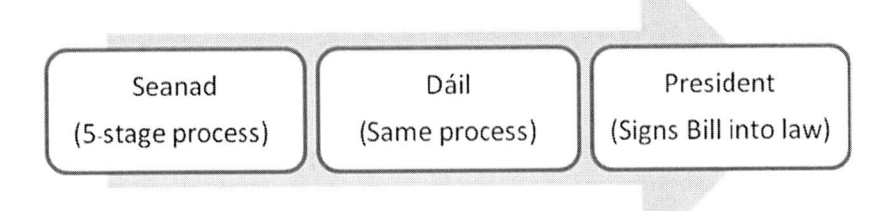

Seanad (5-stage process) → Dáil (Same process) → President (Signs Bill into law)

Money/Taxation Bills

Money Bills are Bills that relate to taxation or relate to spending by the Government. The Ceann Comhairle of the Dáil certifies the Bill as being a Money Bill. The significance of this is that the Seanad has just 21 days to consider these Bills and has no power to reject them. The Seanad can only make recommendations, which can be accepted or rejected by the Dáil. However, the Seanad may challenge the Ceann Comhairle's certification, if the President agrees.

Figure 6.4

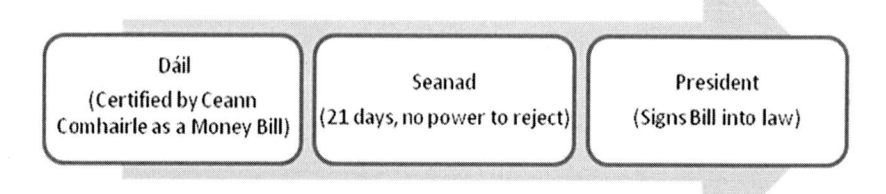

```
[Dáil                    ] → [Seanad                       ] → [President            ]
(Certified by Ceann         (21 days, no power to reject)     (Signs Bill into law)
 Comhairle as a Money Bill)
```

Bills to Amend the Constitution

A proposal to amend the Constitution can only be proposed in the Dáil. A Bill containing such a proposal must not contain any other proposal. Once passed by the Dáil, the Bill then goes to the Seanad for approval. However, before it can be signed into law by the President, it must first be passed by the people in a constitutional referendum.

Figure 6.5

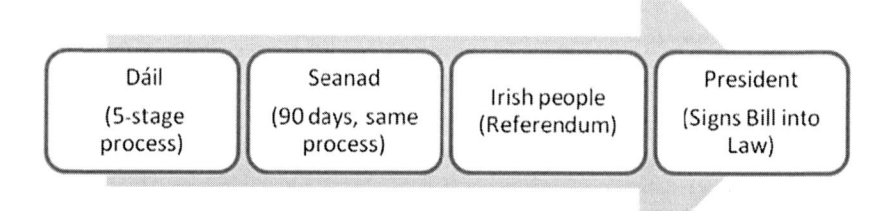

```
[Dáil         ] → [Seanad        ] → [Irish people ] → [President            ]
(5-stage         (90 days, same    (Referendum)       (Signs Bill into
 process)         process)                              Law)
```

Abridged Time Bills

These are Bills which must be passed urgently for the preservation of public peace and security or by reason of national or international emergency. Again, the time for Seanad consideration of these Bills is cut short, or abridged, by the Dáil, with the prior approval of the President. Before the President can approve, he/she must first consult the Council of State. If an abridged time Bill is enacted, it remains in force for 90 days only, unless passed by both Houses of the Oireachtas within these 90 days. This abridged-time procedure cannot be used for Bills to amend the Constitution. This method of making legislation has never been used.

Figure 6.6

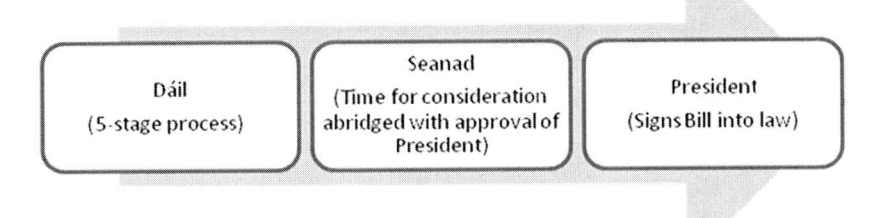

```
[ Dáil              ] → [ Seanad                          ] → [ President            ]
[ (5-stage process) ]   [ (Time for consideration          ]   [ (Signs Bill into law)]
                        [  abridged with approval of      ]
                        [  President)                     ]
```

Private Members' Bills

These are Bills proposed by a member of the Oireachtas other than a Government minister. Unless adopted by the Government, these Bills have little chance of being passed. The process for enacting such Bills is the same as with ordinary Bills.

Consolidation Bills

This is a Bill which brings together or *consolidates* in one Act all of the legislation on a particular topic. These Bills are often introduced in the Seanad. Once the Bill is certified by the Attorney General as not containing any substantive amendment to the law, it goes through the five-stage procedure in the initiating House and is sent to the other House for approval. In the second House, the first three stages are waived and the Bill is debated and voted upon. If passed, it goes to the President for signature.

Figure 6.7

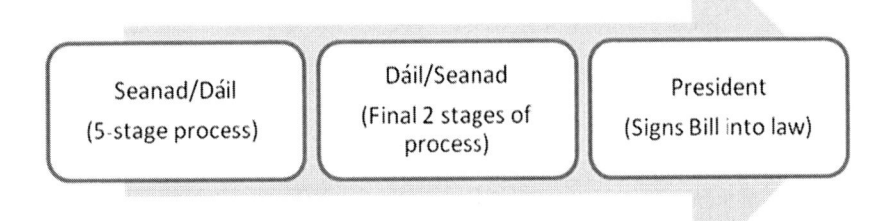

```
[ Seanad/Dáil       ] → [ Dáil/Seanad          ] → [ President             ]
[ (5-stage process) ]   [ (Final 2 stages of   ]   [ (Signs Bill into law) ]
                        [  process)            ]
```

D. Delegated/Secondary Legislation

Introduction

This consists of measures enacted by a person or body to whom the Oireachtas has delegated legislative authority. These measures are known as statutory instruments and are enacted by a Government minister or other administrative body.

In general delegated legislation establishes detailed rules while the Act under which it is made contains general principles.

Figure 6.8

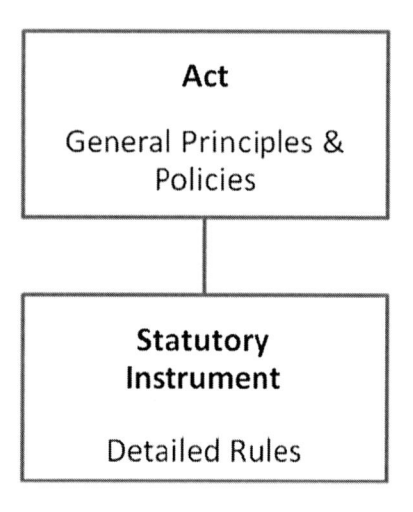

```
┌─────────────────────────────┐
│           Act               │
│                             │
│  General Principles &       │
│        Policies             │
└──────────────┬──────────────┘
               │
┌──────────────┴──────────────┐
│        Statutory            │
│        Instrument           │
│                             │
│      Detailed Rules         │
└─────────────────────────────┘
```

Rationale

Although Article 15.2 of Bunreacht na hÉireann explicitly confers the "sole and exclusive power of making laws for the State" on the Oireachtas, the courts have held that it is permissible in certain circumstances to delegate the power to give effect to the principles and policies established in an Act. It is necessary to delegate this power for a number of reasons:

- Speed and flexibility
  Delegated legislation can be passed more quickly than Acts of the Oireachtas and can respond to pressing issues and emergencies. It can be put into effect quickly and revoked or amended easily if it proves problematic.

- Need for local knowledge
  Laws which are to apply to particular localities and geographical areas benefit from local knowledge, e.g. bye-laws passed by a local authority.

- Lack of time in the Oireachtas
  The Oireachtas has limited time and cannot be expected to go through the legislative process enshrined in the Constitution for every detailed rule which is required. Some statutory instruments are necessary to enact EU laws or commence Acts of the Oireachtas. Others deal with very technical and specific areas and may be quite detailed.

- Planning for Future Contingencies and Changes
  Unanticipated problems may arise with legislation, and statutory instruments may be used to address such issues. Also, changes may be required

to details such as fines and schedules of fees, benefits, etc. These changes are often made using statutory instruments.

In Ireland, delegated legislation takes the form of statutory instruments, which have been defined as instruments "made, issued or granted under a power or authority conferred by statute" (the Interpretation Act 1937). The Statutory Instrument Act 1947 defines a statutory instrument as "...an order, regulation, rule, scheme or bye-law made in exercise of a power conferred by statute."

The number of statutory instruments enacted usually exceeds by multiples the number of Acts passed. For example, in 2012, 53 new Acts of the Oireachtas were enacted, compared to 590 statutory instruments.

Types of Statutory Instrument

There are various types of statutory instrument, each of which has a different function:

Figure 6.9

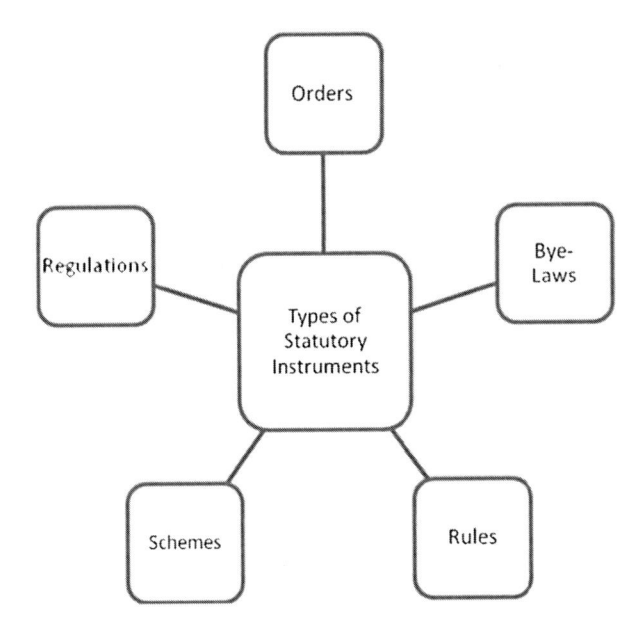

Type of Statutory Instrument	Description
Orders	Orders tend to be made in respect of a single exercise of a delegated power, such as a compulsory purchase order or a commencement order bringing a statute into effect.
Regulations	Regulations are legislative in nature and tend to contain detailed provisions pertaining to general matters which are contained in the parent statute.

Rules	These are legislative in nature and are generally instruments which govern court practice and procedure, such as the Rules of the Superior Courts 1986.
Bye-laws	These are legislative in nature and have been defined as an ordinance "affecting the public, or some portion of the public, imposed by some authority clothed with statutory powers ordering something to be done or not to be done, and accompanied by some sanction or penalty for its non-observance." *Kruse v Johnson* [1898] 2 QB 91. These are often passed by local councils, for example to introduce or change charges and rates or when it is in the interests of the common good of the community that an activity should be regulated or controlled. Local authorities frequently make bye-laws in relation to the control of parking, litter and animals.
Schemes	These tend to be administrative in nature and often consist of numerical material, such as scales of fees and charges.

Control of Statutory Instruments

There are many criticisms of delegated legislation. It is argued that there is a lack of control over the process and that too much power is put in the hands of non-elected representatives, making such legislation undemocratic. Others argue that it is an overused mechanism of making law. However, both the courts and the Oireachtas have a role in controlling delegated legislation.

Control by the Courts

Delegated legislation involves the exercise of a power conferred or delegated by an Act of the Oireachtas. Many cases have come before the Irish courts where it was argued that the delegation of such powers to a minister or other body, by the Oireachtas, was unconstitutional because the delegation was one to make legislation and was thus contrary to Article 15.2 of the Constitution, which vests the sole and exclusive power for making law in the Oireachtas.

In *Cityview Press v An Comhlaire Oiliúna* [1980] IR 381, the extent to which the Oireachtas could delegate its legislative function was considered by the Supreme Court. It held that such delegation is constitutional if the exercise of the delegated power is designed to give effect to the *principles and policies* which are contained in the parent Act. If the law is laid down in the statute and the details are filled in or completed by the designated minister or subordinate body, there is no unconstitutional delegation of legislative power.

In *Laurentiu v Minister for Justice* [1999] 4 IR 26, the Supreme Court held that there are limits to the permissible delegation of legislative power and that the Oireachtas may not abdicate its power to legislate. Where the Oireachtas gives the authority to make regulations to a minister or other body, these bodies are not "law makers", nor do they constitute "subordinate legislatures".

Therefore, the power to enact a statutory instrument is no more than the power to put into effect the views of the Oireachtas which are expressed in the principles and policies of the parent Act. The statutory instrument must be confined to the purposes for which it was conferred. If it goes beyond this, it will be *ultra vires* and unconstitutional.

Additionally, if the Oireachtas grants wide discretion to a minister, but fails to give clear guidance as to the exercise of this discretion, the delegation of power by the Oireachtas is likely to be unconstitutional. In exercising powers delegated by the Oireachtas under an Act, a minister must act "with basic fairness, reasonableness and good faith".

Control by the Oireachtas

In general terms, the Oireachtas does not have a formal role in the enactment of statutory instruments. However, a number of control mechanisms are in place.

First, many Acts under which the power to make statutory instruments is delegated, expressly reserve the right of the Oireachtas to annul the statutory instruments made under that Act. These Acts require the statutory instruments to be laid before one or both Houses of the Oireachtas and they will come into effect automatically unless they are rejected by motion of the Oireachtas.

Secondly, some parent Acts may require a positive motion of acceptance by the Oireachtas, but these are a minority.

There is no Oireachtas committee dedicated to the examination of statutory instruments. Previous committees identified difficulties with statutory instruments, including:

- Poor drafting;
- Lack of explanatory memorandums;
- Lack of correct reference to, or citation of, the relevant statutory authority (parent Act) and;
- Delays in the publication of the statutory instruments.

E. The Interpretation of Legislation

Introduction

While the Oireachtas is charged with enacting legislation in Ireland, the task of interpreting and applying it falls to the courts, whose interpretation enjoys the force of law. When faced with interpreting a piece of legislation, the courts are required to give effect to the intention of the legislature (the Oireachtas).

However, this is not always a straightforward task and several problems may arise when interpreting legislation:

- Language is an inexact method of communication. Words do not have an agreed and consistent meaning and how the word is interpreted may often depend on the context within which it is used;
- The intelligibility of legislation may be an issue. Legislation may contain antiquated language and be the product of several drafts and draftsmen;
- The events before the court may be unforeseen. Technical and social change frequently overtakes legislation which was drafted in the past;
- A broad term may have been used by the Oireachtas and it is up to the courts to decide what the word includes;
- There are difficulties with the Irish statute book. Relevant provisions may be located in a number of different sources and archaic language is often used;
- The draughtsmen tries to anticipate every possible contingency and this adds to the complexity of legislation. Issues often arise when unforeseen events occur as to whether the provision should be interpreted to include/exclude the unforeseen event.

When interpreting legislation, the courts are required to act in a manner that does not infringe upon the legislative function of the Oireachtas.

A court may not add to or delete from the legislation, even where the court is of the opinion that to do so would lead to a fairer result or one which more accurately reflects the intention of the Oireachtas. Additionally, the court cannot in any way amend legislation to cover an unforeseen event or an obvious oversight by the Oireachtas. In *McGrath v McDermott* [1988] IR 258, Finlay CJ stated that "the courts have not got a function to add or delete from express statutory provisions so as to achieve objectives which to the court appear desirable."

Traditional Rules of Interpretation

When interpreting legislation, the courts use a number of canons (rules) of interpretation. In addition to these rules, a number of maxims and presumptions are used and the Interpretation Acts also apply.

These rules of interpretation are general principles which guide the interpretation of legislation by the courts and reflect different approaches used to determine the intention of the Oireachtas.

Traditionally, the courts used three main canons of interpretation: the literal rule; the golden rule; and the mischief rule. These approaches have been overtaken by the two modern approaches to the interpretation of legislation: the literal approach and the schematic/teleological approach.

Nonetheless, it is still important to examine the traditional rules, as the modern approaches reflect the same general principles to statutory interpretation.

Figure 6.10

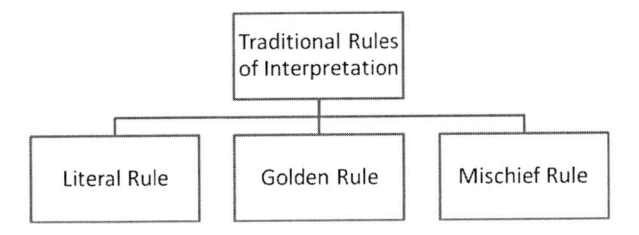

```
          Traditional Rules
          of Interpretation
         /        |        \
   Literal Rule  Golden Rule  Mischief Rule
```

The Literal Rule

This was the main rule of interpretation and required the courts to give a provision its literal, ordinary, natural meaning. The central principle here is that the best way of interpreting intention of the Oireachtas is to follow the literal meaning of the words it has used.

In *Rahill v Brady* [1971] IR 69, Budd J stated that "in the absence of some special technical or acquired meaning, the language of a statute should be construed according to its ordinary meaning."

In the absence of ambiguity or uncertainty, legislation was to be accorded its literal meaning even where it might lead to an undesirable or unjust result. However, a secondary meaning might be adopted where the words were not clear and unambiguous.

The Golden Rule

This provides that, if the application of the literal rule would result in an absurdity or inconsistency, which the Oireachtas could not have intended, then a legislative provision could be given a modified or secondary meaning, in light of the Act as a whole.

In *The People (Attorney General) v McGlynn* [1967] IR 232, Budd J referred to Lord Shaw's decision in *Shannon Realties v St Michael (Ville de)* [1924] AC 185, where he stated that

> … where alternative constructions are equally open, that alternative is to be chosen which will be consistent with the smooth working of the system which the statute purports to be regulating; and that alternative is to be rejected which will introduce uncertainty, friction or confusion into the working of the system.

When adopting the golden rule, the court is not limited to an isolated examination of the provision in question. The long title, preamble and other provisions of the Act may be considered in order to establish the legislative intent, and the provision can be given a modified or secondary meaning in light of the Act 'as a whole'. The court is not, however, permitted to examine extrinsic materials such as parliamentary history. See *Minister for Industry and Commerce v Hales* [1971] IR 30.

In Ireland, s 5 of the Interpretation Act 2005 gives statutory effect to the golden rule.

The Mischief Rule

This rule was laid down in *Heydon's Case* in the 16th century, making it the oldest of the three rules. This rule was devised by the courts at a time when there was a suspicion of statute law. The rule allowed the court to examine the pre-existing common law in order to determine the defect, or mischief, which the statute was designed to remedy. It provided that judges should consider three factors:

- What was the common law before the statute was passed?
- What problem, defect or 'mischief' was the statute trying to remedy?
- What remedy was the legislature trying to provide?

The statute was interpreted in a manner which was appropriate to deal with that defect and put a stop to the problem or mischief that the legislature was addressing.

Principal Approaches to Interpretation

The two main approaches to the interpretation of legislation which are currently used by the Irish courts are as follows:

1. The literal approach;
2. The schematic/teleological approach.

When faced with interpreting legislation, a court will first look to the Interpretation Act 2005 and then to the interpretation section, if any, of the Act in question.

The Interpretation Act 2005 contains a number of rules and definitions which are of general application, thus avoiding the need to specify these matters in each statute individually and assisting the courts when it comes to interpreting legislation.

While this Act does not establish general principles of interpretation, it does refer to two key rules:

- Section 5 declares that, in interpreting an Act that is obscure or ambiguous, or that on a literal interpretation would be absurd or would fail to reflect the plain intention of the Oireachtas, then the provision shall be given a construction that reflects the plain intention of the Oireachtas or parliament concerned, as the case may be, where that intention can be ascertained from the Act as a whole. This gives effect to the golden rule, as discussed above.
- Section 6 of the Act declares that in interpreting legislation:

    a court may make allowances for any changes in the law, social conditions, technology, the meaning of words used in that Act or statutory instrument and other relevant matters, which have occurred since the date of the passing of that Act or the making of that statutory instrument, but only in so far as its text, purpose and context permit.

Section 18 of the Act also provides that:

- Words which import the singular also include the plural and vice versa, unless a contrary intention appears.
- A word which imports the masculine includes the feminine and vice versa, unless a contrary intention appears.
- The word "person" includes both bodies corporate and unincorporated bodies of persons, unless a contrary intention appears.

Additionally, many Acts now contain sections which define particular words/expressions used in the Act. Such sections are referred to as the 'interpretation section' and act as a glossary for the statute. The definition given in the interpretation section of an Act is binding upon the courts. Murnaghan J in *Mason v Levy* [1952] IR 40 at 47 stated that, where an Act provides an interpretation section and a definition, a court "should not depart from the definitions given by the statute and the meanings assigned to the words used in the statute."

Figure 6.11

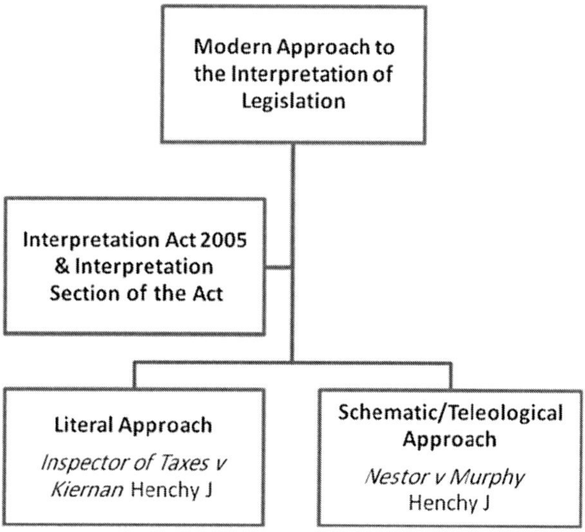

```
                    ┌─────────────────────────┐
                    │   Modern Approach to    │
                    │  the Interpretation of  │
                    │       Legislation       │
                    └───────────┬─────────────┘
                                │
              ┌─────────────────────────────┐
              │   Interpretation Act 2005   │
              │      & Interpretation       │
              │     Section of the Act      │
              └──────┬───────────────┬──────┘
                     │               │
        ┌────────────────────┐  ┌──────────────────────┐
        │  Literal Approach  │  │ Schematic/Teleological│
        │                    │  │      Approach         │
        │ Inspector of Taxes v│  │   Nestor v Murphy    │
        │   Kiernan Henchy J │  │      Henchy J        │
        └────────────────────┘  └──────────────────────┘
```

The Literal Approach

This is the main approach to the interpretation of legislation used by Irish courts and is similar to the old literal rule. This requires the courts to give a provision its literal, ordinary, natural meaning from the context in which it appears. Underlying the literal rule is the view that the best way of interpreting the intention of the Oireachtas is to follow the literal meaning of the words it has used.

The authoritative statement of the literal approach was given by Henchy J in *Inspector of Taxes v Kiernan* [1981] IR 117. Mr Kiernan (the respondent) was a taxpayer who was assessed for income tax under s 78 of the Income Tax Act 1967, which applied to an occupier of land who is a "dealer in cattle." During the relevant year, Mr Kiernan had engaged in intensive pig production at his holding of 27 acres by buying young animals, fattening and then selling them.

The Circuit Court upheld the assessment but stated a case for the opinion of the High Court on the question whether the Circuit Court judge was correct in holding that the respondent had been a dealer in cattle within the meaning of s 78 of the Act of 1967.

The High Court held that the word "cattle" did not include pigs and that, accordingly, the respondent had not been a dealer in cattle. The High Court judgment was then appealed to the Supreme Court which was required to consider whether the expression 'cattle' which was used in the Income Tax Act 1967 included pigs.

In the Supreme Court, Henchy J stated the following three basic rules of statutory interpretation:

i. First, if the statutory provision is directed to the public at large, rather than to a particular class who may be expected to use the word or expression in question in either a narrowed or extended connotation, then, in the absence of internal evidence suggesting the contrary, the word or expression should be given its ordinary or colloquial meaning. However, if an Act is passed with reference to a particular trade, business or transaction and words are used which everybody conversant with that business etc, understand to have a particular meaning, then the words will be construed according to that particular meaning, though it may differ from the common/ordinary meaning of the word;

ii. Secondly, if a word or expression is used in a statute creating a penal or taxation liability and there is looseness or ambiguity attaching to it, the word should be construed strictly, so as to prevent a fresh imposition of liability from being created unlawfully by the use of oblique or slack language;

iii. Thirdly, when a word which requires to be given its natural and ordinary meaning is a simple word, which has widespread and unambiguous currency, the judge construing it should always draw primarily on his own experience of its use. Dictionaries and other literary sources should only be looked at when alternative meanings, regional uses and other obliquities are shown to cast doubt on its ordinary meaning or when there are grounds for suggesting that the meaning of the word has changed since the statute in question was passed.

Upon application of the above principles, the Court held that, as the provisions in question in this case were aimed at the public generally, "cattle" should be given its ordinary and natural meaning. Relying on his own understanding of the word, Henchy J held that "cattle" was to be interpreted as meaning no more than a bovine animal and that, to the ordinary person, sheep, cattle and pigs are distinct forms of livestock.

The principles established by Henchy J have been endorsed in *McGrath v McDermott* [1988] IR 258, in *Texaco (Ireland) Ltd v Murphy* [1991] 2 IR 449 and in *Howard v Commissioners of Public Works* [1994] 1 IR 101, where Blayney J stated that:

> "The cardinal rule for the construction of Acts of Parliament is that they should be construed according to the intention expressed in the Acts themselves. If the words of a statute are themselves precise and unambiguous, then no more can be necessary than to expound those

words in their ordinary and natural sense. The words themselves alone do, in such a case, best declare the intention of the law giver."

The application of the literal approach is changed in the following instances:

i. Where the words in the statute are legal terms of art, in which case they will be given that meaning, rather than their ordinary meaning. For example, in *Minister for Industry and Commerce v Pim Brothers Ltd* [1966] IR 154, the word 'offer' was given its legal meaning, which differed from the popular or ordinary meaning of the word.
ii. Where the statute is directed at a particular class or group of people rather than the public at large, the words are given the meaning which would be understood by that class. In *Minister for Industry and Commerce v Hammond Lane Metal Co Ltd* [1947] Ir Jur Rep 59, the expression 'scrap lead' was assigned the meaning which it would bear in the scrap metal business, that being the class to which the relevant measure was directed, rather than the meaning which the general public might attribute to the word.

Table on Advantages and Disadvantages of the Literal Approach to the Interpretation of Legislation

Advantages of the Literal Approach	Disadvantages of the Literal Approach
Respects the sovereignty of the Oireachtas and its constitutional function as the sole law-making body for the State.	Some terms may have a very clear meaning but it may be unsure how far the word stretches.
Prevents the courts substituting their own will for the intention of the Oireachtas.	It assumes perfect drafting which is not always the case.
	Words are an imperfect method of communication and may mean different things to different people.
	The meaning of words may shift over time.

The Schematic or Teleological Approach

If the application of the literal rule leads to an absurdity, the courts can adopt a different approach. This approach is known as the schematic or teleological approach and involves the courts examining the scheme or purpose of a statutory provision and interpreting the provision in such a way as to give effect to that scheme or purpose and, consequently, the intention of the legislature.

Historically, this approach was expressed in the golden and mischief rules. However, the courts now avoid using terms like "golden rule" and "mischief rule" and refer to the schematic or teleological approach, where the literal rule would lead to an absurdity.

Where the possibility of an absurdity arises, the court may reject the literal interpretation and attribute to the words a secondary, modified meaning which they are capable of bearing. In adopting an alternative, the court may examine the provision in its wider statutory context and may take into account the defect of the pre-existing law.

The authoritative statement of the modern schematic/teleological approach was given by Henchy J in *Nestor v Murphy* [1979] IR 326.

In that case, the defendants were a married couple who, in July 1978, agreed to sell their home, which they held as joint tenants, to the plaintiffs. They signed a contract for the sale of the home which was binding and enforceable. However, they then refused to complete the sale and claimed the contract was void under s 3(1) of the Family Home Protection Act 1976, which states

> where a spouse, without the prior consent in writing of the other spouse, purports to convey any interest in the family home to any person except the other spouse, then ... the purported conveyance shall be void.

The defendants claimed that the contract for the sale of the home was void because the wife did not consent in writing to the sale of the family home before the contract was signed, as required by s 3(1) above.

Henchy J, giving judgment for the Supreme Court, upheld the decision of the High Court ordering specific performance by the defendants of the contract of sale. In his decision, Henchy J conceded that, while a surface or literal appraisal of s 3 (1) might be thought to give support to the defendants' objection to the contract, the basic purpose of the section is to protect the family home by giving a right of avoidance to the spouse who was not a willing party to the transaction. It is directed against the unilateral alienation by one spouse and cannot have been intended by Parliament to apply when both spouses join in the 'conveyance'.

He held that "to construe the sub-section in the way proposed on behalf of the defendants would lead to a pointless absurdity." He went on to outline the practical consequences of such a literal interpretation and described them as being "outside the spirit and purpose of the Act", stating that in such circumstances, a schematic or teleological approach was required.

He held that

> s 3(1) must be given a construction which does not overstep the limits of the operative range that must be ascribed to it, having regard to the legislative scheme as expressed in the Act of 1976 as a whole. Therefore the words of s 3(1) must be given no wider meaning than is necessary [in order] to effectuate the right of avoidance ... It is only by thus confining the reach of the sub-section that its operation can be kept within what must have been the legislative intent.

> In such event no protection is needed for one spouse against an unfair and unnotified alienation by the other of an interest in the family home ... When both spouses join in the 'conveyance', the evil at which the sub-section is directed does not exist. By confining the reach of the sub-section, its operation can be kept within what must have been legislative intent.

In *DPP (Ivers) v Murphy* [1999] 1 IR 98, the Supreme Court considered the interpretation of s 6(1) of the Criminal Justice (Miscellaneous Provisions) Act 1997, which states as follows:

> "S 6(1) Where a person, who has been arrested otherwise than under a warrant, first appears before the District Court charged with an offence, a certificate purporting to be signed by a member [of An Garda Síochána] and stating that that member did, at a specified time and place, any one or more of the following namely—
>
> (a) arrested that person for a specified offence,
> (b) charged that person with a specified offence, or
> (c) cautioned that person upon his or her being arrested for, or charged with, a specified offence,
>
> shall be admissible as evidence of the matters stated in the certificate.

On a literal reading of the provision, a Garda's evidence was necessary in order to confirm that the accused had been arrested "otherwise than under a warrant" and to enable the remainder of the provision to operate in any particular case. In this case, no member of An Garda Síochána had appeared before the court to give evidence as to whether the accused had been arrested otherwise than under a warrant.

However, the DPP argued that the purpose behind introducing the provision was precisely that a Garda would not have to appear in court, thus saving Gardaí the burden of appearing in court to testify on a procedural matter. Before the enactment of this provision, evidence would have been given orally to the court by the arresting Garda.

The High Court, adopting a literal approach, found in favour of the accused. McCracken J stated:

> I would accept that the legislature probably did not intend that evidence of the nature of the arrest would have to be given, but I cannot construe a statute, which is quite clear in its wording, in accordance with what I might perceive as the intention of the legislature. I must give the words their normal meaning.

However, this decision was unanimously reversed by the Supreme Court. Denham J, in her decision, categorised the approach taken by McCracken J as one based on the literal rule, which she considered was not in line with contemporary judicial practice, whereby a purposive approach was preferred. She referred to a passage from the groundbreaking English case of *Pepper v Hart* [1993] AC 593 quoting Lord Griffiths:

> The days have long passed when the courts adopted a strict constructionist view of interpretation which required them to adopt a literal meaning of the language. The courts now adopt a purposive approach, which seeks to give effect to the true purpose of legislation.

Denham J went on state that the literal rule should not apply if it produces an absurd result that thwarts the intention of the legislature.

When the schematic approach is invoked, a court examines the general purpose and scheme of the statute. To do this, the court may examine the long title to the Act, its subject matter and the pre-existing law which it was designed to alter. Once a statutory purpose is identified, the provision in question is interpreted in a manner which is consistent with it and which avoids the absurdity.

One difficulty with this rule is that there is no clear definition of what constitutes an 'absurdity'. If the literal meaning is said to be repugnant, to render the statute unworkable or meaningless or to be grossly unreasonable, then this would probably be an absurdity and result in the adoption of the schematic approach. An absurdity is considered to arise where the literal interpretation leads to a conclusion which, it is thought, could not have been intended by the legislature.

However, something more than the fact that the literal interpretation would lead to an unfair, unreasonable or inequitable result is needed to justify the adoption of the schematic approach and allow the courts to adopt an alternative meaning. Such modification by the courts of statutory language is considered to be a 'usurpation of legislative power' and is only allowable where it is done to implement the 'true' or 'real' intention of the Oireachtas.

It is clear that the identification of an absurdity involves some discretion. What one court finds absurd might not be so found by another court.

Table on Advantages & Disadvantages of the Schematic/Teleological Approach

Advantages of the Schematic/ Teleological Approach	Disadvantages of the Schematic/Teleological Approach
Can prevent an absurd interpretation.	No clear definition/explanation of what constitutes an 'absurdity'.
Prevents possible injustice.	No clarity on when the schematic rule can be invoked.

F. Aids to Interpretation

Whichever approach is adopted by a court to the interpretation of legislation, a number of aids are available to assist with the task. These may be intrinsic/internal (those found within the legislation itself) or extrinsic/external (those found outside the piece of legislation).

Figure 6.12

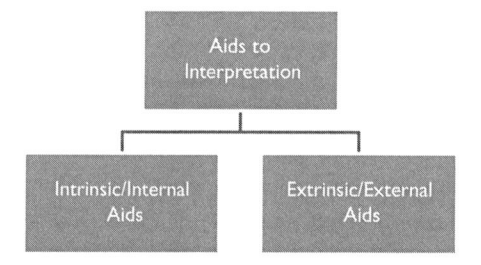

Intrinsic/Internal Aids

These aids include:

- The statute itself;
- Presumptions;
- Rules of language.

The Statute Itself

The wording of the statute in question, including the explanatory notes, long title and preamble to the Act, short title and the interpretation section may provide clues to the meaning of a specific provision.

Presumptions and Rules of Language

A number of presumptions and rules of language are used by the courts when interpreting legislation. These complement the approaches discussed above.

Presumptions

The courts assume that the following presumptions apply to the interpretation of legislation, deriving from the intention of the legislature. All of these presumptions may be rebutted by evidence to the contrary.

Presumption	Meaning
Presumption of Constitutionality	It is presumed that all statutes enacted by the Oireachtas are constitutional unless the contrary is proven. It is presumed that the Oireachtas intends to abide by the Constitution.
Presumption of Compatibility with EU Law	All EU legislation, such as directives and regulations, along with all domestic legislation, should be interpreted in a manner which is compatible with the provisions of the EU treaties.
Presumption of Compatibility with International Law	There is a general presumption that the Oireachtas intended to abide by its international legal obligations when it enacted domestic legislation.
Presumption that all Words Bear a Meaning	It is presumed that the Oireachtas intended that each word in an Act should contribute to its meaning and no words are used without reason.
Presumption that a Statute should be given an 'updated' meaning	It is presumed that the legislature intended that the law be capable of applying to future circumstances. The interpretation of legislation should facilitate statutes being applied to new circumstances.
Presumption against unclear changes in the law	This presumption requires that a change in the law must be achieved clearly either by express statement or by a clear implication.
Presumption that penal statutes be construed strictly	It is presumed that, if the legislature wishes to impose a penalty, it will do so expressly in clear and certain language. Penal statutes should be construed strictly, in a way which leans against the creation or extension of penal liability by implication.
Presumption that revenue statutes should be construed strictly	Any statutory provision which creates a financial liability on the State or individuals must be strictly construed.
Presumption against retrospective effect	Article 15.5.1° of the Constitution prohibits the enactment of retrospective penal legislation.
Presumption against extra-territorial effect	It is presumed that the operation of an Act of the Oireachtas is confined to the territory of the State, unless a contrary intention is shown.

A more detailed description of the presumptions is provided below:

Presumption of Constitutionality

It is presumed that all statutes enacted by the Oireachtas are constitutional unless the contrary is proven. It is presumed that the Oireachtas intends to abide by the Constitution. This presumption was outlined by the Supreme Court in *East Donegal Livestock Mart v Attorney General* [1970] IR 317 and has two main legal effects:

- It assigns the burden of proof to the party alleging invalidity;
- It establishes what is known as a 'double construction rule' for post-1937 statutes — where a court is faced with two reasonable interpretations of a statute, one of which would result in the statute bearing a constitutional meaning and the other of which would render the statute unconstitutional, the former must be adopted.

Additionally, it is presumed that all legislative powers and procedures will be exercised in accordance with the Constitution.

An example of this presumption in action was in *Re JH* [1985] IR 375, where s 3 of the Guardianship of Infants Act 1964 was construed as involving a constitutional presumption, based on Article 42.1, that the best interests of a child are best protected within the family unit unless there is compelling evidence to the contrary.

Presumption of Compatibility with EU Law

All EU secondary legislation, such as directives and regulations, should be interpreted in a manner which is compatible with the provisions of the EU treaties. Additionally, it should follow from the applicability of EU law in the national legal system and its precedence over domestic law that, as a matter for domestic law, a court should interpret all national legislation in a manner which is consistent with the EU treaties. See *Dowling v Ireland* [1991] 2 IR 379.

This is known as the doctrine of *indirect effect* — all domestic courts in the European Union are required to interpret national legislation in conformity with EU law. In *Murphy v Bord Telecom Eireann* [1989] ILRM 53, the requirements of EU law overrode a literal interpretation of the Anti-Discrimination (Pay) Act 1976.

Presumption of Compatibility with International Law

There is a general presumption that the Oireachtas intended to abide by its international legal obligations when it enacted domestic legislation. In *O'Domhnaill v Merrick* [1984] ILRM, Henchy J stated that one must presume that the statute was enacted (there being no indication in it of a contrary intention) subject to the postulate that it would be construed and applied in consonance with the State's obligations under international law, including any relevant treaty obligations.

- Presumption that all Words Bear a Meaning

It is presumed that the Oireachtas intended that each word in an Act should contribute to its meaning and no words are used without reason. In *Cork County Council v Whillock* [1993] 1 IR 231, Egan J held that

> words are not used in a statute without a meaning and are not… superfluous, and so effect must be given, if possible, to all the words used, for the legislature must be deemed not to waste its words or say anything in vain.

- Presumption that a Statute Should be Given an Updated Meaning

It is presumed that the legislature intended that the law be capable of applying to future circumstances. The interpretation of legislation should facilitate statutes being applied to new circumstances and make allowances for changes in the law and in social and technological conditions. This presumption has now been put on a statutory footing in s 6 of the Interpretation Act 2005, which declares that, when interpreting legislation,

> a court may make allowances for any changes in the law, social conditions, technology, the meaning of words used in that Act or statutory instrument and other relevant matters, which have occurred since the date of the passing of that Act or the making of that statutory instrument, but only in so far as its text, purpose and context permit.

- Presumption Against Unclear Changes in the Law

This presumption requires that a change in the law must be achieved clearly and unambiguously, either by express statement or by a clear implication. In the event of any uncertainty or ambiguity, a court should not interpret the statutory provision as changing the law.

- Presumption that Penal Statutes be Construed Strictly

It is presumed that, if the legislature wishes to impose a penalty, it will do so expressly in clear and certain language. Consequently, penal statutes should be construed strictly, in a way which leans against the creation or extension of penal liability by implication. If there are two possible interpretations of a penal statute, the interpretation which does not result in the imposition of a new penalty must be favoured. In *The People (DPP) v Farrell* [1978] IR 13, the Court held that s 30 of the Offences against the State Act 1939 must be strictly construed and refused to assume that the procedural requirements established by that section had been complied with by the Gardaí.

- Presumption that Revenue Statutes Should be Construed Strictly

Any statutory provision which creates a financial liability on the State or individuals must be strictly construed. Henchy J in *Inspector of Taxes v Kiernan* [1981] IR 117, stated that, if a word or expression is used in a statute creating a penal or taxation liability and there is looseness or ambiguity attaching to it, the word should be construed strictly, "so as to prevent a fresh imposition of liability from being created unlawfully by the use of oblique or slack language."

- Presumption Against Retrospective Effect

Article 15.5.1° of the Constitution prohibits the enactment of retrospective penal legislation, stating that the Oireachtas shall not declare acts to be infringements of the law which were not so at the date of their commission. The Supreme Court, in *Hamilton v Hamilton* [1982] IR 266, declared that retrospective legislation is, on its face, unjust, and consequently a statute should be presumed to be prospective only, unless the words express a clear and unambiguous intention to the contrary.

However, not all retrospective legislation will be unjust. The courts are primarily concerned with retrospective statutes which alter the substantive law or which affect vested rights, by retrospectively creating a penal or financial liability, for example.

In *McKee v Culligan* [1992] I IR 233, the Supreme Court held that Article 15.5.1° constitutes an unambiguous prohibition against the enactment of retrospective laws which declares acts to be an infringement of the law, which were not so at the date of their commission. However, the Court clarified that this is not a general prohibition on retrospective legislation: its application is confined to situations where apparently innocent actions are retrospectively construed as constituting infringements of the law.

- Presumption Against Extra-Territorial Effect

It is presumed that the jurisdiction of an Act of the Oireachtas is confined to the territory of the State unless a contrary intention is shown.

Rules of Language

These four rules of language (Latin maxims) have been developed over time to aid statutory interpretation.

Rule of Language/Maxim	Explanation
Expressio unius est exclusio alterius	This means "to express one thing is to exclude another". For example, if an Act expressly includes a particular age group of people, it would by implication exclude all others. In *Kiely v Minister for Social Welfare* [1977] IR 267, Henchy J held that "the fact that Article 11(5) [of the Regulations] allows a written statement to be received in evidence in specified limited circumstances means that it cannot be received in other circumstances."
Noscitur a sociis	"A thing is known by its associates" — a word draws its meaning from the other words around it. Meaning is attributed to a word by reference to the context in which it appears. This maxim is used to give a limited or restricted meaning to general words.
Ejusdem generis	General words which follow specific ones are taken to include only things of the same kind. In *DPP v Farrell* [1978] IR 13, the Court applied the *ejusdem generis* rule to s 30 of the Offences against the State Act 1939, and held that "a Garda Síochána station, a prison or other convenient place" did not include a police car as the general word "place" followed specific words relating to buildings. The maxim was also invoked in *CW Shipping Co Ltd v Limerick Harbour Commissioner* [1989] ILRM 416.
Generalia specialibus non derogant	Under this maxim, a statute which refers to a general subject matter is taken not to affect an Act which applies to a specific topic. This prevents the unintentional repeal or amendment of a specific statutory provision by a later Act which is general in nature. In *McGonagle v McGonagle* [1951] IR 123, O'Byrne J stated that "[i]t is a general rule of construction that a prior statute is held to be repealed, by implication, by a subsequent statute which is inconsistent with and repugnant to the prior statute. This rule, however, does not apply where, as in the present case, the prior statute is special and the subsequent statute general."

Extrinsic/External Aids

These are aids which may be found outside the Act itself. Historically, the courts were reluctant to look outside the Act itself. However, in recent years, this reluctance has subsided and the courts may on occasion look to the following external aids:

Historical Setting/Legislative History

A court may consider the historical setting of the provision in question and its passage through the Houses of the Oireachtas.

Previous Statutes

The court may examine earlier statues dealing with the same subject matter as the statute under consideration.

Reports and Publications of the Law Reform Commission or Other Similar Bodies

Legislation is often preceded by a Law Reform Commission report or reports from other similar bodies, including White Papers, reports from special commissions and tribunals of inquiry. These may be useful for a court when interpreting a subsequent piece of legislation.

Parliamentary Materials

These include records of the proceedings in both Houses of the Oireachtas, parliamentary debates, etc. Historically, these materials could not be used as an aid to interpretation by the courts. However, in recent years, some Irish courts departed from this traditional common law position and consider parliamentary materials when interpreting legislation. In *Wavin Pipes Ltd v Hepworth Iron Co Ltd* [1982] 8 FSR 32, Costello J held that there is no strict rule of construction which requires the court to examine only the words of the statute — a court is permitted in principle to consider the parliamentary history of an Act, including parliamentary debates, to assist in its interpretation.

However, in *Crilly v Farrington* [2001] 3 IR, the Supreme Court unanimously refused to take into account the Oireachtas debates surrounding s 2(1) of the Health (Amendment) Act 1986, the provision in question before the Court. The Supreme Court suggested that such material would undermine the traditional approaches to the interpretation of legislation and presumptions developed by the courts. Additionally, the Court felt that the freedom enjoyed by members of the Oireachtas to debate proposed legislation might be curtailed if they knew such utterances might be examined by the courts, and that statements made by members of the Oireachtas are not sufficiently neutral. Additionally, it could not be said that statements made by one member of one House could not be imputed as the intention of the Oireachtas as a whole. The Court also considered the extra expense which would be incurred by clients if parliamentary debates were to be admissible in such cases.

Dictionaries and Textbooks

These may be consulted to find the meaning of a word or to gather information on the opinions of leading legal academics on a point of law.

International/EU Treaties and Legislation

These may be consulted where domestic legislation is based on international/EU law and/or if the court is following the presumption of compatibility with EU/international law.

Previous Practice/Use of the Words

General practice and commercial usage of a word in the area covered by the legislation may shed light on the meaning of a statutory provision.

CHAPTER SEVEN

COMMON LAW AND PRECEDENT

A. Introduction 115
B. **Justification/Aims** 115
C. **Necessary Conditions for the Operation of Precedent** 116
    An Accurate System of Law Reporting 116
    A Hierarchical Court System 117
    Rules for Deciding which Judgments and which Parts of that
    Judgment to Follow 117
D. **Locating and Understanding Case Law** 117
    Locating and Citing Case Law 117
E. **Binding/Authoritative Precedents** 118
    Ratio Decidendi 119
    Obiter Dicta 120
F. **Non-Binding/Persuasive Precedents** 120
G. **Other Legal Terms to Note** 120
H. **The Operation of *Stare Decisis* in the Irish Courts — Vertical
    and Horizontal Dimensions** 122
    Vertical Dimension 122
    Horizontal Dimension 123
        Strict Approach 123
        Liberal Approach 123
        The Supreme Court 124
        The High Court 126
        The Court of Criminal Appeal 126

Learning Outcomes

Upon completion of this chapter, the student should be able to:

- Describe the operation of precedent or *stare decisis* in the Irish legal system;
- Locate and cite common/case law;
- Differentiate between binding and non-binding precedents;
- Identify and explain the key legal terminology used by the courts in relation to precedent;
- Differentiate between *ratio decidendi* and *obiter dicta*;
- Analyse how the Irish superior courts apply the doctrine of precedent, both vertically and horizontally.

A. Introduction

As a common law system, Ireland relies heavily on case law as a source of legal rules. Indeed, some areas of law are made up almost entirely of legal principles which have been established through case law. Common law consists of decisions handed down by the courts and certain tribunals and adjudicative bodies. The case law which is of most significance in Ireland is the reserved judgments of the Supreme Court, High Court and the Court of Criminal Appeal, which collectively are the Irish superior courts.

The vast body of common law in our legal system was developed throughout the centuries by judges applying the customary law to new situations, using precedent. As our legal system developed, the practice of following the decisions of previous cases became established. This is referred to as the doctrine of *stare decisis* — 'let the decision stand'.

Precedent can be defined as the application of a principle of law as laid down by a higher court on a previous occasion in a similar case. Both civil and common law systems have precedent, but it is has greater weight in common law systems which lack the certainty and specificity of written codes.

When a case comes before a judge, he/she must first establish the facts of the case and secondly, determine how the law applies to those facts. The judge(s) listen to legal argument put forward by the parties and prepares a written decision or judgment on who wins, based on the facts of the case and the application of the relevant law to those facts. In deciding a case, the judge must follow any decision that has been made by a higher court in a case with similar facts. Once a decision has been made on how the law applies to those facts, similar cases should be treated in the same way, following the principle of *stare decisis*.

A system based on precedent restricts the judge and denies him/her the discretion which other decision-makers (e.g. legislators) enjoy. The judge must decide the case on the basis of prior decisions of higher courts. Consequently, decisions reached are not attributable to the inclinations of individual judges but to the existing body of law.

B. Justification/Aims

The practice of *stare decisis* or of following precedent is the principal rule of judicial decision-making in common law systems.

Adopting a doctrine of precedent has a number of advantages:

Figure 7.1 Advantages of a Legal System based on Precedent

Advantage of a Legal System based on Precedent	Explanation
Consistency	It leads to consistency and uniformity of judges' decisions. Previous decisions on similar issues are followed, ensuring stability in the legal system.
Equality	It assures equal treatment before the law, which should be a fundamental aim in all legal systems — similar cases are treated similarly.
Predictability	The law becomes more predictable and it becomes easier to determine the legal merit of a proposed action.
Public confidence	Decisions are attributable to an existing body of case law and not the individual inclinations of judges. This assures greater public confidence.
Certainty	Existing common law principles can only be changed according to the hierarchy of courts.

Strict adherence to the doctrine of precedent may also have a number of disadvantages

Disadvantages of a Legal System strictly based on Precedent	Explanation
Leads to a fossilisation of the law	An inability to depart from previous court decisions can lead to the law becoming stagnant and being unable to adapt to the needs and expectations of society.
Inhibits legal development	A strict adherence to the doctrine of precedent can prevent new legal thinking and inhibit the development of new legal principles.
Frustrates the possibility of doing justice in individual cases	As judges are bound by previous decisions, they may be unable to do justice in individual cases.

C. Necessary Conditions for the Operation of Precedent

In order for precedent to operate successfully, certain requirements must be met. These are as follows:

An Accurate System of Law Reporting

If previous court decisions are to be followed, then they must be recorded accurately and be accessible. Throughout the centuries, a system of law reporting has developed to ensure that decisions handed down are recorded in an accurate manner, thus providing the material which will govern future cases. Various established volumes of law reports exist in Ireland, including the *Irish Reports, Irish Law Reports Monthly, Irish Jurist Reports* and *Irish Law Times*. Most judgments are now also available online, either through subscription databases, www.bailii.org or on www.courts.ie.

A Hierarchical Court System

A hierarchical court system is required to assess the weight of any particular precedent and to decide whether or not a precedent is binding in a later case. The general rule is that lower courts must follow the decisions of higher courts. So, for example, the High Court must follow previous decisions of the Supreme Court and the Court of Criminal Appeal, the Circuit Court must follow previous decisions of the High Court, Court of Criminal Appeal and Supreme Court, etc. This will be examined in more detail below.

Rules for Deciding which Judgments and which Parts of that Judgment to Follow

The process of applying precedents can be complex. No two cases are identical — each offers an individual set of facts which differentiates it from any other. The task of the court is to identify decisions from previous cases which are considered to be similar to the case before it and to apply the legal reasoning from those decisions to the present case. There is some flexibility provided in that courts are required to place the cases in conceptual categories from which the legal issues involved are analysed. Some cases may be conceptually different and consequently a court is not required to follow every decision which preceded it. Rules have been established which dictate whether a decision is binding or non-binding (persuasive). Further principles establish which part of the judgment is binding.

D. Locating and Understanding Case Law

Common/case law consists of decisions handed down by the courts and certain tribunals and adjudicative bodies. The case law of most significance is the reserved judgments of the High Court, Supreme Court and the Court of Criminal Appeal, which are the Irish superior courts.

Locating and Citing Case Law

Case law has become easier to locate in recent years. Traditionally, judgments were available only in printed law reports in law libraries. However, most law reports have now become available online (sometimes for a fee) through various legal databases such as Lexis-Nexis, Justis, Westlaw and Bailii — the British and Irish legal website. Additionally, all of the more recent decisions from the Irish superior courts are now available free to the public on www.courts.ie, the website of the Courts Service of Ireland.

There are two main series of law reports in Ireland:

- The Irish Reports (cited as IR) which began in 1894; and
- The Irish Law Reports Monthly (cited as ILRM) which began in 1976.

Both sets of reports are cited primarily by year. Students may come across the *Irish Law Times Reports*, which were published between 1867 and 1980 (cited as ILTR) and the *Irish Jurist*, which published reports from 1935 to 1965 (cited as Ir Jur Rep).

A typical case citation (or reference) would read: *Reddy v Bates* [1983] IR 141. This means that the parties in this case are *Reddy* (plaintiff) *v Bates* (defendant) and the case is reported in the 1981 series of the *Irish Reports* at page 141.

Judgments from the Irish superior courts are now available free of charge. Neutral citations have been developed to reference these, e.g. *Ryan v Minister for Justice* [2000] IESC 33 – the 33rd judgment delivered by the Supreme Court in 2000. IESC refers to Supreme Court decisions and IEHC refers to decisions of the High Court.

When reading a judgment, the main focus should be on the legal reasoning behind the decision. The reader should be alert to other information contained in the law report, such as:

- Status of the court in which the judgment was given — this is important regarding the weight of the judgment—;
- The date of the judgment (it may be under appeal if it is a recent decision);
- If multiple judgments are given, is it a unanimous or majority decision? Note which members of the court were in agreement and which dissented. Note, compare and contrast the reasoning of the majority and dissenting judgments. This is particularly important in Supreme Court judgments, where a three or five judge court may sit, and each judge is entitled to offer his/her judgment (except in cases about the constitutional validity of legislation). A majority judgment of 3-2 may be reached in a five-judge court, for example, but the majority judges may have expressed different legal reasons for their decision.
- Earlier cases listed in the report often provide useful pointers for further research.

E. Binding/Authoritative Precedents

Precedents are classified either as:

- Binding — a precedent which a later court is required to follow; and
- Non-binding or persuasive — a later court enjoys discretion as to whether or not it should adopt the previous decision.

The main rule is that a court must follow the previous decisions of courts superior to it in the judicial hierarchy. A court is also generally expected to follow the earlier decisions of courts of co-ordinate, or equal, jurisdiction, although courts from time to time, have declared a freedom to depart from their own earlier decisions.

Generally, judgments are structured as follows:

Figure 7.2

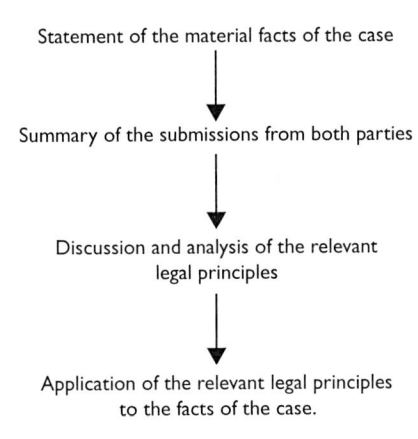

```
Statement of the material facts of the case
                    ↓
Summary of the submissions from both parties
                    ↓
   Discussion and analysis of the relevant
              legal principles
                    ↓
    Application of the relevant legal principles
             to the facts of the case.
```

Many reported judgments also include a headnote, which contains a summation of the facts of the case and the decision and reasoning of the court. It should be noted that these are not prepared by judges, but rather by third parties. Students should therefore always ensure that the entire judgment is read carefully as it is the judgment and not the headnote which is the authoritative statement of the law from the court.

When a court is bound by an earlier decision, it must follow the legal reason or principle of law which led the earlier court to reach its conclusion. This is known as the *ratio decidendi*. Other statements or principles of law which did not lead the earlier court to its conclusion are known as *obiter dicta* and do not need to be followed by a later court.

Ratio Decidendi
The *ratio decidendi* is the legal reason for the decision and is the part of the judgment which is binding. It is the principle of law which was applied to the facts of the case and led the court to its decision. If one judgment is given, as is generally the case in the Circuit Court, High Court and Court of Criminal Appeal, the ratio is the legal reason for the judgment. If multiple judgments are given, it can be more difficult to identify clearly the reason for the decision. In such cases, it is necessary to identify the reason for the decision given by each judge:

- If the judgment is unanimous and the reasoning is similar in all judgments, that is the *ratio*.
- If the judgment is unanimous but the reasoning differs, then the reasoning of the majority is the *ratio*.
- If there is a majority judgment, the reasoning of the majority judges is the *ratio*. Any dissenting judgments, which are delivered by the minority, are not binding on a later court.

Obiter Dicta

Obiter dictum means 'a thing said by the way'. During the course of a judgment, a judge might analyse and discuss various legal principles and theories, which may not be directly relevant to the outcome of the case. These statements of law may be used to illustrate a certain point, to give an example or a possible course of action. Such statements are called *obiter dicta*. They are not the reason for the decision and are not of direct relevance to the outcome of the case. Consequently, these *obiter dicta* are not binding. These statements of law, are, however, of persuasive authority and may be adopted at the option of the later court in the absence of other binding authority.

F. Non-Binding/Persuasive Precedents

A court is not bound by the decisions of courts which are inferior to it. The Supreme Court, for example, is not bound by previous decisions of the Court of Criminal Appeal or the High Court, although they may be persuasive and be adopted at the option of the higher court.

Likewise, as a sovereign nation, Irish courts are not bound by the decisions of foreign courts. However, decisions of foreign courts may be of persuasive authority and may be followed at the option of the Irish court. Decisions of foreign courts, particularly those in other common law jurisdictions, are regularly cited and adopted in Irish courts in the absence of Irish authority, particularly decisions from the British courts and courts in other common law jurisdictions, such as Australia and New Zealand.

G. Other Legal Terms to Note

The following table contains a list and explanation of legal terms which the student will come across when reading case law. It is important to understand these, as they are important in deciding on the value of any precedent which is being proposed.

Legal Term	Meaning
Reverse	When an appeal of a decision is successful, the appellate court is said to have *reversed* the decision of the inferior court. Essentially, the decision of the lower court is replaced by that of the higher court and the decision of the lower court ceases to have any effect.
Res Judicata	This means 'the matter has been decided'. Once a decision is no longer capable of being appealed, it becomes final and the principle of *res judicata* applies. This means that the parties are bound by the decision and, generally, may not seek to have it reopened.
Overrule	Where an appellate court in a later case considers the earlier decision of a lower court to be incorrect, it may overrule that decision. The effect of this is prospective only and it does not affect the position of the parties to the earlier case. In other words, by overruling a case, a court states that it is not to be followed in the future.
Distinguish	A case may sometimes be distinguished from earlier cases which may have been heard, often in the same court. A case is distinguished when a later court discovers a material factual difference between the two cases or a difference in the legal issues involved. If the subject matter or legal issues involved in the two cases differs, the cases are placed in separate conceptual categories and the earlier case does not have to be followed. By distinguishing an earlier decision, a court can confine it to a very precise situation such that it becomes marginal and of limited importance. The court may say that the previous decision should only be followed in the specific set of circumstances in which it occurred. It will often state that the decision is confined to its particular facts and is of no assistance in other cases.
Per Curiam	This means 'by the court' or 'in accordance with the law'. If a decision is reached *per curiam*, it is reached by a judge/court in accordance with the law.
Per Incuriam	This means 'otherwise than in accordance with the law'. In some cases a court may have reached a decision in ignorance of a relevant statutory provision or binding precedent. If this happens, the decision is said to have been reached *per incuriam* and no later court is bound to follow it.
Sub Silentio	This means 'under silence'. If a court has made a decision on a point of law, without its being specifically argued or mentioned in the judgment, it is said to have been decided *sub silentio* and will not be binding on a later court.

H. The Operation of Stare Decisis in the Irish Courts — Vertical and Horizontal Dimensions

Precedent is the accepted method of judicial decision-making in the Irish legal system. There are two dimensions to the system of precedent used in the Irish courts: vertical and horizontal.

Vertical Dimension

It is long established that a lower court is bound by the decisions of higher courts. This operates in the Irish legal system, according to the hierarchy of courts, which is explained below.

Figure 7.3 Hierarchy of courts in Ireland

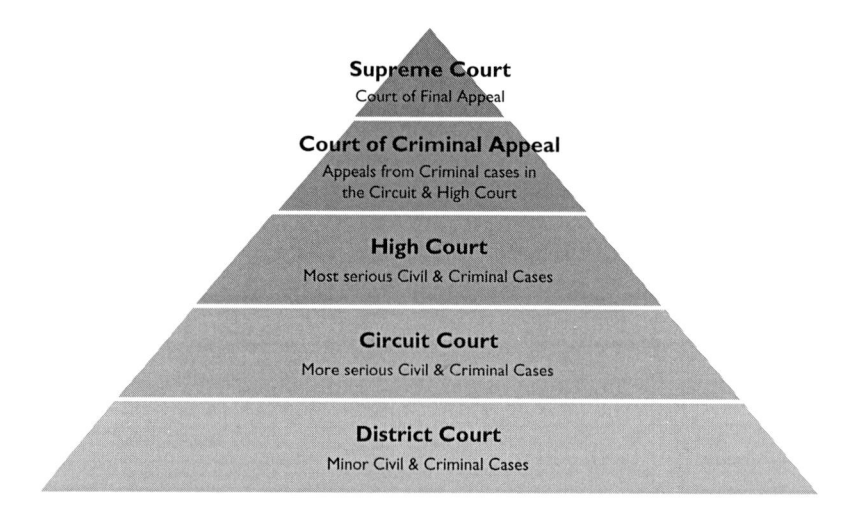

Supreme Court
Court of Final Appeal

Court of Criminal Appeal
Appeals from Criminal cases in the Circuit & High Court

High Court
Most serious Civil & Criminal Cases

Circuit Court
More serious Civil & Criminal Cases

District Court
Minor Civil & Criminal Cases

An inferior court must follow the earlier decisions of superior courts. In practice, this means that:

- The Court of Criminal Appeal must follow Supreme Court decisions;
- The High Court (including the Central Criminal Court) must follow Court of Criminal Appeal and Supreme Court decisions;
- The Circuit Court must follow High Court (including Central Criminal Court), Court of Criminal Appeal and Supreme Court decisions;
- The District Court must follow Circuit Court, High Court (including Central Criminal Court), Court of Criminal Appeal and Supreme Court decisions.

This rule is almost unquestioned. The Supreme Court has rarely had to reprimand the High Court for failure to follow one of its decisions. However, this did occur in *McDonnell v Byrne Engineering Co Ltd*, *The Irish Times*, 3 October 1978, when the Supreme Court strongly criticised the High Court for failing to follow one of its previous decisions, adding that the Supreme Court would "insist that its directions be respected and obeyed."

It is possible that a situation might arise where a lower court is required to follow a decision of a higher court, even though it is believed to be erroneous and it is anticipated that the decision will subsequently be overruled by the Supreme Court. For example, in *DPP v O'Sullivan* [2007] IEHC 248, the High Court followed a previous decision of the Supreme Court, despite a marked reluctance on the part of the Court to do so.

Horizontal Dimension

This concerns the extent to which a court is bound by the decisions of courts of co-ordinate or equal jurisdiction. Should the Supreme Court, for example be bound by its own previous decisions?

Strict Approach

A strict approach to the application of precedent was favoured during 19th century and lasted well into 20th century. Courts of co-ordinate jurisdiction could not depart from an earlier decision given by that court. Such an approach has a number of advantages and disadvantages.

Table on Advantages and Disadvantages to a strict approach to the application of precedent

Advantages to a strict application of precedent	Disadvantages to a strict application of precedent
Greater certainty and stability in the law.	Leads to a fossilisation of the law.
Equal treatment assured.	Inhibits legal development.
Easier to predict the outcome of a case.	Frustrates the possibility of doing justice in individual cases.
Ensures judicial order and continuity.	

Liberal Approach

A liberal approach would allow courts of coordinate jurisdiction to depart from earlier decisions of that court. This would mean, for example, that the High Court could depart from earlier decisions of the High Court, the Court of Criminal Appeal could depart from earlier decisions of the Court of Criminal Appeal, etc. Such an approach also has a number of advantages and disadvantages.

Table on Advantages and Disadvantages to a liberal approach to the application of precedent

Advantages to a liberal application of precedent	Disadvantages to a liberal application of precedent
Allows new legal thinking.	Unsettles the law and creates instability.
Provides for justice to be done in individual cases.	Introduces uncertainty into the legal system.
Allows the development of new legal principles in line with societal changes.	Upsets legitimate expectations.

There is clearly a need to strike a balance between the two approaches. The approach of the Irish courts is considered below.

The Supreme Court

The main issue for examination is whether or not the Supreme Court can depart from its earlier decisions.

Until the 1960s, a strict approach was adopted by the Court and no departure was made from its previous decisions. However, in the mid-1960s, the Supreme Court began to move away from the strict rule of *stare decisis* and adopted a slightly more liberal approach.

The State (Quinn) v Ryan [1965] IR 110 marked the historic first departure from the strict 'rule'. In that case, the constitutionality of s 29 of the Petty Sessions (Ireland) Act 1851 was challenged. The Supreme Court had upheld the validity of that section in two earlier decisions. It was argued by the respondent that, as a result, the state was bound by those decisions.

However, despite the two previous decisions, the Supreme Court held that s 29 was unconstitutional and declared its freedom to depart from its earlier decisions and from a strict adherence to *stare decisis*.

Walsh J reasoned that, when examining the constitutionality of legislation, the Constitution states that it is only in the case of a law, the Bill for which had been referred to the Supreme Court by the President under Article 26 of the Constitution, that there is no longer jurisdiction in any court to question the constitutionality of that law. In other words, the only limit placed on the freedom of the courts to hear challenges to the constitutionality of legislation is in cases of Bills which were subject to an Article 26 reference.

Walsh J held that the implication from this was that all other Bills, which were not subject to an Article 26 reference, may be challenged a number of times before the Supreme Court. The Constitution did not impose a strict rule of *stare decisis* for such Bills. He stated that the Supreme Court:

> should not depart from an earlier decision for any but the most compelling reasons. The advantages of *stare decisis* are many and obvious so long as it is remembered that it is a policy and not a binding unalterable rule.

Although this case marked a new departure, a strict interpretation of the case would limit the Supreme Court's freedom to depart to cases which involve the constitutionality of legislation.

However, the new approach was confirmed soon after this by the Supreme Court's decision in *Attorney General v Ryan's Car Hire Ltd* [1965] IR 642. In that case, the Supreme Court again refused to follow two of its previous decisions.

In his decision in that case, Kingsmill Moore J stated that:

> The law....is based on a system of precedents and there can be no question of abandoning the principle of following precedent as the normal, indeed almost universal, procedure. To do so would be to introduce into our law an intolerable uncertainty. But where the Supreme Court is of the opinion that there is a compelling reason why it should not follow an earlier decision of its own, where it appears to be clearly wrong, is it to be bound to perpetuate the error?..... However desirable certainty, stability and predictability of law may be, they cannot in my view justify a court of last resort in giving a judgment which they are convinced, for compelling reasons, is erroneous.

These judgments indicate that while, in general, the Supreme Court will follow its own decisions, it reserves the freedom to depart from them where there are compelling reasons to do so.

The circumstances in which the Supreme Court would depart from an earlier decision were further elaborated upon in *McNamara v ESB* [1975] IR 1, where the Supreme Court indicated that it would be prepared to depart from previous decisions in light of changing social conditions and legal thinking.

In other cases, however, the Supreme Court has acted more cautiously and has displayed a reluctance to interfere with previous decisions of the court.

In *Mogul of Ireland Ltd v Tipperary North Riding County Council* [1976] IR 260, Henchy J refused to depart from a previous decision, stating:

> the mere fact that a later court, particularly a majority of the members of a later court, might prefer a different conclusion is not in itself sufficient to justify overruling the earlier decision.

The same point was made by the Supreme Court, in *Hynes-O'Sullivan v O'Driscoll* [1989] ILRM 349 where the court expressed concerns about maintaining judicial order and continuity.

From the case law, it appears that the Supreme Court, when composed of five judges, will more readily reconsider the decision of a three-judge Supreme Court. In *Hamilton v Hamilton* [1982] IR 466, the Court stated that a three-judge Supreme Court decision was law, unless and until a different conclusion was reached by a full court of five judges.

The High Court

The question of *stare decisis* in the High Court has not generated much judicial comment. In *Kearns v Manresa Estates Ltd* (Unreported, High Court, 25 July 1975), Kenny J stated:

> although I am not bound by decisions of other judges of the High Court, the usual practice is to follow them unless I am satisfied that they were wrongly decided.

In *Irish Trust Bank Ltd v Central Bank of Ireland* [1976-7] ILRM 50, Parke J was reluctant to depart from an earlier High Court decision. He argued that, unless an earlier decision could be clearly shown to have been wrongly decided, a court of co-ordinate or equal jurisdiction should follow it. The decision not to follow it should normally be made by an appellate court which enjoys the power to overrule it. This appears to reflect the practice in the High Court.

The Court of Criminal Appeal

The Court of Criminal Appeal has declared its freedom to depart from its earlier decisions.

In *The People (Attorney General) v Moore* [1964] Ir Jur Rep 6, the court refused to follow one of its earlier decisions. In his decision in *The People (Attorney General) v O'Neill* [1964] Ir Jur Rep 1, Davitt P stated:

> we are not unmindful of the principle of *stare decisis* and of the desirability of having uniformity in judicial decisions interpreting the law. We think, however, that the interests of justice will be best served by giving effect to our own opinions.

CHAPTER EIGHT

EU Law

A. **Introduction and History** 130
   Introduction 130
   History of the EU 130
      The European Coal and Steel Community 131
      Euratom and the EEC 132
      The Merger Treaty 1965 134
      The Single European Act 1986 134
      The Treaty of Amsterdam 1997 135
      The Treaty of Nice 2000 135
      The Treaty of Lisbon 2007 136
   Membership of the EU 136
B. **Institutions of the EU** 138
   Introduction 138
   The European Parliament 139
   The Council of the EU 141
   The Commission 142
   The European Council 144
   The Court of Justice of the European Union (CJEU) 144
   The European Central Bank 146
   The Court of Auditors 146
C. **Sources of EU Law** 146
   Introduction 146
   Primary Sources of EU Law 147
   Secondary Sources of EU Law 148
      Regulations 148
      Directives 148
      Decisions 148
      Recommendations and Opinions 149
      Case Law of the Court of Justice of the European Union (CJEU) 149
      General Principles of EU Law 150
      International Agreements 150
D. **The Interaction of Irish Law and European Union Law** 150
   Overview 150
   The Doctrine of Supremacy of EU Law 151
   The Doctrine of Direct Effect 153

Introduction 153
Treaty Articles and Direct Effect 153
Regulations and Direct Effect 154
Decisions and Direct Effect 154
International Agreements and Direct Effect 155
Directives and Direct Effect..155
State Liability 156
The *Francovich* Principle..156
Legal Responses to the Eurozone Financial Crisis 157
Withdrawal from the EU 160

Learning Outcomes

Upon completion of this chapter, students will be able to:

- Trace the historical development of the EU from its establishment to its modern incarnation;
- Discuss and explain the functions of the institutions of the European Union;
- Describe the sources of EU law and how they affect upon Irish law;
- Explain the interaction between Irish and EU law.

A. Introduction and History

Introduction

The economies of Europe were left devastated after the Second World War in 1945. The peoples of Europe were therefore determined to ensure that such a catastrophe could never happen again. Economic and political integration between the European States was seen as the best way to achieve this. The United States of America also regarded a union of some type between the European states as both inherently desirable and as a means of countering a perceived communist threat from the Soviet Union. The USA provided financial aid to Europe under what became known as the *Marshall Plan*. The Organisation for Economic Co-Operation was established in 1948 to administer the aid. This led to a high degree of co-operation between the beneficiary States and was an early form of co-operation. Other forms followed, for example the North Atlantic Treaty Organisation (NATO), the primary objective of which was defence; another was the Council of Europe (see chapter 8).

A further critical phase of the European integration was the development of the European Communities. These three Communities were to become what is now the European Union (EU). EU law has become an important source of Irish law through Treaty articles, regulations, directives and decisions, each of which have the force of law in the legal systems of each of the Member States of the EU.

History of the EU

Table on Major Treaties/Events in the Development of the EU

Year	Treaty/Event
April 1951	Six States West Germany, France, Italy, the Netherlands, Belgium and Luxembourg, sign the Treaty of Paris establishing the European Coal and Steel Community (ECSC).
March 1957	The same six States sign the treaties of Rome establishing Euratom and the European Economic Community (EEC) — both entering into force January 1958.
April 1965	The Merger Treaty is signed providing all three Communities with the same institutional structure.
January 1973	Ireland, the United Kingdom and Denmark join the European Communities.
December 1974	The Member States reach agreement on direct elections to the European Parliament.

(*Cont*)

June 1979	The first direct elections to the European Parliament take place.
January 1981	Greece joins the European Communities.
January 1986	Spain and Portugal join the European Communities.
February 1986	The Single European Act is signed: key aim — to speed up European integration (entering into force July 1987).
February 1992	Treaty on European Union (TEU) is signed at Maastricht — creates the European Union (entering into force November 1993).
January 1995	Austria, Finland, and Sweden join the European Union (EU).
October 1997	Treaty of Amsterdam signed: key aim — to consolidate the existing treaties to facilitate enlargement and to bring the EU closer to its citizens (entering into force May 1999).
December 2000	Treaty of Nice signed: key aim — to reform the institutions in preparation for enlargement (entering into force February 2003).
May 2004	Estonia, the Czech Republic, Latvia, Lithuania, Hungary, Poland, Slovenia, Slovakia, Cyprus, and Malta join the EU.
October 2004	The Treaty Establishing a Constitution for Europe is signed by the 25 Member States.
May 2005	France and the Netherlands reject the Constitutional Treaty in referendums (the Treaty is abandoned in summer 2007).
January 2007	Romania and Bulgaria join the EU.
December 2007	Treaty of Lisbon ('The Reform Treaty') is signed by the 27 Member States.
December 2009	Treaty of Lisbon enters into force: key aim — to amend the TEU and to amend and rename the TEC, now called the Treaty on the Functioning of the European Union (TFEU).
July 2013	Croatia joins the EU.

The European Coal and Steel Community

The European Coal and Steel Community (ECSC) was the first European Community. It was created by the Treaty of Paris in 1951. It adopted a 'functional approach' to integration, i.e. sector-by-sector integration — in this case, the coal and steel industries of France and West Germany. The treaty envisaged a mechanism by which the relationship between the two countries could be stabilised. It allowed their coal and steel industries to be closely supervised such that their ability to covertly re-arm would be reduced. France, West Germany, Italy, Belgium, Luxembourg and the Netherlands signed the Treaty in Paris on 18 April 1951. It entered into force on 23 July 1952.

The ECSC Treaty was significant. It represented a move away from the traditional intergovernmental system of co-operation which was a characteristic of international treaties. 'Intergovernmentalism' is a theory of integration under which the participating States take decisions by co-operation and consensus. This is to be distinguished from 'supranationalism', which is a theory of integration which involves power moving from the participating States to separate and distinct institutions created by them. The ECSC was supranational in nature. Four independent institutions were created to administer the ECSC. The power to control the coal and steel industries therefore moved from the participating States, or the Member States, to the four institutions. These institutions comprised a High Authority, an Assembly, a Council and a Court of Justice.

The ECSC created a common market in coal and steel between the six Member States. This involved the removal of all barriers to trade in those goods. Whilst economic co-operation was the immediate focus of the ECSC, the Member States viewed co-operation as a way of achieving the long-term aims of European peace and unity. This is clear from the preamble to the Treaty of Paris which states that the creation of an economic community is a "basis for a broader and deeper community among peoples long divided by bloody conflicts; and to lay the foundations for Institutions which will give direction to a destiny henceforward shared".

Euratom and the EEC

A further two Communities were created in 1957. The European Atomic Energy Community (Euratom) and the European Economic Community (EEC) treaties were signed in Rome in 1957 by the same six members of the ECSC. They entered into force on 1 January 1958. The ECSC, Euratom and the EEC were collectively known as the 'European Communities'.

Euratom sought to ensure the development of atomic energy in a safe and peaceful manner. This required close co-operation in the sector which included the establishment of uniform safety standards. As with the ECSC, the Member States ceded control of their atomic energy industries to four supranational institutions. The Assembly and the Court of Justice were to be common to both Communities.

The EEC was to be administered by four independent institutions to which the Member States had relinquished the right to act independently in certain agreed areas. As with the other two Communities, the Court and the Assembly were shared.

The ECSC and Euratom created a common market in coal and steel and in atomic energy respectively. The EEC, however, was broader in scope. Its purpose was to provide the Member States with the necessary legal and administrative structures to work towards integration of all aspects of their economies. This is clear from the preamble to the EEC Treaty which refers to broader and longer-term objectives, in particular that the Community was determined to lay the foundations of an ever-closer union among the peoples of Europe. Initially the EEC Treaty focused on the creation of a common market. This was evident from Article 2 of the Treaty which stated that "[t]he Community shall have as its task, by establishing a common market, to promote throughout the Community a harmonious development of economic activities."

Since the common market was the primary objective of the EEC Treaty, it was arguably the most important of the three. The Treaty stated that "[t]he common market shall be progressively established during a transitional period of twelve years." Central to the common market was the free movement of goods, persons, services and capital — the 'four freedoms'. Free movement of goods means that Member States must not introduce laws which unreasonably hinder imports and exports among the Member States of the EU. Similarly, free movement of persons means that Member States must not introduce laws which unreasonably hinder the free movement of workers and the self-employed between the Member States. The treaty gives expression to the Member States' intention that free trade between them is to be achieved through the elimination of customs duties and other restrictions on the import and export of goods. This necessitated the removal of protectionist measures introduced over the years by the Member States. These national laws would be displaced through the 'approximation of laws' in order to achieve a common market in which the four freedoms could develop. However, progress on this was slow, primarily due to the requirement for unanimous agreement among the Member States for the adoption of these new EEC laws.

The treaties establishing the European Communities were themselves revised and amended by later treaties. These were: the Merger Treaty 1965; the Single European Act 1986; the Treaty on European Union (the Maastricht Treaty) 1992; the Treaty of Amsterdam 1997; the Treaty of Nice 2000; and the Treaty of Lisbon 2007. These revisions and amendments were carried out by the Member States in order to respond to changing economic, social and political demands.

The Merger Treaty 1965

The Merger Treaty (effective 1967) merged the institutions of the three Communities. This created a common Council of Ministers and a common Commission (which, prior to the enactment of the Treaty, was known as the High Authority). The two remaining institutions, the European Parliament (formerly the Assembly) and the Court of Justice, were already common to all three Communities.

The Single European Act 1986

The Single European Act (SEA) (effective 1987) increased the use of qualified majority voting (QMV). QMV is a voting system in which each Council ministers' vote is 'weighted' such that it reflects the population of the Member State that they represent (see below). This meant that there was a move away from unanimous decision-making. The result was an accelerated pace at which legislation could be passed. In addition, the SEA gave the Commission a key role in the development of the internal market which substantially increased its influence within Europe.

The SEA established a Court of First Instance (CFI) to assist the Court of Justice. It also introduced the new legislative procedure of 'co-operation', which gave the European Parliament (EP) greater influence in the legislative process. The EP was also given a right to veto the accession of new Member States. The treaty recognised the European Council as an institution of the EEC. It was created in 1974 with a membership composed of the heads of State or government of the Member States. It is important to distinguish the European Council from the Council, an entirely separate institution of what is now the EU. It is also important to distinguish the European Council from the Council of Europe.

The SEA formally recognised co-operation in economic and monetary union, social policy, economic and social cohesion, research and technological development and environmental protection. The treaty also set out the foundation for social and political integration. The institutional changes it introduced enhanced the supranational nature of the Communities by increasing the influence of both the Commission and the EP. The Treaty also made QMV the normal method of decision-making within the Council, thereby diluting the influence of individual Member States.

The Treaty on European Union 1992

The Treaty on European Union of 1992 (TEU) (the 'Maastricht Treaty') had two main objectives. First: to maintain the momentum created by the SEA with regard to European integration. Secondly to create a new organisation, built upon the original Communities, to be known as the European Union (EU). The TEU came into effect in 1993. It renamed both the EEC and the EEC Treaty. The EEC Treaty became the EC Treaty, or the Treaty Establishing the European Community, or TEC. This name change indicated that the Community would focus as much on social and political integration as it would on economic integration. The TEU introduced new areas of Community competence, expanded existing ones and provided for institutional and legislative changes. It also introduced the legal framework and timetable for the introduction of European Monetary Union (EMU).

The European Parliament's (EP's) role in the legislative process was increased. This involved extending the use of the co-operation procedure and the introduction of 'co-decision', a new procedure which effectively gave the EP the power to 'veto' legislative proposals from the Commission. Furthermore, the EP was given a right to initiate legislation, which, up to this point, had been the exclusive right of the Commission. The TEU formally recognised the Court of Auditors as a Community institution. It also created the European Central Bank (ECB). The concept of European citizenship was introduced which is given to all nationals of the Member States.

The Treaty of Amsterdam 1997
The Treaty of Amsterdam (ToA) (effective 1999) was a consolidating treaty. It sought to increase the transparency of the EU decision-making processes. It declared that the EU would respect human rights protected by the European Convention on Human Rights (ECHR). The ToA amended the TEC to include non-discrimination provisions which provided the EC with the authority to create secondary legislation to tackle discrimination based on sex, racial or ethnic origin, religion or belief, disability, age and/or sexual orientation. Treaty provisions relating to public health and consumer protection were enhanced. The use of the co-decision procedure by the EP in the legislative process (introduced by the TEU) was simplified and expanded.

The Treaty of Nice 2000
The Treaty of Nice (ToN) (effective 2003) sought, through institutional reform, to facilitate further enlargement of the EU. It extended QMV in the Council. It also introduced a change of procedure, where any decision needed a specified number of votes (the 'threshold') together with the approval of a majority of Member States. The Treaty also placed limits on the size of the Commission and EP.

The Treaty of Lisbon 2007

In 2005, the peoples of France and the Netherlands rejected in referendums a treaty to establish a Constitution for Europe. However, in December 2007, a 'Reform Treaty' was agreed by all 27 Member States in Lisbon (the 'Treaty of Lisbon'). On 12 June 2008, it was rejected by referendum in Ireland, but was passed in a second referendum on 2 October 2009. The Treaty of Lisbon came into effect in December 2009. Its chief aim was described by the Council as completing

> the process started by the Treaty of Amsterdam and the Treaty of Nice with a view to enhancing the efficiency and democratic legitimacy of the Union and to improving the coherence of its action.

It introduced a number of important changes:

- The TEC was renamed the *Treaty on the Functioning of the European Union* (TFEU);
- The number of EU institutions increased from five to seven;
- The Charter of Fundamental Rights was given legal recognition;
- A procedure for withdrawal from the EU by a Member State was provided (Article 50 TEU).

Membership of the EU

The EU currently comprises 28 European countries. As we have seen, the original members — France, West Germany, Belgium, Luxembourg, Italy and the Netherlands laid the foundations in 1951, when they created the European Coal and Steel Community (ECSC). In 1957, they signed the Treaty of Rome, creating the European Economic Community (EEC) and the European Atomic Energy Community (Euratom). The original six were joined by Denmark, Ireland and the UK in 1973, Greece in 1981 and Spain and Portugal in 1986. In the same year, the Member States signed the Single European Act. This treaty developed free movement of goods and people within the Community, creating the single market. It also brought about greater political unity. Finland, Austria and Sweden joined in 1995. Following the Nice Treaty, in 2004 the EU increased its membership from 15 to 25. In 2007, Bulgaria and Romania joined, bringing the membership to 27. Most recently, Croatia joined in July 2013 bringing the membership to 28.

Table on Membership of the EU

Year	Membership of Europe
	Country
1951	Belgium
	France
	Italy
	Luxembourg
	Netherlands
	West Germany
1973	Denmark
	Ireland
	United Kingdom
1981	Greece
1986	Portugal
	Spain
1995	Austria
	Finland
	Sweden
2004	Cyprus
	Czech Republic
	Estonia
	Hungary
	Latvia
	Lithuania
	Malta
	Poland
	Slovakia
	Slovenia
2007	Bulgaria
	Romania
2013	Croatia

The EU operates approval procedures which ensure that new countries are admitted only when they can demonstrate that they will be able fully to play their part as members. Therefore, before a country can accede to the EU, it must satisfy the terms of Article 49 TEU, Article 6 TEU and the Copenhagen Criteria. Article 49 requires that the State be European; Article 6 requires respect for democracy, the rule of law and respect for human rights.

The Copenhagen criteria are:

- The political criterion (respect for democracy and human rights);
- The economic criterion (the need for viable market economies and the capacity to cope with competitive pressure and market forces within the EU);
- The ability to adopt the Union *acquis* (i.e. the adoption, implementation and enforcement of all current EU rules).

Therefore, a candidate country must have a legal system capable of adopting, interpreting and applying EU primary and secondary law. In addition, its economy must be capable of withstanding the competitive pressures of joining the EU. In 1995, the Madrid European Council added the further requirement that the candidate country must have adjusted its administrative structures and systems so as to ensure the effective implementation of the EU *acquis* in practice. There has been recognition recently that the EU itself must be able to cope with continued enlargement.

Table on Potential Future Members of the EU

Country	Date of Application	Current Status
Iceland	16 July 2009	Candidate country: accession negotiations under way since July 2010.
Montenegro	15 December 2008	Candidate country.
Serbia	22 December 2009	Candidate country.
The former Yugoslav Republic of Macedonia	22 March 2004	Candidate country.
Turkey	1 April 1987	Candidate country.
Albania	1 April 2009	Potential candidate country.
Bosnia and Herzegovina	N/A	Potential candidate country.
Kosovo	N/A	Potential candidate country.

B. Institutions of the EU

Introduction

The primary decision-making institutions of the EU are the European Parliament, the Council, the Commission and the Court of Justice. In addition, there are the European Council, the Court of Auditors and the European Central Bank. None of these formed part of the original EEC constitution. These institutions are based in Brussels, except for the Court of Justice which sits in Luxembourg and the European Central Bank which sits in Frankfurt. The Parliament sits in both Strasbourg and Brussels.

Figure 8.1 Institutions of the EU

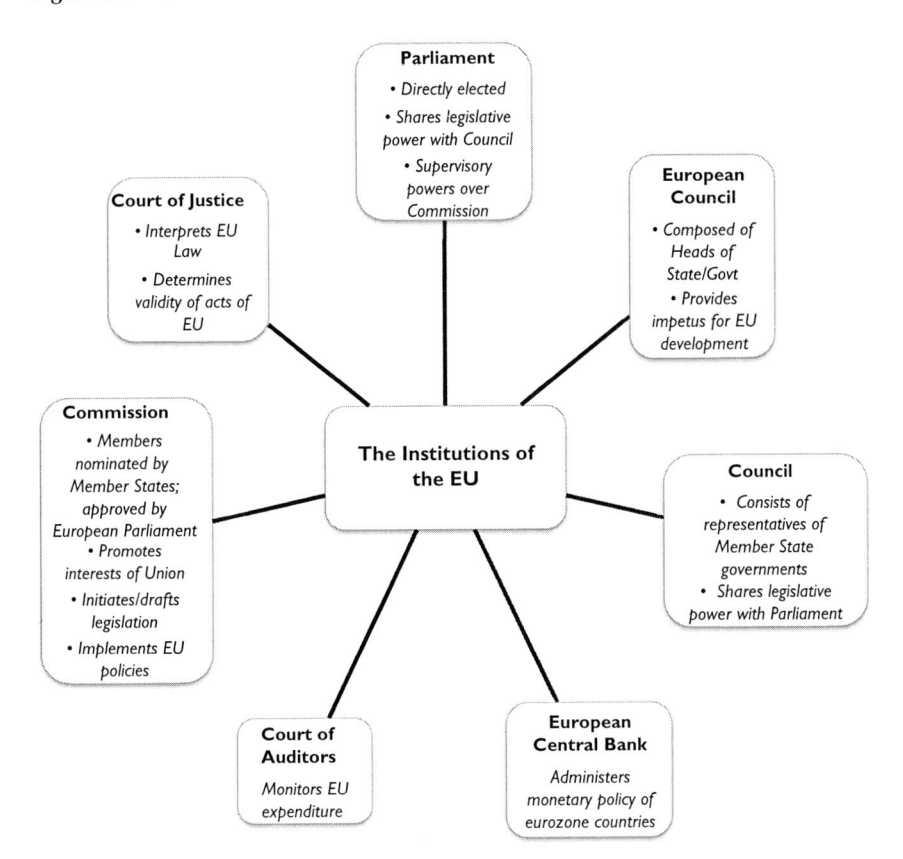

Parliament
- Directly elected
- Shares legislative power with Council
- Supervisory powers over Commission

European Council
- Composed of Heads of State/Govt
- Provides impetus for EU development

Court of Justice
- Interprets EU Law
- Determines validity of acts of EU

Commission
- Members nominated by Member States; approved by European Parliament
- Promotes interests of Union
- Initiates/drafts legislation
- Implements EU policies

Council
- Consists of representatives of Member State governments
- Shares legislative power with Parliament

Court of Auditors
Monitors EU expenditure

European Central Bank
Administers monetary policy of eurozone countries

The Institutions of the EU

The European Parliament

The European Parliament (EP) is made up of 766 Members (MEPs) elected in the 28 Member States of the Union. Since 1979, MEPs have been directly elected for a five-year period. Ireland has 12 MEPs elected by proportional representation. The Member States of the Union are each allocated seats roughly according to their population. The MEPs sit in the EP in political groupings, rather than with MEPs from their own Member State.

In the 2014 European elections, 12 EU Member States will each lose one seat and none will gain any under a draft decision endorsed by the Parliament on 12 June 2013. These reductions are needed to comply with the 751-seat limit set by the Lisbon Treaty and make room for Croatia's MEPs. The remaining three seats have to come from Germany, whose share must go down from 99 seats to 96 — the maximum allowed by the Treaty of Lisbon (see table below).

The powers of the EP have been increased by the Treaty of Lisbon in order to enhance democratic participation in the EU. The EP exercises supervisory power over the Commission. It has a right of veto over the appointment of the Commission as a whole and has the power to dismiss the entire Commission by way of a vote of censure. This issue arose in 1999 when the Commission resigned *en bloc*, in order to avoid a vote of censure as a result of a controversy relating to alleged corruption and mismanagement within the Commission.

The Commission is required to make an annual report to the EP. It must also submit each proposed budget of the European Union to the EP for its approval. The EP may also require Commissioners to answer written or oral questions and it can exercise supervisory powers over the acts of other institutions by instituting legal challenges before the Court of Justice of the European Union (CJEU). The EP also may set up temporary Committees of Inquiry and elect a European Ombudsman to investigate complaints of maladministration against any EU body. On 3 July 2013, Emily O'Reilly, Ombudsman of Ireland, was elected European Ombudsman of the EP. She took up her new post on 1 October 2013.

Table on Allocation of MEPs between Member States

Member State	Current allocation of seats	Proposed allocation for 2014 elections	Difference
Germany	99*	96	−3
France	74	74	=
United Kingdom	73	73	=
Italy	73	73	=
Spain	54	54	=
Poland	51	51	=
Romania	33	32	−1
Netherlands	26	26	=
Greece	22	21	−1
Belgium	22	21	−1
Portugal	22	21	−1
Czech Republic	22	21	−1
Hungary	22	21	−1
Sweden	20	20	=
Austria	19	18	−1
Bulgaria	18	17	−1

Denmark	13	13	=
Slovakia	13	13	=
Finland	13	13	=
Ireland	12	11	−1
Croatia	12	11	−1
Lithuania	12	11	−1
Slovenia	8	8	=
Latvia	9	8	−1
Estonia	6	6	=
Cyprus	6	6	=
Luxembourg	6	6	=
Malta	6	6	=
TOTAL	**766**	**751**	**15**

* *The three extra German seats were part of a transitional arrangement that expires at the end of the current parliamentary term in 2014.*

The Council of the EU

The Council's primary function is that of legislature, which it shares with the EP. Most legislation is passed through the 'ordinary legislative procedure'. Under this procedure the Commission submits proposals for legislation to both the Council and the EP. If the two institutions fail to reach agreement, the proposal will be abandoned.

The composition of the Council is dependent on the subject matter under discussion: if the Council is discussing agriculture matters, each Member State's agriculture minister, or equivalent, will be present. The Member States' representatives in the Council are authorised to commit the government of their State. The Council is supported by a Committee of Permanent Representatives of the governments of the Member States (COREPER). This body is responsible for 'preparing' the work of the Council. In reality, most Council decisions are taken by COREPER and are subsequently approved by the ministers (or equivalent) in Council. The Council represents national interests. The TFEU provides that

> the Council shall, jointly with the European Parliament, exercise legislative and budgetary functions. It shall carry out policy-making and coordinating functions as laid down in the Treaties.

When the Council is required to reach a decision, it may do so by taking a vote. The Council operates three voting systems: simple majority, qualified majority

(QMV) and unanimity. Decisions in the Council are generally taken by QMV. Under this method, each Member State's vote is 'weighted' to reflect the size of its population. This means that a Member State may find itself subject to a decision for which it did not vote. The higher the Member State's population, the more votes it has, but in fact the numbers are slightly weighted in favour of the less populous Member States. A qualified majority is reached when:

- A majority of the 28 Member States vote in favour;
- At least 260 of the possible 352 votes are cast.

Table on Voting Strength of Members States

Voting Strength of Member States in the Council	
Member States	Number of Votes Each
Germany, France, Italy and the United Kingdom	29
Spain and Poland	27
Romania	14
Netherlands	13
Belgium, Czech Republic, Greece, Hungary and Portugal	12
Austria, Bulgaria and Sweden	10
Croatia, Denmark, Ireland, Lithuania, Slovakia and Finland	7
Cyprus, Estonia, Latvia, Luxembourg and Slovenia	4
Malta	3
TOTAL	352

A Member State can ask for a check to determine whether the majority represents a minimum 62 per cent of the total population of the EU. If this is not the case, the proposal cannot be adopted. In votes concerning sensitive matters — such as security and external affairs and taxation — decisions by the Council must be unanimous. This means that one Member State can veto a decision.

From 1 November 2014, a system known as 'double majority voting' will be introduced. For a proposal to be adopted, it will need the support of two types of majority: a majority of Member States and a majority of the total EU population. The Council therefore will adopt a decision when it is approved by at least 55 per cent of Council members comprising at least 15 of them and representing Member States which include at least 65 per cent of the population of the Union. A blocking minority is made up of at least four Member States.

The Commission

The Commission represents and upholds the interests of the EU as a whole. It is the 'guardian of the Treaties'. It oversees and implements EU policies by proposing new laws to Parliament and the Council, managing the EU's budget, allocating funding, enforcing EU law (together with the Court of Justice), and representing the EU internationally, for example, by negotiating agreements between the EU and other countries or trading blocs. It comprises 28 Commissioners, one from each Member State. They are appointed for a renewable period of five years. The Commission President and the High Representative of the Union for Foreign Affairs and Security Policy are also members. It has a total staff of approximately 25,000. Commissioners must be EU citizens. The TFEU requires that each Commissioner be independent, not take instruction from any government or other body, and act only in the interests of the Union. It also provides that the Commission must promote the general interests of the Union and take appropriate initiatives to that end. The Commission is divided into directorates-general (DGs). Each DG is headed by a director-general who reports to the Commissioner with overall responsibility for that DG. The DGs are divided by subject matter (for example, agriculture or transport). Each Commissioner is supported by a *cabinet*.

The Commission's most important function is to initiate legislation. It produces draft legislation which it then sends to the Council and the EP for consideration or approval. If the Council or EP fail to secure agreement on a proposal, the Commission may amend the proposal in line with the other institutions' suggestions. In very limited circumstances, the Commission may act alone in making regulations. These are called 'delegated acts'.

The TFEU makes a distinction between legislative acts, delegated acts, and implementing acts. Regulations, directives, and decisions are legislative acts (Article 289 TFEU). Delegated acts are non-legislative decisions made by the Commission under delegated authority from the Council. The delegation of power to the Commission to make regulations has existed since the creation of the EEC. This is regarded as important for practical purposes. There are policy areas, such as environment, fisheries and agriculture, which require numerous regulations to be passed quickly to respond to rapidly changing circumstances. Such regulations could not be passed with the necessary speed if the normal legislative procedures applied. Consequently, the treaties have empowered the Council to authorise the Commission to enact specific regulations in respect of particular policy areas through a 'parent regulation'. Article 290 TFEU provides:

> A legislative act may delegate to the Commission the power to adopt non-legislative acts of general application to supplement or amend certain non-essential elements of the legislative act… The objectives, content, scope and duration of the delegation of power shall be explicitly defined in the legislative acts.

In addition, the essential objectives of the policy area must be reserved to the legislative act, and cannot be delegated. This means that the Council maintains tight control over what delegated acts the Commission may perform. 'Implementing acts' are defined in Article 291 TFEU. They may be made pursuant to a legislative act or a delegated act. Implementing acts will typically contain the detailed rules necessary to execute, or 'implement', legislative or delegated acts.

The Commission ensures that EU legislation and policy are put into effect at national level. If a Member State is in breach of its EU obligations, the Commission has the power to investigate. It will encourage Member States to remedy such breaches informally. As a last resort, the Commission may bring the Member State before the CJEU.

The Commission also manages the EU's annual budget. It acts as negotiator on behalf of the EU in relation to trade and cooperation agreements with third countries or other trading blocs.

The Commission's importance in the day-to-day running of the EU cannot be overstated. It has significant influence over its development and direction. Its power to initiate legislation means that it can largely determine the legislative programme of the EU. It is itself, however, subject to the treaties and supervision of the EP.

The European Council
The European Council (EC) is comprised of the heads of State or government of the Member States. They are assisted by their foreign ministers, along with the President of the Commission. They hold ad hoc meetings, known as 'summits', twice a year. It has its own elected President. The High Representative of the Union for Foreign Affairs and Security Policy also takes part in the work of the EC. It is based in Brussels.

The treaties define the role of the EC as providing the Union with the necessary impetus for its development and providing that it shall define the general political guidelines thereof. The EC has a critical function in ensuring that agreement between the Member States is reached in the event of failure at a lower level. The EC is regarded as an important force within the EU in that it determines its long-term policy direction and provides it with political leadership. For example, it was agreement at EC level that resulted in the creation of monetary union.

The Court of Justice of the European Union (CJEU)
The Court was originally known as the European Court of Justice (ECJ). In November 1989, a Court of First Instance (CFI) was created to assist it. Collectively, the courts are now known as the 'Court of Justice of the European Union' (CJEU). The CJEU is therefore made up of the Court of Justice (the Court), the General

Court (GC) (formerly the CFI) and 'specialised courts'. The CJEU sits in Luxembourg and comprises judges and advocates-general (AGs). Whilst it is the judges who adjudicate upon disputes and issue the judgments, the AGs assist the judges by issuing non-binding written opinions to them before they make their decisions. Each court also has a president and registrar. The judges, one from each Member State, hold office for a period of six years, renewable every three years. The treaties state that judges must be persons whose independence is beyond doubt. The TFEU requires the judges to be individuals who

> possess the qualifications required for appointment to the highest judicial offices in their respective countries or who are jurisconsults of recognised competence.

Academic lawyers may therefore be appointed. The Court has eight AGs. The rules for appointment and qualification of AGs are the same as those for judges. The Court's deliberations are held in secret and a single judgment only is issued.

The role of the CJEU is stated in the treaties as ensuring that, in the interpretation and application of the treaty, the law is observed. Typically, two types of actions may be brought before the Court: direct actions and preliminary references. Direct actions can include those brought by the Commission against Member States considered to have failed to fulfil their EU obligations. They can also include actions brought by other EU institutions or individuals seeking to challenge the validity of acts of the EU institutions. Preliminary references are made by national courts in respect of disputes before them where the interpretation or validity of EU law requires determination. The CJEU will give a ruling on the matter. The CJEU is not a court of appeal against decisions of the domestic courts of the Member States: it does not substitute its decision for the domestic court's decision. It merely provides an interpretation of EU law which assists the domestic court in making its ruling.

The Court uses a purposive, or teleological, approach to interpretation of EU law. This approach was explained in the *CILFIT* case (Case 283/81) thus:

> every provision of [EU] law must be placed in its context and interpreted in the light of the provisions of [EU] law as a whole, regard being given to the objectives thereof.

As a result of this approach, the Court is regarded as having taken a dynamic approach in 'filling the gaps' in EU legislation. This has led to claims of judicial activism by the Court. Such decisions as *Van Gend and Loos* (Case 26/62) and *Costa v ENEL* (Case 6/64) are undoubtedly far-reaching decisions. In these cases, the

Court developed the fundamental principles of direct effect and supremacy of EU law (see below).

The European Central Bank

The European Central Bank (ECB) was established by the TEU 1992. It is an institution of the EU. Its primary function is the administration of the monetary policy of the Eurozone. The ECB, along with the national central banks of the Eurozone states, make up the European System of Central Banks (ESCB) — the central banking system of the euro area. The main objective of the ESCB is to maintain price stability and to safeguard the value of the euro. The ECB determines and implements monetary policy by controlling interest rates and the money supply. It also controls foreign reserves and issues euro banknotes.

The Court of Auditors

The Court of Auditors (CoA) was established by the Budgetary Treaty of 1975. Although described as a 'court', it has no judicial functions. It was made an institution by the TEU in 1992. It comprises one member from each Member State. Members must be appropriately qualified and their independence beyond doubt. The CoA scrutinises the EU's budget and expenditure. Each Union institution and subsidiary body that has access to or expends Union funds is subject to the scrutiny of the CoA. It seeks to ensure that all legal requirements in relation to expenditure of Union funds are observed and that such expenditure is appropriate and reasonable. It publishes an annual report in which it sets out ways in which improvements in budgetary management and expenditure may be achieved. The CoA also provides the Council and EP with a Statement of Assurance, which affirms that EU funds have been spent appropriately and that value for money has been achieved.

C. Sources of EU Law

Introduction

EU law can be divided into primary and secondary law. The treaties are the primary source of EU law. These include all the treaties enacted to create the original European Communities and those enacted to amend them. The treaties provide the legal framework for the EU by setting out the specific rules and policy objectives which are then expanded by the secondary sources of EU law. The secondary sources include secondary legislation as enacted by the institutions of the Union, case law from judgments of the CJEU, general principles of law as declared by the CJEU and international agreements entered into by the Union with third parties.

Figure 8.2 Sources of EU Law

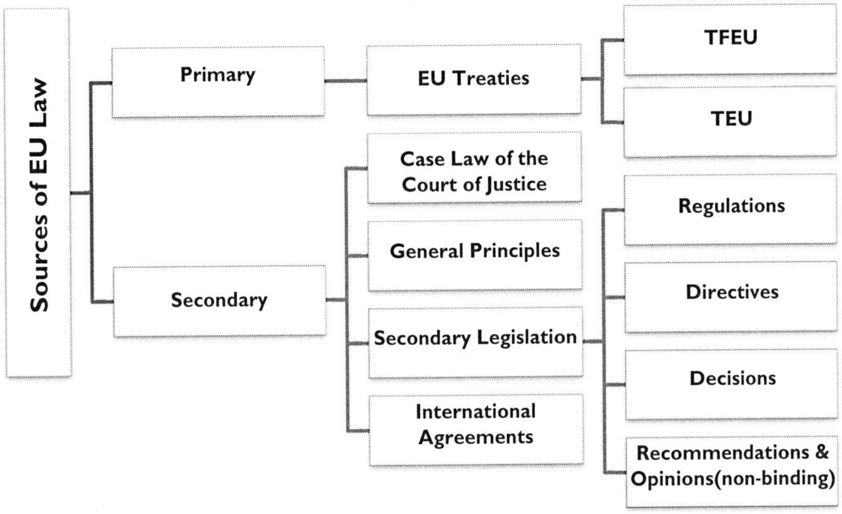

Sources of EU Law
- Primary
  - EU Treaties
    - TFEU
    - TEU
- Secondary
  - Case Law of the Court of Justice
  - General Principles
  - Secondary Legislation
    - Regulations
    - Directives
    - Decisions
    - Recommendations & Opinions (non-binding)
  - International Agreements

Primary Sources of EU Law

The TFEU and the TEU set out the treaty framework on which the EU is based. These treaties now represent the primary law of the EU. Only the Member States can develop and amend the treaties. They can be amended through one of two amendment procedures: the 'ordinary revision procedure' or the 'simplified revision procedure' (Article 48 TEU). The ordinary revision procedure involves the consideration of a proposed amendment by a Convention, composed of representatives of national parliaments, heads of State, the EP, and the Commission. Alternatively, the proposed amendment can be put before an intergovernmental conference (IGC) comprising representatives of the Member States. Before any amendment to a treaty can come into effect, it must be ratified by the Member States under their respective constitutions. The simplified revision procedure applies only to proposed amendments in respect of Part Three of the TFEU. This relates to Union policies and internal actions. This area of EU law is seen as politically less sensitive than other treaty provisions. Under this procedure, the EC may adopt an amendment, which is normally done by unanimity, after consulting the EP and the Commission. The ECB will also be consulted if it relates to a monetary issue. The EC notifies the Member States of the proposed amendment. That amendment cannot enter into force until it is approved by the Member States in accordance with their respective constitutional requirements. If no objection to it is raised within six months, the EC may adopt the amendment, provided the agreement of the EP is also given.

Secondary Sources of EU Law

The secondary sources of EU law comprise regulations, directives, decisions, recommendations and opinions. Regulations, directives and decisions are binding acts. Recommendations and opinions are non-binding acts and are sometimes referred to as *soft law*. Secondary sources of EU law are, generally, proposed by the Commission and enacted by the EP and Council under the 'ordinary legislative procedure' (known as *co-decision* prior to the enactment of the Treaty of Lisbon). As we have seen, in certain circumstances the Commission can make secondary legislation itself, but only under delegated authority.

Regulations

Article 288 TFEU provides that a regulation shall have general application and it shall be binding in its entirety and directly applicable in all Member States. Therefore they will have full effect throughout the EU, in every Member State. They are 'directly applicable', which means that they take effect automatically in each Member State without the need for domestic implementing measures. The CJEU has stated that Member States must not pass any implementing measures as this may result in a Member State placing a different interpretation on the regulation to that which was intended (Case 34/73, *Variola*). Regulations are effective legal instruments for achieving uniformity of EU law throughout the Member States.

Directives

Article 288 TFEU provides that:

> A directive shall be binding, as to the result to be achieved, upon each Member State to which it is addressed, but shall leave to the national authorities the choice of form and methods.

Directives, therefore, do not have general application and so do not have to be addressed to all Member States. Unlike regulations, they are not directly applicable. The rights and obligations created by directives can only become effective once they have been incorporated into the domestic law of the Member States under their constitutional requirements. Directives place an obligation on Member States to ensure that the particular policy objective of the directive is achieved by a particular date. Domestic authorities may decide on the exact method of implementation (for example, constitutional amendment, statute, statutory instrument). Directives are an effective legal instrument for achieving harmonisation, rather than strict uniformity.

Decisions

Article 288 TFEU states: "A decision shall be binding in its entirety. The decision which specifies those to whom it is addressed shall be binding only on them."

A decision is similar to a regulation in that it has direct applicability, requiring no domestic implementing measures in order for it to take effect. All decisions must be published in the Official Journal, taking effect on a prescribed date or on the twentieth day following the decision's publication.

Recommendations and Opinions

Unlike the other secondary sources of EU law, recommendations and opinions are not legally binding. Article 288 TFEU provides that they have no binding force. They are, however, persuasive and are generally taken into account by the national courts.

Figure 8.3 Summary of Secondary Legislation

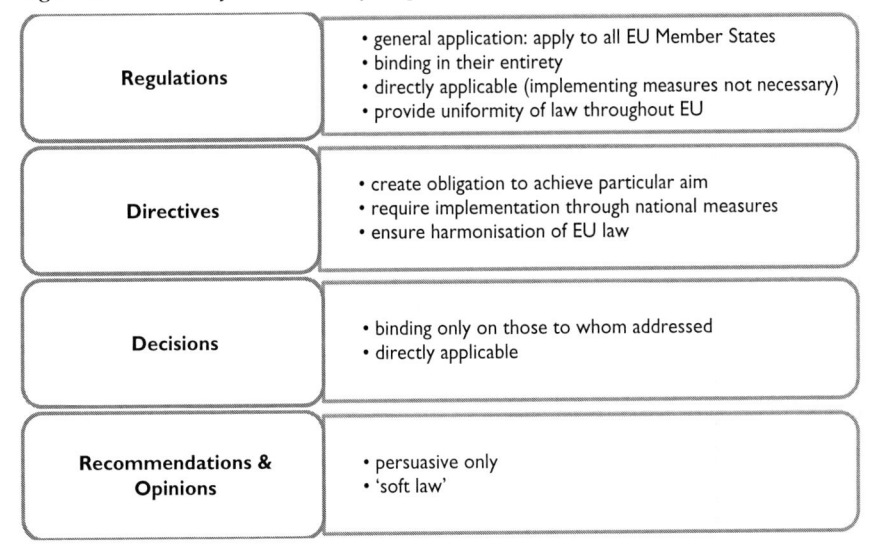

Regulations	• general application: apply to all EU Member States • binding in their entirety • directly applicable (implementing measures not necessary) • provide uniformity of law throughout EU
Directives	• create obligation to achieve particular aim • require implementation through national measures • ensure harmonisation of EU law
Decisions	• binding only on those to whom addressed • directly applicable
Recommendations & Opinions	• persuasive only • 'soft law'

Case Law of the Court of Justice of the European Union (CJEU)

Article 19 TEU sets out the CJEU's function: to ensure that, in the interpretation and application of the treaties, the law is observed. Since the treaties and secondary legislation are often broadly drafted with relatively little detail, the CJEU, through its powers of interpretation, has filled in the gaps in legislation. It has therefore played a key part in the development of the EU legal system and bringing about the 'constitutionalisation' of the treaties. It has done this through its purposive, or teleological, method of interpretation, primarily under its jurisdiction to provide preliminary rulings. Unlike the common law courts, there is no formal system of precedent. The Court may depart from its own past decisions. In the interests of consistency, however, it tends not to do so.

General Principles of EU Law

General principles of law have been developed by the CJEU in order to assist it where the written sources of law (primary and secondary) are insufficiently detailed. General principles have been applied by the Court in the interpretation of EU legislation and in determining the validity of secondary legislation. Some of these have subsequently been formally recognised by being included in the treaties. General principles have been held to include equality (non-discrimination), fundamental rights, proportionality, subsidiarity and legal certainty.

International Agreements

International agreements entered into by the EU bind the institutions of the EU and its Member States. The EU has authority to enter into such agreements with third countries (and other trading blocs) because it enjoys legal personality under Article 47 TEU.

D. The Interaction of Irish Law and European Union Law

Overview

Ireland joined the European Communities in 1972. Its membership took effect from 1 January 1973. That membership was authorised by the Third Amendment of the Constitution Act 1972. This amendment also gave EU law primacy over Irish law by allowing for the passing of the European Communities Act 1972. Section 2 of the 1972 Act provides that, from 1 January 1973, the treaties governing the European Union and the existing and future acts adopted by the EU institutions shall be binding on the State and form part of its domestic law. By virtue of s 3 of the 1972 Act a Minister of State is authorised to make regulations to enable s 2 to have full effect. It is therefore the 1972 Act that gives the force of law in Ireland to laws made by the EU institutions. Without the 1972 Act, Ireland would be a member of the EU in international law only and the laws of the EU would not have effect in the domestic law of the State. Furthermore, without the Third Amendment to the Constitution, the 1972 Act would be unconstitutional by virtue of Article 15.2 of the Constitution.

The Twenty-eighth Amendment of the Constitution (Treaty of Lisbon) Act 2009, which allowed the State to ratify the Treaty of Lisbon, restated the primacy of EU law by amending Article 29.4 as follows:

> No provision of this Constitution invalidates laws enacted, acts done or measures adopted by the State, before, on or after the entry into force of the Treaty of Lisbon, that are necessitated by the obligations of membership of the European Union referred to in subsection 5 of this section or of the European Atomic Energy Community, or prevents laws enacted, acts done or measures adopted by—

(i) the said European Union or the European Atomic Energy Community, or institutions thereof,
(ii) the European Communities or European Union existing immediately before the entry into force of the Treaty of Lisbon, or institutions thereof, or
(iii) bodies competent under the treaties referred to in this section,

from having the force of law in the State.

Article 29.4 of the Constitution therefore provides that no provision in the Constitution can invalidate any laws enacted, acts done or measures adopted by the State which are necessitated by its obligations of membership of the EU. This provision effectively immunises EU law from constitutional challenge.

The founding treaties of the European Union did not directly address the matter of supremacy of EU law. Member States originally assumed that EU law would have the same domestic effects as other sources of international law. This would have meant that the status of EU law would have been determined by each Member State's own constitutional system. In dualist states, such as Ireland, international law can only bind individuals if that law has been incorporated into the domestic law. It was originally assumed by the Member States that the EEC Treaty would bind the State but not provide enforceable rights to individuals unless specifically incorporated into the domestic law. In monist States (such as the Netherlands), once ratified, international law automatically becomes part of the domestic law. In such States, it was assumed that EEC law automatically became part of the State's domestic legal system. This would have given rise to a situation where different Member States treated EU law differently domestically. Recognising this possibility, the CJEU developed two fundamental principles upon which the effectiveness of EU law rests: direct effect and supremacy, or 'primacy'.

The Doctrine of Supremacy of EU Law

In *Van Gend en Loos* (Case 26/62) [1963] ECR 1, the CJEU explained that EU law constitutes

> a new legal order... for the benefit of which the States have limited their sovereign rights, albeit within limited fields.

In that case, the CJEU gave direct effect to a treaty article prohibiting the introduction of customs duties. The treaty article in question was negative in nature and did not require any further implementing measures to give it effect in national (Dutch) law. The CJEU recognised that allowing Members States to apply conflicting national law rather than EU law would undermine the ability of the EU to achieve its objectives. Thus the doctrine of supremacy of EU law was established.

In *Costa v ENEL* (Case 6/64) [1964] ECR 585, the CJEU described the supremacy of EU law in this way:

> By creating a Community of unlimited duration, having its own institutions, its own personality, its own legal capacity and capacity of representation on the international plane and, more particularly, real powers stemming from a limitation of sovereignty or a transfer of powers from the States to the Community, the Member States have limited their sovereign rights, albeit within limited fields, and have thus created a body of law which binds both their nationals and themselves. The integration into the laws of each Member State of provisions which derive from the Community, and more generally the terms and spirit of the Treaty, make it impossible for the States, as a corollary, to accord precedence to a unilateral and subsequent measure over a legal system accepted by them as a basis of reciprocity.

This judgment confirmed that, where national law and EU law conflict, EU law must take precedence, even where the national law has been enacted subsequent to EU law. This ruled out the possibility of national law taking precedence under the doctrine of implied repeal (where later law is presumed to have automatically repealed earlier conflicting law).

The principle of supremacy came under threat in the case of *Internationale Handelsgesellschaft* (Case 11/70) where the German court questioned the legal basis for the principle of supremacy. It expressed concern that fundamental rights in the German constitution could be overruled by EU law. The German courts appeared to reserve the right not to give primacy to EU law where it conflicted with fundamental German constitutional rights. However the CJEU ruled that EU law is supreme over all forms of national law — constitutional or ordinary. The CJEU did, however, accept that such fundamental rights were an integral part of the general principles of law whose protection would be ensured within the structure and objectives of the EU. Therefore, from the CJEU's point of view, fundamental rights similar to those in the German constitution were also part of EU law. A conflict between the two would therefore be unlikely.

This position was further elucidated by the CJEU in *Simmenthal* (Case 106/77) [1978] ECR 629. Here, an Italian court was required to apply EU law which prohibited import charges despite subsequent domestic legislation authorising the levying of such charges. The CJEU ruled:

> Every national court must, in any case within its jurisdiction, apply Community law in its entirety and protect rights which the latter confers on individuals, and must accordingly set aside any provision of national law which may conflict with it, whether prior or subsequent to the Community rule.

Simmenthal is a significant decision because the Italian court in that case did not have jurisdiction under the Italian constitution to dis-apply national legislation which conflicted with EU law. Only the Italian constitutional court had such jurisdiction. Despite this, the CJEU ruled that the Italian court was required to dis-apply national law and not wait for a ruling from the Italian constitutional court. The effect of *Simmenthal* is that it confers on domestic courts jurisdiction which they may not have under domestic law. A similar situation arose in *Factortame* (Case C-213/89, *R v Secretary of State for Transport ex parte Factortame Ltd (Factortame (No 2))*. In that case, the CJEU stated that a national rule must be set aside by the national court if that rule interferes with an EU law right. The House of Lords (sitting as the final court of appeal for the United Kingdom) was required to dis-apply a British Act of Parliament which conflicted with EU law, despite the fact that the United Kingdom courts had no such power under the British constitution.

The Irish courts, for their part, have consistently upheld the supremacy of EU law. In *Meagher v Minister for Agriculture and Food* [1994] 1 IR 329, Blayney J stated:

> It is well established that Community law takes precedence over our domestic law. Where they are in conflict, it is the Community law which prevails.

The Doctrine of Direct Effect

Introduction

The doctrine of direct effect of EU law was established in *Van Gend en Loos* (Case 26/62). Van Gend (a company based in Utrecht) imported goods from Germany into the Netherlands. It was required under Dutch law to pay customs duties on the goods. Van Gend challenged the legality of the duty. The Dutch tax tribunal referred the matter to the CJEU. The CJEU declared that EU law constituted a new legal order of international law, which conferred both rights and obligations on individuals, as well as on the participating Member States, without the need for implementing legislation. The Court added that domestic courts must protect these rights. In other words, EU law had direct effect in that it could be invoked by individuals before domestic courts. *Van Gend* set out the criteria necessary for a provision of EU law to have direct effect (the *Van Gend* criteria):

- It must be clear and precise;
- It must be unconditional;
- It must not be subject to any further implementing measures.

Treaty Articles and Direct Effect

Treaty articles are capable of direct effect providing they comply with the *Van Gend* criteria. In addition, the CJEU has ruled that rights and obligations contained in treaty articles may be enforced both against the State and public bodies, known as 'vertical direct effect', and against private bodies and individuals, known as 'horizontal direct effect'. Horizontal direct effect of treaty articles was established in *Defrenne v Sabena* (Case 43/75). In this case, Defrenne, an air hostess, was seeking compensation from Sabena, her employer, for low pay she had received in comparison with male workers. She relied on Article 119 EEC which contained the principle of equal pay for equal work. The CJEU held that she could rely on the Treaty article, despite the fact that Sabena was a private body.

Regulations and Direct Effect
Article 288 TFEU appears to give regulations direct effect. It describes a regulation as being of general application…binding in its entirety and directly applicable in all Member States. A Regulation is therefore clearly intended to take immediate effect without the need for further implementation. Regulations are automatically part of the domestic law of Member States. This is 'direct applicability'. Member States do not need to take further steps to implement them. Regulations operate both between the individual and the state (vertical direct effect) and between citizen and citizen (horizontal direct effect). However, if a regulation requires implementation, it may not have direct effect. This occurred in *Azienda Agricola Monte Arcosu v Regione Autonoma della Sardegna* (case C-403/98). In that case, regulations left it to the Member States to define the word 'farmer'. This gave the Member States too much discretion for the provision to have direct effect.

Where the criteria for direct effect are satisfied, a regulation may be invoked vertically or horizontally. For example in *Antonio Munoz Cia SA v Frumar Ltd* (case C-253/00) a regulation laid down the standards by which grapes are classified. Munoz brought civil proceedings against Frumar which had sold grapes under labels which did not comply with the relevant standard. The regulation did not confer rights specifically on Munoz. Rather it applied to all operators in the market. A failure by one operator to comply with the regulation could have adverse consequences for other operators in the market. The CJEU held that, since the purpose of the regulation was to keep products of unsatisfactory quality off the market, and ensure the full effectiveness of the regulation, it must be possible for a trader to bring civil proceedings against a competitor to enforce the regulation. The CJEU therefore confirmed in this case that regulations, by their very nature, operate to confer rights on individuals which must be protected by the domestic courts.

Decisions and Direct Effect
Decisions, as is the case with regulations, are directly applicable. However, Article 288 TFEU provides that they can be binding only on those to whom they are addressed. They may be addressed to Member States, individuals or incorporated bodies. The CJEU has stated that decisions will be directly effective against an addressee, providing they fulfil the *Van Gend* criteria.

International Agreements and Direct Effect

The law in this area is not entirely settled. However the CJEU has suggested in *Kupferberg* (Case 104/81) that international agreements may have direct effect if the circumstances so require.

Directives and Direct Effect

Directives must satisfy the *Van Gend* criteria in order for them to be directly effective. Although the final criterion would appear to preclude directives from having direct effect, the CJEU has held that, once the deadline for implementation has passed, the directive may be capable of direct effect (*Ratti* (Case 148/78)).

Unlike treaty articles and regulations, directives are only capable of vertical direct effect (against the State), not horizontal direct effect (against individuals). This was made clear by the CJEU in *Marshall v Southampton and Southwest Hampshire Area Health Authority*. Ms Marshall wished to enforce rights in the Equal Treatment Directive (Council Directive (76/207/EEC)) against her employer before an Employment Tribunal. The tribunal referred the matter to the CJEU asking if Ms Marshall could rely on the directive. The CJEU held that she could because she was seeking to rely on the directive vertically, as her employers were a public body and therefore part of the State. Had her employers been a private party, with no connection to the State, she would not have been able to rely on it. The CJEU has construed 'the State' widely. In *Marshall*, a health authority was held to be part of the state. In *Fratelli Constanzo* (Case 103/88) regional and local government were held to be part of the State and, in *Johnston v Chief Constable of the RUC* (Case 222/84), the Chief Constable was so held. The CJEU went further in *Foster v British Gas* (Case C-188/89). British Gas at the time was a statutory corporation. The UK authorities claimed that it was not part of the state for the purposes of the direct effect of directives. The CJEU disagreed. It laid down the following guidelines for determining whether or not a body was an 'emanation' of the State such that a directive might be relied upon against it:

- The body has been made responsible for providing a public service; and/or
- The body is subject to the authority or control of the State; and/or
- The body has special powers beyond those which result from the normal rules applicable to relations between individuals

In *Doughty v Rolls-Royce* [1992] 1 CMLR 1045, the English Court of Appeal held that, although Rolls-Royce at the relevant time was wholly owned by the British State, it was not an 'emanation of the State' because the company neither provided a public service nor had any of the 'special powers' referred to in the *Foster v British Gas* guidelines.

The fact that directives were not capable of horizontal direct effect reduced their effectiveness as legal instruments. To circumnavigate this limitation, the CJEU developed the principle of 'indirect effect'. In *Von Colson* (Case 14/83), the CJEU relied on Article 4 TFEU which states that Member States are required to "take all appropriate measures…to ensure the fulfilment of the obligations arising out of this Treaty" and also to "facilitate the achievement of the [EU's] tasks." The CJEU declared that, in light of this provision, domestic courts were under an obligation to interpret and apply domestic law in a manner that was consistent with the wording and purpose of directives. It developed the doctrine in *Marleasing* (Case C-106/89) by ruling that national legislation which had been interpreted by a domestic court in the light of a non- or incorrectly implemented directive can be relied upon, not only by an individual against the state, but also against another individual, even where such domestic law predates a directive and was not intended to implement it. This appears to allow for horizontal direct effect of directives by allowing unincorporated directives to be enforced against individuals.

Figure 8.4 The Relationship between EU Law and National Legal Systems – Key Concepts

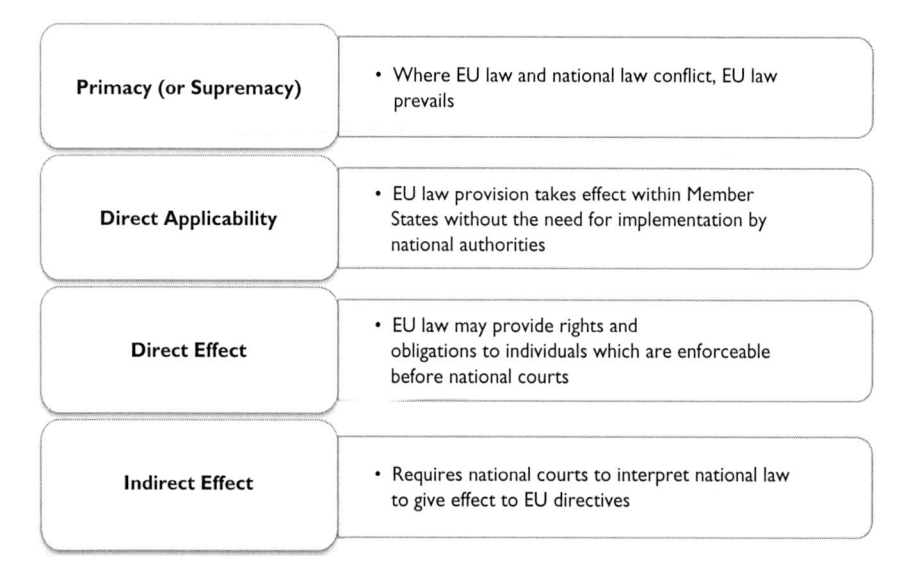

Primacy (or Supremacy)	Where EU law and national law conflict, EU law prevails
Direct Applicability	EU law provision takes effect within Member States without the need for implementation by national authorities
Direct Effect	EU law may provide rights and obligations to individuals which are enforceable before national courts
Indirect Effect	Requires national courts to interpret national law to give effect to EU directives

State Liability

The *Francovich* Principle

In Cases C-6 and 9/90, *Francovich and Bonifaci v Italy (Francovich)*, the CJEU held that, should a Member State fail to incorporate a directive into domestic law, an individual who suffers damage as a consequence of that failure may claim compensation from that Member State. This right to compensation was, however, subject to a number of criteria, namely:

- The directive must be intended to confer rights on the individual;
- The content of the right must be identifiable by reference to the directive; and
- There must be a causal link between the State's breach and the damage suffered.

The CJEU's judgment in *Francovich* reinforces Member States' obligations under the treaties and also provides a further incentive to Member States to ensure that EU law rights are not denied to individuals.

The *Francovich* case related to a Member State's failure to fulfil its obligations in relation to directives only. However in *Brasserie du Pecheur SA v Germany* and *R v Secretary of State for Transport ex parte Factortame Ltd and Others* (Cases C-46 and C-48/93), the CJEU ruled that damages could also be available where a Member State had failed to fulfil obligations derived from other sources of Union law. The CJEU set down the following criteria for such cases:

- The rule of law infringed must be intended to confer rights on individuals;
- The breach must be sufficiently serious; and
- There must be a direct causal link between the State's breach and the damage suffered.

The CJEU also stated that the principle applied to any organ of the State responsible for the breach or omission, whether it be legislative, executive or judicial (*Kobler v Austria*, Case C-224/01 [2003] ECR I-10239).

Legal Responses to the Eurozone Financial Crisis

Following the European debt crisis which began in 2008, a number of Eurozone countries experienced difficulty funding their public sector borrowing requirements due to unsustainable borrowing costs on the international bond markets. This financial instability presented a risk to the Eurozone banking system and the single currency itself. To manage this risk, in May 2010, the EU responded by establishing special funds to provide emergency financial assistance to those states. The European Financial Stabilisation Mechanism (EFSM) was created by Council Regulation, and agreement to create the European Financial Stability Facility (EFSF) was reached by international treaty between the euro area Member States. The EFSF was established as a private company and incorporated in Luxembourg under Luxembourgish law. It came into effect on 7 June 2010. The first Eurozone state to receive assistance was Greece in spring 2010. It was feared that Greece would default on its sovereign debt, thereby triggering a banking crisis across the Eurozone due to the fact that a number of Eurozone banks held Greek sovereign bonds.

The EFSM and EFSF were mandated to provide financial assistance to Eurozone Member States that needed it ('programme countries'). The EFSM and EFSF were established as temporary measures. In October 2010, however, it was decided to create a permanent rescue fund: the European Stability Mechanism (ESM). The ESM came into existence on 8 October 2012 following the signing of the ESM treaty in July 2011. In order to confirm the legal validity of the ESM treaty in light of the 'no bailout' rule in the TFEU, all EU Member States agreed to amend the TFEU. The validity of this amendment under EU law was challenged in *Pringle v Ireland* (C-370/12) [2013] but the CJEU confirmed that it was valid under EU law. The ESM is now the main instrument to finance new programmes. As of 1 July 2013, the European Stability Mechanism (ESM) is the sole and permanent mechanism for responding to new requests for financial assistance by euro area Member States. The European Financial Stability Facility (EFSF) may no longer engage in new financing programmes or enter into new loan facility agreements. The EFSF will remain active in financing the ongoing programmes for Portugal, Ireland and Greece. The EFSF will be dissolved and liquidated when all financial assistance provided to euro area Member States and all funding instruments issued by the EFSF have been repaid in full. The ESM currently provides financial assistance to Spain for the recapitalisation of its financial institutions and financial assistance to Cyprus.

To further seek to ensure the stability of the Eurozone financial system, 25 Member States of the EU adopted the *Treaty on Stability, Coordination and Governance in the Economic and Monetary Union*. This was not an EU treaty, but an international treaty, because the UK and the Czech Republic were not parties to it. The treaty contains a 'fiscal compact' which commits the signatory states to introduce rules on budgetary deficits to their national constitutions. A referendum on the treaty was held in Ireland in May 2012 in order to ensure its validity under the Irish Constitution. It was approved by the people.

Table on Key Dates in the Eurozone Financial Crisis

Date	Event
9 May 2010	The European Financial Stability Facility (EFSF) treaty is agreed by Eurozone states: key objective — to provide temporary financial assistance to euro area Member States
11 May 2010	The European Financial Stabilisation Mechanism (EFSM) is created by Council Regulation (EU) No 407/2010.
May 2010	Greece becomes the first programme country of the EU/IMF with a €110bn loan
7 June 2010	EFSF comes into effect

28 November 2010	Ireland becomes a programme country with a loan of €85bn
7 April 2011	Portugal becomes a programme country with a €78bn loan
11 July 2011	Treaty establishing the ESM agreed by the 17 Eurozone countries: key objective – to provide permanent rescue fund for Eurozone countries
26 October 2011	Second programme for Greece of €172.6bn EFSF loan agreed
2 March 2012	The Treaty on Stability, Coordination and Governance in the Economic and Monetary Union (the 'stability treaty') is signed by 25 of the 27 EU Member States: it is an international treaty, not an EU treaty
31 May 2012	Referendum in Ireland on *Treaty on Stability, Coordination and Governance in the Economic and Monetary Union Bill 2012* (Thirtieth Amendment of the Constitution); it is approved by the people
25 June 2012	Cyprus makes an official request for financial assistance from the EU/IMF
27 June 2012	Irish Constitution is amended (following referendum of 31 May) to allow for ratification of the 'stability treaty'
20 July 2012	EFSF disburses assistance to Spain for bank recapitalisation (€39.468bn)
11 Dec 2012	EFSF's disbursement to Spain is transferred to the ESM
5 Feb 2013	ESM's second disbursement to Spain for bank recapitalisation (€1.865bn). This is the first time the ESF permanent rescue fund is used
28 March 2013	Cyprus agrees a €10bn loan from the ESM/IMF following its banking crisis (€9bn from the ESM/€1bn from the IMF)

Source of Funds for Ireland's Programme of Financial Support

Source	€Billion
National Pension Reserve Fund	17.5
EFSM	22.5
EFSF	17.7
Bilateral contributions from the United Kingdom of €3.8 billion, Sweden: €0.6 billion, and Denmark: €0.4 billion	4.8
IMF	22.5
Total Loan	**85**

Withdrawal from the EU

Only one country has ever left the EU: Greenland, in 1985. Greenland joined as a province of Denmark in 1972. It attained home rule in 1979. In 1982, the people of Greenland voted to leave the EU. Withdrawal was complete by 1985. A similar situation could arise in relation to Scotland. On 18 September 2014, a referendum will be held there on the question of whether Scotland should become an independent state. Scotland is part of the EU because it is a constituent part of an existing Member State: the UK. If it leaves the UK, it is probable that it will cease to be part of the EU. If so, and Scotland wished to join the EU as an independent country, it would have to make an application to do so under Article 49 TEU. This would require a Treaty of Accession requiring unanimous approval of the EU Member States. In addition, in early 2013 the British Prime Minister David Cameron, gave an undertaking to hold a referendum in 2017 on the UK's membership of the EU. Opinion polls suggest that it is unlikely that the British people would vote to leave the EU. However, the prospect of the UK withdrawing from the EU is now at least a possibility.

Prior to the Treaty of Lisbon, there was no formal exit process for Member States that wished to leave the EU. In the UK, repeal of the European Communities Act 1972 has been cited as the simplest way for the UK to withdraw from the EU. It is this statute that gives effect to EU law in UK domestic law (the Irish European Communities Act 1972 achieves the same objective in respect of EU law in Ireland). Such repeal, however, would not remove the UK from the EU. The UK would continue to be a member of the EU in international law. This is because the EU is a treaty-based organisation. The EU could legitimately claim that the UK was in breach of its treaty obligations due to its failure to apply EU law domestically. In such circumstances, to effect a complete withdrawal from the EU, the UK would have to follow one of the methods of withdrawal from an international treaty set out in the Vienna Convention on the Law of Treaties (VCLT) 1969.

The Treaty of Lisbon, however, provides an alternative mechanism for withdrawal. It has inserted an exit process into the treaties as Article 50 TEU. It states that any Member State may withdraw from the EU under its own constitutional requirements. A Member State which decides to withdraw is required to notify the European Council of its intention. The EU would then negotiate and conclude an agreement with that Member State. That agreement would set out the arrangements for withdrawal, taking account of the framework for the withdrawing Member State's future relationship with the EU. The treaties would then cease to apply to that Member State from the date of entry into force of the withdrawal agreement or, failing that, two years after the original notification to withdraw, unless the European Council, in agreement with the Member State concerned, unanimously decided to extend that period.

However, if the UK left the EU it could still benefit from something close to the four freedoms (free movement of goods, persons, services, and capital) under membership of the agreement on the European Economic Area (EEA). The EEA brings together the EU Member States and the member states of the European Free Trade Association (EFTA) in a European free trade area. The EEA provides for the inclusion of EU legislation in all policy areas of the EU single market. As well as the four freedoms, it covers competition and state aid rules, and policies including consumer protection, company law, the environment, social policy and statistics. The EEA also guarantees equal rights and obligations within the single market for citizens and economic operators in the EEA. Moreover, the EEA requires that its provisions be interpreted in conformity with the relevant rulings of the Court of Justice of the European Union. Consequently, members of the EEA are effectively subject to significant amounts of EU law without being members of the EU. However, if the UK was not a member of the EU, it would not be subject to the EU's common fisheries policy (CFP) or the common agricultural policy (CAP). Outside the CFP, the UK would be able to reassert sovereign rights over its territorial waters, including the fisheries and natural resources therein. Accordingly, the UK would be able to exclude EU fishermen from UK waters. Likewise, UK fishermen would not have automatic access to EU fisheries. Outside the CAP, the UK would have to support its own farmers exclusively from its own tax base.

The consequences of withdrawal from the EU cannot be stated with precision. As we have seen, a former EU Member State may find itself indirectly subject to EU law through the EEA, but it would not be able to exercise influence over the making of that law because it would have no EU Commissioner; nor would it have representation in the Council of the EU, the European Council or the European Parliament.

CHAPTER NINE

INTERNATIONAL LAW INCLUDING THE EUROPEAN CONVENTION OF HUMAN RIGHTS

A. Introduction 166
B. Public and Private International Law..166
C. Sources of International Law 167
    Treaties/International conventions..168
    Customs 168
    General Principles of Law 169
    Judicial Decisions 169
    The Teachings of Legal Scholars and Publicists 169
D. Monism and Dualism..170
E. The Status of and Incorporation of International Law into Irish Law 170
    Customary International Law 170
    International Agreements 172
F. Ireland and International Organisations..173
    The Council of Europe..173
    The United Nations Organisation 174
        The General Assembly..174
        The Security Council 175
        The Economic and Social Council (ECOSOC) 175
        The Secretariat..175
        The International Court of Justice (ICJ) 176
    Other International Organisations of which Ireland is a Member...............176
        The International Monetary Fund...176
        The World Bank 177
        The General Agreement on Tariffs and Trade (GATT) 177
        The World Trade Organisation (WTO) 178
G. The European Convention on Human Rights..178
    Rights and Freedoms Guaranteed by the Convention 179
H. Incorporation of the Convention into Irish Law — The European Convention on Human Rights Act 2003 179
I. International Tribunals 182
    The International Criminal Court (ICC) 182
    Other International Criminal Tribunals...182

J.	**Withdrawal from an International Treaty**	183
K.	**Private International Law**	184
	Jurisdiction	184
	Applicable System of Laws	184
	Codification and Harmonisation of Private International Law	185
	EU Law and Private International Law	185

International Law Including the European Convention of Human Rights

Learning Outcomes

Upon completion of this chapter, students should be able to:

- Understand the meaning and concept of *international law*;
- Describe the nature, basis, and function of international law;
- Identify the sources of international law;
- Appreciate the role and functions of the European Convention of Human Rights;
- Explain the role of international law in domestic Irish law;
- Discuss the interrelation between the European Convention on Human Rights and Irish law.

A. Introduction

International law is a body of rules and principles that States accept as binding on them and which they commonly observe in relation to one another.

This definition indicates that international law applies to nations or States only. However, international organisations, such as the United Nations, can also apply the rules and principles of international law and have international law applied to them. Although such organisations are themselves composed of nations or States, they may also be legal persons and potentially the subjects of international law.

The application of international law has limitations. For example, under the Rome Statute of the International Criminal Court, human beings cannot apply international law in the same way that states and international organisations can. Despite the fact that certain categories of human being, for instance diplomats and officials of international organisations, enjoy some international rights and privileges that ordinary persons do not, they cannot appear before the International Court of Justice (ICJ) or conclude treaties on their own behalf — although they may do so as State officials.

International law performs a range of functions. These include encouraging friendly relations among States and promoting the peaceful resolution of disputes between them. The maintenance of international peace and security is also a key function. This aim is given expression in Article 1 of the UN Charter. It states that one of the objectives of the organisation is:

> to maintain international peace and security, and to that end: to take effective collective measures for the prevention and removal of threats to the peace, and for the suppression of acts of aggression or other breaches of the peace, and to bring about by peaceful means, and in conformity with the principles of justice and international law, adjustment or settlement of international disputes or situations which might lead to a breach of the peace…

B. Public and Private International Law

The term 'international law' is used to refer to two distinct areas of legal discipline. One is 'public international law' which is the 'law of nations' and deals with relations between sovereign States. It is the body of legal rules applying between States. The other is 'private international law', or 'conflict of laws'. This branch of international law deals with relations between individuals or legal persons, such as corporations, in which the laws of more than one State may be applied. Private international law concerns rules developed by States to deal with such matters as transactions and contracts involving private nationals of one State and another State, which may contain some foreign elements.

Figure 9.1

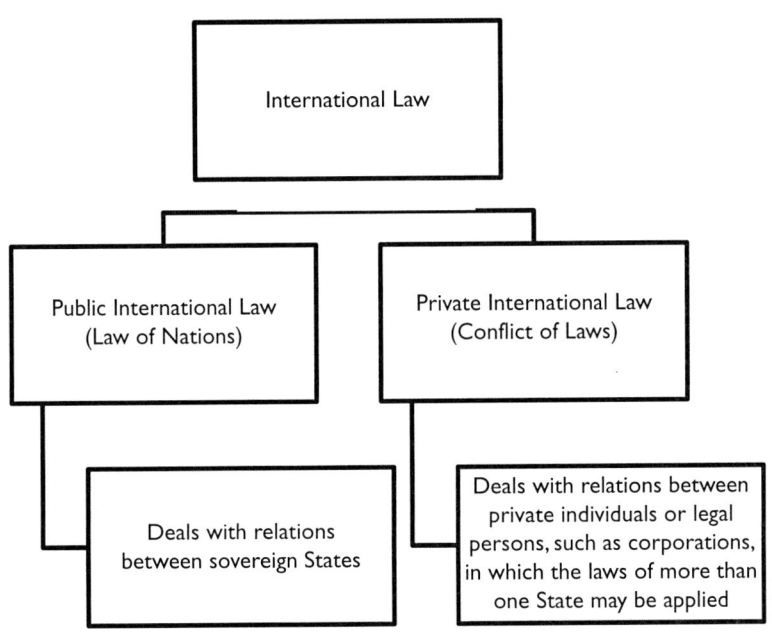

```
                        ┌─────────────────────┐
                        │  International Law  │
                        └──────────┬──────────┘
                    ┌──────────────┴──────────────┐
          ┌─────────┴──────────┐        ┌─────────┴──────────┐
          │ Public International│        │Private International│
          │  Law (Law of Nations)│       │  Law (Conflict of Laws)│
          └─────────┬──────────┘        └─────────┬──────────┘
          ┌─────────┴──────────┐        ┌─────────┴──────────────┐
          │  Deals with relations│       │ Deals with relations    │
          │  between sovereign   │       │ between private         │
          │  States              │       │ individuals or legal    │
          │                      │       │ persons, such as        │
          │                      │       │ corporations, in which  │
          │                      │       │ the laws of more than   │
          │                      │       │ one State may be applied│
          └──────────────────────┘       └─────────────────────────┘
```

C. Sources of International Law

The formally recognised sources of international law are set out in Article 38(1) of the Statute of the International Court of Justice as follows:

(a) International conventions, whether general or particular, establishing rules expressly recognised by the contesting States;
(b) International custom, as evidence of a general practice accepted by law;
(c) The general principles of law recognised by civilised nations;
(d) Subject to the provisions of Article 59, judicial decisions and the teachings of the most highly qualified publicists of the various nations, as subsidiary means for the determination of rules of law.

Under Article 38(2), if the parties to a dispute before the Court all agree, they can invite the Court not to apply any of the instruments listed above to the case in question. Article 59 provides that decisions have no binding force except between the parties and in respect of that particular case.

Figure 9.2

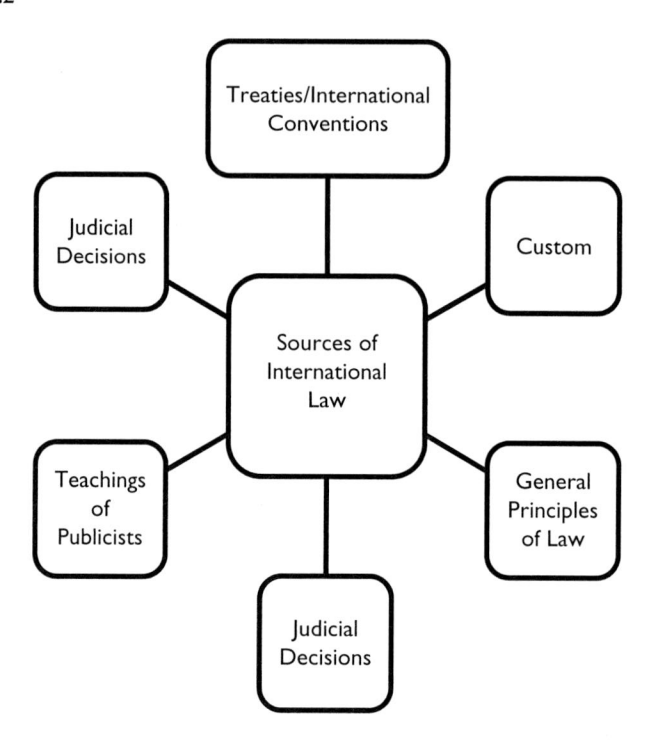

```
                    ┌─────────────────┐
                    │ Treaties/International │
                    │   Conventions   │
                    └─────────────────┘
    ┌──────────┐           │            ┌──────────┐
    │ Judicial │           │            │          │
    │ Decisions│───┐   ┌───────┐   ┌────│  Custom  │
    └──────────┘   │   │Sources│   │    └──────────┘
                   └───│  of   │───┘
                       │Int'l  │
                   ┌───│ Law   │───┐
    ┌──────────┐   │   └───────┘   │    ┌──────────┐
    │Teachings │───┘       │       └────│ General  │
    │   of     │           │            │Principles│
    │Publicists│           │            │  of Law  │
    └──────────┘   ┌─────────────┐      └──────────┘
                   │  Judicial   │
                   │  Decisions  │
                   └─────────────┘
```

Treaties/International conventions

A *treaty* is an international agreement concluded between States in written form and governed by international law. Treaties may be embodied in a single instrument or in two or more related instruments. Therefore, treaties may not always be called 'treaties'. They have been described as 'protocols', 'pacts', 'general Acts', 'accords', 'statutes', 'declarations', 'charters' and 'covenants'. Treaties between states exist usually in written form, although there is no requirement that they be contained in a single document. Treaties can be amended, reduced, or supplemented by means of a lesser treaty.

Some examples of international treaties to which Ireland is a party are: the UN Charter, Rome Statute of the International Criminal Court, European Convention for the Protection of Human Rights and Fundamental Freedoms, Convention Relating to the Status of Refugees and the Convention on the Rights of the Child.

Customs

There is no universally accepted definition of 'customary law'. However, Article 38(1) of the ICJ Statute sets down two criteria for indicating the existence of customary international law: general practice and the acceptance of this practice as 'law'. These two criteria are commonly referred to as 'state practice' and *opinio juris* respectively. It would therefore appear that, for there to be custom amounting to international law, it would be necessary that a usage of that custom be generally practised by States and that the practice be accepted by those States, and other States, as creating a legal obligation.

General Principles of Law
The term 'general principles of law' can refer to general principles of either international law or domestic law. Examples of general principles are: the principle of good faith, estoppel, proportionality, the right to a fair hearing or the duty to exhaust local remedies. This is a difficult area of international legal practice because not all such principles have attained international recognition.

Judicial Decisions
Article 38(1) of the ICJ Statute identifies judicial decisions as one of the two subsidiary sources of international law which the Court can apply when adjudicating upon disputes. The Court can only do this in the context of Article 59 of the Statute which states: the decision of the Court has no binding force except between the parties and in respect of that particular case. The implication of this is that the doctrine of precedent, something lawyers in common law jurisdictions are familiar with, does not apply to the ICJ because, by virtue of Article 59, the ICJ's previous decisions do not bind it. Furthermore, it is arguable that the decisions of domestic courts are included in the term judicial decisions mentioned in Article 38(1). This is because domestic courts have been active in establishing rules which have been applied on the international plane, such as fundamental human rights and diplomatic immunity.

The Teachings of Legal Scholars and Publicists
The writings and teachings of publicists are generally regarded as showing evidence of the law. Many modern legal scholars recognise the important contribution some of the earlier legal scholars have made to the development of international law, such as Grotius, Vattel and Gentili. Grotian theory of international law has been characterised as giving:

> equal weight to what States actually do, to habit and custom and to the course of dealing between parties, which contribute significantly to whatever system of law; and no less to what States are — or what they must do because of their nature. [Clive Parry, "The function of law in the international community", in M Sorenson (ed.) *Manual of Public International Law* (London: Macmillan, 1968) p 26]

Gilbert Charles Gidel (1934), for example, is acknowledged as giving the concept of the 'contiguous zone' authority and coherence. The contiguous zone is recognised as giving jurisdiction to a state beyond its territorial seas for special purposes.

D. Monism and Dualism

According to monism (or 'monist theory'), international law and domestic law are part of the same legal order: that is both systems co-exist within the domestic legal system. In a monist system, international law is superior to domestic law. Where there is a conflict between the two, international law prevails.

Dualism (or 'dualist theory'), on the other hand, holds that international law is not superior to domestic law. Under a dualist system, a domestic court is bound to apply international law to a case before it only if national constitutions so provide. Ireland operates a dualist system in relation to international agreements. Article 29.6 of the Irish Constitution provides: "No international agreement shall be part of the domestic law of the State save as may be determined by the Oireachtas". Consequently, no such agreement can be part of Irish domestic law unless and until the Oireachtas so decides.

E. The Status of and Incorporation of International Law into Irish Law

Customary International Law

The Constitution makes a distinction between two types of public international law:

- Principles of customary international law; and
- International agreements.

Principles of customary international law are incorporated through Article 29.3, whereas Article 29.6 requires that international agreements be incorporated into domestic law by statute in order to have legal force within the State. As regards possible conflict between a principle of customary international law and the provisions of domestic legislation, the Irish courts, along with most common law jurisdictions, operate a presumption that legislation is not intended to contravene international law. Article 29.3 of the Constitution provides: "Ireland accepts the generally recognised principles of international law as its rule of conduct in its relations with other States". Barr J in *ACT Shipping (Pte) Ltd v Minister for the Marine* [1995] 3 IR 406 at 422-423 explained the position in this way:

> ... Established principles of customary international law may be part of Irish [domestic] law provided that they are not contrary to the Constitution, statute law or the common law.

In that case, the *MV Toledo*, the plaintiff's ship, had been damaged during a transatlantic voyage. The captain and crew were airlifted to safety. A salvage tug was sent to try to save the ship. The captain of the tug sought permission to tow her into Cork but, fearing pollution, the minister refused. The *MV Toledo* was eventually beached on the Cornish coast and subsequently scuttled off the Bay of Biscay. The plaintiff sued the minister for damages for the ship's loss alleging that the minister's refusal was unlawful and resulted in the damage. The plaintiff claimed that, under customary international law, a foreign commercial vessel in serious distress had a right to safe refuge in an adjacent State and that this rule formed part of Irish domestic law by virtue of Article 29.3 of the Constitution. The plaintiff claimed that the minister had failed to observe that law. Barr J accepted the principle that, if customary international law recognised the right claimed by the plaintiff, it would form part of Irish domestic law. The State would therefore be liable for its failure to observe it. However, Barr J held, *inter alia*, that the content of the rule had changed over time in that the modern law was concerned primarily with risk to life, rather than risk to economic interests. Since the threat in this case was to the plaintiff's economic interests only, there was no clear obligation on the State to give refuge to the ship.

The generally recognised principles of international law therefore do not constitute a fixed code of laws: they will change in accordance with variations in the practice of the various States. Thus, Article 29.3 of the Constitution imports into Irish domestic law the relevant principles in their current form, not their form when the Constitution was enacted in 1937.

The operation of Article 29.3 was also considered in *Horgan v Ireland* [2003] 2 IR 468. Here, the State's provision of Shannon airport as a stopover for US military aircraft was challenged. The plaintiff argued that the provision of the airport for these purposes breached the rules of customary international law on neutrality. The plaintiff relied on Article 29.3. Kearns J, in approving the existing case law, accepted that customary international law could form part of Irish domestic law by virtue of Article 29.3. He observed:

> One can only conclude [...] that principles of international law enter domestic law only to the extent that no constitutional, statutory or judge-made law is inconsistent with the principle in question. Where a conflict arises, the rule of international law must in every case yield to domestic law.

Customary international law can be invoked by a foreign State to protect its position in this State. This occurred in two cases: *Canada v Employment Appeals Tribunal* [1992] 2 IR 484 and *McElhinney v Williams* [1995] 3 IR 382. In each of these cases, the respective governments invoked the doctrine of sovereign immunity as defences to proceedings brought against them before an Irish forum.

In *Canada v Employment Appeals Tribunal*, a chauffeur employed by the Canadian embassy in Dublin had been dismissed. He claimed that his dismissal was unfair. He took an action for unfair dismissal against the Canadian government before the Employment Appeals Tribunal. The Canadian government argued that the tribunal lacked jurisdiction in the matter. It claimed that Canada enjoyed sovereign immunity and this had not been waived. The tribunal rejected this argument. The government of Canada subsequently withdrew from the proceedings and the tribunal found in the chauffeur's favour. In subsequent proceedings, this decision was upheld by the High Court but reversed by the Supreme Court. It took the view that, even if the doctrine of sovereign immunity had narrowed in its scope over time, it would still apply, albeit in its current form, by virtue of Article 29.3.

Similarly, in *McElhinney v Williams*, the government of the United Kingdom invoked the principle of sovereign immunity in respect of a claim against it by the plaintiff. In the High Court, Costello P dismissed the plaintiff's claim on the basis that the principle of sovereign immunity could apply.

International Agreements

As we have seen, customary international law is not treated in the same way in the Constitution as international agreements, such as treaties. According to Article 29.6, international agreements can only be part of the domestic law of the State if incorporated into it by the Oireachtas.

International agreements create obligations between States that are parties to those agreements. As a result of Ireland's dualist approach to international agreements, such agreements do not confer legal rights on individual citizens in Ireland. Consequently, the Irish courts are precluded from giving legal force to international agreements unless incorporated. This dualist approach to international agreements can be seen in a number of cases relating to the European Convention on Human Rights prior to the enactment of the European Convention on Human Rights Act 2003. The Convention had been invoked on several occasions in support of arguments challenging the constitutionality of legislation. The Irish courts consistently affirmed that the Convention — an unincorporated international agreement — could not be applied by them in cases where its provisions were invoked by litigants.

In *In Re Ó Laighléis* [1960] IR 93 the Supreme Court set out the constitutional position on unincorporated international agreements. In this case, the applicant had been interned under the Offences against the State (Amendment) Act 1940. He could not challenge the constitutionality of the Act as its provisions had been upheld as constitutional by the Supreme Court in 1940 on an Article 26 reference (*In Re the Offences against the State (Amendment) Bill 1940* [1940] IR 470). The applicant then sought an inquiry into the lawfulness of his detention under Article 40.4 of the Constitution. He asserted that his internment under the Act was in conflict with the right to liberty under Article 5 of the Convention and the right to a fair trial under Article 6. The Supreme Court, however, held that domestic legislation could not be displaced by the State becoming a party to the Convention. The Court could not give effect to the Convention if it was contrary to domestic law because, as an unincorporated international agreement, it was not part of the domestic law of the State.

The decision in Ó Laighléis was followed in a number of cases. In *Norris v Attorney General* [1984] IR 36, for example, the plaintiff had instituted proceedings challenging the constitutionality of sections of the Offences against the Person Act 1861 which criminalised certain homosexual acts, even if carried out in private by consenting adults. The High Court dismissed the plaintiff's challenge in 1980. The following year the European Court of Human Rights in *Dudgeon v United Kingdom* (1981) 4 EHRR 149 held that the sections in question, which were at that time still in force in Northern Ireland, were in conflict with the right to privacy under Article 8 of the Convention. When the *Norris* case came before the Supreme Court in 1983, the plaintiff cited *Dudgeon* in support of his argument that the sections of the 1861 Act were invalid. He argued that the decision by the European Court of Human Rights in *Dudgeon* should be regarded by the Supreme Court as more than a persuasive precedent and should be followed. The Supreme Court disagreed. It ruled by a 3-2 majority that the impugned sections of the 1861 Act were not unconstitutional. O'Higgins CJ stated that the ruling in *Dudgeon* was not relevant to a decision on the constitutionality of the impugned sections of the 1861 Act. The Court, following Ó Laighléis, made it clear that the Convention (at that time) did not form part of domestic law and therefore could not be relied upon by the plaintiff. Six years later, in *Norris v Ireland* (1988) 13 EHRR 186, the European Court of Human Rights held that the impugned sections of the 1861 Act were in conflict with Article 8 of the Convention. The judgment of the European Court of Human Rights in *Norris* was given effect by the Oireachtas when it enacted the Criminal Law (Sexual Offences) Act 1993 which decriminalised consensual sexual acts between males.

F. Ireland and International Organisations

The Council of Europe
The Council of Europe was founded on 5 May 1949 by ten countries, one of which was Ireland. The Council now has a membership of 47 European countries. It is based in Strasbourg, France. It adopted the European Convention on Human Rights (ECHR or 'Convention') which Ireland ratified on 25 February 1953. The Convention entered into force on 3 September 1953. It is a treaty by which the

Member States of the Council of Europe undertake to respect fundamental rights and freedoms. The Convention established the European Court of Human Rights, which is also based in Strasbourg. The Council of Europe is entirely separate and distinct from the European Union and its institutions. Similarly, the European Court of Human Rights is entirely separate and distinct from the Court of Justice of the European Union (CJEU). The European Court of Human Rights exercises jurisdiction over the ECHR, whereas the CJEU exercises jurisdiction over EU law.

The United Nations Organisation

The United Nations (UN) was established in San Francisco in 1945, following the Second World War, by 51 countries. Ireland acceded in 1955. It is now based in New York and (as of June 2013) has 193 members. The organisation was established by the Charter of the UN. Article 1 of the Charter sets out its purposes, which include:

- To maintain international peace and security;
- To develop friendly relations among nations;
- To cooperate in solving international problems and in promoting respect for human rights, and;
- To be a centre for harmonising the actions of nations.

Article 2 requires its members to:

- Fulfil their obligations to the UN in good faith;
- Settle international disputes peacefully;
- Refrain from the threat or use of force in their international relations;
- Assist the UN in carrying out its functions.

Article 2 also makes it clear that the UN is not, in general, authorised to intervene in matters which are essentially within the domestic jurisdiction of any State.

The Charter establishes a number of institutions whose purpose is to carry out the functions of the UN. These are: the General Assembly, the Security Council, the Economic and Social Council (ECOSOC), the Secretariat and the International Court of Justice (ICJ).

The General Assembly

This is the main deliberative body of the UN. All Member States are represented and each has one vote. Matters are decided by simple majority, though some require a two-thirds majority. The Assembly can discuss and make recommendations on matters relating to the UN Charter. It cannot compel any Member State to act. The Assembly determines policies and agrees programmes for the Secretariat. It approves the UN budget and peacekeeping operations and supervises development activities. It also appoints the Secretary-General.

The Security Council
The UN Charter gives primary responsibility for maintaining international peace and security to the Security Council, which may meet whenever peace is threatened. It has 15 members — five permanent and ten elected. The permanent members are: China, France, Russia, the United Kingdom and the United States. The remaining ten are elected by the General Assembly for two-year terms. Decisions require nine votes. A decision cannot be taken in the event of a negative vote by a permanent member. This is referred to as the 'veto'. When a complaint concerning a threat to peace is brought before it, the Council can recommend that the parties try to reach agreement by peaceful means. In doing so, the Council may: set out principles for such an agreement; carry out investigations and mediation; dispatch a mission; appoint special envoys; or request the Secretary-General to seek a peaceful settlement of the dispute. If hostilities occur, the Council may issue ceasefire directives or dispatch military observers or a peacekeeping force.

The Council may impose enforcement measures such as economic sanctions, arms embargoes, financial penalties and restrictions; travel bans; severance of diplomatic relations; blockades; and, if necessary, pursue collective military action. The Council may also recommend to the General Assembly the appointment of the Secretary-General and, together with the Assembly, elect the judges of the International Court of Justice. Resolutions of the Security Council are binding on all members.

The Economic and Social Council (ECOSOC)
This organ consists of fifty-four States elected from and by the General Assembly. It is the UN's primary forum for discussion of economic and social issues. It advises the General Assembly on economic and social matters in respect of which it can make recommendations. It has a particular focus on development.

The Secretariat
This organ services the other principal organs of the United Nations and administers the programmes and policies laid down by them. At its head is the Secretary-General, who is appointed by the General Assembly on the recommendation of the Security Council for a five-year, renewable term. It administers peacekeeping operations, mediates on international disputes, surveys economic and social trends and problems and prepares studies on human rights and sustainable development. As of 30 June 2012, the Secretariat had 42,887

staff members around the world. As of 2013, the UN has 16 peace operations deployed on four continents.

The International Court of Justice (ICJ)

This is the principal judicial organ of the UN. It was established in June 1945 by the UN Charter and began work in April 1946. The seat of the Court is at the Peace Palace in The Hague in the Netherlands. Of the six principal organs of the UN, it is the only one not located in New York. The Court comprises 15 judges who are elected for terms of office of nine years by the General Assembly and the Security Council. It is assisted by a registry, its administrative organ. Its official languages are English and French. Its decisions are final and not subject to appeal.

The ICJ has two categories of jurisdiction: contentious and advisory. Under its contentious jurisdiction, only States may appear before it. Under its advisory jurisdiction, organs of the UN and specialised agencies are entitled formally to request the opinion of the ICJ in order to obtain clarification of disputed words or phrases in legal documents. This would imply that States may not seek an advisory opinion from the ICJ directly. However, they could do so through the organs of the UN or its specialised agencies. As a matter of principle, the ICJ cannot exercise jurisdiction over a case without the consent of the parties. The fact that a State is a member of the UN means that it is bound by the ICJ Statute. This does not, however, mean that the State has given its consent to the ICJ to hear cases involving itself, though a State can give its consent through agreement or conduct. If there is disagreement between the parties to a dispute as to the meaning or scope of a judgment of the ICJ, the Court can, at the request of either party to the case, interpret its own judgments.

Other International Organisations of which Ireland is a Member

The International Monetary Fund

The IMF came out of the United Nations Monetary and Financial Conference (the 'Bretton Woods Conference') which was held at Bretton Woods, New Hampshire, USA, in July 1944. The conference resulted in agreements requiring the setting up of GATT, the International Bank of Reconstruction and Development (IBRD) and the IMF. The IMF sought to help to develop an international monetary system. The Bretton Woods agreement also envisaged the establishment of the World Bank as a sister institution. The main purposes of the IMF are to promote international monetary co-operation, facilitate the expansion of balanced growth of international trade and promote exchange-rate stability. The IMF's main functions are to conduct surveillance and provide conditional financial support and technical assistance. Surveillance entitles the IMF to undertake an assessment of a country's economic policies and prepare a report to advise that country accordingly. Conditional financial support enables the IMF to provide loans to Member States. The purpose of 'conditionality' arises due to the fact that a country with external payment problems is spending more than it is taking in. Therefore, unless economic reform takes place, that situation will not be corrected. Conditionality makes financial support contingent upon implementation by a Member State of adjustment policies prescribed by the IMF. Ireland became a member of the IMF in 1957.

The World Bank
The World Bank also emerged from the Bretton Woods conference. It originally comprised only the IBRD but now includes the International Development Association (IDA). The purposes of the World Bank are to assist in the reconstruction and development of territories of members by facilitating investment of capital for productive purposes, including the restoration of economies destroyed or disrupted by war, the reconversion of productive facilities to peacetime needs and the encouragement of the development of productive facilities and resources in less developed countries. The World Bank provides low-interest loans and interest-free credit facilities to developing countries. Developed countries, however, may also benefit from World Bank loan facilities. The IDA's primary purpose is to promote economic development, increase productivity and thus raise standards of living in the less developed areas of the world. It can provide loans to meet important developmental requirements on terms which are more flexible than those of conventional loans. The IDA seeks to further the developmental objectives of the IBRD and supplement its activities.

The General Agreement on Tariffs and Trade (GATT)
In the 1940s, the International Trade Organisation (ITO) was proposed as a mechanism for regulating international trade. At conferences in New York, Geneva and Havana in 1946, 1947 and 1948 respectively, it was proposed that GATT would establish the ITO as an organisation to implement GATT. However, the US Congress refused to pass the ITO Charter, but it passed GATT provisionally. In 1947, GATT was formally agreed. It remained a provisional agreement until 1995 when it was replaced by the World Trade Organisation (WTO). GATT was a multilateral trade treaty. Its basic goal was to promote free international trade by establishing rules that limited national impediments to trade. A dispute resolution mechanism was established under the treaty to deal with complaints against members of GATT who did not follow those rules. A major weakness of the dispute resolution mechanism was that it was subject to long delays and, in any case, its decisions were not enforceable. This meant that it was rarely used. By 1994, a new GATT agreement brought about significant improvements to the original 1947 agreement. One of these was the creation of an institutional mechanism for the resolution of all disputes between the Member States of GATT. It was called the WTO.

The World Trade Organisation (WTO)
The WTO is an international organisation. It has become a major force in the development of an international economic system in general and international trade in particular. The WTO has a range of organs, functions and responsibilities that make it an effective mechanism for the promotion of international trade. Its constitution is a treaty and the legal obligations that apply to its members are treaty obligations. The WTO is governed by a Ministerial Conference and a General Council which comprise the Member States. The dispute settlement mechanism under the WTO as set out in the GATT agreement of 1994 is intended to address many of the shortcomings of the original 1947 GATT agreement.

The WTO is based in Geneva, Switzerland. It was formally established on 1 January 1995 and has a current membership of 159 countries. Its key functions are to: administer WTO trade agreements; provide a forum for trade negotiations; handle trade disputes; monitor national trade policies; provide technical assistance and training for developing countries; and cooperate with other international organisations.

G. The European Convention on Human Rights

The European Convention on Human Rights (ECHR), as mentioned above, was adopted in 1950 and entered into force in 1953. It was the first international treaty that comprehensively dealt with human rights. The first international complaints procedure and international court, the European Court of Human Rights, were created under the ECHR. This was done under the Council of Europe which was founded in 1949 to promote European integration.

Judges of the European Court of Human Rights are elected for six years. The number of judges is determined by the number of high contracting parties to the Convention. The judges serve in an independent personal capacity and do not represent their State of nationality. The Court is subject to its own rules of procedure and is composed of four sections: the Committee; the Chamber; the Grand Chamber; and the Committee of Ministers. The Chamber and Grand Chamber, on hearing a case, include an *ex officio* judge from the State party concerned. He or she provides expert advice on the position in domestic law. All judges give reasons for their decisions. Separate opinions are permitted when a decision is not unanimous. The jurisdiction of the Court extends to all matters concerning the interpretation and application of the Convention and the protocols thereto (Article 32).

Rights and Freedoms Guaranteed by the Convention

The following table summarises the main rights/freedoms protected by the European Convention on Human Rights.

Article	Right/Freedom Protected*
Article 2	The right to life
Article 3	Prohibition on torture
Article 4	Prohibition on slavery and forced labour
Article 5	The right to liberty and security of the person
Article 6	The right to a fair trial
Article 7	Prohibition on punishment without law
Article 8	The right to respect for private and family life
Article 9	The right to freedom of thought, conscience and religion
Article 10	The right to freedom of expression
Article 11	The right to freedom of assembly and association
Article 12	The right to marry
Article 13	The right to an effective remedy
Article 14	Prohibition on discrimination
Article 15	Derogation from the Convention in times of emergency

The Convention allows for some of these rights to be qualified by State authorities in certain circumstances such as national security, public safety, the economic well-being of the country, the prevention of disorder or crime, the protection of health or morals or the protection of the rights and freedoms of others.

H. Incorporation of the Convention into Irish Law — The European Convention on Human Rights Act 2003

The European Convention on Human Rights Act 2003, which came into force on 31 December 2003, enables provisions of the European Convention for the Protection of Human Rights and Fundamental Freedoms 1950 (ECHR) to be given effect in Irish domestic law. The enactment of the 2003 Act has resulted in litigants in Ireland being able to rely upon the Convention and the jurisprudence of the European Court of Human Rights in cases where their fundamental rights are in issue. Although many of the rights protected by the Convention are also protected by the Constitution, Irish constitutional law and European human rights law together can provide litigants with significantly greater protection of their fundamental rights than was the case prior to the enactment of the 2003 Act.

Section 2 of the 2003 Act requires that the courts, when "interpreting and applying" any statutory provision and any rule of law must, as far as possible, do so in a manner compatible with the State's obligations under the Convention provisions. 'Statutory provision' is defined to include any provision of a statute, or any order, regulation, rule, licence or bye-law created under a statute (s 1(1)). Rule of law includes common law rules. Section 4 requires courts to take judicial notice of the Convention provisions and of judgments of the European Court of Human Rights or any decision of the Committee of Ministers established under the Statute of the Council of Europe on any question in respect of which it has jurisdiction. A court must also, when interpreting and applying the Convention provisions, take due account of the principles laid down in such judgments or decisions.

Section 3(1) places a statutory duty on organs of the State to perform its functions in a manner compatible with the State's obligations under the Convention provisions unless there is a rule of law stating that this is not required. Under s 3(2), if a court determines that there has been a breach of statutory duty under s 3(1), it can award damages to an individual who has suffered loss and no other remedy in damages is available.

It is clear that the 2003 Act does not 'incorporate' the ECHR into domestic law as such. In *Re McKerr* [2004] UKHL 12, [2004] 1 WLR 807 at para 63, Lord Hoffmann explained the position in relation to the United Kingdom Human Rights Act 1998:

> ... the Convention, as an international treaty, is not part of English domestic law ... That proposition has been in no way altered or amended by the 1998 Act. Although people sometimes speak of the Convention having been incorporated into domestic law, that is a misleading metaphor... What the Act has done is to create domestic rights expressed in the same terms as those contained in the Convention. But they are domestic rights, not international rights. Their source is the statute, not the Convention. They are available against specific public authorities, not the United Kingdom as a State. And their meaning and application is a matter for the domestic courts, not the court in Strasbourg.

In *Lelimo v Minister for Justice, Equality and Law Reform* [2004] 2 IR 178 at 188, Laffoy J, in considering Lord Hoffman's speech in *Re McKerr*, stated:

> Lord Hoffmann's reasoning can be adopted in considering the effect of the coming into force of section 3(1) of the European Convention on Human Rights Act, 2003, which is the analogue in this jurisdiction of section 6(1) of the Human Rights Act, 1998 in the United Kingdom.

In *Dublin City Council v Fennell* [2005] 1 IR 604, Kearns J described incorporation as having taken place in Ireland at a 'sub-constitutional level' in the form of indirect or interpretive incorporation adopted by the Act of 2003. This form of incorporation is similar to the form of incorporation adopted in the United Kingdom by the United Kingdom Human Rights Act 1998. The European Convention on Human Rights Act 2003, being a statute, is subject to the provisions of the Constitution. Where the 2003 Act and the Constitution conflict, the Constitution prevails. The Supreme Court, in *Dublin City Council v Fennell*, held that the 2003 Act is not retrospective in effect. Therefore, breaches of the Convention which occurred prior to the coming into force of the 2003 Act cannot be subject to the Act's provisions. This could be the case even where the breach is continuing in nature (see *Foy v An t-Ard Chláraitheoir* [2007] IEHC 470).

Section 5 of the 2003 Act allows a court to make a declaration of incompatibility where it finds that legislation or a rule of law is incompatible with the State's obligations under the Convention. Where a court makes such a declaration, the Taoiseach must ensure a copy of the court order is laid before each House of the Oireachtas within 21 sitting days. A declaration of incompatibility does not affect the validity of the law in question. It continues to have effect until such time as it is either amended by the Oireachtas or struck down by the courts as unconstitutional. Section 6(1) of the Act obliges parties to proceedings in which a declaration of incompatibility under s 5 is sought to notify both the Irish Human Rights Commission (IHRC) and the Attorney General of the proceedings.

Recent examples of where declarations of incompatibility were made are *Foy v An t-Ard Chláraitheoir* [2007] IEHC 470 and *Donegan v Dublin City Council* [2012] IESC 18. In *Foy*, the applicant was a transgender woman. She was refused a birth certificate with her new name and gender. The Irish High Court found that the existing statutory regime for civil registration failed to respect her private life as protected by Article 8 of the Convention. Since no remedy existed in Irish law, the Court made a declaration of incompatibility stating that the existing Irish law was not compatible with the Convention. In *Donegan*, the Court determined that a declaration of incompatibility was appropriate in relation to s 62(3) of the Housing Act 1966. It provides for a statutory procedure for the repossession of a local authority dwelling. The State appealed the decision to the Supreme Court but the Supreme Court agreed with the High Court that there was a breach of Article 8 of the Convention on the grounds that the applicants had no other adequate legal remedy available to them in relation to the local authority's decision to evict them. In July 2013, in order to address the human rights issues raised in *Foy*, the Oireachtas published the Legal Recognition of Gender Bill 2013. Its purpose is to provide transgender persons with legal recognition of their preferred gender.

I. International Tribunals

The International Criminal Court (ICC)

The development of international criminal law, in modern times, is generally considered to have started with the Nuremberg trials following the Second World War. After the First World War, attempts had been made to bring the German Kaiser to trial, but these were unsuccessful. Following the Second World War, international tribunals were successfully established and, for the first time, held individuals to account for crimes committed during the Second World War. The Nuremberg tribunal was not, however, permanent. It was not until the establishment of the International Criminal Court (ICC) on 17 July 1998 that the first treaty-based international criminal court came into being. One-hundred-and-twenty States adopted the Rome Statute — the legal basis of the Court. It is an independent international organisation. It is not part of the United Nations system. Its seat is at The Hague in the Netherlands.

The ICC is funded primarily by States but it also receives voluntary contributions from governments, international organisations, individuals, corporations and other entities. The Rome Statute entered into force on 1 July 2002 after ratification by 60 countries. The ICC is independent and permanent. It tries persons accused of the most serious crimes of international concern, namely genocide, crimes against humanity and war crimes. It is a Court of last resort. It will not act if a case is investigated or prosecuted by a national judicial system unless the national proceedings are not genuine. This conclusion might be reached if formal proceedings were undertaken solely to shield a person from criminal responsibility. A referendum to amend the Constitution for Ireland to accept the jurisdiction of the International Criminal Court was held on 7 June 2001. It was approved by the people.

Other International Criminal Tribunals

As a result of the war in the Balkans, the international community established its first post-war international criminal tribunal. In May 1993, the UN Security Council adopted a resolution which established the International Criminal Tribunal for the Former Yugoslavia (ICTY). This had power to prosecute persons responsible for serious violations of international humanitarian law committed in the territory of the former Yugoslavia since 1991. The International Criminal Tribunal for Rwanda (ICTR) was established in 1994, also by a UN Security Council resolution, following the genocide in Rwanda. It was given the power to prosecute persons responsible for serious violations of international humanitarian law committed in the territory of Rwanda. In addition, Rwandan citizens responsible for such violations committed in the territory of neighbouring States in 1994 could also be prosecuted. Later, a Special Court for Sierra Leone (SCSL) was established by a UN Security Council Resolution in 2000. It was given power to prosecute persons who bear the

> greatest responsibility for serious violations of international humanitarian law and Sierra Leonean law committed in the territory of Sierra Leone since 13 November 1996, including those leaders who, in committing such crimes, have threatened the establishment of and implementation of the peace process in Sierra Leone.

It is expected that the ICC will replace both the ICTY and the ICTR once their mandates expire.

J. Withdrawal from an International Treaty

A State which is a party to a treaty may terminate its participation in that treaty. Termination may be voluntary or automatic. A voluntary termination occurs where a State decides to bring that treaty to an end. An automatic termination occurs where an act of one state automatically ends the treaty, unless otherwise provided for in the treaty itself or agreed by the parties to it. This area of international law is governed by the Vienna Convention on the Law of Treaties (VCLT). Article 54 VCLT states that the termination of a treaty or the withdrawal of a party may take place in conformity with the provisions of the treaty or, at any time, by consent of all parties. Termination of a treaty may also occur by 'denunciation'. Article 56 VCLT provides that a denunciation occurs where a State avows publicly that it is no longer bound by the treaty. At least twelve months' notice of the State's intention to denounce or withdraw from the treaty must be given.

Article 60 VCLT allows one party to a bilateral treaty to invoke a 'material breach' by the other party as a ground for terminating the treaty or suspending its operation in whole or in part. In the case of multilateral treaties, a material breach by one of the parties entitles the other parties by unanimous agreement to suspend the operation of the treaty in whole or in part either in relations between themselves and the defaulting State, or as between all the parties. Termination of a treaty may also occur by a supervening event.

Article 61(1) VCLT entitles parties to a treaty to terminate it if circumstances occurring after the conclusion of the treaty make performance impossible as a result of a permanent disappearance or destruction of an object indispensable for the execution of the treaty.

Article 62 VCLT allows termination of a treaty in case of a fundamental change of circumstances. This could arise where a change has occurred that has totally altered the original intention of parties to a treaty to the extent that performance of the treaty would be futile.

K. Private International Law

The term 'private international law', or the 'conflict of laws', denotes the rules which are intended to resolve conflicts between laws of different jurisdictions in domestic courts. Strictly speaking, this is a part of Irish law, rather than international law. It deals with cases involving a foreign element. This area of law is concerned primarily with civil rather than criminal law matters. Conflict of laws deals with questions such as: (a) whether the Irish courts have jurisdiction over a particular case; (b) what system of law should be applied; and (c) the recognition and enforcement of judgments of foreign courts.

Jurisdiction

When a conflict of laws arises, a court must decide whether it has jurisdiction to hear the case. The traditional approach has been that the appropriate court to hear the case is the one which is most convenient. This will usually mean that jurisdiction lies with the State which has the greatest connection to the dispute. A court has discretion not to hear a case if it concludes that it is not a convenient forum. This is known as the doctrine of *forum non conveniens*. It is a common law doctrine whereby the court may refuse to exercise its right of jurisdiction because, for the convenience of the parties and in the interests of justice, an action should be brought in a different jurisdiction. Where a dispute arises as to the appropriate forum for the case to be heard, and a party to the litigation seeks a stay in the proceedings, the test to be applied is whether or not justice requires that the action be stayed: *Doe v Armour Pharmaceutical Co Inc* [1994] 1 ILRM 416.

In *Doe v Armour Pharmaceutical Co Inc*, the doctrine of *forum non conveniens* was considered. In that case, the plaintiffs had haemophilia. They claimed that they had become HIV-positive due to the use of a blood-clotting agent manufactured by the defendant, an American corporation. They alleged negligence on the part of the defendant in the manufacture of the agent. They instituted proceedings seeking damages before the New York courts. The court in New York dismissed their actions on the basis of *forum non conveniens*. The court there made this decision subject to the condition that the defendant accepted that the plaintiff could institute proceedings in New York again if the Irish courts declined jurisdiction. The Irish High Court accepted jurisdiction. This was upheld in the Supreme Court.

Applicable System of Laws

Once jurisdiction is decided, the applicable law must then be determined by that forum. Procedural issues are normally decided based on the law of the forum. The applicable substantive rules may be determined with reference to foreign law.

In tort cases, for example, common law jurisdictions typically apply the law of the forum, whereas civil law jurisdictions tend to apply the law applicable in the jurisdiction in which the tort occurred.

Codification and Harmonisation of Private International Law

The UN General Assembly established the United Nations Commission on International Trade Law (UNCITRAL) in 1966. Its function is to propose conventions and uniform laws on international trade. A number of important conventions have resulted, for instance the 1980 Vienna Convention on Contracts for the International Sale of Goods. Other organisations are the Rome Institute for the Unification of Private Law (UNIDROIT) and the Hague Conference on Private International Law, which carry out similar functions. The UNIDROIT 1980 Convention on the Law Applicable to Contractual Obligations was implemented in Irish law by the Contractual Obligations (Applicable Law) Act 1991. The 1993 Convention on Protection of Children came out of The Hague Conference. It has been incorporated into Irish law by the Protection of Children (Hague Convention) Act 2000. Similarly, Hague Convention provisions on inter-country adoption have been incorporated into Irish law by the Adoption Act 2010. Other examples of the codification of private international law are conventions concerning the environment. One example of this is the Sea Pollution Act 1991 which incorporated the International Convention for the Prevention of Pollution from Ships (MARPOL) 1973 (the 'London Convention') into Irish law.

EU Law and Private International Law

Where applicable, rules of private international law in EU Member States have been displaced by EU law. For instance, Council Regulation 44/2001 (Brussels II Regulation) applies uniform rules across the EU in relation to jurisdiction and enforcement of judgments in respect of most civil and commercial matters. The general rule, set out in the 2001 Regulation, is that persons domiciled in a Member State shall, irrespective of nationality, be sued in the courts of that Member State. Choice of law in relation to contracts is also governed by EU law.

CHAPTER TEN

OTHER SOURCES OF LAW

A. Introduction 189
B. Custom 189
C. Canon Law...190
D. Commentaries and Academic Writing...191

Learning Outcomes

Upon completion of this chapter, the student should be able to:

- Explain the difference between primary and secondary sources of law;
- Describe secondary sources of law including custom, canon law, commentaries and academic writings and explain how these interact with the legal system.

A. Introduction

The sources of law examined above (the 1937 Constitution, legislation, common law, EU law and international law) are all known as primary or formal sources of law.

There are other influences or sources of law which must also be considered. These are often referred to as secondary sources of law. They do not enjoy force of law, but may be important nonetheless. These secondary sources may influence the interpretation of a law by a court/adjudicative body or may be incorporated into law via legislation. These sources of law are often referred to for their instructive value and for the references they provide to relevant primary sources of law. Secondary sources of law include the following:

Figure 10.1

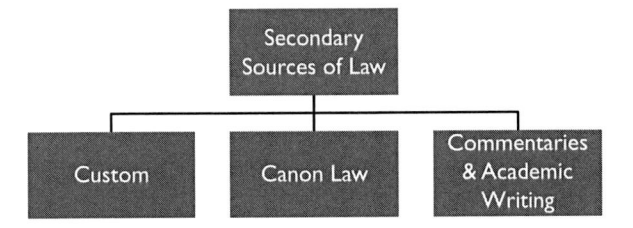

```
              Secondary
             Sources of Law
        ┌────────┼────────┐
                              Commentaries
     Custom   Canon Law     & Academic
                                Writing
```

B. Custom

The adoption of the common law system in Ireland gradually eliminated the old Brehon law system, which was based primarily on custom. However, customary law still has a role in the common law system which exists today, and the common law courts have demonstrated an acceptance of the legal existence of customs.

A custom is often defined as a habitual practice which, by virtue of continuous existence and general acquiescence, acquires legal force. The courts will, in certain circumstances, recognise custom as a source of law.

In order for the custom to be given force of law by the courts, it must:

- Be certain and clear;
- Have existed continuously;
- Exist in a particular locality (not throughout the State) in respect of a particular matter. Other general matters are governed by the ordinary common law — custom is only ever a source of local law;
- Have been exercised openly and as of a right;
- Be consistent with other local customs;
- Be obligatory if the custom creates a specific duty, rather than discretionary;
- Not conflict with any legislation/constitutional provisions.

Custom and practice may be implied as terms of a contract of employment where they are so universal that "no workman would be supposed to have entered into the service without looking to it as part of the contract" (*Devonald v Rosser & Sons* [1906] 2 KB 728). An employer may be able to establish a right to lay off an employee without pay only where such custom is "reasonable, certain and notorious" (*Lawe v Irish Country Meats Ltd* [1998] ELR 266). In *Carroll v Dublin Bus* [2006] ELR 149, it was held that the right of an employee to be placed on rehabilitative duties derived from established custom and practice and therefore constituted a term of his contract of employment.

C. Canon Law

This is the law of the Catholic Church and is one of the oldest continuously functioning legal systems in the Western world. It has its own laws, courts, lawyers and judges. Canon law, which governs the Catholic Church, is found primarily in a single codified volume called the 'Code of Canon Law'.

Canon law exists separately from the secular law of the State and does not enjoy force of law. However, some Irish laws have been heavily influenced by canon law, particularly in the area of marriage. Canon law, as the basic law of the Catholic Church, was codified in 1917 under Benedict XV and later, in 1983, by Pope John Paul II.

In Ireland, in *O'Callaghan v O'Sullivan* [1925] 1 IR 90, the Supreme Court held that:

> the Canon Law of the Roman Catholic Church is foreign law, which must be proved as a fact and by the testimony of expert witnesses according to the well-settled rules as to proof of foreign law (Kennedy CJ).

That case related to the removal of a parish priest by the Bishop of Kerry. Both parties accepted that the relationship between them was subject to canon law. The Court held, *inter alia*, that the decree of removal of the parish priest was not illegal because it was proved to the satisfaction of the Court that the decree was authorised by canon law. More recently, in 2004, Desmond Cardinal Connell, Archbishop Emeritus of Dublin, said that canon law enjoys the same status as foreign law, recognised as law enacted by a sovereign independent authority residing in the Holy See (*The Irish Times*, 31 May 2004). Earlier, in 2002, the Bishop of Killaloe, Dr Willie Walsh, said that confidentiality in the relationship between priest and bishop, although protected by canon law, did not take precedence over civil law (*The Irish Times*, 6 September 2002).

D. Commentaries and Academic Writing

In some instances, leading commentaries and academic writings are treated as an authoritative source of law. This is principally the case where there is no formal primary source of law on the issue in dispute. Authoritative legal textbooks by distinguished legal writers, legal dictionaries and encyclopaedias and scholarly journals are all useful sources of law for the student, practitioner and court. International commentaries and academic writings are also very useful in the absence of domestic law. These sources of law are persuasive, rather than binding, and the courts can adopt or reject their propositions.

Section D

Personnel of the Law

CHAPTER ELEVEN

Personnel of the Law

A. Introduction 198
B. The Judiciary 198
    Introduction 198
    Judicial Hierarchy and Composition 198
        Judicial Hierarchy 198
        Judicial Composition of the Courts 199
    Appointment and Qualifications 200
        Appointment 200
        Qualifications 201
    Judicial Independence 202
    Remuneration 203
    A Judicial Council/Commission 204
    Immunity from Suit and Contempt of Court 204
    Termination of Judicial Appointments 204
        Retirement 205
        Resignation 205
        Impeachment 205
C. The Jury 207
    Introduction 207
    Composition 207
    Function 208
    The Verdict 208
    Advantages and Disadvantages of a Jury System 209
    Reform 209
D. The Legal Profession 211
    Introduction 211
    Barristers 211
        Introduction 211
        Admission to the Profession 212
        The Law Library 214
        Advocacy and Negotiation 214
        Mode of Dress 214
        Junior Counsel and Senior Counsel 214
        Discipline and Conduct 215

Solicitors..216
　　Introduction..216
　　Role of a Solicitor 216
　　Admission to the Profession 217
　　Discipline and Conduct 219
　　Advertising...219
　　'No Foal, No Fee' Litigation 220
Law Clerks and Legal Executives 220
　　Law Clerks..220
　　Registered Legal Executives..220
Reform of the Profession 221
　　Introduction...221
　　The Competition Authority — Study of Competition
　　　　in Legal Services, December 2006..221
　　The Legal Services Ombudsman...222
　　The Legal Services Regulatory Authority 223
　　Fusion of the Profession...224

E. **The Law Officers**...225
　The DPP: Director of Public Prosecutions 225
　　Introduction...225
　　Appointment 225
　　Functions..225
　　Structure of Office...226
　The Attorney General 226
　　Introduction...226
　　Appointment 227
　　Functions..227
　　Structure of Office...228

F. **Other Personnel**..228
　An Garda Síochána 228
　The Probation Service 229
　County Registrars...229
　District Court Clerk...230
　Court Clerks 230
　The Courts Service of Ireland 230

Learning Outcomes

Upon completion of this chapter, the student should be able to:

- Discuss the critical role of judges in the Irish legal system, describing their appointment and main functions and comprehending the importance of the independence of the judiciary;
- Explain the role of the jury in the Irish legal system;
- Describe and differentiate between the two branches of the legal profession in Ireland, and analyse proposals for reform of the profession;
- Identify and explain the key functions of the law officers of the State — the DPP and the Attorney General;
- Appreciate the role played by other personnel in the Irish legal system, including An Garda Síochána, the Probation Service, County Registrars and Court Clerks and the Courts Service.

A. Introduction

This chapter will introduce the student to the personnel, both professional and voluntary, who work in the Irish legal system. The role of court adjudicators (judges and juries), along with the legal profession (barristers and solicitors) will be examined. The role of the Director of Public Prosecutions and the Attorney General, as law officers of the State will also be discussed.

B. The Judiciary

Introduction

Judges play a crucial role under the Irish Constitution and in the Irish legal system. Article 34.1 of the Constitution tasks judges with the role of administering justice in Ireland.

Article 34.1:

> "Justice shall be administered in courts established by law by judges appointed in the manner provided by this Constitution, and, save in such special and limited cases as may be prescribed by law, shall be administered in public."

Articles 34, 35 and 36 of the Constitution establish the constitutional framework within which judges are appointed and must operate.

Judicial Hierarchy and Composition

Judicial Hierarchy

The hierarchy of courts gives rise to a system of judicial hierarchy. The Courts of Justice Act 1924 establishes the hierarchy between judges of the various courts, with the Chief Justice of the Supreme Court holding the highest ranking judicial office.

Table on Order of Judicial Hierarchy

Judge	Court
The Chief Justice	Supreme Court
The President of the High Court	High Court
The Ordinary judges of the Supreme Court who are former Chief Justices according to priority of appointment as Chief Justice	Supreme Court
The Ordinary judges of the Supreme Court (in order of appointment)	Supreme Court

The Ordinary judges of the High Court (in order of appointment)	High Court
The President of the Circuit Court	Circuit Court
The Ordinary judges of the Circuit Court (in order of appointment)	Circuit Court
The President of the District Court	District Court
Ordinary judges of the District Court	District Court

Table on Judicial Composition of the Courts

	Supreme Court	High Court	Circuit Court	District Court
President	Chief Justice (President of the Supreme Court) Seven year limit on term as chief	President of the High Court	President of the Circuit Court	President of the District Court
Judges	Nine ordinary judges	36 ordinary judges	37 ordinary judges	63 ordinary judges
Ex-officio members	The President of the High Court	The Chief Justice The President of the Circuit Court	President of the District Court	
Composition when hearing cases	Five judges, unless Chief Justice directs that three judges can hear the case Five judges reserved for major legal issues/constitutional law cases All judges may hear Article 26 reference	In civil cases, normally judge only, but the President of the High Court may direct that any case may be heard by two or more judges In criminal cases, judge and jury of 12	In civil cases, one judge only In criminal cases, judge and jury of 12	One judge only, in both civil and criminal matters

(Continued)

	Supreme Court	High Court	Circuit Court	District Court
	The SC is collegiate court — always consists of a number of judges and not just one			
Retirement Age	70	70	70	65
	Judges appointed prior to the coming into operation of the Court & Court Officers Act 1995 may continue in office until aged 72	Judges appointed prior to the coming into operation of the Court & Court Officers Act 1995 may continue in office until aged 72		The judge may apply to a committee to have this extended on a year-to-year basis

Appointment and Qualifications

Appointment

Article 35.1 of the Constitution provides that all judges in Ireland shall be appointed by the President, who acts on the advice of the Government in this regard.

The Judicial Appointments Advisory Board was established by law under s 13 of the Court and Court Officers Act 1995 to identify and inform the Government about suitable barristers and solicitors who have applied for a judicial appointment.

Membership of the Judicial Appointments Board consists of:

- The Chief Justice;
- President of the High Court;
- President of the Circuit Court;
- President of the District Court;
- The Attorney General;
- A practising barrister;
- A practising solicitor; and
- Three Ministerial appointments.

In most cases, the Government decides who to appoint as a judge after it has been advised by the Judicial Appointments Advisory Board. In reality, the Government controls judicial appointments and many of those appointed to judicial office in the past have political connections.

Qualifications

No specific requirements regarding judicial qualifications are set out in the Constitution. Article 26.1 leaves it to legislation to set out the minimum qualifications required. The Court and Court Officers Act 2002 sets out the minimum qualifications as follows:

Table on Minimum Qualifications Required for Judicial Appointment by Court

Supreme Court	High Court	Circuit Court	District Court
A practising barrister or solicitor for at least 12 years.	A practising barrister or solicitor for at least 12 years.	A practising barrister or solicitor for at least 10 years.	A practising barrister or solicitor for at least 10 years.
Or	Or	Or	Or
A person who was at any time in the last two years a judge of the ECHR, the ICC, the ECJ, the CFI or an Advocate-General and who was a practising barrister or practising solicitor before appointment to the office.	A person who was at any time in the last two years a judge of the ECHR, the ICC, the ECJ, the CFI or an Advocate-General and who was a practising barrister or practising solicitor before appointment to the office.	A judge of the District Court. Or A county registrar, who has practised as a barrister or solicitor for at least 10 years.	A person who has practised as a barrister or solicitor for at least 10 years and now holds an office to which only practising barristers or solicitors would be appointed.
Or	Or		
A person who was at any time during the last two years a judge of an international tribunal in accordance with the	A person who was at any time during the last two years a judge of an international tribunal in accordance with the		

(Continued)

Supreme Court	High Court	Circuit Court	District Court
International War Crimes Tribunals Act 1998 and who was a practising barrister or practising solicitor before appointment to the office.

Or

A judge of the Circuit Court for at least two years. | International War Crimes Tribunals Act 1998 and who was a practising barrister or practising solicitor before appointment to the office.

Or

A judge of the Circuit Court for at least two years. | | |

In practice, judges usually have many more years of experience than indicated above before they are appointed. If a judge lacks any of the appropriate qualifications or is wrongly appointed, then a conviction by that judge may be set aside. For example, in *State (Walsh) v Murphy* [1981] 1 IR 275, a judge was past the statutory retirement age when he handed down a conviction. The conviction was later set aside on this basis.

Judicial Independence

Judicial independence is of central importance to any legal system. Judges, once appointed, must act independently. The Constitution has a number of measures to ensure judicial independence:

- Article 34.5.1° of the Constitution requires all judges to make the following declaration upon appointment: "In the presence of Almighty God I, (name), do solemnly and sincerely promise and declare that I will duly and faithfully and to the best of my knowledge and power execute the office of Chief Justice (or as the case may be) without fear or favour, affection or ill-will towards any man, and that I will uphold the Constitution and the laws. May God direct and sustain me."
- Article 35.2 states that "all judges shall be independent in the exercise of their judicial functions and subject only to this Constitution and the law."
- Article 35.3 provides that "no judge shall be eligible to be a member of either House of the Oireachtas or to hold any other office or position of emolument."

If there is even a perception of bias, a judge should excuse him/herself from the case. In *Dublin Wellwoman Centre Ltd v Ireland* [1995] 1 ILRM, the Supreme Court held that Carroll J in the High Court ought not to hear a case concerning access to information to abortion due to the fact that there could be an appearance of bias. Carroll J had previously chaired a Commission on the Status of Women and, as chairwoman, wrote a letter to the Taoiseach on behalf of the Commission supporting the right of access to abortion counselling and information. The Supreme Court held that, even though there was no suggestion that there would be actual bias, the judge should recuse him/herself where there was even the appearance of bias.

In *Kenny v Trinity College* [2008] 2 IR 40, the Supreme Court overturned its previous decision to strike out an objection against planning permission for a new development on the grounds that a reasonable person would have perceived there to have been bias in the case. It had emerged that a brother of Murray J, who had given the judgment in the Supreme Court, was a partner in the architectural firm which designed the development.

Remuneration

Another element in the protection of the independence of the judiciary was Article 35.5 of the Constitution which stated that "the remuneration of a judge shall not be reduced during his continuance in office." This was designed to protect the judiciary from being subject to cuts or threatened cuts in pay if they handed down decisions which displeased the Government. However, following a referendum in 2011 to allow reductions in judges' salaries (but only in the context of a pay cut for other public servants on similar incomes), the Twenty-Ninth Amendment of the Constitution (Judges' Remuneration) Act 2011 came into effect. This replaced the old Article 35.5 with the following:

Article 35.5

1. The remuneration of judges shall not be reduced during their continuance in office save in accordance with this section.
2. The remuneration of judges is subject to the imposition of taxes, levies or other charges that are imposed by law on persons generally or persons belonging to a particular class.
3. Where, before or after the enactment of this section, reductions have been or are made by law to the remuneration of persons belonging to classes of persons whose remuneration is paid out of public money and such law states that those reductions are in the public interest, provision may also be made by law to make proportionate reductions to the remuneration of judges.

According to the Department of Finance, the average pay for judges in the Supreme, High, Circuit and District Courts in 2012 equates to €223,036.68 per judge.

A Judicial Council/Commission

The Judicial Council Bill was published in 2009. The Bill proposes the establishment of a Judicial Council, representative of the judiciary of all the courts. The Bill also proposes the establishment of a code of judicial ethics and a process for the investigation of complaints of breaches of that code by members of the judiciary. There is to be lay involvement in this process.

These provisions, if enacted, would not displace the constitutional or legislative provisions concerning the impeachment of judges. Where investigation of a particular allegation discloses that there may have been a sufficiently serious breach to merit impeachment, the matter will be referred to the Oireachtas, which has sole responsibility for the impeachment process. Where investigation shows a less serious breach of ethics, the Bill will provide for a range of lesser steps that can be taken, including giving advice, issuing a reprimand or recommending changes of practice or procedure as it considers appropriate.

The proposed council will also oversee judicial studies, the sharing of information between judges on matters such as sentencing, library services and related matters. The proposed Bill is the subject of continuing consultation.

Some members of the judiciary have also proposed that a new Judicial Commission be established on a constitutional basis, which would take responsibility for judges' appointments, their terms and conditions and discipline.

Immunity from Suit and Contempt of Court

It is accepted at common law that a judge is immune from any claims arising from any acts or omissions whilst acting in his/her judicial capacity, such as negligence or defamation. This was reiterated by the Supreme Court in *McIlwraith v Fawsitt* [1990] 1 IR 343.

Additionally a judge may have recourse to the contempt of court doctrine to protect his/her independence. If a judge becomes aware of any possible interference with the administration of justice, he/she may initiate a prosecution for, try and convict a person for contempt of court.

Termination of Judicial Appointments

A judge may be removed from office or terminate his/her appointment in the following ways:

Figure 11.1 Termination of Judicial Appointments

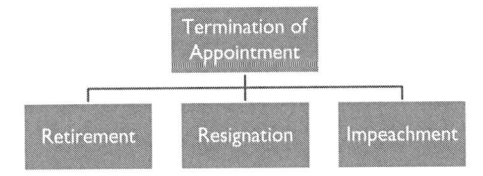

```
        Termination of
         Appointment
    ┌─────────┼─────────┐
 Retirement Resignation Impeachment
```

Retirement

A judge must retire when he/she reaches the retirement age, as set out in figure 11.1 above. There is a long settled principle that a retired judge does not practise in a court of equal or lower jurisdiction to that in which he sat as a judge.

Resignation

A judge may also resign his/her office or may leave office to take up another judicial post. If a judge wishes to resign office, he/she must do so in writing under his/her own hand addressed to the President and transmitted to the Taoiseach (see s 6 of the Courts (Establishment and Constitution) Act 1961).

Impeachment

The procedure for removing a judge from office is broadly outlined in the Constitution. A judge may be removed from office only for stated misbehaviour or incapacity after resolutions have been passed in both Houses of the Oireachtas. The President will then remove the judge from office.

Article 35.4.1° states that "a judge of the Supreme Court or the High Court shall not be removed from office except for stated misbehaviour or incapacity, and then only upon resolutions passed by Dáil Éireann and by Seanad Éireann calling for his removal." Legislation has extended this procedure to include judges in the lower courts also.

Article 35.4.2° provides that:

> (t)he Taoiseach shall duly notify the President of any such resolutions passed by Dáil Éireann and by Seanad Éireann, and shall send him a copy of every such resolution certified by the Chairman of the House of the Oireachtas by which it shall have been passed.

Article 35.4.3° states that, upon receipt of such notification and of copies of such resolutions, "the President shall forthwith, by an order under his hand and Seal, remove from office the judge to whom they relate"

It is not certain exactly what incapacity and stated misbehaviour is. It has been suggested that incapacity suggests medical unfitness for office. The words "stated misbehaviour" appear to include misconduct both on and off the bench — for example, taking bribes or a conviction for a serious criminal offence.

The question of impeaching a judge has rarely arisen in Irish law. However, there have been two occasions on which the issue arose.

The first was the so called "Sheedy Affair", which resulted in the resignation of Supreme Court Judge Hugh O'Flaherty. O'Flaherty J intervened on behalf of Mr Philip Sheedy, who had been convicted and sentenced to four years' imprisonment for causing death by dangerous driving and driving under the influence of alcohol, to have his sentence reviewed. After the intervention by O'Flaherty J, Mr Sheedy's case was re-listed by the Dublin County Registrar and his sentence was reviewed and remitted before Cyril Kelly J and not Matthews J, as would be the correct procedure. Neither the gardaí nor the DPP were informed of the review or the fact that Mr Sheedy was released.

The DPP brought a High Court challenge to Kelly J's decision to release Mr Sheedy in February 1999. Prior to the case being heard, Mr Sheedy had voluntarily returned to prison. On the basis of the DPP's High Court challenge, John O'Donoghue, then Minister for Justice, asked Chief Justice Liam Hamilton to investigate the affair. The Chief Justice's report was published on 16 April 1999. In it, Chief Justice Hamilton stated that Kelly J's handling of the matter and O'Flaherty J's intervention compromised the administration of justice. The Chief Justice was critical of O'Flaherty J, whose actions he deemed to be "open to misinterpretation."

Initially, O'Flaherty J refused to resign, and instead wrote to the Chairman of the Oireachtas Committee on Justice, Equality and Women's Affairs asking to make a statement to the committee as soon as possible. However, he resigned from the Supreme Court the following day, preventing an almost certain impeachment. On 20 April, Kelly J and Michael Quinlan, the Dublin County Registrar, also resigned their positions.

The second occasion on which the issue of impeachment of a judge arose in the Irish legal system was in the case of Judge Brian Curtin, a Circuit Court judge. He had been acquitted on charges of possession of child pornography when a garda raid on his home had been carried out using a search warrant which was ruled invalid because it had expired. The evidence against Judge Curtin was consequently excluded as being inadmissible and Judge Curtin was acquitted of all charges. A motion to impeach him was launched in the Dáil. The impeachment process commenced and a joint Oireachtas committee began its investigations. Judge Curtin challenged the constitutionality of this process and appealed to the Supreme Court, which refused his claim. In November 2006, facing questions by the joint Oireachtas committee, he resigned on health grounds and ended the impeachment process before it could conclude.

C. The Jury

Introduction

A jury is a body of sworn persons summoned to decide questions of fact in a judicial proceeding. The role, therefore, of a jury is to determine whether, on the facts of the case, a person is guilty or not guilty of the offence with which he or she has been charged. The jury must weigh up the evidence presented and decide what actually happened. The judge directs the jury as to the relevant law and the jury then returns a verdict based on the evidence.

A jury is not required in every legal case. Article 38.5 of the Constitution states that

> Save in the case of the trial of offences under section 2 (minor offences), section 3 or section 4 of this Article (offences to be tried at the Special Criminal Court or military tribunals), no person shall be tried on any criminal charge without a jury.

Therefore there is a constitutional right to trial by jury for indictable criminal offences which are not tried by a Special Criminal Court or by a military tribunal. Persons charged with minor offences will not be tried by jury, nor will persons who are brought before the Special Criminal Court.

In civil matters, juries are only used in defamation, assault, false imprisonment and malicious prosecution cases. However, for the vast majority of civil cases, there is no jury and it is the judge who decides the outcome of the case.

Composition

A jury consists of 12 members of the public, one of whom is selected as foreman of the jury by the members of the jury before the case starts. The foreman acts as an informal chairperson and spokesperson for the jury. The 12 jurors in a case are selected from a number of people who have been called to do their jury service on that day. The Juries Act 1976 set out the rules regarding eligibility for jury service in Ireland, which have been criticised for being unduly exclusionary and not representative of the community. The Law Reform Commission has issued a report making recommendations in this regard. Section 23 of the Courts and Civil Law (Miscellaneous Provisions) Act 2013 provides that a judge in the Circuit Court or the Central Criminal Court may appoint a jury of 15 persons in a criminal trial which is likely to exceed two months in duration. This is in order to ensure that there will be a sufficient number of jurors (i.e. 12) to remain properly constituted for the purpose of giving a verdict in that trial.

Function

The jurors must decide whether, on the facts of the case, a person is guilty or not guilty of the offence with which he or she has been charged. At all stages during the trial, jurors must remain impartial and independent and must not be influenced by any other person.

During the trial, the jurors may take notes and ask questions of the judge, if necessary. Once the evidence is taken, the jury will be directed by the judge on legal matters and must reach a verdict only on the evidence introduced in court. The jurors must take, and act upon, the legal directions from the trial judge.

The Verdict

At the conclusion of the trial, the jurors are given an issue paper, which states the issues that the jury must consider in reaching its verdict. The jury is taken into the jury room and allowed no outside communication, with the exception of notes to the Court registrar. They may keep a copy of the indictment, the exhibits and their notes. Jurors may send out notes asking for the law to be further explained or for the judge to remind them of the details of the evidence. They will then be brought back into the court for the judge to give them such assistance as he/she can, but there can be no new evidence at this stage. All statements which are made in the jury room are confidential.

In reaching its verdict in a criminal trial, the jury must be satisfied that the person is guilty beyond reasonable doubt. If the case is a civil case, the jury must be satisfied with its verdict on the balance of probabilities.

It is not necessary that a jury be unanimous in its verdict. In a criminal case, a majority verdict of at least 10 will suffice if they agree on a verdict after considering the case for a reasonable time (not less than two hours). In a civil trial, a verdict may be reached by a majority of nine of the 12 members.

When the jury has reached its decision, it will return to the court and the verdict will be read out by the foreman. The jury has no role in sentencing, which is left to the trial judge. In civil cases, the jury decides how much money should be awarded in damages.

Advantages and Disadvantages of a Jury System

Table on Advantages and Disadvantages of a Jury System

Advantages	Disadvantages
Encourages public participation in the administration of justice.	Some jurors may not be competent to perform the task.
Allows a citizen to be tried by his/her peers.	Possible bias, for example, in favour of attractive members of the opposite sex or against ethnic minorities.
Provides protection against politically – motivated or oppressive prosecutions.	Compulsory nature of jury service may cause resentment amongst jurors, who as a result may not fully engage with the role.
Adds greater certainty to the legal system – no reasons are given, so decision is not open to dispute or misrepresentation.	Juries may award excessive damages, particularly in defamation cases.
	Distress to jury members caused by evidence produced in serious criminal trials.
	Possible manipulation, intimidation or interference with jurors or their family members by defendants.

Reform

The Law Reform Commission's *Report on Jury Service 2013* examined a number of topics concerning jury service, including:

- Qualification for jury service (the commission examined concerns that the existing law and processes for jury selection do not involve selection of juries from panels that are representative of the community. For example, the current jury panels compiled under the *Juries Act 1976* are limited to Irish citizens and exclude long-term residents including EU citizens).
- The categories of persons who are ineligible for jury service and persons who are excusable as of right from jury service. (For example, the 1976 Act allows a wide group of persons, such as doctors, nurses, teachers and public servants, to be excused "as of right" from jury service in Ireland).
- Deferral of jury service.
- Disqualification from jury service arising from criminal convictions.
- Jury tampering (the commission examined concerns that the general right to inspect jury panel lists means jury members are open to intimidation or jury tampering).
- Juror misconduct, including independent investigations such as internet searches (the commission examined concerns about the extent to which the

availability of wireless technology might allow jurors in the jury room to search online for information about an accused, rather than limit their decision to the evidence presented).
- Juror expenses.
- Lengthy and complex jury trials; and
- Empirical research on the jury process.

The final report published by the Commission contains 56 recommendations and includes a draft *Juries Bill* intended to implement these recommendations. The following are the key recommendations in the report, which may be grouped under the following headings: selection for, excusal from and deferral of jury service; juror expenses; jury tampering and misconduct; lengthy and complex jury trials; and empirical research on the jury process:

- Selection for, excusal from and deferral of jury service:
  o Jury panels should be based on the electoral registers for Dáil, local and European elections, which would allow not only Irish citizens but also EU citizens and other long-term residents to be selected for jury service. The report recommends a minimum residency requirement of at least five years. This would add about 200,000 persons to those qualified for jury service.
  o Jurors should be able to read, write, speak and understand English to the extent that they can carry out their functions, and they should be reminded of this when summoned for jury service.
  o The existing blanket excusal from jury service "as of right" for many professionals and public servants should be repealed, and be replaced by an individualised excusal "for good cause."
  o Jurors should be allowed deferral of service for up to 12 months to facilitate those who have good reasons to decline jury service when they are initially summoned.
  o A person with a disability should be eligible for jury service unless, taking account of permissible and practicable assisted decision-making supports and accommodation that are consistent with the right to a trial in due course of law, the disability would mean that he or she could not perform the duties of a juror.
  o The number of objections to jurors without the need to give any reason (peremptory challenges), which is currently seven for both the prosecution and the defence, should be retained, and pre-trial questionnaires to jurors should continue to be prohibited.
- Juror expenses:
  o A modest daily flat rate payment should be paid to jurors to cover their travel and subsistence costs, and the Government should consider

what other means could be used to alleviate the financial burden that jury service involves for small businesses and self-employed persons, including the use of tax credits and insurance.
- Jury tampering:
  o To address concerns regarding jury tampering, the right to inspect the jury panel should be limited to legal advisers four days before the start of a trial and the law on jury tampering should be set out in a single comprehensive offence.
- Juror misconduct:
  o Juries should be given a specific warning not to access the internet during a trial and such inappropriate enquiries should be made a specific offence.
- Lengthy and complex jury trials:
  o A court should be allowed to empanel up to three additional jurors where the judge estimates that the trial will extend beyond three months.
- Empirical research on the jury process:
  o Research should be carried out on matters such as jury representativeness, juror comprehension, juror management and juror capacity and competence. This research should be subject to appropriate confidentiality safeguards to ensure that jury deliberations are not revealed.

D. The Legal Profession

Introduction
In Ireland, the legal profession is divided into two branches: solicitors and barristers. This historical division was carried over from the English system. However, very few other common law jurisdictions continue with the division. There is a significant distinction between the two branches of the profession.

In the vast majority of cases, a member of the public seeking legal advice must first consult a solicitor, who offers legal advice and prepares a case for court. Barristers are not permitted to take instructions from a member of the public, subject to a number of exceptions. Barristers offer specialist legal opinion and act as court advocates.

Barristers

Introduction
Barristers are known collectively as 'the Bar'. Individually, they are referred to as barristers or counsel. They are traditionally regarded as the senior branch of the profession.

A barrister has a number of functions, including:

- Representing his/her client in court;
- Providing legal opinions/advice regarding proposed court actions in court or on almost any legal issue;
- Drafting pleadings, preparing legal submissions, questioning witnesses in court by way of examination-in-chief and cross-examination;
- Negotiating settlements in civil disputes.

Barristers may also represent their client's case outside the courtroom setting, for example in arbitrations, mediations, tribunals, investigations and disciplinary hearings.

All barristers are members of the Bar of Ireland and most are also members of the Law Library, situated in and around the Four Courts building in Dublin. Unlike the solicitors' branch of the profession, the Bar in general is not regulated by statute.

Admission to the Profession

The Honorable Society of King's Inns, which was established in Dublin in 1541, controls admission to the profession and provides post-graduate legal training for those who wish to practise at the Bar. The King's Inns is the oldest institution of legal education in Ireland. The law school of King's Inns provides the course of education by successful completion of which one may be admitted to the degree of Barrister-at-Law and thereby entitled to be called to the Bar of Ireland. Admission to the Barrister-at-Law degree course is via an entrance exam. To be eligible to take the entrance exam, a candidate must hold either an approved law degree or the Society's Diploma in Legal Studies.

In additions the applicants must show that, in the course leading to these degrees, he/she has passed the following subjects:

- Land law (including law of succession);
- Equity;
- Administration law;
- Company law;
- Law of the European Union;
- Jurisprudence.

Applicants who do not have an approved law degree must first complete a two-year part-time Diploma in Legal Studies at King's Inns, before taking the entrance examination.

All applicants who are eligible for entry to the Barrister-at-Law degree course will be required to sit an entrance examination in five subjects namely:

- Law of contract;
- Criminal law;
- Irish constitutional law;
- Law of torts;
- Law of evidence.

Places on the Barrister-at-Law degree course are then allocated in order of merit, subject to a maximum number of places.

On successful completion of the degree course, students are conferred with the degree of Barrister-at-Law. Only holders of the degree may be called to the Bar by the Chief Justice and admitted to practise in the courts of Ireland as a member of the Bar of Ireland.

Before entering the Law Library, a barrister must ensure that an established barrister of at least five years' standing has agreed to act as a 'master' for the new member of the Law Library. The barrister must spend at least one legal year as a pupil of an experienced junior barrister, although many spend two years. This period is known as 'devilling'. The pupil barrister is known as a 'devil', while the experienced barrister is referred to as the 'master'. During the pupil stage, the master will introduce the devil to the general practice of the Law Library, legal and court work. The devil will be required to assist with drafting pleadings and other documents for court. The devil will assist in all aspects of the master's practice and will attend court with the master as a means of learning the role of a barrister. Devils do not get paid for this work.

Figure 11.2 Qualification as a Barrister

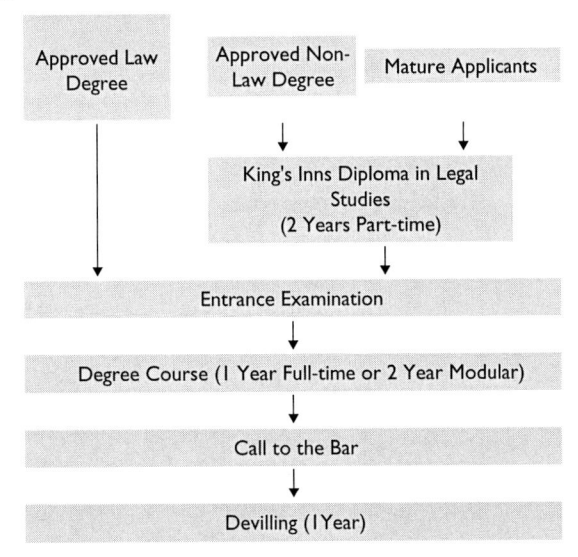

```
┌──────────────┐   ┌──────────────┐   ┌──────────────────┐
│ Approved Law │   │ Approved Non-│   │ Mature Applicants│
│    Degree    │   │  Law Degree  │   │                  │
└──────┬───────┘   └──────┬───────┘   └────────┬─────────┘
       │                  ↓                    ↓
       │         ┌────────────────────────────────┐
       │         │ King's Inns Diploma in Legal   │
       │         │            Studies             │
       │         │        (2 Years Part-time)     │
       │         └────────────────┬───────────────┘
       │                          ↓
       │         ┌────────────────────────────────┐
       └────────→│     Entrance Examination       │
                 └────────────────┬───────────────┘
                                  ↓
                 ┌────────────────────────────────────────┐
                 │ Degree Course (1 Year Full-time or     │
                 │          2 Year Modular)               │
                 └────────────────┬───────────────────────┘
                                  ↓
                 ┌────────────────────────────────┐
                 │         Call to the Bar        │
                 └────────────────┬───────────────┘
                                  ↓
                 ┌────────────────────────────────┐
                 │        Devilling (1 Year)      │
                 └────────────────────────────────┘
```

The Law Library

When a person is called to the Bar, he or she is admitted to practise as a Barrister-at-Law or 'junior counsel'. Barristers in Ireland may not join together to form groups or 'chambers' of barristers as is the practice in England and Wales. Barristers in Ireland act as sole traders and instead form 'the Law Library'. All barristers should be members of the Law Library to practise as a barrister. Membership of the Law Library entitles members to accommodation (offices) and access to legal textbooks upon payment of an annual membership fee.

Advocacy and Negotiation

Advocacy is a particularly important skill for barristers, especially in criminal cases. However, much of a barrister's time is spent on paperwork (preparation of pleadings). Additionally, the vast majority of civil cases are settled before a court hearing. Therefore the ability to give advice on legal problems, to draft pleadings and having strong negotiation skills, are just as essential.

Mode of Dress

Another distinctive feature of barristers is their style of dress. Until 1996, barristers were required by statute to wear a wig, usually made of horsehair, as well as a black gown over dark dress. The shirt or blouse worn generally has a winged collar and, in place of a tie, the barrister wears white bands. Throughout the 1980s, the wearing of wigs was subject to significant debate. A 1990 Fair Trade Commission report found that the wig created an element of intimidation for those unaccustomed to appearing in court and recommended that barristers no longer wear wigs. Section 49 of the Courts and Court Officers Act 1995 now states that the wearing of wigs by members of the Bar 'shall not be required' and it is therefore a matter of discretion for each barrister.

Junior Counsel and Senior Counsel

The bar is divided into two branches, junior counsel, which is known as the 'outer Bar', and senior counsel, which is the 'inner Bar'. The move from junior counsel to senior counsel is known as 'taking silk', as the gown worn by senior counsel is made of silk, rather than the poplin gown worn by junior counsel. The letters 'SC' are usually inserted after name of a senior counsel but 'JC' is not used after names of junior counsel, who are referred to as barristers-at-law. Progression to the rank of senior counsel is not automatic and is only usually considered after about 15 years' practice. A barrister wishing to take silk must apply to the Chief Justice and Attorney General for admission to the inner Bar. A barrister is called to the inner Bar by the Chief Justice in the Supreme Court, on the approval of the Government, which acts on the advice of the Attorney General who liaises with the chairman of the Bar Council. Approval is not automatic, but members of the Bar do not apply to take silk without first making informal inquiries as to their chances of approval.

When accepted into the inner Bar, the barrister is granted letters patent by the Government.

The main difference between junior and senior counsel is that junior counsel draft pleadings and conduct cases generally in the lower courts. The functions of a senior counsel include scrutinising draft pleadings and conducting the more difficult cases in the High Court and Supreme Court. The majority of senior counsel are known for their courtroom expertise.

Another difference between junior and senior counsel is in the amount of payment they receive. The fee for a junior counsel has traditionally been two-thirds of the fee charged by a senior counsel, except where the latter is charging a special fee due to the length or difficulty of a particular case, in which case they are entitled to be paid more.

Discipline and Conduct

Disciplinary matters at the Bar are regulated by the Bar Council of Ireland, which has adopted a Code of Conduct and Disciplinary Code for the Bar of Ireland. The Bar Council is a non-statutory body, elected annually by the members of the Bar. A chairman is also elected to chair important committees and to represent the Bar. The Bar Council issues a Professional Code of Conduct which is amended from time to time by the members themselves.

Under this code of conduct, barristers are not normally allowed to take instructions directly from lay clients, although in the case of contentious matters, they are allowed to have preliminary consultations with clients once a solicitor is present. Consequently, barristers are largely dependent upon solicitors for work.

The Code of Conduct of the Bar Council obliges a barrister to uphold the interests of his client "without regard to his own interests or any consequences to himself or any other person". Furthermore, written or oral communications between a barrister/solicitor and a client are legally privileged if made in the context of contemplated or pending litigation.

The Code of Conduct includes rules regarding the following:

- Duty not to mislead a court in any manner;
- Prohibitions on touting and advertising his or her services to the public;
- Client confidentiality;
- Fees;
- Code of Conduct between members of the Bar.

Complaints of misconduct by a barrister against another barrister are considered by the Bar Council's Professional Practices Committee, which now includes lay members. This committee has extensive powers and may impose fines, issue admonishments and suspend or exclude members from the Law Library.

Complaints of misconduct from the public, solicitors and other clients are considered by the Barristers' Professional Conduct Tribunal. The Tribunal can impose penalties if it finds that a barrister has been guilty of breaching the Code of Conduct or of breaching proper professional standards.

Solicitors

Introduction

Solicitors represent the second branch of the legal profession. Although originally connected to the barrister's profession, the Incorporated Law Society of Ireland was formed in 1830 to secure the independent existence of solicitors as a separate and distinct profession. In 1898, the Solicitors (Ireland) Act established the Incorporated Law Society of Ireland on a statutory footing and charged it with the control of admission, education and discipline of solicitors. In 1994, it was renamed the Law Society of Ireland.

The Law Society of Ireland is the professional regulatory body for solicitors. It exercises statutory functions under the Solicitors Acts 1954 to 2008 in relation to the education, admission, enrolment, discipline and regulation of the solicitors' profession.

Role of a Solicitor

Solicitors are in the front line dealing with the public and are the first point of contact when a person requires legal advice, conveyancing or the drafting of a will. Much of the work of a solicitor involves non-contentious business that does not involve court cases or other dispute resolution.

As regards contentious business, solicitors tend to specialise in legal work which involves the preparation of cases for court, rather than advocacy, although many solicitors act as advocates for their clients, particularly in the lower courts. Solicitors will prepare a case for court, manage communications on behalf of the client, file court documents, organise witnesses, etc.

In large firms of solicitors, particularly those dealing with commercial law, a wide range of services is offered, including international litigation or arbitration, the formation of private companies, the flotation of companies on the stock exchange, tax advice and planning and other areas of commercial law.

If required, a solicitor will instruct and 'brief' a barrister for a case by sending him/her all of the necessary documents and information pertaining to a particular case. A solicitor may also consult a barrister for a specialist legal opinion. It is usual for a solicitor to instruct a barrister for cases in the Circuit Court, High Court and Supreme Court. Since 1971, solicitors have the same right as barristers to appear in any court, including the High or Supreme Court. However, very few take full advantage of this right. Despite attempts to encourage solicitors to make fuller use of their right of audience, changes in practice have not been very significant.

Solicitors may be appointed as judges in both the District and Circuit Courts and to the High Court and Supreme Court is also possible.

Unlike barristers, who must operate as sole traders, solicitors are allowed to join together to form partnerships and are allowed to advertise their services. The Law Society has a code of conduct to regulate how solicitors conduct their business.

Admission to the Profession

There are four steps to qualification as a solicitor:

Figure 11.3 Steps to Qualification as a Solicitor

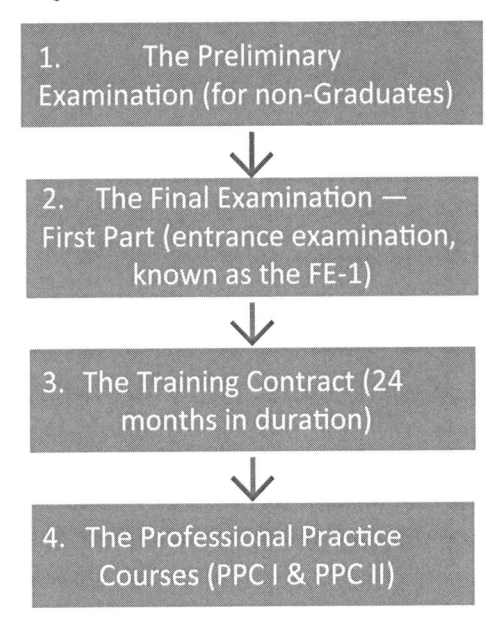

1. The Preliminary Examination (for non-Graduates)

↓

2. The Final Examination — First Part (entrance examination, known as the FE-1)

↓

3. The Training Contract (24 months in duration)

↓

4. The Professional Practice Courses (PPC I & PPC II)

- Stage 1: The Preliminary Examination (for non-Graduates)

University graduates from Ireland and the United Kingdom or holders of degrees (regardless of the discipline) awarded by the Higher Education and Training Awards Council (HETAC) are exempt from this examination, as are most foreign graduates and law clerks who have at least five years' experience and hold a diploma in legal studies, or an equivalent qualification, or have in excess of ten years' experience (diploma in legal studies not required).

For those who are not exempt, the examination consists of the following papers:

- English;
- Irish Government and politics;
- General knowledge.

■ Stage 2: The Final Examination — First Part

The FE-1 is the entrance examination to the Law Society of Ireland. Only those who have passed or gained exemption from the Preliminary Examination can sit this examination. Students must pass papers in the following eight 'core' subjects:

Table on FE-1 Entrance Examinations

| Constitutional law | Criminal law | Equity | Law of contract |
| Company law | Real property | Law of tort | European Union law |

The Law Society of Ireland previously offered exemptions for students who passed these 'core' subjects in their law degrees in the Republic of Ireland. However, in *Bloomer and Ors v Incorporated Law Society of Ireland* [1995] 3 IR, it was held that this constituted discrimination on the grounds of nationality contrary to Article 6 of the EC Treaty, as students from Northern Ireland were not receiving similar exemptions. Following this case, the Law Society removed exemptions for all students. In *Abrahamson and Others v Law Society of Ireland and the Attorney General* [1996] 2 IR 403, the court restored the position prior to Bloomer for those already in the system based on their legitimate expectation. Currently, no exemptions from these examinations are offered to law graduates.

■ Stage 3: The Training Contract (24 Months in Duration)

During stage 3, the trainee solicitor spends 24 months undergoing in-office training. It is up to the trainee solicitor to secure the training contract with a training solicitor.

Training solicitors are required to provide the trainee solicitor with reasonable and appropriate instruction and experience in areas prescribed by the Law Society.

Before being eligible to start the training programme, applicants must apply to the Law Society for consent to start training. Evidence must be provided of good character, and any criminal convictions must be disclosed.

- Stage 4: The Professional Practice Courses (PPC I & PPC II)

In addition to completing the 24 months of in-office training, the trainee solicitor must also complete two professional practice-orientated training courses:

- The Professional Practice Course I (PPC I)

This must be completed before the 24 month training contract period begins. Applicants must secure a training contract before they can apply for a place on the PPC I.

- The Professional Practice Course II (PPC II)

Eleven months into the 24-month training period, the trainee returns to the Law School to attend the PPC II. This course is 12 weeks in duration and is counted as part of the 24-month training period.

Having completed the PPC II, the trainee must return to the office of the training solicitor and complete the outstanding period of time — ten months if the trainee has not gained credit for work done prior to PPC I, or six months if credit has been obtained.

Discipline and Conduct

Discipline and conduct of the profession is regulated by the Law Society. The Solicitors' Disciplinary Tribunal may investigate allegations of misconduct against a solicitor. The members of the Solicitors Disciplinary Tribunal, which is independent of the Society, are appointed by the President of the High Court and include lay members.

The Solicitors Disciplinary Tribunal has limited judicial powers and its primary function is to establish whether misconduct is proved. Where there is a finding of misconduct, the Tribunal itself can impose a sanction on the solicitor (which can include a direction to pay restitution of a sum not exceeding €15,000 to any aggrieved party) or the Tribunal may refer its finding and recommendation to the President of the High Court who ultimately will decide on the nature of the sanction to be imposed on the solicitor. The President of the High Court may suspend the solicitor for a period of time if required, or may strike him/her off the roll of solicitors.

Other complaints, e.g. overcharging, are heard by the Law Society only, which may order repayment. There is a right of appeal to the High Court.

Advertising

The Solicitors Acts 1954 – 2008 prevent advertising by solicitors which:

- Is likely to bring the profession into disrepute;
- Is in bad taste;
- Reflects unfavourably on other solicitors;
- Is false or misleading;
- Is contrary to public policy;
- Consists of unsolicited approaches to individuals for business.

Advertisements designed to encourage personal injury claims are prohibited and any breaches of the regulations may be regarded as a disciplinary matter.

'No Foal, No Fee' Litigation

'No foal, no fee' refers to cases (usually personal injury cases) where solicitors are involved on the basis that the client will not be charged a professional fee if the claim is unsuccessful. This practice was widely criticised and s 9(a) of the Solicitors (Advertising) Regulations 2004 (SI No 518 of 2002) prohibits the publication of an advertisement by a solicitor which includes words or phrases including:

- "no win, no fee";
- "no foal, no fee";
- "free first consultation";
- "most cases settled out of court" ;
- "insurance cover arranged to cover legal costs" or;

> other words or phrases of a similar nature which could be construed as meaning that legal services involving contentious business would be provided by the solicitor at no cost or reduced cost to the client.

This is designed to discourage misleading advertisements where clients may not be aware that, if they lose a claim, they will have to pay all of the costs of the other party.

Law Clerks and Legal Executives

Law Clerks

Under s 59 of the Solicitors Act 1954, activities normally associated with solicitors may be done by any person employed by a solicitor if acting under the solicitor's directions. This allows for 'law clerks' to engage in a lot of work connected with conveyancing and certain court work under the direction of a solicitor. Many law clerks progress to being qualified solicitors after a period of time.

Registered Legal Executives

Legal executives (sometimes referred to as 'paralegals') carry out similar work to a law clerk. Legal executives are regulated in Ireland by the Irish Institute of Legal Executives, which is the professional body representing Registered Legal

Executives in Ireland. In order to register as a legal executive, a certain amount of experience and completion of certain academic courses is required.

Reform of the Profession

Introduction

There have been two major reports into the possible reform of the legal profession in Ireland:

1. Fair Trade Commission Report into the Restrictive Practices in the Legal Professions 1990;
2. The Competition Authority — Study of Competition in Legal Services, December 2006.

In addition, a number of OECD reports have criticised competition in the legal profession, including the OECD Report in Professional Services, 1999, and the OECD Competitive Restrictions in Legal Professions Report, 2007.

The Competition Authority — Study of Competition in Legal Services, December 2006

The Competition Authority's Report, published in December 2006, found that:

- The legal profession was permeated with numerous serious and disproportionate restrictions on competition;
- The current regulatory bodies have a conflict of interest;
- The legal profession had more restrictions than most other professions in Ireland;
- The legal profession in Ireland had more restrictions placed on it than in most other common law countries.

It stated that many of the restrictions are:

- Largely imposed and/or enforced by the profession itself;
- Anti-competitive;
- Unjustified;
- In need of reform.

The Competition Authority made a large number of recommendations for reform, including the following:

- Abolition of the educational monopolies enjoyed by King's Inns and the Law Society in respect of professional legal education;
- Removal or amendment of the rule requiring barristers to be sole traders;

- Either the broadening of the Bar Council's Direct Professional Access Scheme, or the abolition of the prohibition on direct access of the public to barristers' services;
- Amendment of the restriction on the provision of conveyancing services by persons other than solicitors firms and practising solicitors (e.g. financial services institutions);
- Removal of the restriction on partnerships between barristers and solicitors;
- Removal of the restriction on lawyers holding the titles of barrister and solicitor simultaneously;
- Abolition of the rule which prevents barristers engaging in occupations inconsistent with full-time practice at the Bar;
- Abolition of the rule which confines membership of the Law Library to full-time practising barristers;
- Removal of all restrictions on barrister and solicitor advertising, or of all except specified minimum restrictions;
- New criteria for allowing entry of lawyers qualified outside the EU;
- The establishment of a transparent scheme for the awarding of the title of senior counsel, together with the opening up of the title to solicitors;
- The provision by barristers of fee information to clients in advance;
- Abolition of the requirement on certain applicants to acquire the Diploma in Legal Education before sitting the King's Inns entrance examination;
- An independent, transparent accountable regulator — new Legal Services Commission proposed.

Some of the recommendations above concerning fee information, widening of the direct access scheme, the removal of the monopoly on conveyancing and new criteria for allowing the entry of lawyers qualified outside the EU have been implemented. Additionally, moves are afoot to create a new Legal Services Ombudsman and a new Legal Services Regulatory Authority to further erode the restrictive practices in the profession.

The Legal Services Ombudsman

The Legal Services Ombudsman Act 2009, which created the office of a Legal Services Ombudsman to oversee the handling by the Law Society of Ireland and the Bar Council of complaints by clients of solicitors and barristers, was signed by the President on 10 March 2009. However, the Legal Services Ombudsman has yet to be appointed and no commencement order has been signed for the Act.

If commenced, the legislation will introduce an independent review of the operation of the legal profession's complaints systems. A complaint may be made to the Ombudsman concerning the handling of the initial complaint against the solicitor or barrister. Following an investigation, the Ombudsman may issue directions or make recommendations to the Bar Council and Law Society. The

Ombudsman may direct those bodies to reinvestigate a complaint or, in the case of the Law Society, refer it to the Solicitors Disciplinary Tribunal for an inquiry on the ground of alleged misconduct. The Ombudsman will also monitor and report annually to the Minister for Justice and the Oireachtas on the adequacy of the admissions policies of both professions.

The Legal Services Regulatory Authority

The Legal Services (Regulation) Bill, which was published in 2011, proposes the establishment of a new:

- Legal Services Regulatory Authority;
- Complaints committee;
- Independent disciplinary tribunal for the legal profession; and
- Office of Legal Costs Adjudicator.

The proposed new regulatory authority will have 11 members, seven of them lay, and is to be independently appointed. It will report to the Minister for Justice and relevant Oireachtas committees.

It will be able to establish sub-committees, including a complaints committee, to which clients may go in the first instance. Informal resolution of disputes will be encouraged. If a dispute goes to a hearing of the complaints committee, it may impose a series of minor sanctions.

Figure 11.4 Proposed Organisation of the Legal Services Regulatory Authority

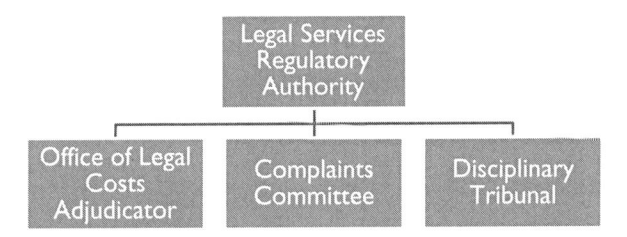

If the matter is more serious, the regulatory authority will refer it to the disciplinary tribunal, which will also be appointed by the Minister for Justice and will have a lay majority. This will have the same power as the High Court to compel witnesses and order the production of documents.

The disciplinary tribunal will have at its disposal a range of sanctions similar to those available at the moment to the Solicitors Disciplinary Tribunal, including the referral of the legal practitioner to the High Court for striking off.

The new regulatory authority will also be charged with preparing or approving codes of conduct for the two branches of the legal profession, deciding on levels of professional indemnity insurance and supervising entry into the professions.

It will review the provision of professional legal education and prepare a report for the minister on how this is to be delivered in future, and by whom, potentially ending the monopoly on legal education exercised by the Law Society and the King's Inns.

In relation to legal costs, legal practitioners will be obliged to outline what these are likely to be in advance and, where there is a dispute, this will be adjudicated by a legal costs adjudicator.

The Bar Council has criticised the Bill, claiming it will reduce competition and increase legal costs.

Fusion of the Profession
Should the profession be fused to remove the distinction between the two branches of the profession and to create one profession of a 'lawyer', as has happened in most other common law jurisdictions, with the exception of England and Wales?

This issue was considered by the Fair Trade Commission Report into the Restrictive Practices in the Legal Professions 1990, which examined the arguments for and against fusing the profession. In the United Kingdom, consideration is also being given to merging the two professions. Since the introduction of the Legal Services Act 2007 in the UK, the distinction between the professions has been reduced considerably, with the Act being seen by many as a step toward a fused legal profession.

The possible advantages and disadvantages to merging the professions into one are outlined below:

Table on some possible advantages and disadvantages of a fused legal profession

Advantages	Disadvantages
Reduce the cost of legal services for the client.	Loss of specialist expertise.
Common training programme for legal professionals would allow greater choice and flexibility for graduates upon completion.	Reduction in the standard of advocacy.
Greater efficiency and less duplication of work.	Loss of professional detachment by barristers.

(Continued)

All other common law countries, with the exception of England and Wales, have a fused profession, which includes a body of specialist advocates.	Reduced access to legal services — the best barristers would join the largest firms in the cities, making their expertise unavailable to most people.
	Reduction in the number of specialist advocates might make it more difficult to secure suitable judicial appointments.

E. The Law Officers

There are two law officers in the Irish State: the Director of Public Prosecutions, who holds a statutory office, and the Attorney General, who is a constitutional office holder.

The DPP: Director of Public Prosecutions

Introduction

The DPP is the Director of Public Prosecutions. The office is created by statute. He/she prosecutes most serious crimes in the name of the Irish people.

Prior to 1976, all serious criminal offences in Ireland were prosecuted in the name of the Attorney General, under Article 30.3 of the Constitution. Article 30 also permits legislation to authorise a person other than the Attorney General to prosecute serious crimes in the name of the people. Section 2 of the Prosecutions of Offences Act 1974 created the independent office of the Director of Public Prosecutions to act instead of the Attorney General in this regard.

Appointment

The DPP is appointed by the Government. To be appointed, the DPP must have practised as a barrister or as a solicitor for at least ten years. Once appointed, the DPP acts independently of the Government and does not resign when a government falls. This is important as it ensures continuity in office. The DPP can be removed from office by the Government, but only on grounds of ill health or misconduct.

Functions

The DPP enforces the criminal law in the courts on behalf of the people of Ireland. He/she directs and supervises public prosecutions on indictment in the courts and gives general direction and advice to the Garda Síochána in relation to summary cases.

He/she decides, based on the file of evidence produced by An Garda Síochána, whether or not to prosecute in serious criminal matters. The DPP makes decisions independently of all other bodies and institutions, including both the Government and the Garda Síochána, and decisions are taken free from political or other influence. Whilst decisions of the DPP which involve the exercise of discretion are generally regarded as unreviewable by the courts, there have been some limited incursions into the DPP's immunity in a small number of exceptional cases (see *Norris v Attorney General* [1984] IR 36 and 81 per McCarthy J (*obiter dicta*); *State (O'Callaghan) v Ó hUadhaigh* [1977] IR 42; *Eviston v DPP* [2002] 3 IR 260; [2002] 1 ILRM 134 (HC); [2003] 1 ILRM 178 (SC); and *E(G) v DPP* [2008] IESC 61 (30 October 2008).

Most serious crimes must be prosecuted in the name of the people at the instance of the DPP, e.g. *People (DPP) v Walsh*. However, some offences which may give rise to sensitive political issues still require the consent of the Attorney General to prosecute.

Structure of Office

Figure 11.5 Structure of the Office of the DPP

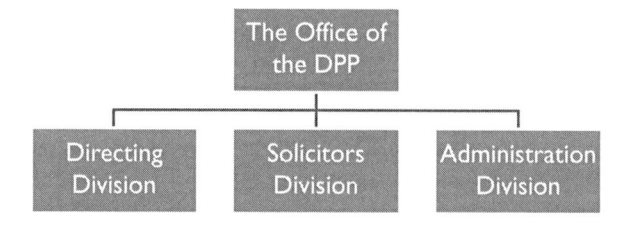

```
           The Office of
             the DPP
    ┌────────────┼────────────┐
 Directing    Solicitors   Administration
 Division     Division      Division
```

The Office of the DPP has three main divisions:

- The Directing Division — comprises barristers and solicitors who examine criminal investigation files and decide whether or not a prosecution should be taken;
- The Solicitors Division — comprises prosecution solicitors and legal executives who prepare and conduct cases on behalf of the DPP in all courts sitting in Dublin. Cases heard in courts sitting outside Dublin are prepared and conducted by a local State solicitor;
- The Administration Division — comprises general service civil service grades providing support and other services to the Office.

The Attorney General

Introduction

Article 30 of the Constitution creates the office of Attorney General. The Attorney General is the legal adviser of the Government in matters of law and legal opinion. He/she also performs other functions conferred on him/her by law.

Appointment

Article 30.2 provides that the Attorney General is appointed by President, on nomination of the Taoiseach. The Attorney General is conventionally a practising member of the Bar and a Senior Counsel. He/she usually ceases private practice once appointed.

The Attorney General is not a member of the Government, although he/she will often attend cabinet meetings. The Attorney General also becomes 'leader of the Bar', which is a ceremonial position conferred upon him/her by the Bar Council of Ireland.

The Attorney General usually holds office for the same period of time as the Taoiseach who nominated him/her. The Attorney General retires from office when the Taoiseach who appointed him/her resigns, but may continue to carry on his/her duties until the successor to the Taoiseach is appointed.

The Attorney General may at any time resign from office by placing his/her resignation in the hands of the Taoiseach for submission to the President. The Taoiseach may also request the resignation of the Attorney General and, if he/she refuses, the President may terminate his/her appointment on the advice of the Taoiseach.

Functions

The main role of the Attorney General is to act as the legal advisor of the Government in matters of law and legal opinion. Although appointed by the Government, he/she must act independently. The Attorney General scrutinises all proposed legislation and advises the Government in an international context about legal affairs. The Attorney General also plays an important role regarding extradition requests. The Attorney General also represents the public in the assertion of or protection of public rights, and defends constitutional and public right actions on behalf of the State. The Attorney General may also sometimes act to vindicate constitutional or public rights, e.g. *Attorney General v X* [1992] 1 IR 1.

Article 30.3 of the Constitution provides that:

> All crimes and offences prosecuted in any court constituted under Article 34 of this Constitution other than a court of summary jurisdiction shall be prosecuted in the name of the People and at the suit of the Attorney General or some other person authorised in accordance with law to act for that purpose.

However, since the enactment of the Prosecution of Offences Act 1974, the responsibility for the prosecution of indictable criminal offences is mainly in the hands of the Director of Public Prosecutions who is, by law, independent of the Attorney General and the State.

Structure of Office

The Attorney General is supported by the Office of the Attorney General, which is made up of a number of the following:

- The Attorney General's Office containing the advisory counsel to the Attorney General;
- The Office of Parliamentary Counsel to the Government containing the parliamentary counsel who draft legislation and have responsibilities in the area of statute law revision;
- The Chief State Solicitor's Office (CSSO) containing the solicitors representing the Attorney and the State. The Chief State Solicitor is a civil servant who acts as the Attorney General's solicitor. He/she represents the State and instructs barristers on behalf of the State. The State also appoints solicitors at a local level to represent the State. These are known as 'State solicitors'.

Figure 11.6 Structure of the Office of the Attorney General

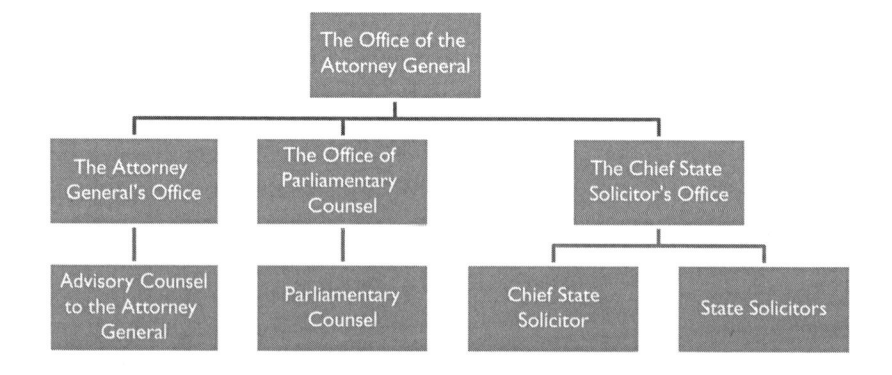

F. Other Personnel

An Garda Síochána

An Garda Síochána, the Irish police force, plays a crucial role in the policing of the Irish State. Within the Irish legal system, the functions of An Garda Síochána are to:

- Conduct independent criminal investigations;
- Conduct most summary prosecutions in the District Court in relation to minor offences;
- Prepare and submit files to the Solicitors Division of the DPP's Office (Dublin cases) or to the local State solicitor (cases outside Dublin) in relation to more serious offences;
- Police the State and provide State security.

In order to achieve these objectives, the law has vested in An Garda Síochána various legal powers, including the power to search premises and to arrest and/or question a suspect.

The Minister for Justice, Equality and Law Reform is accountable to the Oireachtas for the performance of An Garda Síochána. A government appointed Garda, known as the Garda Commissioner, is responsible for the day-to-day running of the force. The Commissioner has Deputy and Assistant Commissioners.

The Probation Service

The Probation Service, which is part of the Department of Justice, Equality and Law Reform, assesses and manages criminal offenders in the community, facilitating the re-integration of ex-offenders on behalf of the Courts Service and the Prison Service. It provides probation supervision, community service, offending behaviour programmes and specialist support services to adult and young offenders, which aim to stop the commission of further offences. The Probation Service also works in prisons and detention centres. It is managed by the Director of the Probation Service.

County Registrars and Court Clerks

County Registrars

A County Registrar has responsibility for the administration and management of Circuit Court offices within his/her own county. Appointed by the Government, the County Registrar also performs a number of quasi-judicial functions, such as:

- Entering judgments in default;
- Dealing with the taxation of costs;
- Dealing with probate matters;
- Dealing with matters in relation to the land registry;
- Acting as returning officer during general elections.

Appeals against the decision of a Country Registrar are made directly to a Circuit Court judge.

Court Clerks

District Court Clerk

A District Court Clerk administers the work of the District Court. He/she signs all summonses issued by the Gardaí on behalf of the DPP. The District Court Clerk may also arrange special sittings of the District Court out of normal working hours. Additionally the District Court Clerk is registrar of clubs and licensed premises in his/her district.

Court Clerks

The Court Clerk is responsible for a variety of administrative tasks concerned with the day-to-day running of the court. As registrar of court sittings, they call cases, swear in witnesses, prepare warrants for signatures and record the orders of the judge.

The Courts Service of Ireland

The Courts Service was established as an independent corporate organisation, following the enactment of the Courts Service Act 1998.

The Court Service has a number of functions, including to:

- Manage the courts;
- Provide support services for the judges;
- Provide information on the courts system to the public;
- Provide, manage and maintain court buildings;
- Provide facilities for users of the courts.

Section E

The Administration of Justice in Ireland

CHAPTER TWELVE

THE ADMINISTRATION OF JUSTICE IN IRELAND: AN INTRODUCTION

A. Introduction 235
B. The Administration of Justice in Ireland — Main Features 235
C. Administration of Justice in Public 236

Learning Outcomes

Upon completion of this chapter, students should be able to:

- Identify and discuss the main features of the administration of justice in Ireland;
- Explain the *in camera* rule and its operation in the Irish legal system, and elucidate proposals for its reform.

A. Introduction

The Irish Free State, Saorstát Éireann, was established in 1922. Articles 64 to 73 of the 1922 Free State Constitution set out the basic court structure of the new state. The Courts of Justice Act 1924 was enacted to provide the details for the operation of the new court system. The 1924 Act made provision for the establishment and jurisdiction of the following courts: the Supreme Court; the Court of Criminal Appeal; the High Court; the Circuit Court; and the District Court. In 1937, the Constitution of Ireland, Bunreacht na hÉireann, replaced the 1922 Constitution. Articles 34 to 37 of the new Constitution retained the basic structure of the system set out in 1922. However, legislation re-establishing the court system under Article 34.1 of the 1937 Constitution was declared to be necessary by the Supreme Court in *The State (Keegan) v Minister for Justice* [1954] IR 207. This ruling was given effect by the Courts (Establishment and Constitution) Act 1961. This Act carried forward the existing court system which had been created by the 1924 Act. The Courts (Supplemental Provisions) Act 1961, which was passed at the same time, clarified and updated the jurisdiction of the various courts.

B. The Administration of Justice in Ireland — Main Features

Article 34.1 of the 1937 Constitution provides:

> Justice shall be administered in courts established by law by judges appointed in the manner provided by this Constitution, and, save in such special and limited cases as may be prescribed by law, shall be administered in public.

This provision is fundamental to the administration of justice in Ireland. It requires that justice only be administered in a court which has been established under the Constitution, by properly appointed judges and that justice should generally be done in public.

The meaning of the term 'administration of justice' was considered by the High Court in *McDonald v Bord na gCon (No 2)* [1965] IR 217. In that case, Mr McDonald challenged the constitutionality of s 47 of the Greyhound Industry Act 1958. This provision empowered Bord na gCon to exclude a person from: (a) being on any greyhound racetrack; (b) being at any authorised coursing meeting (c) being at any public sale of greyhounds. Mr McDonald argued that this provision allowed the Board to exercise judicial power. In the High Court, Kenny J held in favour of Mr McDonald. He ruled that the 'administration of justice' had the following characteristic features:

1. A dispute or controversy as to the existence of legal rights or a violation of the law;

2. A determination or ascertainment of the rights of the parties or the imposition of liabilities or the infliction of a penalty;
3. The final determination (subject to appeal) of legal rights or liabilities or the imposition of penalties;
4. The enforcement of those rights or liabilities or the imposition of a penalty by the Court or by the executive power of the state which is called on by the Court to enforce its judgment;
5. The making of an order by the Court which, as a matter of history, is an order characteristic of courts in this country.

Article 37.1 of the 1937 Constitution provides:

> Nothing in this Constitution shall operate to invalidate the exercise of limited functions and powers of a judicial nature, in matters other than criminal matters, by any person or body of persons duly authorised by law to exercise such functions and powers, notwithstanding that such person or such body of persons is not a judge or a court appointed or established as such under this Constitution.

This provision authorises persons other than judges or courts to exercise 'limited' functions and powers of a judicial nature. This allows certain specified civil disputes to be adjudicated upon outside of the court system. It is clear, however, that only the courts can deal with criminal matters. In addition, Article 38 requires that criminal trials be held 'in due course of law', that minor offences may be tried in courts of summary jurisdiction and that, subject to certain exceptions, a person charged with a non-minor offence cannot be tried without a jury.

C. Administration of Justice in Public

Article 34.1 of the Constitution provides that courts must in general sit in public, save in such special and limited cases as may be prescribed by law. Henchy J, in *Re R Ltd* [1989] ILRM 759, considered the meaning of this provision. He said:

> The actual presence of the public is never necessary, but the administration of justice in public does require that the doors of the court must remain open so that members of the general public may come and see for themselves that justice is done.

This is based on the maxim that justice must not only be done, but must be seen to be done. The administration of justice in public is regarded as necessary to ensure public confidence in the administration of justice, to act as a deterrent to would-be wrongdoers and to provide necessary accountability and transparency.

Article 34.1, however, allows for certain hearings to be conducted in private. A sitting other than in public is described as being *in camera*. Members of the public, as well as the media, are generally excluded from *in camera* hearings. Attendance is restricted to the judge and jury (if applicable), the court registrar or clerk, the parties to the proceedings and their representatives. Exceptions to the public administration of justice are provided for in statute. For example, s 45(1) of the Courts (Supplemental Provisions) Act 1961 provides that the following matters may be heard *in camera*: applications of an urgent nature for *habeas corpus*, bail, prohibition or an injunction; matrimonial causes and matters (e.g. divorce, judicial separation or nullity); lunacy and minor matters, and proceedings involving the disclosure of a secret manufacturing process. In addition, s 205 of the Companies Act 1963 provides that High Court cases involving a claim of minority oppression in companies may be held *in camera* where the court is of the opinion that a public hearing "would involve the disclosure of information the publication of which would be seriously prejudicial to the legitimate interests of the company." The urgency of the case or sensitivity of the material involved is the justification for *in camera* hearings in such cases.

Any publication which would identify parties involved in *in camera* proceedings or reveal sensitive information discussed in such hearings would amount to contempt of court. Other restrictions apply in the context of criminal proceedings. In proceedings on indictment, restrictions apply to the information which may be published concerning the defendant once proceedings have been initiated. In prosecutions for rape and sexual offences, the trial judge is required to exclude the general public, but *bona fide* members of the media as well as court officers may attend the hearing. The verdict is announced in public but the names of the defendant and complainant may only be published by the media with court authorisation.

In *Roe v Blood Transfusion Service Board* [1996] 1 ILRM 555, Laffoy J held that the plaintiff, Brigid McCole, was required to use her real name in litigation, rather than a pseudonym. In *Irish Times Ltd v Ireland* [1998] 1 IR 359, the Supreme Court held that a trial judge had no general power to impose a ban on contemporaneous reporting of court proceedings. The Circuit Court judge in that case had made an order forbidding the media from reporting evidence given in court, whilst also stating that the case was not being held *in camera*. The Supreme Court took the view that any harm caused by improper reporting could be remedied by the trial judge giving appropriate directions to the jury, or by applying the contempt of court jurisdiction available to him.

Part 2 of the Courts and Civil Law (Miscellaneous Provisions) Act 2013, which was signed into law on 24 July 2013, will, when commenced, amend the *in camera* rule in order to provide greater transparency in the administration of family and child care proceedings by allowing press access to the courts in family, child care and adoption hearings. Such access is subject to certain restrictions and prohibitions. These include a prohibition on the publication of material which could lead to the identification of the parties or children involved.

CHAPTER THIRTEEN

Structure of the Irish Court System

A. Introduction 241
B. The Superior Courts — The High Court and the Supreme Court 241
C. Courts of Local and Limited Jurisdiction 242
D. Statutory Regulation of Court Business 243
E. Jurisdiction of the Courts — First Instance and Appellate 243
    First Instance Jurisdiction of the Courts 243
    Appellate Jurisdiction of the Courts 243
        The Constitutional Framework 243
        De novo Hearing 243
        Appeal on a Point of Law 244
        Findings of Fact 244

Learning Outcomes

Upon completion of this chapter, students should be able to:

- Identify the constitutional and legislative provisions establishing the Irish court system;
- Distinguish between the superior courts and courts of local and limited jurisdiction, and comprehend the importance of that distinction;
- Differentiate between the first instance and appellate jurisdiction of the courts.

A. Introduction

The basic outline of the court system is set out in Articles 34-38 of the Constitution. These provisions identify by name the High Court and Supreme Court. Courts with 'local and limited jurisdiction' are referred to, but not identified by name. Article 34.2 provides: 'The Courts shall comprise Courts of First Instance and a Court of Final Appeal.' This provision envisages that there should be courts with first instance jurisdiction and at least one final court of appeal.

B. The Superior Courts — The High Court and the Supreme Court

Article 34.3 and Article 34.4 set out the key powers and functions of the High Court and Supreme Court.

Article 34.3.1° provides:

> The courts of first instance shall include a High Court invested with full original jurisdiction in and power to determine all matters and questions whether of law or fact, civil or criminal.

Article 34.3.2° provides:

> Save as otherwise provided by this Article, the jurisdiction of the High Court shall extend to the validity of any law having regard to the provisions of this Constitution, and no such question shall be raised (whether by pleading, argument or otherwise) in any court established under this or any other Article of this Constitution other than the High Court or the Supreme Court.

Article 34.4.1° provides:

> The Court of Final Appeal shall be called the Supreme Court.

Article 34.4.3° provides:

> The Supreme Court shall, with such exceptions and subject to such regulations as may be prescribed by law, have appellate jurisdiction from all decisions of the High Court, and shall also have appellate jurisdiction from such decisions of the courts as may be prescribed by law.

Article 34.4.4° provides:

> No law shall be enacted excepting from the jurisdiction of the Supreme Court cases which involve questions as to the validity of any law having regard to the provisions of this Constitution.

The High Court is therefore conferred with "full original jurisdiction in and power to determine all matters and questions whether of law or fact, civil or criminal". The High Court also has the power to determine whether any law is constitutionally valid. The Supreme Court, as the final court of appeal, has appellate jurisdiction from all decisions of the High Court. There is a constitutional prohibition on the Oireachtas introducing any law which limits the Supreme Court's appellate jurisdiction from the High Court in any case in which the constitutionality of a law is in issue. The Constitution envisages that the Supreme Court may also be a final court of appeal from courts other than the High Court.

Since the High Court and Supreme Court are specifically identified in the Constitution, it follows that neither can be abolished by statute — only by constitutional amendment. This protection does not apply to courts not specifically identified, namely courts of 'local and limited jurisdiction'.

The reference to 'full original jurisdiction' in relation to the High Court in Article 34.3.1° implies that its jurisdiction goes further than that which is expressly conferred by statute. This is consistent with the fact that judges of the High Court and Supreme Court occasionally exercise the 'inherent jurisdiction' of those courts. The concept of 'inherent jurisdiction' relates to powers exercised by the High Court in the pre-1922 court system when Ireland was part of the United Kingdom. The Court of King's Bench exercised certain 'inherent' powers arising from the royal prerogative. These powers were considered to be intrinsic to the Court because they were not conferred by statute. An example of the apparent exercise of inherent jurisdiction in the Supreme Court occurred in *Holohan v Donohoe* [1986] IR 45. In that case, the Supreme Court held that it could, where the circumstances required, substitute its own award of damages for that given by the High Court, even though it had not been expressly conferred with such power by statute.

C. Courts of Local and Limited Jurisdiction
Article 34.3.4° provides:

> The Courts of First Instance shall also include Courts of local and limited jurisdiction with a right of appeal as determined by law.

This provision provides for the establishment of courts other than the High Court and the Supreme Court. The 1922 Constitution and the Courts of Justice Act 1924 created the Circuit Court and District Court. The 1937 Constitution ensured their continuation under the new Constitution. They were formally re-established by the Courts (Establishment and Constitution) Act 1961. As is clear from the wording of Article 34.3.4°, these courts do not have the 'full' jurisdiction with which the High Court and the Supreme Court are endowed. The term 'local and limited' indicates that their jurisdiction would be limited in terms of geography and the seriousness of the cases they could hear. Since they are created by statute, it follows that their powers derive from statute only.

D. Statutory Regulation of Court Business

Article 36 of the Constitution allows for the statutory regulation of such matters as the number of judges of the High Court and Supreme Court, their remuneration, retirement age and pension entitlements. It also allows for regulation of the number of the judges of all other courts and their terms of appointment, the constitution and organisation of the courts, the distribution of jurisdiction and business among the courts and judges, and all matters of procedure.

E. Jurisdiction of the Courts — First Instance and Appellate

First Instance Jurisdiction of the Courts

The first instance, or original, jurisdiction of the courts concerns the designation by law of a court to hear a particular matter in the first place. The statutory bases for this element of the courts' jurisdiction are the Courts of Justice Act 1924, the Courts (Supplemental Provisions) Act 1961, the Courts and Court Officers (Amendment) Act 2007 and the Courts and Civil Law (Miscellaneous Provisions) Act 2013. In addition, a number of pre-independence statutes contain important provisions setting out the jurisdiction of the courts in Ireland, in particular the Petty Sessions (Ireland) Act 1851, the Summary Jurisdiction Act 1857 and the Supreme Court of Judicature (Ireland) Act 1877.

Appellate Jurisdiction of the Courts

The Constitutional Framework

Article 34.3.4° provides that courts of local and limited jurisdiction are to have a right of appeal as may be determined by law. Article 34.4.3° provides that the Supreme Court has appellate jurisdiction from all decisions of the High Court "with such exceptions and subject to such regulations as may be prescribed by law". Legislation has augmented these provisions.

There are two types of appeal which may be made in the Irish legal system: full rehearing (*de novo* hearing) and appeal on a point of law.

De Novo Hearing

A *de novo* hearing takes place where the case is reheard in full in a higher court. *De novo* hearings are possible in respect of cases heard at first instance in the District Court or the Circuit Court. A *de novo* hearing in the Circuit Court following an appeal from the District Court will be heard in full, including any oral evidence from witnesses. This gives the appellant the opportunity effectively to re-run the trial in the Circuit Court. However, whilst the Circuit Court may reach a different decision from that reached in the District Court, its jurisdiction is confined to that which is conferred on the District Court.

Appeal on a Point of Law

An appeal on a point of law involves the higher court determining a matter of law only. Matters of fact will not generally be re-opened. The appellate court will not hear oral evidence from witnesses. It will review a transcript of the evidence as taken by the stenographer at the trial which is subject to appeal. The appellate court will examine the findings of fact made by the lower court and will therefore be in a position to determine whether the findings of fact are supported by the evidence which was given before the lower court. If the appellate court is satisfied that the evidence given provides a foundation for the findings of fact made, it will not generally interfere with those findings. This is because the appellate court does not have the advantage of observing the demeanour of witnesses as they give evidence. The trier of fact in the lower court would have been able to do this and would therefore have been in a better position than the appellate court to ascertain the veracity and persuasiveness of the witnesses.

Findings of Fact

For the purpose of an appeal, facts may be divided into two categories. First, there are primary or basic facts. These are determinations of fact depending on the assessment by the trial judge of the credibility and quality of the witnesses. It is for the determination of those facts that an oral hearing takes place. Because the finding of those facts depends upon the oral evidence accepted by the trial judge, the appellate court will not normally interfere with those findings. This is so even if the appellate court deems different findings to be more appropriate, or even if the findings made seem to the appellate court to be incorrect. It is only when the findings of primary fact cannot reasonably be held to be supported by the evidence that the appellate court will interfere.

Secondly, there are secondary, or inferred, facts. These are facts which do not follow directly from an assessment or evaluation of the credibility of the witnesses or the weight to be attached to their evidence. Instead they derive from inferences drawn from the primary facts. Once the primary facts have been established by oral evidence at trial, their consequences or implications for the purpose of the matters in issue must be determined by a process of deduction from the facts found or admitted, rather than by an assessment of the witnesses or of the weight or persuasiveness of their evidence. In regard to such secondary facts, the advantage of the trial judge who sees and hears the witnesses is less important. Consequently, the appellate court will feel free to draw its own inferences if it considers that the inferences drawn by the trial judge were not correct. Such secondary facts include all matters which are derived from the primary facts.

An example of an appellate court drawing different inferences from findings of primary fact by a lower court is *Hanrahan v Merck Sharp & Dohme Ltd* [1988] ILRM 629. In that case, the plaintiffs were dairy farmers. They, and their farm animals, suffered respiratory illnesses. They claimed in an action before the High Court that the illnesses were caused by emissions from the defendant's factory. After evaluating the scientific evidence adduced by the defendant and the expert and sensory evidence adduced by the plaintiff, the High Court judge concluded that the plaintiffs had failed to discharge the burden of proof, so they lost their case. On appeal, the Supreme Court took the view that the High Court judge should have given less priority to the defendant's scientific evidence and more weight to the plaintiff's expert evidence and direct sensory evidence. On this basis, whilst not disturbing the findings of primary fact, the Supreme Court drew different inferences from the evidence and largely found for the plaintiff, substantially reversing the decision of the High Court (see generally *Northern Bank Finance Corporation Ltd v Charlton* [1979] IR 149; *Browne v Bank of Ireland Finance Ltd* [1991] 1 IR 431; *Hay v O'Grady* [1992] 1 IR 210; *M v M* [1979] ILRM 160; *Norris v Attorney General* [1984] IR 36, per Henchy J; *In Re DG, an Infant; OG v An Bord Úchtála* [1991] 1 IR 491; and *JM and GM v An Bord Úchtála* [1988] ILRM 203).

CHAPTER FOURTEEN

Civil Courts: Jurisdiction and Procedure

A. Introduction 250
B. The First Instance Jurisdiction of the Courts in Civil Cases 250
    The District Court..250
        General 250
        General and Monetary Jurisdiction..251
        Family Proceedings 251
        Commercial and Consumer Protection — General Jurisdiction.............251
        Commercial and Consumer Protection — Small Claims Jurisdiction ...251
        Environmental Matters 251
        Renewal of Intoxicating Liquor Licences 252
        Land and Equity Matters...252
    The Circuit Court..252
        General 252
        General and Monetary Jurisdiction..252
        Family Proceedings 253
        Environmental Matters 253
        New Intoxicating Liquor Licences 253
        Commercial and Consumer Protection 254
        Land and Equity Matters...254
        Landlord and Tenant..254
        Malicious Injuries 254
        Local Government Elections and Petitions 254
    The High Court...254
        General 254
        General Monetary Jurisdiction 255
        Constitutional Cases...255
        Judicial Review 255
        Family Proceedings 256
        Company and Personal Insolvency Matters..256
        The Commercial Court...256
        Equity and Chancery Matters 257
        Wardship...257
        Oireachtas Election and Referendum Petitions...257

The Supreme Court 258
   General 258
   Incapacity of the President 258
   Reference of Bills by the President to the Supreme Court........................258
C. **Appellate Jurisdiction of the Courts in Civil Cases** 259
   Civil Cases Originating in the District Court..259
   Civil Cases Originating in the Circuit Court..260
   Civil Cases Originating in the High Court 260
   Court of Justice of the European Union...261
D. **Civil Process** 266
   Procedure in Civil Litigation 266
      Pleadings — Introduction..266
      High Court Pleadings 267
      Circuit Court Pleadings 268
      District Court Pleadings 269
      Settlement of Cases..269
      Payments into Court 269
      Reforms to the Civil Justice System 270

Civil Courts: Jurisdiction and Procedure

Learning Outcomes

Upon completion of this chapter, students will be able to:

- Identify the basis of jurisdiction in the civil courts;
- Explain the first instance jurisdiction of the Irish courts in civil cases;
- Discuss the appellate jurisdiction of the Irish courts in civil cases;
- Describe the main rules of legal procedure in civil cases;
- Identify the remedies which may be awarded by the courts in civil cases and discuss the basis upon which those remedies are awarded.

A. Introduction

This chapter examines the jurisdiction of the Irish courts to resolve civil disputes between parties. It also examines procedure used in civil cases and the remedies which may be awarded by the courts where they are satisfied on the balance of probability that a civil wrong has been proven.

B. The First Instance Jurisdiction of the Courts in Civil Cases

The first instance, or original, jurisdiction of the courts concerns the designation by law of a court to hear a particular matter in the first place. Three courts have first instance jurisdiction to hear civil cases in Ireland. They are the High Court, the Circuit Court and the District Court.

The Courts and Civil Law (Miscellaneous Provisions) Act 2013 was signed into law by the President on 24 July 2013. Part 3 of the Act amends the monetary jurisdiction of the District Court and Circuit Court. At the time of writing, Part 3 of the Act has not been brought into force. The civil jurisdiction of the District Court in contract and most other matters is, for the time being, where the claim or award does not exceed €6,348.69. The 2013 Act will increase this to €15,000. With regard to the Circuit Court, its civil jurisdiction is a limited one unless all parties to an action consent, in which case the jurisdiction is unlimited. Otherwise, the limit of the Circuit Court's jurisdiction, for the time being, relates mainly to actions where the claim does not exceed €38,092.14 and the rateable valuation of land does not exceed €254. The 2013 Act will increase the Circuit Court's monetary jurisdiction from €38,092.14 to €75,000, except in personal injuries actions, which will be capped at €60,000. The monetary jurisdiction limits mentioned below are those that are in force as at July 2013.

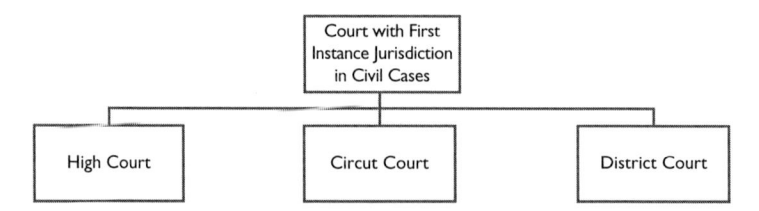

```
            Court with First
           Instance Jurisdiction
              in Civil Cases
    ┌───────────────┼───────────────┐
 High Court     Circut Court    District Court
```

The District Court

General

The District Court is a court of local and limited jurisdiction within the meaning of Article 34.3.4° of the Constitution. It derives its jurisdiction from statute, primarily s 77 of the Courts of Justice Act 1924, carried forward by s 33 of the Courts (Supplemental Provisions) Act 1961 as amended, and s 4 of the Courts Act 1991.

General and Monetary Jurisdiction

The District Court is empowered to award damages not exceeding €6,348.69 in cases of contract, breach of contract and tort cases (except the tort of defamation, seduction, malicious prosecution and false imprisonment). Where the parties to an action before the District Court consent in writing, the Court is conferred with jurisdiction in excess of this limit by virtue of the s 4 (c) of the Courts Act 1991.

Family Proceedings

In family law proceedings, the District Court's jurisdiction is limited. It does not have jurisdiction to grant a decree of divorce, judicial separation or nullity. These matters are reserved for the Circuit Court and High Court. However, where judicial separation proceedings have already been initiated, the parties may apply to the District Court for variation of maintenance. The court, in the circumstances, may award maintenance to a spouse up to a maximum of €500 per week and to a maximum of €150 per week per child. The court also has jurisdiction relating to the disposal of household chattels up to a value of €6,348.69 in proceedings under s 9 of the Family Home Protection Act 1976.

Commercial and Consumer Protection — General Jurisdiction

The District Court has jurisdiction to deal with civil claims under the Hotel Proprietors Act 1963 and the Consumer Credit Act 1995. Such claims are subject to the €6,348.69 limit as to the amount of damages that may be awarded.

Commercial and Consumer Protection — Small Claims Jurisdiction

The small claims procedure is set out in Ord 53A of the District Court Rules 1997. The rules provide for an initial application to the Small Claims Registrar, a clerk of the District Court. He or she is empowered to attempt to reach a compromise between the parties in dispute. The application can be made online. A fee of €25 applies. A small claim is defined as one involving a claim not exceeding €2,000. It must come within one of the three categories of claim in Ord 53A. These are:

- Consumer contracts, such as the retail purchase of goods, but not a claim arising from an alleged breach of a hire purchase or leasing agreement;
- A minor property damage claim in tort, provided the claimant is not a body corporate and excluding personal injuries claims; and
- A claim by a tenant for the return of rent deposit or any sum known as *key money*, unless the claim is a dispute which can be referred to the Private Residential Tenancies Board.

Environmental Matters

The District Court has jurisdiction to deal with claims for damages arising under the Local Government (Water Pollution) Acts 1977 and 1990. Such claims are subject to the €6,348.69 limit for an award in damages.

Renewal of Intoxicating Liquor Licences

Normally, the holder of an intoxicating liquor licence may obtain a renewal of most liquor licences from the Revenue Commissioners. However, such a licence holder must make an application to the District Court to obtain a certificate stating that he or she is a fit person to continue to hold a licence only in certain circumstances, for example, where an objection is made in relation to the licence renewal.

Land and Equity Matters

The District Court's jurisdiction is limited to cases of ejectment for non-payment of rent or overholding in any class of tenancy, provided that the rent does not exceed €6,358.69 per annum. The District Court does not have jurisdiction to determine title to property: nor does it have jurisdiction in relation to other connected matters generally described as the equity jurisdiction.

The Circuit Court

General

The Circuit Court, like the District Court, is a court of local and limited jurisdiction within the meaning of Article 34.3.3°. It can only deal with matters which have been expressly assigned to it by legislation.

General and Monetary Jurisdiction

By virtue of s 22 of the Courts (Supplemental Provisions) Act 1961, the Circuit Court is conferred with the same jurisdiction as that exercised by the High Court in a number of areas. These are set out in the Third Schedule to the 1961 Act. The Circuit Court's jurisdiction extends to all claims in contract or tort, including those which are made outside the jurisdiction of the District Court, namely the tort of defamation, seduction, slander of title, malicious prosecution and false imprisonment.

There are two limitations on the jurisdiction of the Circuit Court. First, it is limited to an award of damages not exceeding €38,092.14. However, parties to an action can, if they consent, confer unlimited jurisdiction on that court. A similar provision exists in relation to a civil claim in the District Court. The Circuit Court also has exclusive and unlimited jurisdiction in applications for new commercial tenancies. The Court may also award unlimited compensation in claims relating to discrimination on grounds of gender.

The Circuit Court is precluded from hearing matters at first instance where exclusive jurisdiction is given to another court in those matters. For example, s 22 of the Courts (Supplemental Provisions) Act 1961 confers extensive jurisdiction on the Circuit Court concurrently with the High Court. However, Article 34.3.2° of the Constitution confers exclusive jurisdiction on the High Court in determining the constitutional validity of any law. Similarly, s 4 of the Courts (No 2) Act 1986 has conferred on the District Court exclusive jurisdiction in the renewal of intoxicating liquor licences. The Circuit Court may not therefore hear such applications at first instance.

Family Proceedings
Section 5 of the Courts Act 1981 conferred on the Circuit Court the jurisdiction to award a decree of divorce *a mensa et thoro*, or 'judicial separation' (Judicial Separation and Family Law Reform Act 1989). The objective of the 1981 Act appears to have been that all such cases be heard in the Circuit Court. However, it was held in *R v R* [1984] IR 296 that the High Court had concurrent jurisdiction in these areas by virtue of its inherent jurisdiction conferred by Article 34.3.2° of the Constitution. The plaintiff in that case was seeking various orders against her husband. She wished to bring proceedings in the High Court. She sought custody of, and maintenance for, the children; maintenance for herself; and an order barring her husband from the matrimonial home. The lower courts, under the relevant statutes, clearly had jurisdiction over these matters. They were the only courts mentioned in the statutes as having jurisdiction. The question to be determined was whether the High Court was excluded. If it was, was this constitutionally permissible? The High Court held that the statutes in question were to be construed in accordance with the presumption of constitutionality. They could be declared invalid only if they were incapable of interpretation and effective implementation consistent with the Constitution. The statutes, however, contained nothing restricting or removing any jurisdiction from the High Court. By virtue of Article 34.3.1°, the High Court retained jurisdiction over claims such as the plaintiff's. However, it was open to the High Court to decline to hear the proceedings on the grounds that relief was available in the lower courts. The Judicial Separation and Family Law Reform Act 1989 gave legislative effect to the decision in *R v R* by conferring concurrent jurisdiction on the Circuit Court and High Court in judicial separation proceedings. Section 53 of the Courts and Court Officers Act 1985 conferred, for the first time, jurisdiction on the Circuit Court in nullity cases. Section 38 of the Family Law (Divorce) Act 1996 conferred jurisdiction on the Circuit Court in divorce cases. This jurisdiction is concurrent with the High Court.

Environmental Matters
The Circuit Court, like the District Court, is empowered to deal with claims for damages arising under the Local Government (Water Pollution) Acts 1977 and 1990. The Circuit Court limit in respect of claims and awards of €38,092.14 applies.

New Intoxicating Liquor Licences
The Circuit Court has exclusive jurisdiction to hear applications for new intoxicating liquor 'on-licences' within the meaning of the Licensing Acts 1833 to

2004. The District Court has exclusive jurisdiction in respect of applications for renewal of intoxicating liquor licences (see above).

Commercial and Consumer Protection

The Circuit Court, along with the District Court, is empowered to deal with civil claims under the Hotel Proprietors Act 1963 and the Consumer Credit Act 1995. The Circuit Court limit in respect of claims and awards of €38,092.14 applies.

Land and Equity Matters

The Circuit Court has jurisdiction in matters relating to title to land and certain actions for ejectment where the rateable valuation of the land does not exceed €254. In cases involving the grant of probate or the administration of an estate, the dissolution of a partnership, the specific performance of contracts, the partition or sale of land or an action relating to property in which an injunction is sought, the Circuit Court has jurisdiction where the subject matter does not exceed €38,092.14.

Landlord and Tenant

The Circuit Court has jurisdiction to determine claims for new leases irrespective of the amount of rent payable or the value of the property in question. This jurisdiction applies to both business and private leases. In cases where a claim is made in respect of arrears of rent, the Court's jurisdictional limit of €38,092.14 applies. In matters before the Court relating to land and equity, the jurisdiction of the court is where the rateable valuation of the land in question is not greater than €254.

Malicious Injuries

The Circuit Court has been conferred with exclusive jurisdiction by the Malicious Injuries Acts 1981 and 1986. Prior to 1986, property owners could claim compensation from local authorities for damage maliciously caused to their property. However, under the Malicious Injuries (Amendment) Act 1986, a claim may now only be made where the damage is caused in the course of a riot or arising from the activities of an unlawful organisation or an organisation advocating the use of violence related to Northern Ireland.

Local Government Elections and Petitions

The Local Elections (Petitions and Disqualifications) Act 1974, as amended, confers jurisdiction on the Circuit Court for the purpose of petitions challenging the validity of an election to a local authority.

The High Court

General

Article 34.3.1° of the Constitution confers the High Court with "full original jurisdiction in and power to determine all matters and questions whether of law or fact, civil or criminal". Notwithstanding the reference to "full original jurisdiction", the inferior courts can be, and have been, assigned functions over certain matters by statute. Article 34.3.1° has the effect of ensuring that the High Court retains at least some jurisdiction over matters in which the inferior courts appear to have been given exclusive first instance jurisdiction. The High Court's jurisdiction in this sense may be by way of appeal or through its supervisory role of judicial review. This issue was considered in *Tormey v Ireland* [1985] IR 289. In that case, the plaintiff had been returned for trial to the Circuit Criminal Court. He wished to be tried in the Central Criminal Court (the High Court). Section 31 of the Courts Act 1981 had removed the right to elect for trial in the Central Criminal Court. The plaintiff questioned whether s 31 of the 1981 Act was consistent with Article 34.3.1° which conferred "full original jurisdiction" on the High Court. The Supreme Court rejected the plaintiff's claim. It held that Article 34.3.1° should not be given a literal meaning. The Court took the view that the High Court retained an original jurisdiction under Article 34.3.1° through its power of judicial review of trials heard in the Circuit Court or through its power to make declaratory orders.

As we have seen in *R v R* [1984] IR 296, it was held that the High Court retained its 'full' jurisdiction under Article 34.4.1° even where the Courts Act 1981 had appeared to confer exclusive jurisdiction on the Circuit Court in certain family law matters. Consequently, there is doubt as to whether any statute which purports to confer exclusive jurisdiction upon the inferior courts in respect of an entire subject matter can be constitutionally valid having regard to Article 34.3.1° of the Constitution.

General Monetary Jurisdiction
The High Court is the appropriate court to hear cases involving claims for damages in excess of €38,092.14. This is the effect of s 2 of the Courts Act 1991 which sets the upper limit imposed on the jurisdiction of the Circuit Court.

Constitutional Cases
As we have seen, Article 34.3.2° of the Constitution confers on the High Court the exclusive jurisdiction to determine the constitutional validity of legislation. It is the only Court in the court system upon which such jurisdiction is conferred, apart from the Supreme Court which can hear such cases on appeal from the High Court. The Supreme Court has no first instance (original) jurisdiction in this area. Constitutional cases must go to the High Court first.

Judicial Review
Article 34.3.1° of the Constitution, which confers 'full' jurisdiction on the High Court, extends to it the general power to supervise the inferior courts and administrative decisions of public bodies and tribunals by way of judicial review. The High Court can review decisions of the inferior courts in relation to both civil and criminal matters. Judicial review of decisions of the inferior courts and

administrative decisions of public bodies seeks to ensure that those courts and administrative bodies stay within the jurisdiction conferred on them by law. In *Murren v Brennan* [1942] IR 466, Gavan Duffy J expressed the view that Article 34.3.1° confirmed and entrenched the supervisory jurisdiction of the High Court. He believed that statutory provisions purporting to exclude the High Court were invalid, in particular a statutory provision making a minister's decision on a legal matter 'final'. He said that such provisions could not "exclude the constitutional jurisdiction of the High Court in a case deemed by the High Court to call for interference" (at 476). That view appears to have been put beyond doubt by *Tormey v Ireland* [1985] IR 289.

Family Proceedings
The High Court has concurrent jurisdiction with the Circuit Court in respect of family law matters by virtue of the 'full' jurisdiction conferred on it by Article 34.3.1 of the Constitution. As we have seen, the court in *R v R* [1984] IR 296 has made this position clear. Consequently some divorce, judicial separation, and nullity cases are heard in the High Court, while others are heard in the Circuit Court.

Company and Personal Insolvency Matters
The Companies Act 1963 confers exclusive jurisdiction on the High Court in respect of the winding-up of companies established under that Act. Under the Companies Act 1990, the High Court has exclusive jurisdiction in respect of the appointment of an examiner to a company. Under the Bankruptcy Act 1988, the High Court has exclusive jurisdiction in dealing with bankruptcy cases, irrespective of the amount involved.

The Commercial Court
In 2004, the Rules of the Superior Courts (Commercial Proceedings) 2004 (SI No 2 of 2004) established the Commercial Court list. It is referred to as the 'Commercial Court'. This is an administratively separate list of commercial cases valued in excess of €1 million. It seeks to achieve the resolution of large-scale commercial litigation in a speedy and efficient manner. It uses 'judicial case management' to do so. This approach was advocated for England and Wales by Lord Woolf in his report *Access to Justice: Report to the Lord Chancellor on the Civil Justice System in England and Wales* ('The Woolf Report', July 1996). The Commercial Court applies pre-trial procedures which seek to identify key matters at issue between the parties at the earliest possible stage. Also, the presiding judge is empowered to adjourn the matter for up to 28 days to allow the parties to consider mediation, conciliation or arbitration. The judge may do this of his or her own motion or upon request by the parties. Case management conferences may be held prior to trial upon direction of

the judge. This is to seek to ensure that the proceedings are prepared for trial "in a manner which is just, expeditious and likely to minimise the cost of the proceedings" (Rules of the Superior Courts, Ord 63A, r 14 (1)). Pre-trial conferences may also be held in which the judge may determine what steps, if any, need to be taken in order to prepare the case for trial. At this stage, the judge may give directions in order to ensure that all necessary arrangements are made for trial. A trial date may also be set at this stage. Parties who delay may be subject to cost sanctions.

Equity and Chancery Matters

The High Court has jurisdiction over claims concerning land and land ownership. This jurisdiction is subject to the concurrent jurisdiction of the Circuit Court. Prior to 1922, chancery matters had been dealt with by the Chancery Division of the High Court. The High Court under the 1937 Constitution has no divisions as such. By contrast, the English High Court has three divisions: Chancery, Queen's Bench and Family. In Ireland, chancery matters are dealt with separately from other cases. They are heard by judges with expertise in this area. Chancery judges of the High Court also hear company law cases.

Wardship

Jurisdiction in wardship proceedings has been vested in the High Court. A person may be made a ward of court in circumstances where they are unable to look after themselves. They may be minors or persons suffering mental illness or brain injury. A person may be made a ward of court where it is thought desirable to obtain independent protection of their property interests. When a person is made a ward of court, all important matters affecting their welfare become the responsibility of the court. In wardship proceedings, the trial judge must decide issues relating to the welfare of the ward. The proceedings must be fair and in accordance with constitutional justice. The High Court is empowered to administer any property of the ward, as well as determine other matters concerning their future. The High Court's jurisdiction in wardship proceedings is derived originally from the Lunacy Regulation (Ireland) Act 1871. The Courts (Supplemental Provisions) Act 1961 describes the jurisdiction as lunacy and minor matters. Section 9 (4) of the 1961 Act provides that the words "ward of court" or "person of unsound mind" be substituted for the word "lunatic" in the 1871 Act.

Oireachtas Election and Referendum Petitions

Section 132 of the Electoral Act 1992 designates the High Court as the appropriate court to which petitions may be brought challenging the validity of any election to the Oireachtas. Similarly, s 42 of the Referendum Act 1994 designates the High Court as the court to which petitions may be brought challenging the validity of any referendum result.

The Supreme Court

General

The Supreme Court is the court of final appeal in Ireland. Its jurisdiction therefore is primarily appellate. However, it has two areas of first instance jurisdiction conferred on it by the Constitution: determining the incapacity of the President and Article 26 references. Apart from these two matters, the Supreme Court has no first instance jurisdiction.

Incapacity of the President

Under Article 12.3.1°, the Supreme Court may determine the permanent incapacity of the President. A Supreme Court of not less than five judges is required to determine that matter should it arise, which it has not.

Reference of Bills by the President to the Supreme Court

As mentioned, Article 26 empowers the President to refer a Bill — or any specified provision or provisions — to the Supreme Court for a ruling on its constitutional validity. Article 26 cannot be used in respect of Money Bills, Constitution amendment Bills or Bills passed under Article 24 (the abridgment provision). All other Bills will potentially fall within its scope. Such a reference must be made not later than seven days from the date of the Bill's presentation for signature (Article 26.1.2°).

The purpose of Article 26 is to provide a speedy decision-making process to determine the constitutional validity of a legislative proposal. The procedure involves the Supreme Court hearing arguments *pro* and *contra* the Bill's validity. The arguments are put by the Attorney General (or counsel on her behalf) and by counsel assigned by the court. Normally the Supreme Court assigns one team of counsel to argue against the validity of the Bill. There was one exception. In the case of the abortion information Bill, *In Re-Article 26 and the Regulation of Information (Services outside the State for Termination of Pregnancies) Bill 1995* [1995] 1 IR 1, the Court assigned one team to oppose the Bill on the basis of the right to life of the unborn and a second team to oppose it on the basis of the right to life of the mother.

A particular difficulty in Article 26 referrals is that the court has no concrete dispute between parties before it. Therefore it will not normally be able to consider evidence as to how the Bill might operate in practice. This means that the court conducts its proceedings in a necessarily hypothetical environment. It considers entirely abstract problems which are quite unlike other cases that come before the court. Unlike most ordinary cases, Article 26 references are characterised by an absence or shortage of concrete facts. The court therefore has to consider abstract materials in order adequately to examine the social, economic, fiscal and other features of the proposal that may be critical to an understanding of how the Bill will operate when enacted. These difficulties were expressed by Higgins CJ when he delivered the Court's judgment in *Re Article 26 and the Housing (Private Rented Dwellings) Bill 1981* [1983] IR 181. In that case, he expressed doubts about the appropriateness of the Article 26 machinery for certain types of Bill.

There are, however, advantages to the procedure. If a Bill was signed into law by the President without being referred under Article 26, there could be a long delay before a person with the requisite *locus standi* and the necessary resources to fund a challenge to the statute appeared. If the statute was invalidated many years after its enactment, there could be real difficulty untangling the many decisions made under it. An example is the Electoral (Amendment) Bill 1983. That Bill was held to be unconstitutional on an Article 26 reference (*The Electoral (Amendment) Bill 1983* [1984] IR 268). If that measure had been struck down as unconstitutional after becoming law and after a general election in which unqualified persons had voted, the consequences may have been significant.

C. Appellate Jurisdiction of the Courts in Civil Cases

Civil Cases Originating in the District Court

Both forms of appeal, i.e. an appeal *de novo* or an appeal on a point of law, are available for cases heard at first instance in the District Court. Either party may appeal to the High Court on a point of law. A further appeal to the Supreme Court on a point of law is also possible. Alternatively, either party may obtain a *de novo* hearing on appeal to the Circuit Court. In such cases, the decision of the Circuit Court is generally final, although that decision may be subject to judicial review to the High Court.

As mentioned above, an appeal on a point of law lies from the District Court to the High Court by way of case stated. A case stated takes the form of a written document which includes the question(s) of law to be determined by the High Court. Either party may make such a request while the case is in progress. This is known as a 'consultative case stated'. A request may also be made at the end of the District Court hearing when a final determination of the case has been made. A District Court judge must make a referral if requested. The question of law is then referred to, and considered by, the High Court. Its decision is then returned to the District Court for final determination of the matter. A District Court judge's refusal to state a case may itself be subject to judicial review.

On a consultative case stated, the decision of the High Court can be appealed from the High Court to the Supreme Court, but only if the High Court judge grants leave. However, on a case stated to the High Court after the District Court has made a final determination, a further appeal may be made to the Supreme Court without the need to seek leave from the High Court judge. Appeal by way of case stated after final determination in the District Court is therefore more common.

Figure 14.1 Civil Appeals from the District Court

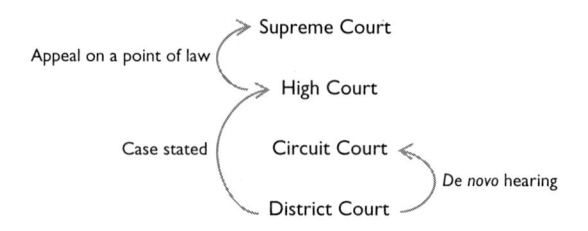

```
                              → Supreme Court
        Appeal on a point of law (
                              → High Court

        Case stated ( Circuit Court ←
                                    ) De novo hearing
                      District Court
```

Civil Cases Originating in the Circuit Court

Either party to civil proceedings before the Circuit Court may seek a *de novo* hearing in the High Court. There is no further appeal from the High Court to the Supreme Court as of right. However, if either party applies to the High Court judge for leave to appeal to the Supreme Court, the judge may refer any question of law to the Supreme Court if he or she thinks it proper to do so. If such a referral takes place, the High Court judge must adjourn making a final decision in the case.

Alternatively, either party in an action before the Circuit Court may appeal on a point of law to the Supreme Court by way of case stated. If such an appeal is made, the Circuit Court judge must adjourn making a final decision in the case, although he or she may continue to hear evidence. The question of law referred is considered by the Supreme Court and then remitted to the Circuit Court for final determination of the matter.

Figure 14.2 Civil Appeals from the Circuit Court

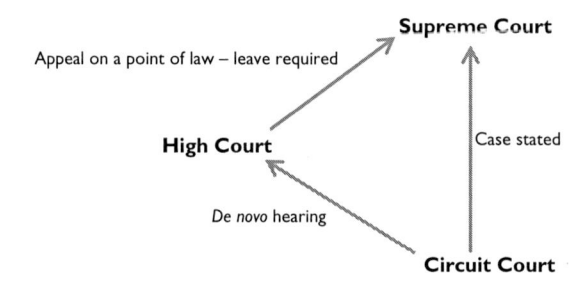

```
                                           Supreme Court
                                                ↑
   Appeal on a point of law – leave required ↗
                                                    Case stated
              High Court
                      ↖
                       De novo hearing
                                           Circuit Court
```

Civil Cases Originating in the High Court

An appeal on a point of law to the Supreme Court is the only appeal available in respect of cases originating in the High Court. By virtue of Article 34.4.4°, the

Supreme Court always has jurisdiction to hear appeals from the High Court in constitutional matters. Article 34.4.3° creates an appellate jurisdiction in the Supreme Court "from all decisions of the High Court", subject to "such exceptions and... regulations as may be prescribed by law". It is therefore constitutionally permissible for the Oireachtas to legislate for exceptions to the Supreme Court's jurisdiction, except for constitutional matters.

Appeals from the High Court to the Supreme Court in cases involving claims for damages will usually centre on liability and/or quantum. If the Supreme Court allows an appeal on the issue of liability, it may order a retrial of the matter in the High Court. If it allows an appeal on the issue of quantum, it may, instead of referring the matter back to the High Court, determine the appropriate quantum of damages itself. In these circumstances, the Supreme Court is said to exercise its inherent jurisdiction under Article 34.4.3° of the Constitution.

Figure 14.3 Civil Appeals from the High Court

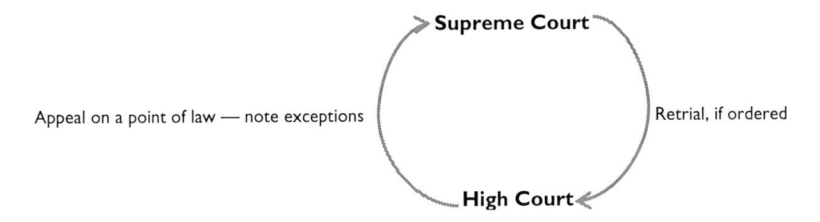

Supreme Court

Appeal on a point of law — note exceptions

Retrial, if ordered

High Court

Court of Justice of the European Union
The Court of Justice of the European Union (CJEU) interprets EU law to ensure it is applied in the same way in all EU Member States. It also settles legal disputes between EU governments and EU institutions. Individuals, companies or organisations can also bring cases before the Court if they feel their rights have been infringed by an EU institution. The Court has one judge per Member State. It is assisted by eight 'advocates-general' whose function is to present opinions on the cases brought before the Court. They must do so publicly and impartially. The reasoned opinions do not bind the judges of the Court. The Court issues single rulings with no dissenting judgments.

Each judge and advocate-general is appointed for a term of six years, which can be renewed. The governments of EU Member States agree on whom they wish to appoint. To help the Court cope with the large number of cases brought before it, a General Court deals with cases brought forward by private individuals, companies and some organisations, and cases relating to competition law. In addition, the EU Civil Service Tribunal rules on disputes between the EU and its staff.

The development of the EU legal order has largely been achieved through the co-operation of the CJEU and the domestic courts through the preliminary rulings procedure under Article 267 of the Treaty on the Functioning of the European Union (TFEU). These rulings are usually made following a preliminary reference from a Member State's courts. The CJEU has jurisdiction to give preliminary rulings concerning the interpretation of the treaties, the validity and interpretation of acts of the EU institutions and certain other matters. The preliminary rulings procedure is the primary mechanism through which the CJEU offers guidance to domestic courts and tribunals as to the meaning and effect of EU law. Questions referred to the CJEU must be limited to the interpretation or validity of a provision of EU law because the CJEU does not have jurisdiction to interpret domestic law or determine its validity.

Article 267 TFEU states that a court or tribunal of a Member State may make a preliminary reference. The Treaty does not define 'court or tribunal'. The CJEU has however laid down guidelines in its case law. It has said that a body need not be classified as a court in domestic law in order to be a court or tribunal for the purposes of making preliminary references. In *Doris Saltzmann* (Case C-178/99) [2001] ECR I–4421, the CJEU said that the following factors were to be taken into account in determining whether a body is a court or tribunal for the purposes of making a reference:

- Whether the body is a permanent body;
- Whether it is exercising functions of a judicial nature;
- Whether its jurisdiction is compulsory (in this sense, arbitrators are not courts or tribunals as their jurisdiction derives, not from a compulsory regime, but the terms of a private contract);
- Whether the body is independent;
- Whether the body's procedure is *inter partes*;
- Whether the body applies rules of law.

An example of the CJEU's reasoning in this area is *Broekmeulen v Huisarts Registratie Commissie* (Case 246/80) [1981] ECR 2311. In that case, a Dutch citizen qualified as a doctor in Belgium. He applied to register as a medical practitioner in Holland. His application was refused by the Dutch Medical Association (DMA). He appealed to the Dutch Appeals Committee for General Medicine. Both of these bodies were private associations. In practice, it was not possible for him to practise in Holland without registration by the DMA. When the appeal came before the appeals committee, it made a preliminary reference. The committee was not regarded as a court under Dutch law. However, its proceedings were adversarial in character, it allowed legal representation and its decisions, even though subject to a right of appeal to the domestic courts, were regarded as final. The CJEU held that the Appeals Committee was a 'court or tribunal' within the meaning of Article 267. Therefore it was entitled to make a reference. The CJEU also referred to the quasi-judicial nature of the proceedings before the committee, and the fact that it was exercising functions of a public or quasi-public nature which could affect the exercise of EU rights — in this case free movement of persons within the EU.

Although any court or tribunal may refer questions to the CJEU under Article 267, a distinction must be made between those courts or tribunals which *may* refer and those which *must*. Under Article 267(3), where a question concerning the interpretation of EU law is raised

> in a case pending before a court or tribunal of a Member State, against whose decisions there is no judicial remedy under national law, that court or tribunal shall bring the matter before the [CJEU].

Thus, for all courts other than those covered by Article 267(3), referral is discretionary. In most cases, therefore, national courts have a choice as to whether to refer questions to the CJEU. As we have seen, decisions of domestic courts which are disputed may be appealed through the domestic appeals system. It is only when a case can go no further within the domestic legal system that the mandatory obligation to refer under Article 267 arises. In Ireland, the Supreme Court is the final court of appeal for Irish cases; consequently an obligation to refer will arise in relation to cases before it where a matter of EU law is in issue. It is, however, possible for a court below the Supreme Court to be a court "against whose decisions there is no judicial remedy under national law". This might happen if leave to appeal is required and that leave is refused. It is thought that, in such circumstances, because that case can go no further, Article 267(3) would apply and the obligation to refer would arise. This occurred in *Costa v ENEL* (Case 6/64) [1964] ECR 585; [1964] CMLR 425 where a decision of the Italian magistrates' court could not be appealed because the sum of money involved in the case was too small. In *Lyckeskog, Criminal Proceedings* (Case C-99/00) [2002] ECR I-4839, the CJEU held that, where there was a right for a party to seek to appeal against the decision under challenge, that was not a final court. It followed that, if there was no right to appeal against the decision, then that court was a 'final court' for the purposes of Article 267(3). This would be so irrespective of that court's position in the judicial hierarchy.

As we have seen, in general, a 'final' court or tribunal must make a reference where a ruling on the interpretation of EU law is necessary to enable it to make a decision in the matter. However, where there has been a previous ruling on a point of EU law, there will be no need for a domestic court to refer the same point to the CJEU again (see *Da Costa en Schaake NV v Nederlandse-Belastingadministratie*

(Cases 28-30/62) [1963] ECR 31; [1963] CMLR 224 and *CILFIT Srl v Ministero della Sanitá* (Case 283/81) [1982] ECR 3515, [1983] 1 CMLR 472). Similarly, the court or tribunal need not refer if the doctrine of *acte clair* applies. That is, the meaning of the provision of EU law in question is so clear that no reference is necessary. As mentioned, this is so even in respect of matters before courts of final appeal or courts against whose decision no appeal is available. In *CILFIT*, the CJEU summarised its case law by saying that there was no need to refer if the matter was (a) irrelevant, (b) materially identical to a question already the subject of a preliminary ruling, or (c) so obvious as to leave "no scope for reasonable doubt".

In Ireland, no appeal is possible against a decision of an Irish court or tribunal to refer, or not to refer, a question by way of preliminary reference to the CJEU. The Supreme Court in *Campus Oil v Minister for Energy & Others* [1983] IR 88 made this clear. In that case, the High Court made a reference to the CJEU seeking an interpretation of certain treaty provisions. Walsh J rejected an attempt by the defendants to have the Supreme Court overturn the High Court's decision to refer to the CJEU. He said:

> The [domestic] judge has an untrammelled discretion as to whether he will or will not refer questions for a preliminary ruling under Article [267] and in doing so he is not in any way subject to the parties or any other judicial authority.

It is clear therefore that it is within the exclusive discretion of the trial judge to refer or not, as the case may be.

In addition, while the domestic judge may consult and seek the assistance of counsel in framing the wording of a reference, the judge is not required to consult anyone, not even the parties, if he or she does not wish to do so. The precise wording of the reference is entirely a matter for the domestic judge. In practice, the reference may be made by the judge at the invitation of one or other of the parties, though the judge can make the reference of his or her own volition — even if both parties object.

Therefore, since parties in proceedings before an Irish court have no automatic right to a preliminary reference to the CJEU, the CJEU cannot be said to have appellate jurisdiction in respect of Irish cases. Once the CJEU makes its ruling, the domestic court is nevertheless obliged to apply it; but the application of that ruling is exclusively a matter for the domestic court. It should be noted however that, if a domestic court of a Member State fails to apply EU law, including rulings of the CJEU, that Member State can be brought before the CJEU by the European Commission for failing to fulfil its treaty obligations.

Summary of the Civil Jurisdiction of the Courts

Civil Jurisdiction of the Courts	
Court	Main Areas of Jurisdiction
Supreme Court	• Appeals from decisions of the High Court in proceedings commenced in the High Court; • Matters referred to it by way of case stated from the Circuit Court or High Court; • Article 12 of the Constitution — the Court, consisting of not less than five judges, can establish whether the President of Ireland has become permanently incapacitated; • Article 26 of the Constitution — the Court may receive a reference by the President (after consultation with the Council of State) of Bills of the type prescribed in the Article for a decision as to whether any such Bill or specified provision or provisions of the Bill is or are repugnant to the Constitution.
High Court	• Power to determine all matters and questions whether of law or fact; • Power to determine the constitutional validity of any law; • Appeals from the Circuit Court; • Judicial review of the decisions of certain tribunals, public bodies and inferior courts; • Power to make rulings on questions of law submitted by the District Court.
Circuit Court	• Limited jurisdiction unless all parties to an action consent, in which event the jurisdiction is unlimited; • Actions where the claim does not exceed €38,092.14; • Rateable valuation of land does not exceed €252.95; • Family law proceedings: e.g. judicial separation, divorce, nullity and appeals from the District Court on these matters — custody and access orders, maintenance and barring orders; • Applications for protection and barring orders made directly to the Court; • Applications to dispense with the three month notice period of marriage; • Appeals from decisions of the District Court with some exceptions — appeals proceed by way of a full rehearing — the decision of the Circuit Court is final; • Appeals from the decisions of the Labour Court and the Employment Appeals Tribunal.

Court	Main Areas of Jurisdiction
District Court	• Claims/awards not exceeding €6,348.69; • Safety orders and barring orders under the Domestic Violence Act 1996 and 2002; • Custody and access orders and the appointment of guardians under the Guardianship of Infants Act 1964, as amended by the Status of Children Act 1987; • Award of maintenance to a spouse and child(ren) under the Maintenance of Spouses and Children Act 1976 (as amended); the maximum that can be awarded to a spouse is €500 per week and for a child € 150 per week; the court can direct that all payments be made through the District Court office, make attachment of earnings orders or issue a warrant for the arrest of the defaulting debtor; • Orders under the Child Care Act 1991, on application from the HSE; • Licensing: liquor and lottery.

D. Civil Process

Procedure in Civil Litigation

Pleadings — Introduction

Pleadings are the formal written documents used in civil actions by the plaintiff or defendant which set out their claims. They are usually drafted by counsel and delivered alternatively by the parties to each other. They set out the allegations of fact upon which the parties to the action base their case. The primary purpose of pleadings is to delineate the issues between the parties and to ensure that the parties know the case they have to meet and that they will not be put at a disadvantage by the introduction of matters which are not set out in the pleadings. Pleadings should generally not contain matters of law. The High Court in *Hanley v Newsgroup Newspapers Ltd* [2004] 1 IR 471 stated that

> The function of pleadings is to ascertain with precision the matters upon which the parties differ and the points on which they agree and thus to arrive at certain clear issues on which both parties require a judicial decision.

Pleadings must be accurately drafted. Poor drafting can result in dismissal of the action by the court. This could have serious consequences for the plaintiff if the relevant limitation period expires before the error is detected thereby precluding the initiation of fresh proceedings.

High Court Pleadings

Pleadings in the High Court include an originating summons, statement of claim, defence, counterclaim, reply and petition. These are set out in the Rules of the Superior Courts (RSC) 1986, Ord 125, r 1.

A petition is a written application to the court for a remedy. It is used to commence proceedings in particular cases, e.g. in matters relating to the Companies Acts. These might be petitions for bankruptcy or winding up, or matters relating to matrimonial causes, patents, wardship proceedings or matters concerning professional disciplinary bodies.

An originating summons may be plenary, summary or special. A plenary summons is used for cases requiring pleadings and oral evidence. It must be used for certain types of claims e.g. claims for unliquidated damages (i.e. unascertained damages to be determined by the court). The chief method by which facts contained in the plenary summons are disputed is by way of oral evidence. A summary summons is used for proceedings to be heard by way of affidavit. This would be used typically in claims for liquidated damages (i.e. a fixed and ascertained amount, usually set out in a contract) or for the recovery of possession of land. A special summons is used mainly for equity claims. These might relate to probate matters or the administration of trusts.

In personal injuries cases, the parties are required to swear a verifying affidavit to verify the truthfulness of the assertions in the pleadings. If it emerges that the contents of the pleadings are untrue, the party in question may have committed an offence under s 25 of the Civil Liability and Courts Act 2004. The plaintiff must lodge the verifying affidavit not later than 21 days after the service of summons. Similarly, the defendant must lodge a verifying affidavit not later than 21 days after the service of the defence, or later if the parties so agree or the court directs.

In response to a plenary summons, the defendant must enter an 'appearance'. This is a document which is an instruction to the court that an appearance should be entered for the defendant and that the defendant intends to defend the claim. The plaintiff then files his statement of claim. This is a written statement by the plaintiff stating the facts on which he relies to support his claim against the defendant. It also sets out the relief (remedy) he claims. The plaintiff may amend his statement of claim only once without leave (RSC Ord 28, r 2). The statement of claim must be served within 21 days after service of the summons. If the plaintiff fails to do this, the defendant may apply to dismiss the action for want of prosecution. There is no need for any further statement of the matters pleaded if they are pleaded in the statement of claim with sufficient particularity. The court may allow a plaintiff to alter or amend his pleadings at any stage in the proceedings, at which point unpleaded matters may be introduced, but only where the court considers that the amendments are necessary for the purpose of determining the real questions of controversy in the litigation (*Croke v Waterford Crystal* [2005] 1 ILRM 321) and, in the case of a late amendment to the statement of claim, there is no real injustice to the other party.

A defence is a written statement in reply to a statement of claim. It must be served by the defendant within 28 days of delivery of the statement of claim or from the time limited for appearance, whichever is later (RSC Ord 21, r 1). Facts which are not denied specifically or by necessary implication are taken to be admitted. If the defendant fails to serve a defence, the plaintiff may be permitted to enter judgment. The court may allow a defence to be amended if it can be done without injustice to the other party. If the defendant wishes to serve a counterclaim against the plaintiff, he must state the grounds supporting the counterclaim in his defence. The plaintiff may then answer a defence or counterclaim with a reply. A reply must be delivered within 14 days from delivery of the defence. A reply will not be necessary where all the material statements of fact in the relevant pleading are merely to be denied and put in issue (RSC Ord 23, r 1).

Once all pleadings have been served by all parties, pleadings are deemed closed. The action can then be set down for hearing and placed in the Legal Diary.

In the course of proceedings, either party is entitled to obtain possession of documents within the control of the other party through the process of 'discovery'. Discovery is normally obtained by application by one party to the other, in writing, requesting that discovery be made voluntarily. An order for discovery may be made by the court where one party has failed to make such discovery (RSC Ord 31, r 12).

In the pre-trial phase, one party may pose formal questions to the other party for an answer in order to further define a disputed matter. These are called 'interrogatories'. They are written questions, answerable on affidavit, which a party may, with leave, put to the other party to the proceedings. The objective is to obtain admissions and to limit the scope of the other party's case. They also seek to avoid unfairness where one party has the knowledge and ability to prove facts which are important to the opposing party's case and that party lacks the knowledge or ability to prove those facts.

Circuit Court Pleadings
In the Circuit Court, pleadings consist of the indorsement of claim on the Civil Bill, defence, or defence and counterclaim. The Civil Bill is similar in content and

structure to the statement of claim from the plaintiff in High Court proceedings. The defendant may file a defence, which is similar to the High Court defence. These are set out in the Circuit Court Rules 2001.

District Court Pleadings
In the District Court, the pleadings (although they are not described as such) consist of the civil summons, which sets out concisely the nature of the plaintiff's claim and the grounds upon which that claim is being made, notice of intention to defend, set-off or counterclaim, interpleader and third-party procedure (District Court Rules 1997).

Settlement of Cases
A significant number of civil claims do not progress to court hearings. This is because they are either settled or a compromise between the parties is reached. In many cases a letter before action, or a 'solicitor's letter', will be sufficient to bring about a settlement. Even where proceedings are initiated, settlements can be reached early on. However, it is not unknown for cases to be settled 'on the steps of the court'.

Such out-of-court settlements may be attractive when compared to the potential cost of going to trial. Some of the factors parties may take into account in deciding whether to settle include: the possible length of the trial and its attendant costs; the length of time it will take to get to trial; the risk of unfavourable publicity at trial; the possibility of having to disclose sensitive documents; and the risk of the costs of both sides being imposed on the losing party.

Payments into Court
Order 22, RSC sets out the procedure for payments into court in High Court actions. The purpose of this is to encourage early settlement of cases in order to avoid the expense and court time involved in a full trial. In effect, the defendant can make a payment into court in full and final settlement of the plaintiff's claim. This is referred to as a 'payment in' or a 'lodgment'. If the plaintiff fails or refuses to accept the payment in or fails at the full hearing of the action to obtain an award which is more than the sum paid in, the plaintiff will be penalised as to costs. In such circumstances, the plaintiff will have to bear his own costs from the date of payment in and also discharge the defendant's costs from that date, unless the court orders otherwise. A similar procedure is followed in the Circuit Court. The fact that a payment in has been made is not disclosed to the judge (or jury, if there is one) trying the case.

An example of the operation of the payment into court rules in England and Wales, which are similar to those in Ireland, is *Roache v News Group Newspapers Limited and Others* [1998] EMLR 161. In that case, the plaintiff, William Roache, was a well-known actor in the television drama series *Coronation Street*. The defendants had published an article in the *Sun* newspaper which claimed that he was boring, self-satisfied and hated by the other members of the cast. The plaintiff brought proceedings for libel. Three weeks before trial the defendants paid a total of £50,000 into court in full and final settlement of the plaintiff's claim. The plaintiff refused to accept and proceeded to full trial. At trial the jury awarded the plaintiff precisely the same sum — £50,000. The plaintiff sought an injunction against re-publication, which the defendants resisted. The trial judge granted the injunction. The plaintiff then asked for his costs of action while the defendants asked for their costs after the date of the payment in. The judge ordered that the plaintiff should have his costs since he had had to pursue the matter to judgment in order to obtain an injunction. The defendants appealed. The Court of Appeal held that the defendants had been the substantial winners at trial in that they had held the award to a sum no greater than what was already on offer. The Court of Appeal took the view that the injunction was of no significance because the defendants did not intend to re-publish anyway. In addition, the Court was satisfied that the main reason the plaintiff pursued the matter to full trial was for larger damages. Accordingly, the defendants were entitled to their costs from the date of the payment in. The plaintiff therefore had to pay his own legal costs of £120,000 plus the costs of the defendants from the date of the payment in. Mr Roache then sued his solicitors arguing that they had given him negligent advice. He lost that case too, by which time it is thought that his total costs had escalated to some £300,000 (*The Guardian*, Wednesday, 14 April 1999). Although this case is a rather extreme and unusual one, it does illustrate the risks plaintiffs may run in not accepting payments into court in full and final settlement of their claims.

Reforms to the Civil Justice System

In July 1996, Lord Woolf, the then Master of the Rolls (President of the Civil Division of the Court of Appeal for England and Wales), produced his final report to the Lord Chancellor on the civil justice system in England and Wales. It was entitled Access to Justice and is known as 'The Woolf Report'. That report defined the problems with the civil justice system in England and Wales as follows:

> The defects I identified in our present system were that it is too expensive in that the costs often exceed the value of the claim; too slow in bringing cases to a conclusion and too unequal: there is a lack of equality between the powerful, wealthy litigant and the under-resourced litigant. It is too uncertain: the difficulty of forecasting what litigation will cost and how long it will last induces the fear of the unknown; and it is incomprehensible to many litigants. Above all it is too fragmented in the way it is organised since there is no one with clear overall responsibility for the administration of civil justice; and too adversarial as cases are run by the parties, not by the courts and

the rules of court, all too often, are ignored by the parties and not enforced by the court.

Similar criticisms have been made of the Irish civil justice system. The Woolf Report led to the enactment of the Civil Procedure Act 1997 in the United Kingdom. This led to the introduction of new rules of court, the Civil Procedure Rules (CPR) 1998. They came into effect in 1999. They sought to streamline and simplify civil procedure in all the courts, to maximise efficiency and minimise delay. A key feature of the new approach was the introduction of judicial case management. This involves judges becoming much more actively involved in the litigation process, rather than being observers or referees. The Woolf report explained judicial case management as being:

> ... the court taking the ultimate responsibility for progressing litigation along a chosen track for a predetermined period during which it is subjected to selected procedures which culminate in an appropriate form of resolution before a suitably qualified judge. Its overall purpose is to encourage settlement of disputes at the earliest appropriate stage; and, where trial is unavoidable, to ensure that cases proceed as quickly as possible to a final hearing which is itself of strictly limited duration.

In Ireland, reforms similar to the Woolf reforms were considered by the Working Group on a Courts Commission. The Working Group produced six reports between 1995 and 1998. These reports led to the enactment of the Courts Service Act 1998, which established the Courts Service. The Courts Service has the following functions:

- To manage the courts;
- To provide support services for the judges;
- To provide information on the courts system to the public;
- To provide, manage and maintain court buildings; and
- To provide facilities for users of the courts

The Working Group thought that the introduction of judicial case management in Ireland should be considered. As mentioned above, the Rules of Court that established the Commercial Court (Rules of the Superior Courts (Commercial Proceedings) 2004 (SI No 2 of 2004)) now largely applies judicial case management methods in the Commercial Court.

CHAPTER FIFTEEN

CRIMINAL COURTS: JURISDICTION AND PROCEDURE

A. Introduction 275
B. First Instance Jurisdiction of the Courts in Criminal Cases 275
    Introduction..275
    The District Court..276
        General 276
        Offences Triable 'Either Way' 276
        The Children's Court..277
        Sending Forward for Trial 277
    The Circuit Court...277
        General 277
        Transfers of Trial to the High Court 277
    The High Court (Central Criminal Court) 278
    Special Criminal Courts..278
C. Appellate Jurisdiction of the Courts in Criminal Cases 280
    Appeal from Summary Trials in the District Court 280
    Appeals From Trials on Indictment — The Court of Criminal Appeal 281
        Appeal Against Conviction...282
        Appeal Against Sentence...282
        Miscarriage of Justice 283
        Appeals by the Prosecution..283
    The Doctrine of Double Jeopardy 283
D. Court Procedure in Criminal Cases 288
    The Prosecutorial System 288
    Summary Trial and Trial on Indictment 289
    Summary Prosecution..290
    Prosecution on Indictment..290
    The District Court in Criminal Litigation 292
    Sending Indictable Offences Forward for Trial 292
    Remands on Bail...292
    The Indictment..293
    Arraignment..293
    Pleas..293
    The Role of the Victim in Criminal Litigation................................294

Learning Outcomes

Upon completion of this chapter, students should be able to:

- Explain the basis of jurisdiction in the criminal courts;
- Differentiate between summary and indictable offences;
- Explain the first instance jurisdiction of the Irish courts in criminal cases;
- Discuss the appellate jurisdiction of the Irish courts in criminal cases;
- Describe the main rules of legal procedure which apply in criminal cases.

A. Introduction

In this chapter, the jurisdiction of the Irish courts in criminal matters is considered, along with the rules of criminal procedure.

B. First Instance Jurisdiction of the Courts in Criminal Cases

Introduction

The mandatory language of Article 34.3.4° of the Constitution (The Courts of First Instance shall… include courts of local and limited jurisdiction…) obliged the Oireachtas to create courts of local and limited jurisdiction. The Courts (Establishment and Constitution) Act 1961 created the District Court and the Circuit Court. These courts have limited jurisdiction. The wording of Article 34.3.4°, however, also requires that the jurisdiction be "local" as well as limited. This implies that their jurisdiction is confined to a defined geographical area. Consequently they are local in their actual operation. Each District or Circuit Court judge has jurisdiction only to hear cases brought against defendants living in, or which arise from the events occurring or property situated in, the relevant District or Circuit. In *Grimes v Owners of SS Bangor Bay* [1948] IR 350, the former Supreme Court held that this was sufficient to satisfy the local and limited requirements of Article 64 the 1922 Constitution.

The jurisdiction of the courts in criminal cases depends on whether the offence in question is classifiable as summary or indictable. Summary offences are also known as 'minor' offences. This is the term used in Article 38.2 of the Constitution which provides that minor offences may be tried summarily. In criminal cases, the District Court's jurisdiction is exclusively a summary one over minor offences. The Circuit Court, on the other hand, has an extensive jurisdiction over indictable offences. The right to trial by jury normally attaches to such offences.

The following courts have first instance jurisdiction in criminal matters:

Figure 15.1 Courts with First Instance Jurisdiction in Criminal Matters

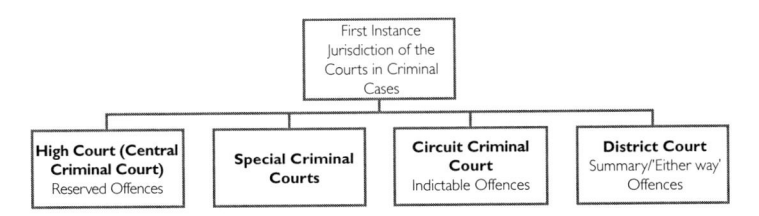

```
                    First Instance
                  Jurisdiction of the
                  Courts in Criminal
                        Cases
   ┌──────────────────┬──────────────────┬──────────────────┐
High Court (Central    Special Criminal   Circuit Criminal      District Court
 Criminal Court)           Courts              Court         Summary/'Either way'
Reserved Offences                        Indictable Offences      Offences
```

The District Court

General

The District Court is a court of local and limited jurisdiction within the meaning of Article 34.3.4° of the Constitution. Article 38.2 provides that minor criminal offences may be tried by courts of summary jurisdiction. The District Court is therefore empowered to hear and determine minor criminal matters. Road traffic offences and minor assaults would be examples. The District Court deals with a very large number of such cases. In 2011, the District Courts throughout the country disposed of 468,525 criminal cases and 372,706 in 2012.

The Constitution does not distinguish between minor and non-minor offences. However, the Supreme Court in two decisions (*Melling v Ó Mathghamhna* [1962] IR 1 and *Conroy v Attorney General* [1965] IR 411) has provided guidance. It identified two factors relevant in making the distinction:

1. The severity of the punishment authorised by law;
2. The moral quality of the acts required to constitute the offence in question, i.e. manifestly serious offences, such as murder, manslaughter and rape, could not be regarded as minor.

Consequently, the practice of the legislature in creating criminal offences triable summarily has been to limit the maximum prison sentence to 12 months. In relation to fines, up to €5,000 has been provided for in legislation on summary conviction.

Offences Triable 'Either Way'

Some indictable offences may be tried summarily. The Schedule to the Criminal Justice Act 1951 specifies offences which, although indictable, may be tried in the District Court. These are referred to as 'either way' offences. Assault causing actual bodily harm, minor sexual assaults and obtaining goods by false pretences are examples. In order for an indictable offence to be tried before the District Court, the following conditions must be fulfilled:

1. The judge of the District Court must be satisfied that the offence is suitable to be tried summarily. The judge must examine the factual circumstances relating to the particular alleged offence. He/she then decides whether those circumstances make the offence a minor offence;
2. The accused must be informed of the right to have the case tried before a jury and he/she must not object to having the case tried before the District Court;
3. In some cases, the consent of the Director of Public Prosecutions is required. This could arise where there is damage to property over a certain limit or where there has been an alleged assault with intent to resist arrest.

The Children's Court

The District Court is referred to as the Children's Court in the following circumstances:

1. When dealing with minor offences alleged against children, i.e. those under the age of 18 years; or
2. When dealing with applications for orders relating to a child where the attendance of the child is necessary.

The Children's Court can deal with indictable offences, but not homicide. It may also deal with an offence within the jurisdiction of the Central Criminal Court where the judge is satisfied that the offence is a minor one fit to be tried summarily and the child consents to it being so tried (s 75 of the Children Act 2001).

Sending Forward for Trial

The District Court 'sends forward' non-minor, indictable criminal matters which cannot be tried in the District Court.

The Circuit Court

General

Serious indictable criminal cases are tried before the Circuit Court. Article 38.5 of the Constitution provides that non-minor criminal offences must, in general, be tried before a judge and jury. The Circuit Court, when exercising its criminal jurisdiction, is often referred to as the 'Circuit Criminal Court', although it has no formal designation as such. The Circuit Court is empowered to try all indictable offences which the High Court may hear, with the exception of certain specified offences which are exclusively within the jurisdiction of the High Court. These are referred to as 'reserved offences'. They include treason, murder, attempted murder and conspiracy to murder. In addition, since the coming into force of the Criminal Law (Rape) (Amendment) Act 1990 in 1991, the High Court has been conferred with exclusive jurisdiction over other offences, for instance, rape and aggravated sexual assaults.

Transfers of Trial to the High Court

Under s 32 of the Court and Court Officers Act 1995, an application can be made by the prosecution or the accused to transfer a trial from the Circuit Court to the High Court. There is no automatic right to transfer. An application must be made to the Circuit Court judge. The right to transfer is therefore restricted. The High Court consequently generally hears only the 'reserved' offences and the Circuit Court generally hears all other serious indictable offences, such as manslaughter, robbery and other serious offences against the person and property. The decision to grant a transfer is entirely in the Circuit Court judge's discretion. The constitutionality of s 32 of the 1995 Act was upheld in *Todd v Murphy* [1999] 2 IR 1.

The High Court (Central Criminal Court)

As we have seen, Article 34.3.1° of the Constitution invests the High Court with full original jurisdiction in all matters, civil or criminal. Article 38.5 provides that non-minor criminal offences must, in general, be tried before a judge and jury. Consequently, when the High Court sits as a criminal court, it comprises a High Court judge sitting with a jury. When sitting as a first instance criminal court, the High Court is known as the Central Criminal Court.

Section 25 (2) of the Courts (Supplemental Provisions) Act 1961 provides that the High Court has exclusive jurisdiction to deal with certain offences. The effect of s 25 (2) is that the Circuit Court has full jurisdiction to deal with indictable offences except those which are reserved to the High Court.

The High Court has exclusive jurisdiction over the following 'reserved offences':

- Treason (as defined by Article 39 of the Constitution);
- An offence under s 2 or s 3 of the Treason Act 1939 (encouraging, or concealing knowledge of, treason);
- Offences under s 6, s 7 or s 8 of the Offences against the State Act 1939 (usurpation of the functions of government, obstruction of government and obstruction of the President, respectively);
- Murder, attempted murder and conspiracy to murder; and
- Piracy.

The High Court has also been conferred with exclusive jurisdiction in the following categories of offences:

- Offences under the Geneva Conventions Act 1962;
- Offences under the Genocide Act 1973;
- Offences under the Criminal Justice (United Nations Convention against Torture) Act 2000;
- The offence of murder under s 2 of the Criminal Justice (Safety of United Nations Workers) Act 2000;
- Offences under s 6 and s 7 of the Competition Act 2000 (abuse of a dominant position and entering into anti-competitive agreements); and
- Rape, aggravated sexual assault and attempted aggravated sexual assault, as defined in the Criminal Law (Rape) (Amendment) Act 1990.

Special Criminal Courts

Article 38.3.1° authorises the Oireachtas to legislate for the establishment of special criminal courts in order to try offences in cases where it may be determined in accordance with such law that the ordinary courts are inadequate to secure the effective administration of justice and the preservation of public peace and order.

By virtue of Article 38.3.2° the Oireachtas may legislate for the constitution, powers, jurisdiction and procedure of these courts.

The key statutory provisions governing the special criminal courts are contained in Part V of the Offences against the State Act 1939. The composition of special criminal courts is regulated by s 39. Under s 39 (1), each court must consist of an uneven number of members, not being less than three. In *McGlinchey v Governor of Portlaoise Prison* [1988] IR 671, the Supreme Court held that persons who, on appointment to the Special Criminal Court, were serving judges, but had since retired, could lawfully continue to sit as members of that court.

Section 43 of the 1939 Act invests a special criminal court with jurisdiction to try and to acquit or convict any person lawfully brought before that Court for trial under this Act. Section 43 also confers ancillary jurisdiction on the court, such as the power to sentence convicted persons to suffer the punishment provided by law in respect of such offence and the power to admit to bail, to administer oaths, and to punish persons for contempt of court, whether committed in the court's presence or not.

Special criminal courts are not permanent. They come into existence only when Part V of the 1939 Act is in force following a Government proclamation to that effect. This has occurred on two occasions. The first was in 1939. Those courts ceased to operate in 1946, although the 1939 proclamation was not revoked at that time. The courts were revived in 1961 to deal with the 'border campaign' of the IRA. In 1962, the 1939 proclamation was revoked and Part V of the 1939 Act ceased to be in force. A new proclamation was made in 1972. It again brought Part V of the 1939 Act into force. This time a single Special Criminal Court was established. The Special Criminal Court as we know it today has been in existence since then — 1972. It deals primarily with subversive type offences connected, for the most part, to Northern Ireland, and with offences where it may not be possible to have a jury trial, perhaps because of threats to jurors.

The Special Criminal Court established in 1972 comprises three judges of the ordinary courts, usually one High Court judge, one Circuit Court judge and one judge of the District Court. The High Court judge presides. A number of challenges to the constitutional validity of special criminal courts have not succeeded (*Re the Criminal Law (Jurisdiction) Bill 1975* [1977] IR 129; *Eccles v Ireland* [1985] IR 545; *McGlinchey v Governor of Portlaoise Prison* [1988] IR 671; *Kavanagh v Government of Ireland* [1996] 1 IR 321; and *Gilligan v Ireland* [2001] 1 ILRM 473).

The Court has, however, been subject to criticism by the United Nations Human Rights Committee. In July 2000, the performance of the Irish government in the promotion and the protection of civil and political rights was examined by the committee. It was concerned about the continued existence of the Special Criminal Court and its powers under the Offences against the State Act 1939 (Part V). It said that the continued existence of the court was difficult to justify by the exigencies of the political situation in Ireland. It recommended that the court be reviewed.

In 2002, the Committee to Review the Offences against the State Acts 1939–1998 and Related Matters produced a report which considered that there was a continued need for the Special Criminal Court in light of the Belfast Agreement 1998 ('Good Friday Agreement') and the St Andrews Agreements of 2004. The committee recommended the retention of the court with minor modifications taking into account continued terrorist threats and threats posed by serious organised crime. The Committee also recommended that the court lapse automatically after three years unless the Oireachtas renewed it. These proposals have not been acted upon by Government.

C. Appellate Jurisdiction of the Courts in Criminal cases

As with civil cases, two types of appeal are possible: a *de novo* hearing or an appeal on a point of law.

Appeal from Summary Trials in the District Court

A *de novo* hearing in the Circuit Court is generally only available in the event of a conviction in the District Court. In such instances, the decision of the Circuit Court is, generally, final. It may not be appealed. It may, however, be subject to judicial review. Only the defendant may bring such an appeal to the Circuit Court (s 18 of the Courts of Justice Act 1928, as amended by s 58 of the Courts of Justice Act 1936). The prosecution can appeal an acquittal in the District Court only in limited circumstances. This would typically be in relation to 'regulatory' offences under fisheries or health and safety at work legislation. In most cases, however, an acquittal by the District Court cannot be appealed by the prosecution. The prosecution can, of course, utilise the case stated procedure to the High Court.

An appeal on a point of law by way of case stated lies to the High Court from decisions of the District Court in criminal matters. Either the prosecution or defence can bring such an appeal. The point of law must be referred to the High Court for determination by the District Court judge, unless he or she considers the request to be frivolous. The appeal may be made either while the criminal trial is still in progress in the District Court by way of consultative case stated, or when the judge has made a final determination in the case at the end of the District Court hearing.

Where a consultative case stated has been brought the decision of the High Court can then be appealed to the Supreme Court, but only where the High Court judge grants leave to appeal (s 52 (2) of the Courts (Supplemental Provisions) Act 1961). An appeal from the High Court to the Supreme Court may be made without the need to seek leave to appeal from the High Court judge where the case stated has not been made to the High Court until *after* a final determination of the matter by the District Court.

Figure 15.2 Appeals from criminal trials in the District Court

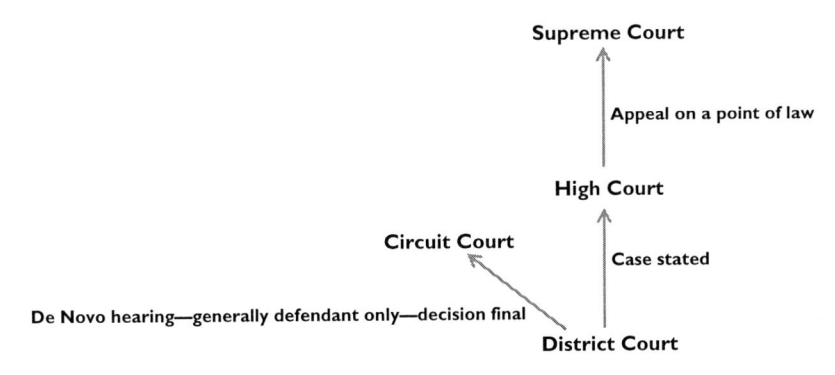

```
                                          Supreme Court
                                               ↑
                                               | Appeal on a point of law
                                               |
                                          High Court
                                               ↑
                           Circuit Court        |
                              ↖                 | Case stated
                                                |
          De Novo hearing—generally defendant only—decision final
                                          District Court
```

Appeals From Trials on Indictment — The Court of Criminal Appeal

Indictable offences are the most serious offences. They are normally tried in the Circuit Court, the Central Criminal Court and the special criminal courts, when in operation. The appeal system in respect of trials on indictment differs from the appeal system in respect of civil and criminal cases heard in the District Court. Appeals against conviction or sentence from the Circuit Court, the Central Criminal Court and the special criminal courts are heard by the Court of Criminal Appeal. A further appeal to the Supreme Court is possible, if leave is granted.

Figure 15.3 Appeals from Trials on Indictment

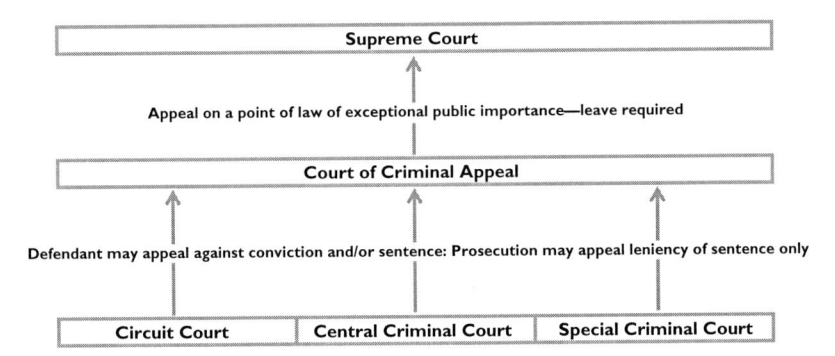

```
┌─────────────────────────────────────────────────────────────────┐
│                        Supreme Court                            │
└─────────────────────────────────────────────────────────────────┘
                                ↑
        Appeal on a point of law of exceptional public importance—leave required
                                │
┌─────────────────────────────────────────────────────────────────┐
│                    Court of Criminal Appeal                     │
└─────────────────────────────────────────────────────────────────┘
         ↑                      ↑                      ↑
 Defendant may appeal against conviction and/or sentence: Prosecution may appeal leniency of sentence only
         │                      │                      │
┌────────────────┬──────────────────────────┬─────────────────────┐
│ Circuit Court  │  Central Criminal Court  │ Special Criminal Court │
└────────────────┴──────────────────────────┴─────────────────────┘
```

The Court of Criminal Appeal was established by the Courts (Supplemental Provisions) Act 1961. It comprises three judges: a Supreme Court judge (either the Chief Justice or another Supreme Court judge nominated by the Chief Justice) and two judges of the High Court, nominated by the Chief Justice. The Court of Criminal Appeal is a superior court of record. This means that it is a court which has the records of its acts and judicial proceedings maintained and preserved and which has power to fine and imprison for contempt of its authority (Courts (Supplemental Provisions) Act 1961 s 7, s 8 and s 21; Courts Act 1971, s 13 respectively.) In an appeal against conviction, the Court of Criminal Appeal and, on further appeal, the Supreme Court, has three options:

- Dismiss the appeal;
- Quash the conviction and release the defendant; or
- Quash the conviction and order a retrial.

The following appeals may be brought to the Court of Criminal appeal:

Figure 15.4 Types Appeal from Trial on Indictment to the Court of Criminal Appeal

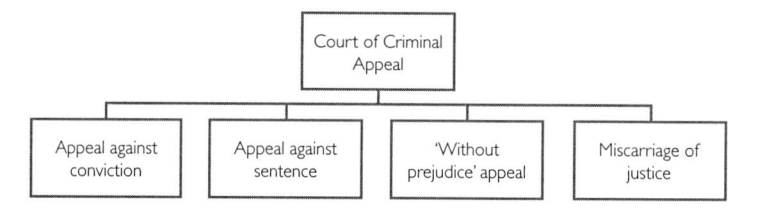

```
                    Court of Criminal
                         Appeal
    ┌──────────────┬──────────────┬──────────────┐
  Appeal against  Appeal against  'Without      Miscarriage of
   conviction      sentence     prejudice' appeal   justice
```

Appeal Against Conviction
Persons convicted on indictment in the Circuit Court, the Central Criminal Court (the High Court) or the special criminal courts when in operation may appeal that conviction to the Court of Criminal Appeal. Leave to appeal must be granted first. The trial judge (or judges, in the case of a special criminal court) may grant a certificate stating that the case is a fit case for appeal. If a trial judge refuses (or judges refuse, in the case of a special criminal court) to issue a certificate, the convicted person may appeal *that* decision to the Court of Criminal Appeal itself. That court may then grant leave to appeal. An appeal will be primarily on a point of law. If the Court of Criminal Appeal allows the appeal, it is empowered either to order a retrial or enter an acquittal of the defendant and order his release (Criminal Procedure Act 1993, s 3).

Appeal Against Sentence
A convicted person may appeal against sentence to the Court of Criminal Appeal. Such appeals involve inviting the court to determine whether the sentence imposed

at trial was within the range of sentences deemed appropriate to the particular crime and the particular convicted person. It is also open to the prosecution to appeal against the leniency of a sentence (Criminal Justice Act 1993, s 2).

Miscarriage of Justice

A convicted person, who believes their conviction to be a miscarriage of justice, may appeal to the Court of Criminal Appeal on that basis. The Criminal Procedure Act 1993 establishes a statutory mechanism to review convictions in such circumstances. Section 2(1)(b) of the 1993 Act sets out the basis for appeals. It is where the convicted person "alleges that a new or newly-discovered fact shows that there has been a miscarriage of justice in relation to the conviction or that the sentence imposed is excessive." The 1993 Act provides for a full hearing in the Court of Criminal Appeal at which any new or newly-discovered evidence may be examined. Section 9 of the 1993 Act provides for the payment of compensation to a person whose conviction has been quashed. Such compensation can be paid where the court has certified that a newly-discovered fact shows that there has been a miscarriage of justice.

Appeals by the Prosecution

Section 21 of the Criminal Justice Act 2006 (amending s 34 of the Criminal Procedure Act 1967) provides for appeals by the prosecution. The effect of this provision is that the prosecution may refer a question of law arising during a criminal trial to the Supreme Court for determination. If the Supreme Court finds that there was an error of law in the trial, a verdict of not guilty cannot be disturbed. Furthermore, the identity of the person found not guilty cannot be revealed during the prosecution appeal process unless that person gives their consent.

The prosecution may also bring a 'without prejudice' appeal to the Supreme Court in relation to a point of law arising in respect of a decision of the Court of Criminal Appeal. The point of law must be certified as being one of exceptional public importance and it must be desirable in the public interest to bring it (Criminal Justice Act 2006, s 22). 'Without prejudice' in this context means that a decision favourable to the person found not guilty will not be disturbed. The purpose of such appeals is to clarify the law for future cases. The prosecution's right to appeal the leniency of a sentence (mentioned above) is not affected (s 59 of the Criminal Justice Act 2007). However, the Criminal Procedure Act 2010 has made significant changes to prosecution appeal rights (see below: *The Doctrine of Double Jeopardy*).

The Doctrine of Double Jeopardy

The doctrine of double jeopardy is a common law rule that requires that a person should not face repeated prosecution for the same offence. However, a person may be charged with different offences arising from the same act. These offences may be of commission or omission, but the person usually cannot be punished twice for the same offence. The doctrine applies to the bringing of identical or similar charges. It does not apply to the prosecution of charges which may have similar or identical evidence involved: *In the Matter of NIB (No 2)* [1999] 2 ILRM 443.

The traditional approach in respect of the double jeopardy rule in Ireland has been about striking a balance between the people's right to prosecute a case to a jury verdict on the one hand, and guarding against the potential unfairness of repeated trials on the other hand. This balance was achieved by limiting the permissible number of trials, which end in jury disagreement, to two trials. A third trial which was preceded by two trials in which the jury failed to reach agreement, may not constitute a 'trial in due course of law' as provided for in Article 38.1 of the Constitution. This was the position adopted by the court in *DS v Judges of the Cork Circuit Court* [2008] 4 IR 379. In that case, there were two previous trials before two juries. This first jury was unable to reach a verdict. The second failed to reach agreement. The question was whether a third trial should be prohibited. The Supreme Court held that there was no statutory limit on the number of times a person might be prosecuted where a jury had failed to reach a verdict. The Court declined to make any hard and fast rule as to the number of prosecutions that were permissible. It made it clear that it was primarily a matter for the DPP as to whether to prosecute. The Court's duty was to protect due process. It held that a balance must be drawn between competing public interests: one was the public interest in prosecuting an accused and the other was the integrity of due process by guarding against the dangers of repeated trials. The Court stated that a third trial was not, *per se*, a breach of a trial in due course of law, but it held that, on the facts of that particular case, it was correct to uphold the decision of the High Court to prohibit a third trial.

By contrast, in *AP v DPP* [2011] IESC 2, the Supreme Court held that the applicant was not entitled to prohibit a fourth trial after the jury had been discharged in his first three trials because inadmissible and prejudicial evidence had been given. The Court accepted that the DPP's decision was exceptional, but it held that there was no rule which held that a fourth trial was an abuse of process *per se*.

In England and Wales, however, the double jeopardy rule was reversed in respect of criminal offences by the Criminal Justice Act 2003. It provides for the reopening of criminal prosecutions in circumstances where new and compelling evidence has come to light following an acquittal. In Ireland, the double jeopardy rule has effectively been ended by the Criminal Procedure Act 2010. The Act does so by introducing three retrial procedures:

- New evidence retrial;
- Tainted acquittal retrial; and
- A with-prejudice prosecution appeal.

The Act now permits the DPP to make an application in serious cases for a retrial after acquittal for relevant offences where new and compelling evidence later emerges. New and compelling evidence is defined as that which is reliable, of significant probative value and such that a jury might reasonably be satisfied beyond a reasonable doubt of the person's guilt in respect of the offence concerned.

Relevant offences include serious crimes such as murder, manslaughter, rape, genocide, trafficking, offences against the State, organised crime, aggravated burglary and robbery, arson and damaging property. Under the 2010 Act, the DPP may make an application for a retrial where the previous acquittal was tainted by the commission of an offence against the administration of justice. Such an offence could be corruption, witness intimidation or jury tampering. The DPP may make only one such application for a retrial. A retrial must be in the public interest. The evidence of guilt must be compelling for a retrial to take place. Unlike the position in England and Wales, these provisions are not retrospective.

The Criminal Procedure Act 2010 allows the DPP or Attorney General to appeal to the Supreme Court on a point of law regarding a direction of the Court of Criminal Appeal or the exclusion of evidence. The Act also introduces a with-prejudice right of appeal against acquittals following trial on indictment. It is only available to the prosecution in certain circumstances, for example, where there is a real prospect of a conviction, i.e., where there is sufficient evidence on which a jury may convict. This appeal procedure is also available in the case of erroneous rulings by a trial judge which result in a judge directing an acquittal or weakening the prosecution case that is put to the jury. The Act specifies the types of rulings that may be appealed and the standard that must be reached before a with-prejudice appeal may be lodged by the DPP or granted by the Supreme Court. The Supreme Court is required to consider the interests of justice when assessing the matter.

Table on Summary of Criminal Jurisdiction of the Courts (both First Instance and Appellate)

Criminal Jurisdiction of the Courts	
Court	Jurisdiction
Supreme Court	• Determination of questions of law referred to it by way of case stated from the Circuit Court; • Appeal from the Court of Criminal Appeal only where the Court of Criminal Appeal itself, or the Attorney General or Director of Public Prosecutions, certifies that the Court's decision involves a point of law of exceptional public importance and that it is desirable, in the public interest, that an appeal should be taken to the Supreme Court on that point of law; • Determination of a question of law where a verdict in favour of an accused person is found by direction of the trial judge, and the Attorney General, without prejudice to the verdict in favour of the accused, refers the question of law to the Supreme Court (s 34 of the Criminal Procedure Act 1967); • Determination of a question of law on a reference by the Attorney General under s 34 of the Criminal Procedure Act 1967 or where the decision of the Central Criminal Court relates to the constitutional validity of any law; • With-prejudice prosecution appeals made under the Criminal Procedure Act 2010.
Court of Criminal Appeal	• Appeals from persons convicted on indictment in the Circuit or Central Criminal Court where they (the appellant) obtain a certificate from the trial judge that the case is a fit one for appeal; where a certificate is refused, the Court of Criminal Appeal itself, on appeal from this refusal, may grant leave to appeal; an appeal may be made against sentence only, conviction only or against both sentence and conviction; • Appeal against conviction or sentence by the Special Criminal Court; • Appeals from the DPP on grounds of alleged undue leniency of a sentence under s 2 of the Criminal Justice Act 1993; • Appeals alleging a miscarriage of justice lodged under s 2 of the Criminal Procedure Act 1993.

(Cont'd)

Central Criminal Court	• 'Reserved offences' ○ treason (Article 39 of the Constitution); ○ an offence under s 2 or s 3 of the Treason Act 1939; ○ offences under s 6, s 7 or s 8 of the Offences against the State Act 1939; ○ murder, attempted murder or conspiracy to murder; ○ piracy; ○ offences against the Geneva Conventions Act 1962; ○ offences under the Genocide Act 1973; ○ rape, aggravated sexual assault and attempted aggravated sexual assault, as defined in the Criminal Law (Rape) (Amendment) Act 1990; ○ murder under s 2 of the Criminal Justice (Safety of United Nations Workers) Act 2000; ○ offences under s 6 and s 7 of the Competition Act 2002.
Special Criminal Court	• 'Scheduled offences' under s 36 of the Offences against the State Act 1939 (offences which the ordinary courts are deemed inadequate to deal with within the terms of Article 38.3 of the Constitution) ○ Current list of scheduled offences: ▪ any offence under the Criminal Damage Act 1991; ▪ any offence under s 7 of the Conspiracy and Protection of Property Act 1875; ▪ any offence under the Explosive Substances Act 1883; ▪ any offence under the Firearms Acts 1925 to 1990; ▪ any offence under the Offences against the State Act 1939; and ▪ certain offences under the Offences against the State (Amendment) Act 1998.
Circuit Court	• Same jurisdiction as the Central Criminal Court in all indictable offences except 'reserved offences'; • Appeals *de novo* from the Distrcit Court.

(Cont'd)

Court	Jurisdiction
District Court	• Summary offences — offences for which there is no right of trial by judge and jury; • Indictable offences tried summarily — with the consent of the accused and the DPP, and the judge being of the opinion that the facts constitute a minor offence; • Indictable offences — other than certain offences including rape, aggravated sexual assault, murder, treason and piracy where the accused pleads guilty and the DPP consents, and the judge accepts the guilty plea — otherwise the accused is sent forward to the Circuit Court on his signed plea of guilty for sentencing; • Indictable offences not tried summarily — a book of evidence is served on the accused — the judge considers the book of evidence and any submissions on behalf of the defence or the prosecution — if the judge is of the opinion that there is a sufficient case to answer, the accused is sent forward to the Circuit Court or Central Criminal Court for trial.

D. Court Procedure in Criminal Cases

The Prosecutorial System

As we have seen, minor criminal offences are prosecuted by way of summary trial, whereas more serious criminal offences are prosecuted by way of trial on indictment. Article 38 of the Constitution provides that a person charged with a criminal offence is entitled to a trial with a jury except in the case of minor offences which may be tried by courts of summary jurisdiction. The effect of Article 38 is that serious criminal offences are tried in the Circuit Court or the Central Criminal Court, while minor criminal offences are generally tried in the District Court by way of summary trial.

In England and Wales, the Crown Prosecution Service is responsible for prosecuting criminal cases investigated by the police in that jurisdiction. Ireland, however, does not have such a centralised, or 'unitary', prosecution system. Most criminal investigations are carried out by the Gardaí, but other State agencies have been given prosecutorial functions by statute. The Gardaí may prosecute minor offences before the District Court, though in practice, such cases are presented by counsel in private practice upon instruction by the Chief State Solicitor or State Solicitor. The Gardaí, after investigating a serious offence, prepare a file which is sent to the DPP who then decides whether a criminal prosecution should take place. Such cases also will normally be prosecuted by counsel in private practice upon being briefed by the Chief State Solicitor or State Solicitor.

The table below gives some examples of state bodies which have been given prosecutorial powers by statute. These are normally confined to summary proceedings.

Table on State Bodies with Prosecutorial Powers

Prosecuting Authority	Authorising Statute
Director of Consumer Affairs	Consumer Credit Act 1995 s 14, as amended by the Central Bank and Financial Service Authority of Ireland Act 2003 s 35, Schedule 1.
Minister for the Marine and Natural Resources	Mineral Development Act 1999, s 4.
Minister for Agriculture, Food and Rural Development	National Beef Assurance Scheme Act 2000, s 26.
Equality Authority	Equal Status Act 2000, s 44.
Minister for Public Enterprise	Electronic Commerce Act 2000, s 6(1),
Minister for Enterprise, Trade and Employment	Copyright and Related Rights Act 2000, s 11(1).
Minister for the Environment, Heritage and Local Government	Unclaimed Life Assurance Policies Act 2003, s 5(4).
Fire Authority (e.g. county councils)	Licensing of Indoor Events Act 2003, s 16.
Environmental Protection Agency	Environmental Protection Agency Act 1992, s 11.

Summary Trial and Trial on Indictment

The common law historically categorised criminal offences as felonies or misdemeanours. Felonies were crimes at common law which carried the death penalty in addition to the forfeiture of the land and goods of the offender. All other crimes were misdemeanours. Many crimes were classified as felonies by statute. The Forfeiture Act 1870 generally abolished forfeiture but the distinction between the two classes of crime remained. However, over time, that distinction became increasingly blurred in that some very serious crimes were classified as misdemeanours, while some less serious crimes were classified as felonies. Notwithstanding this, felonies generally carried heavier penalties. The Criminal Law Act 1997, s 3(1) abolished all distinctions between felonies and misdemeanours. The effect of this statute is that the existing law relating to misdemeanours is applied to all offences. In addition, the power of arrest without warrant, which applied to felonies, is effectively retained by the designation of a new class of serious offences called 'arrestable offences'. An 'arrestable offence' is defined in s 2(1) of the 1997 Act as an offence for which a person may, under any enactment, be punished by imprisonment for a term of five years or by a more severe penalty, and it includes an attempt to commit such an offence.

The practice since the enactment of the 1937 Constitution has been to attach penalties to offences depending on whether they were indictable or summary rather than felonies or misdemeanours. The abolition of the distinction between felonies and misdemeanours was not retrospective (Interpretation (Amendment) Act 1997).

Summary Prosecution

As indicated, most minor offences are prosecuted by the Gardaí. However, at common law, any person has the power to initiate and prosecute a criminal charge by means of private prosecution under the title 'common informer'. The Gardaí in some cases operate under this designation to initiate prosecutions in the absence of clear statutory authorisation to do so. Section 8 of the Garda Síochána Act 2005 authorises any Garda to institute summary prosecutions in the name of the DPP. The Gardaí are required to follow particular or general directions given to them by the DPP in relation to such prosecutions. At any stage of such proceedings, the DPP may take over the prosecution from the Gardaí.

Summary prosecutions are initiated by a summons which is issued by a person authorised by legislation e.g. a District Court clerk on application by, usually, a member of An Garda Síochána. The summons will allege that a particular named person has committed an offence. It will contain the allegation of the offence together with relevant information, such as the date and location of the alleged offence. The summons forms the basis of the charge brought before the District Court. Other relevant evidence may accompany the summons, for example the results of blood tests in relation to a road traffic offence involving driving with excess alcohol. Generally, no further information will be provided to the defence by the prosecution at that stage.

Prosecution on Indictment

In respect of indictable offences, the Gardaí have been conferred with wide-ranging powers of arrest and detention under various statutory provisions. Persons arrested by the Gardaí on suspicion of indictable offences may be questioned whilst in custody. Legislative and constitutional protections for persons in custody apply, e.g. the right to silence. Generally, the decision as to whether to prosecute lies in the hands of the DPP. It appears that private prosecutions brought by 'common informers' can only be brought as far as the return for trial stage by the judge of the District Court. Thereafter, the matter is in the hands of the DPP. Decisions of the DPP not to prosecute, or to prosecute, are decisions in which the courts are reluctant to interfere by way of judicial review, although there is a limited number of exceptions (see for example *State (McCormack) v Curran* [1987] ILRM 225; *Eviston v DPP* [2002] 3 IR 260; [2002] 1 ILRM 134 (HC); [2003] 1 ILRM 178 (SC); *State (O'Callaghan v Ó hUadhaigh* [1977] IR 42; *Dunphy (a Minor) v DPP* [2005] 3 IR 585; [2005] IESC 75).

Historically, the DPP did not disclose reasons why prosecutions did, or did not, take place. However, in 2000 the DPP published, for the first time, general factors taken into account in deciding whether to prosecute (annual report of the Director of Public Prosecutions 1999). These included whether there was sufficient evidence to indicate the likelihood of conviction and whether a prosecution was in the public interest. Ultimately, the DPP's decision is final. Private prosecutions cannot, as we have seen, proceed beyond the District Court, although in theory, the DPP's consent could be given for such prosecutions to proceed further.

In 2008, however, the DPP introduced a policy on giving reasons for decisions not to prosecute in cases involving death. During 2011, the DPP received 12 requests for reasons. This new policy was something of a departure from previous practice whereby reasons for decisions not to prosecute were given only to the Gardaí or other investigators, but not to families of the deceased. The table below provides a breakdown of the disposal of files received by the DPP in 2009, 2010 and 2011 (as of August 2012). The Gardaí and specialised investigating agencies submit files either directly to the DPP's Solicitors Division or to the local state solicitor for a direction on whether or not to prosecute. Depending on the seriousness of the offence and the evidence disclosed in the file, the DPP takes decisions as follows:

- **No Prosecution:** A decision not to prosecute is made. The most common reason not to prosecute is because the evidence contained in the file is not sufficient to support a prosecution;
- **Prosecute on Indictment:** It is decided to prosecute in the Circuit, Central or Special Criminal Courts;
- **Summary Disposal:** The offence is to be prosecuted in the District Court;
- **Under Consideration:** Files in which a decision has not been made. This figure includes those files in which further information or investigation was required before a decision could be made. Further information is sought more often than not to strengthen the case, rather than because of any deficiency in the investigation.

Table on Disposal by DPP of files by number of suspects subject of files received

Disposal by DPP of files by number of suspects subject of files received						
Direction Made	2011	%	2010	%	2009	%
No Prosecution Directed	4,751	37%	4,668	37%	4,266	35%
Prosecution on Indictment Directed	3,611	28%	3,793	30%	3,891	33%
Summary Disposal Directed	4,231	33%	4,071	32%	4,159	32%
Total of Files Disposed	12,593	99%	12,532	100%	12,316	100%
Under Consideration	135	1%	45	0%	28	0%
Total	12,728		12,577		12,344	

Source: Office of the Director of Public Prosecutions annual report 2011.

The District Court in Criminal Litigation

Once a decision to prosecute has been made, the accused person will be brought before the District Court. There they will be formally charged. Where the offence is indictable, the District Court judge may deal with the matter summarily, if empowered to do so. If not, he or she will send the case forward for trial on indictment. If the accused person pleads guilty in the District Court to an offence which cannot be tried summarily, the District Court judge will send the case forward to the Circuit Court for sentencing only. The Criminal Justice Act 1951, Schedule 1, specifies certain offences which, although triable on indictment, can also be tried in the District Court. These are referred to as indictable offences triable summarily, or 'either way' offences.

Sending Indictable Offences Forward for Trial

If the indictable offence cannot be dealt with summarily, s 6 of the Criminal Procedure Act 1967 requires that the prosecution provide to the defence all the evidence which the prosecution intends to use at trial. This material is known as the 'book of evidence'. It includes a statement of the charges, a list of the witnesses the prosecution proposes to call at trial and their statements, and a list of exhibits, such as photographs, and any other relevant material such as forensic evidence, including DNA evidence, if any. The accused cannot be sent forward for trial until the book of evidence has been served. Service of the book of evidence will automatically lead to the case being sent forward to either the Circuit Court or the Central Criminal Court.

Remands on Bail

Prior to the enactment of the Bail Act 1997, an accused person was usually entitled to be remanded on bail. They would therefore be free up to the time of trial. The judicial policy behind this approach was to give expression to the presumption of innocence and the right to liberty under Article 40.4 of the Constitution, unless the accused person was likely to present a flight risk or interfere with potential witnesses. To address public disquiet over this situation, the Bail Act 1997 was enacted following a constitutional amendment in 1996. The 1997 Act provides that a court can refuse bail where a person is charged with a serious offence "if the court is satisfied that such a refusal is reasonably considered necessary to prevent the commission of a serious offence by that person". 'Serious offence' is defined as: murder; manslaughter; rape and other serious sexual assaults; other offences against the person, such as assault causing harm, harassment, false imprisonment and child abduction; sexual offences; some public order offences; various explosives and firearms offences; theft offences; some road traffic offences, such as dangerous driving causing death and taking a vehicle without authority; various forgery offences; various offences against the State; and drug trafficking offences.

The Indictment

The Criminal Justice (Administration) Act 1924 specifies the form of most indictments. The 1924 Act also provides that defects in an indictment may be rectified at any time, provided that this does not cause injustice to the defendant.

The principal elements of the indictment are the statement of offences (counts) which are charged. Each count is written in two parts: the statement of the offence and the particulars of the offence. The statement of the offence sets out the nature of the offence. Where the offence is created by statute, it is necessary to specify the legislation, as amended. The particulars of the offence then set out the circumstances in which it is alleged that the defendant committed the offence. These are not always as specific as the particulars in a civil pleading. For example, in the case of a murder, the precise date of the murder may not be known. Therefore, the particulars may simply state 'on a date unknown'. This is entirely acceptable for the purposes of particulars on the indictment.

Arraignment

It is not until an accused has been brought before the trial court that the formal reading of the indictment takes place. This is called the arraignment. It involves calling the person before the court, reading the indictment and asking the accused whether he or she pleads guilty or not guilty. If the accused pleads not guilty at this stage, a jury is empanelled to hear the case. An accused may withdraw a plea of guilty entered in the District Court and plead not guilty to the trial court.

Pleas

If the accused has pleaded guilty, the trial judge will impose sentence on the accused. The expectation of a lesser sentence may encourage an accused person to enter a guilty plea. In effect, a guilty plea carries a discount on what the normal sentence might otherwise be after a full criminal trial. Such discounts apply even in respect of serious offences, such as rape. Where a guilty plea is made in such a case, the court will generally allow some discount on the basis that the victim has not been required to face the ordeal of giving evidence in a trial.

The Role of the Victim in Criminal Litigation

In Ireland, as in other common law systems, court procedure is adversarial: the judge plays the role of impartial referee between two sides in a contest that takes place in the courtroom. The adversarial system operates in both civil and criminal litigation, but is particularly pronounced in the criminal process. Litigation is conducted between the prosecution, representing the people, and the defendant, or accused.

A victim is not a party to criminal proceedings, though he or she may be a witness. The treatment of victims in criminal proceedings has been the subject of much criticism. They may not be kept fully informed of the progress of investigations or court hearings, unless they are called as a witness. In addition, victims of rape and sexual assault can be subjected to rigorous cross-examination by defence counsel which could be traumatic for them. To address some of these concerns, the Department of Justice and Equality has introduced a Charter and Guide to the Criminal Justice System. It is based on the EU Framework Decision on the Standing of Victims in Criminal Proceedings (2001).

The Charter describes the criminal justice system from a crime victim's point of view. It sets out the victim's rights and entitlements to the services provided by the various State agencies working with crime victims. A 'victim' is defined in the charter as a natural person who has suffered harm, including physical or mental injury, emotional suffering or economic loss, directly caused by acts or omissions that are in violation of the criminal law of a Member State of the European Union. The charter is made up of a number of individual charters setting out what victims can expect from the relevant State services, what they can do if those services to not meet their expectations, and the role of the services in question. The key services are: the Crime Victims Helpline; An Garda Síochána; the Courts Service; the Director of Public Prosecutions; the Probation Service; the Prison Service; the Legal Aid Board; the Coroner Service; and the Criminal Injuries Compensation Tribunal.

Another important development in respect of sexual assault cases is contained in the Sex Offenders Act 2001, Part 6. It provides for separate legal representation for complainants in rape and other sexual assault cases in circumstances where an application is made by the defendant to adduce evidence or to cross-examine the complainant about his or her sexual history. In addition, the Criminal Law (Rape) Acts 1981-1990 provide that the complainant's sexual history may only be introduced into a trial with leave of the trial judge.

CHAPTER SIXTEEN

PROCEDURAL MATTERS AND EVIDENCE

A. General 297
B. The Requirement for *Locus Standi* or 'Standing' 298
C. Limitation Periods..299
D. Standards of Proof..301
E. **Rules of Evidence** 302
    Overview 302
    Hearsay Evidence...303
    Opinion Evidence..304
    Statutory Intervention in the Rules of Evidence..305

Learning Outcomes

Upon completion of this chapter, students should be able to:

- Identify the primary objectives of civil and criminal actions;
- Describe the main requirements for *locus standi* in litigation;
- Explain the significance of limitation periods;
- Distinguish between the civil and criminal standards of proof;
- Outline key rules which determine the admissibility of evidence in civil and criminal proceedings.

A. General

Court procedure differs, depending on whether the matter is civil or criminal. Civil matters tend to involve private law disputes, such as torts (civil wrongs) or contract matters. Criminal matters, on the other hand, involve the prosecution of persons for committing wrongs against society or the public in general. For this reason, crimes are classified as public law matters. Criminal prosecutions are usually initiated by the DPP or An Garda Síochána on behalf of the State. Private prosecutions by a private individual are possible, but rare.

In a civil claim, the person initiating the claim is, in general, called the 'plaintiff' whilst the party against whom the claim is brought is called the 'defendant'. In some instances, such as family cases, the parties may be described as 'petitioner' and 'respondent' or, in judicial review cases, 'applicant' and 'respondent'. In criminal matters the parties are referred to as the 'prosecution' on the one side and 'defendant' or 'accused' on the other. Those initiating proceedings must notify the other party in advance. This is so that those subject to the action will know what case they face and can prepare a defence. Civil claims can be taken by or against natural persons or incorporated bodies, such as companies. Similarly, as with natural persons, incorporated bodies may be subject to criminal prosecution. This could typically happen in relation to 'regulatory' offences, such as breaches of environmental law.

One event can give rise to both civil and criminal proceedings. For example, a driver involved in a road traffic accident in which he or she is at fault may be subject to criminal prosecution by An Garda Síochána. In addition, that driver may also be subject to civil proceedings by the injured person where they seek compensation for the injuries they have suffered in the accident. The criminal and civil actions would be separate proceedings. Another example is that of public nuisance, which is both a tort and a crime.

In general, civil actions seek to compensate, whereas criminal proceedings seek to punish. In civil actions, apart from monetary compensation, a range of other remedies may be available, such as injunctions and declarations. In criminal actions, punishment can mean the imposition of a sentence of imprisonment and/or a fine. In a civil claim, any award of damages is paid by the defendant to the injured party (the plaintiff) whereas, in criminal proceedings, a fine is paid by the wrongdoer to the State, rather than the victim. This underscores the distinction between civil and criminal actions. However, in respect of criminal cases, the Irish courts have discretion, under s 6 of the Criminal Justice Act 1993, to order a convicted person to pay compensation to any person who has suffered personal injury or loss arising from the commission of an offence. Unfortunately, this provision is of little benefit to the victims of impecunious offenders. However, a non-statutory criminal injuries compensation scheme administered by the Criminal Injuries Compensation Tribunal is available. This, however, can only make payments for special damages, e.g. medical expenses or loss of earnings. Payments for general damages, e.g. pain and suffering, are not available under the scheme.

In civil cases, where a plaintiff loses a personal injuries action, the defendant is described as 'not liable'. If the plaintiff succeeds, the defendant is found liable. In criminal cases, if the prosecution loses, the defendant is described as 'not guilty' or is acquitted. If the prosecution is successful, the defendant is described as 'guilty'.

B. The Requirement for *Locus Standi* or 'Standing'

Parties seeking to initiate civil or criminal proceedings must have an interest in the outcome of those proceedings. That is, they must have *locus standi*, or standing, to bring the case at all. In most instances, the parties clearly meet the requirement of *locus standi* and it will not normally be an issue. For example, in a personal injuries action, the plaintiff will be the person claiming damages (monetary compensation) for injuries which they allege were caused by the defendant. Clearly, both parties are involved in the dispute. Similarly, in a contract case, the plaintiff and defendant might be in dispute over the terms of an agreement entered into by them. In a criminal case, the parties are, on the one hand, the prosecution, representing the People and, on the other hand, the accused, or defendant, the alleged perpetrator. In such cases, the question of *locus standi* is not in issue. In other types of case, the question of *locus standi* can be important.

In criminal cases where the proceedings are commenced by the DPP at public expense, witnesses for the prosecution are not parties to the proceedings. Consequently, they are precluded from seeking to impugn any orders made due to the fact that they lack *locus standi*: *Shannon v McGuinness* [1999 HC] 3 IR 274. It has also been held that the DPP does not have *locus standi* to bring proceedings for recovery of a penalty imposed by the Income Tax Act 1967, s 128 (now the Taxes Consolidation Act 1997, s 987, as amended).

With regard to *locus standi* in respect of constitutional cases, the Supreme Court has set down guidelines in two leading cases. In *State (Lynch) v Cooney* [1982] IR 337, where the plaintiff was challenging the constitutionality of legislation, the Supreme Court held that the question as to whether a person has *locus standi* ('sufficient interest') to maintain proceedings is a mixed question of fact and law.

In other words, the Court was required to take into account both the precise circumstances of the plaintiff and the character or type of law they were challenging. In the earlier case of *Cahill v Sutton* [1980] IR 269, the plaintiff had also challenged the constitutionality of a legislative provision. In that case, the Supreme Court stated the primary rule as being that:

> The person challenging the constitutionality of the statute, or some other person for whom he is deemed by the court to be entitled to speak, must be able to assert that, because of the alleged unconstitutionality, his or that other person's interests have been adversely affected, or stand in real or imminent danger of being adversely affected, by the operation of the statute.

However, the courts have also held that a party not directly affected, but who has a *bona fide* concern and interest in an actual or threatened infringement of the Constitution has *locus standi* in proceedings to enforce the provisions of the Constitution (*SPUC v Coogan and Others* [1989] ITLR(SC)). Also, where a person is an aggrieved person, he, by definition, has *locus standi* (*Chambers v An Bord Pleanála and Sandoz* [1992] ILRM 296 (SC)).

Locus standi in relation to applications for judicial review of administrative action is governed by Order 84, r 20 (4) of the Rules of the Superior Courts 1986 (SI No 15 of 1986). This provision provides that leave to apply for judicial review shall not be granted unless the applicant has a sufficient interest in the matter to which the application relates. There are limited statutory exceptions to this. For example, s 50 (4) (b) of the Planning and Development Act 2000 (as amended) requires that the High Court shall not grant leave unless it is satisfied that the applicant has a substantial interest in the matter.

C. Limitation Periods

Various time limits are set down within which court proceedings must be initiated. For civil cases, the Statute of Limitations Acts 1957 to 2000 set out the rules that limit the various periods of time available to a person to initiate various civil claims. The 1957 Act contains the relevant limitation periods for many, though not all, civil actions. Limitation periods can be postponed due to infancy or disability, or extended in the case of part payment, fraud or mistake.

The limitation periods allow the plaintiff a specific amount of time, running from a specified date, within which to bring an action against the defendant. The plaintiff will usually begin civil proceedings by issuing an originating document in the appropriate court office. Once proceedings have been commenced, the limitation period stops running.

If the plaintiff does not begin proceedings within the limitation period, the defendant has a full defence to the plaintiff's claim by arguing that the plaintiff is out of time, or statute-barred. This is irrespective of whether the plaintiff has a valid claim. The limitation period, therefore, operates as a procedural defence to a claim that has been brought outside the relevant time limit. For example, for a civil claim based on breach of contract, the limitation period in the Statute of Limitations is six years from the date of the breach. If the plaintiff begins the claim six years and one day after the breach, the defendant may raise this and have the claim dismissed because it is statute-barred under the 1957 Act. Similarly, for a personal injuries claim arising from a road traffic accident, the limitation period is two years from the date of the accident. If the plaintiff begins this type of claim two years and one day after the accident, the defendant may raise this and have the claim dismissed on the grounds that it is statute-barred (Statute of Limitations (Amendment) Act 1991, s 3, as amended by the Civil Liability and Courts Act 2004, s 7). In *Hegarty v O'Loughran* [1990] 1 IR 148, the Supreme Court held that a cause of action in personal injuries cases accrues when there is a wrong committed and damage is suffered. The Statute of Limitations (Amendment) Act 1991 preserves the existing date of accrual for an action for personal injuries but adds to it a date of knowledge of the person injured on which the limitation period begins to run (s 3 (1)).

With regard to criminal actions, it is necessary to distinguish between summary offences and indictable offences. In the case of a summary offence, generally, the Gardaí must make a complaint to the District Court within six months of the offence being committed. These offences include most road traffic offences such as exceeding the speed limit, illegal parking and fixed charge notices. However, in recent years, for particular offences, a period of up to one year has been set down, with some legislation allowing up to two years. With regard to indictable offences, s 7 of the Criminal Justice Act 1951 states that the time limits that are provided for summary offences do not apply to indictable offences. Technically, therefore, there is no time limit for the commencement of proceedings in the case of an indictable offence unless specific legislation provides one.

It is important to note that if there has been an unreasonable delay in prosecuting an offence, the judge may decide to dismiss the case. In making this decision, the judge considers whether the delay has reduced the chances of a fair trial. This could occur in circumstances where the delay means that key witnesses are no longer available to give evidence or if the delay renders their memory of relevant events unreliable. In civil cases, the court retains an inherent jurisdiction to dismiss a claim even if it is taken within the limitation period on the basis that it would be unjust to the defendant. This could happen where, in a personal injuries action, the limitation period is suspended due to the infancy of the plaintiff, resulting in a long period of time elapsing between the wrong occurring and the commencement of proceedings (see *O'Domhnaill v Merrick* [1984] IR 151 and *Toal v Duignan* [1991] ILRM 135).

Table on Examples of Limitation Periods

Action	Limitation period
Simple contract	6 years
Quasi-contract	6 years
Speciality contract	12 years
Tort (other than personal injuries for defamation)	6 years
Personal injuries cases in tort	2 years
Recovery of land	12 years
Recovery of arrears of conventional rent	6 years
Redemption of mortgage	12 years
Damages in respect of defective products	3 years
Damages arising from breach of implied condition arising from defective motor vehicle	2 years

D. Standards of Proof

In general, in a civil case, any particular issue—as well as the overall question of liability—is determined by establishing the issue or the question of liability on the balance of probability. In a criminal case, all issues to be determined by the court, including the question of guilt, must be proved beyond reasonable doubt.

The balance of probability is therefore the normal standard of proof in civil proceedings. It is often referred to as the 'civil standard of proof'. This standard of proof operates whereby a party, upon whom the burden of proof rests, is entitled to a decision in his favour in that issue if he establishes the proof of the matter on the balance of probability. In criminal cases, where the burden of proof rests with the prosecution, the guilt of the accused must be proved beyond reasonable doubt. The accused is therefore entitled to an acquittal if his evidence raises sufficient doubt as to his guilt. In criminal cases where the burden of proof on any issue rests with the accused, the standard of proof is on the balance of probability — see *The People (Attorney General) v Byrne* [1974] IR 1. 'Beyond reasonable doubt' is often referred to as the 'criminal standard of proof'.

The burden of proof therefore is the obligation that is placed upon a particular party of proving the relevant facts in any case, civil or criminal. The obligation of establishing a case generally rests on the party asserting that case.

The distinction between the civil and criminal standards of proof can come into sharp focus where civil and criminal actions flow from a single event. An example would be road traffic accidents. If a driver is alleged to have caused a road traffic accident through careless driving and is prosecuted before the District Court, he will be entitled to an acquittal if the prosecution fails to prove his guilt beyond reasonable doubt — the criminal standard. Even if this happens, a person injured in that road traffic accident may still succeed in a civil action for damages against that driver. This is because the injured person, the plaintiff in the civil action, is only required to prove that the driver, the defendant, was at fault to the (lower) civil standard — the balance of probability.

E. Rules of Evidence

Overview

Evidence in civil and criminal proceedings must, in general, be given under oath (Oaths Act 1888). Giving false evidence under oath constitutes the criminal offence of perjury. Children under the age of 14 may give unsworn evidence (Criminal Evidence Act 1992, s 27 and the Children Act 1997, s 28).

Oral evidence is considered to be highly probative. This is because the demeanour of witnesses giving that evidence can be observed by the tribunal of fact — either a judge or jury. Furthermore, that evidence can be tested under cross-examination. In these circumstances it is possible to test the veracity of the statements they make. Sworn evidence may also be given in writing in the form of a sworn affidavit. This is a document that is sworn before a Commissioner for Oaths. Any untrue statements in an affidavit are subject to the law of perjury in the same way as oral evidence given in court.

Witnesses called upon to give evidence in both civil and criminal trials are called in a particular sequence. In civil trials, the witnesses for the plaintiff will be called by the plaintiff's lawyer to give their evidence first. They will then be questioned by the plaintiff's lawyer. This is called 'examination-in-chief'. The plaintiff's witnesses may then be cross-examined by the defendant's lawyer. The defendant's witnesses will then be called by the defendant's lawyer. They will then be questioned by the defendant's lawyer (also examination-in-chief). The defendant's witnesses may then be cross-examined by the plaintiff's lawyer. A similar procedure applies in criminal trials, with the prosecution calling its witnesses first.

The defendant is entitled to refuse to give evidence in a criminal trial. At the end of the evidence for the prosecution, the case may go to the jury. The jury must then make a decision without the benefit of hearing the defendant's version of events. Since the defendant is presumed to be innocent of the charges against him, it is entirely a matter for the prosecution to prove, through its evidence, the defendant's guilt beyond reasonable doubt. Should the prosecution fail to do so, the defendant will be entitled to an acquittal.

The law of evidence seeks to regulate what may be adduced before the court in order to prove facts. It comprises the rules which govern the presentation of facts and proof in proceedings before a court.

Evidence may be direct or circumstantial. Direct evidence is evidence of a fact in issue. A fact in issue, in civil proceedings, is that which is alleged by one party and denied by the other in the pleadings. In criminal proceedings, it is the constituent elements of the offence alleged by the prosecution and the facts alleged by the defence and denied by the prosecution. Direct evidence may be a statement by a person who observed an event with his senses. Circumstantial evidence is evidence of a fact relevant to the fact in issue, in the sense that it is evidence from which the fact in issue may be inferred.

The policy objective underpinning rules of evidence is to ensure that evidence adduced before the court is reliable and relevant such that it will offer the best opportunity of yielding an outcome that is true and fair, whether in civil or criminal proceedings. In general, relevant evidence is admissible, whereas irrelevant evidence is inadmissible. There are, of course, exceptions to this general proposition. These exceptions relate, primarily, to hearsay evidence and opinion evidence.

Hearsay Evidence
Hearsay evidence is evidence of a fact which has not been perceived by a witness with his own senses, but asserted by him to have been stated by another person. Evidence will be hearsay if it is offered to prove the truth of facts stated in that evidence. Generally, it will not be admissible. It may, however, be admissible if its purpose is to show that the statement was made, rather than to prove the truth of the statement.

Therefore, hearsay evidence is, in general, not admissible where it is sought to be introduced to a trial to prove the truth of the matter in dispute. This means that, in general, where it is desired to prove the truth of some disputed fact, evidence of what was said by some person not called as a witness, or of what was stated in some document executed by such a person, will not generally be admitted. For example, in a murder case a witness would not generally be permitted to say that, John Smith (some third person not called as a witness) said that he had seen the accused do it. The reason for this rule is said to be that, if such evidence were admitted, there would be no way of testing its veracity, for the speaker or the writer of the statement was not necessarily on oath when he made it, and there is no way of testing the credibility or truthfulness of a person who is not present for cross-examination.

As mentioned, the hearsay rule only operates to exclude evidence when it is sought to be introduced as proof of the truth of the facts in the statement. There is no objection to its introduction for any other purpose, provided that it is otherwise relevant: as, for instance, to prove the fact that the disputed statement was made. Thus, if in an action for defamation A claims that B called him a thief, it will be in order for a witness to testify that he heard B make this remark — since what is in issue is not whether A is a thief, but whether B made the remark — a fact about which the witness can give evidence at first hand.

In an exception to the hearsay rule, information contained in a document is *prima facie* admissible in criminal proceedings as evidence of any facts contained in it. The information must have been compiled, whether on computer or otherwise, in the course of a business and must have been supplied, either directly or indirectly, by someone who had, or may reasonably be supposed to have had, personal knowledge of the matters dealt with in the document recording the information (Criminal Evidence Act 1992, s 5). The term 'business' is defined in the 1992 Act to include any trade, profession or other occupation carried on, for reward or otherwise, either within or outside the State. It also includes the performance of functions by or on behalf of: (a) any person or body remunerated or financed wholly or partly out of moneys provided by the Oireachtas; (b) any institution of the EU; (c) any national or local authority in a jurisdiction outside the State; or (d) any international organisation. In *Director of Corporate Enforcement v Bailey* [2007] IEHC 365; [2008] 2 ILRM 13, it was held that the report of a tribunal of inquiry is not admissible under the public documents exception to the hearsay rule on the basis that a tribunal report expresses opinions.

The Law Reform Commission has recommended that hearsay evidence should generally be admissible in civil cases (LRC 25 of 1988). This is already generally the case in England and Wales (United Kingdom Civil Evidence Act 1995, s 1).

Opinion Evidence

Generally, opinion evidence is inadmissible. There are, however, exceptions. The evidence of 'expert' witnesses in which evidence is given of their opinion on certain matters within their area of expertise is admissible. A medical practitioner in a negligence action, for example, may express an opinion as to whether a particular treatment or procedure was carried out in accordance with generally accepted standards of medical practice. In criminal cases, 'ordinary' witnesses, as opposed to 'expert' witnesses, may not express an opinion on the evidence that they give.

Statutory Intervention in the Rules of Evidence

The Oireachtas has intervened with legislation which seeks to encourage the more efficient conduct of litigation so that lengthy court hearings may be avoided. The Criminal Justice Act 1984 provides for proof of certain matters by way of formal statement (s 21) and formal admission (s 22). Statements or omissions under these provisions are not sworn statements. They do not relate to the admission of confessions as evidence. In addition, in personal injuries actions, both parties are required to disclose to each other and to exchange medical and other expert reports that are relevant to the case. This procedure requires that the parties disclose to each other any report or statement from any expert intended to be called to give evidence of medical or paramedical opinion in relation to any matter in the case or from any other expert of the evidence intended to be given by that expert in relation to an issue in that case. Such documents may be directly relevant to the strength or weakness of the parties' cases: nevertheless they must be given to the other party. This is notwithstanding the availability of privileges under the discovery rules (Rules of the Superior Courts (No 6) (Disclosure of Reports and Statements) 1998 (SI No 391 of 1998).

CHAPTER SEVENTEEN

Decisions of the Courts: Remedies and Enforcement

A. **Civil Matters — Remedies and Enforcement** 309
    Introduction 309
    Damages 309
    Injunction 310
    Specific performance 311
    Declaration 312
    Enforcement of Court Judgments 312
        General 312
        Court Orders and their Enforcement 312
B. **Criminal Matters — Punishment and Enforcement** 314
    Punishment — General 314
    Fines 316
    Imprisonment 317
    Probation 318
    Community Service 318
    'Regulatory' Offences 318
    Extra-Jurisdictional Criminal Enforcement 319
C. **Contempt of Court — Civil and Criminal** 319
    General 319
    Civil Contempt 319
    Criminal Contempt 319
D. **Judicial Review** 320

Learning Outcomes

Upon completion of this chapter, the student should be able to:

- Describe the key remedies and enforcement mechanisms available in civil cases;
- Describe the main types of punishment and enforcement mechanisms available in criminal cases;
- Discuss the distinction between civil and criminal contempt;
- Explain the nature of judicial review, including grounds and remedies.

A. Civil Matters — Remedies and Enforcement

Introduction

Once the court decides that some recognised legal wrong has been committed — for example a contract has been breached or a breach of duty in negligence has occurred — it may grant a remedy. Remedies in civil matters include damages (monetary compensation), injunctions, declarations and specific performance.

Figure 17.1 Remedies in Civil Cases

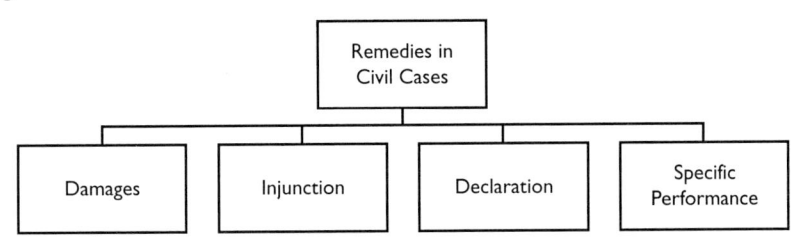

```
                    Remedies in
                    Civil Cases
    ┌──────────┬──────────┴──────────┬──────────────┐
  Damages   Injunction           Declaration     Specific
                                                 Performance
```

Damages

Damages (monetary compensation) are the most common remedy sought in civil actions. They seek to place the plaintiff in the position he or she was in before the legal wrong was committed (*Robinson v Harman* [1848] 1 Exch 850). This principle is known as *restitutio in integrum*. An example is *Wall v Hegarty* [1980] ILRM 124. In that case, the defendants were a firm of solicitors. They prepared a will on behalf of the plaintiff's uncle. The plaintiff was a beneficiary under that will. The will was declared invalid because it was negligently prepared. The plaintiff therefore lost an expected inheritance of £15,000. The Court held that the defendants owed the plaintiff a duty of care in the preparation of the will. Because they failed in that duty, the plaintiff was awarded damages of £15,000. This put the plaintiff into the position he would have been in had the negligent act not taken place.

Damages in personal injuries claims may be general or special. General damages are non-pecuniary losses, for example damages for pain and suffering. Special damages are pecuniary losses. They must be expressly pleaded and proved, for example, loss of earnings or medical expenses.

Since the enactment of the Personal Injuries Assessment Board Act 2003, all personal injuries claims are referred, in the first instance, to the Injuries Board, a statutory body established under the 2003 Act (See chapter 20.) A claimant may, however, proceed to the court system if:

- The claim does not fall within the scope of the Personal Injuries Assessment Board Act 2003;

- The action is one to which the 2003 Act applies but the respondent does not consent to an assessment;
- The Board refuses to deal with the claim; or
- The claimant or respondent declines to accept the assessment

The Personal Injuries Assessment (Amendment) Act 2007 provides that, where a claimant rejects an assessment by the Injuries Board and where he or she fails in subsequent legal proceedings to obtain more, he or she will not be entitled to costs. In addition, the 2007 Act provides that no legal costs are to be allowed for the making of an application to the Injuries Board.

In some instances, the court may make an award of exemplary or punitive damages. This could arise in exceptional circumstances where there has been a conscious and deliberate violation of rights or where the court is satisfied that the defendant intended to profit over and above that which would have been awarded to the injured party.

The court, in making an award of damages, may also order the payment of interest on all or part of that sum from the date of the cause of action to the date of judgment (s 22 of the Courts Act 1981).

Injunction

An injunction is an order of the court directing a party to an action to do, or to refrain from doing, a particular thing. An injunction may be prohibitory or mandatory. A prohibitory injunction is a restrictive or preventative injunction which forbids the party subject to it from doing or continuing a wrongful act. A mandatory injunction is a compulsory injunction which directs the party subject to it to perform a positive act. Injunctions may be perpetual, interim or interlocutory.

A perpetual injunction is a permanent injunction after the hearing of an action. An interim injunction restrains the party subject to it until some specified time. An interlocutory injunction is a temporary injunction usually granted pending trial of the action. It is usually only granted where the balance of convenience lies in favour of granting it and where the recoverable damages would not be an adequate remedy (see *Campus Oil Ltd v Minister for Industry & Energy (No 2)* [1983] IR 88. The difficulty in assessing damages is not in itself a ground for characterising the awarding of damages as an inadequate remedy (*Curust v Loewe GmbH* [1993] ILRM 723; [1994] 1 IR 450).

The injunction was developed as an equitable remedy by the courts of equity to prevent one party from interfering with the rights of another. As indicated, it supplements the remedy of damages which is available at common law. In trespass cases, in particular where the trespass is continuing, the plaintiff may seek an injunction to restrain the defendant from further acts of trespass. In such a case, damages would not necessarily be an adequate remedy.

A *quia timet* injunction may be granted by the court to prevent some future action by the defendant which is feared or threatened, which if done, would cause the applicant substantial damage, and for which damages would not be an adequate remedy. The applicant must show a strong possibility of serious damage. The cost to the defendant must also be considered by the court. It is granted by the court in advance of the feared act of the defendant.

A *Mareva* injunction is a type of interim injunction granted on an *ex parte* basis. It restrains a defendant — who is not within the jurisdiction, but who has assets within it — from removing those assets from the jurisdiction pending trial of an action for debt (*Mareva Compania Naviera v International Bulk Carriers* [1980] 1 All ER 213). A *Mareva* injunction will only be granted if the plaintiff shows he has an arguable case, that he is likely to succeed in the action and that the anticipated disposal of the defendant's assets is for the purpose of preventing the plaintiff from recovering damages and not merely for the purpose of carrying on a business or discharging lawful debts (*O'Mahony v Horgan* [1996] 1 ILRM 161).

An *Anton Piller Order* is a type of mandatory injunction. It is normally granted *ex parte* without notice being given to the defendant. It requires the defendant to permit the plaintiff or his agents to enter his premises to examine documents, computer drives or other articles, and remove any items that belong to the plaintiff. The purpose of this injunction is to prevent the defendant from removing or destroying stolen or pirated material before an action comes to trial (see *Anton Piller KG v Manufacturing Process Ltd* [1976] Ch 55; [1976] 2 WLR 162; [1976] 1 All ER 779).

Specific Performance
Specific performance is an equitable discretionary remedy. It operates where a party to an agreement is compelled by an order of the court to perform his obligations according to the terms of that agreement. This could occur, for example, in contracts for the sale, purchase or lease of land (*Nestor v Murphy* [1979] IR 326). It is particularly appropriate in contracts where the subject matter is unique and a substitute is not readily available. Specific performance will not be granted where damages are an adequate remedy or where the court cannot supervise the execution of the contract (e.g. a building contract). Nor will it generally be granted where the contract is for personal services.

Declaration

The remedy of declaration developed originally as a private law remedy in the Chancery courts prior to the Judicature Act. It is of equitable origin and is therefore discretionary in character. In Ireland, it has its modern origins in the Chancery (Ireland) Act 1865, s 155. That provision is substantially reproduced in Ord 19, r 29 of the Rules of the Superior Courts. A plaintiff may apply to the court for a declaration to determine the rights or status of a person. In this jurisdiction, declaration may be used in constitutional claims, where for example, the plaintiff seeks a declaration that a particular statutory provision is unconstitutional.

Enforcement of Court Judgments
General

Where a creditor (a person to whom a debt is owed) successfully sues a debtor (the person who owes the debt), the court is said to give judgment in favour of the creditor and against the debtor. The creditor is then referred to as the 'judgment creditor' and the debtor as the 'judgment debtor'. In such circumstances, a range of mechanisms is available to judgment creditors to enforce, or 'execute', those judgments. The judgment creditor may seek to use several such mechanisms at the same time. In general, once the creditor obtains a judgment order, the judgment can be enforced. Enforcement orders can be issued by court offices. Judgment creditors generally have 12 years from the date of the judgment to seek enforcement orders. However, if the judgment order was issued six or more years earlier, the judgment creditor may have to apply to the court for 'leave to issue execution'. Once issued, enforcement orders are generally valid for a year and may then be renewed. Most debts are collected by Sheriffs, County Registrars and Revenue Sheriffs, often under the authority of an order.

Court Orders and their Enforcement

Sheriffs enforce judgments in the counties of Cork and Dublin; County Registrars enforce them elsewhere. Sheriffs are self-employed persons who are paid for their enforcement work on a commission basis. The system is called 'poundage'. Their fees are set out in statutory instruments (Sheriff's Fees and Expenses Order (SI No 644 of 2005)) made under the Enforcement of Court Orders Act 1926. This provides for various fixed fees and a scale of fees related to the amount involved.

County Registrars are civil servants. Their main function is to organise the business of the Circuit Court in their areas. They also act as Returning Officers for elections and referendums.

Revenue Sheriffs enforce debts owed to the Revenue Commissioners (tax debts). They can do this on the basis of a certificate of liability issued by the Collector

General (the official in the Revenue Commissioners responsible for collecting taxes). They do not need a court order. Revenue debts can also be collected in the normal way if there is a court order.

Table on Orders/Mechanisms Available to Judgment Creditors through the Courts

Order/Mechanism	Description
Fieri facias or *Fifa* order (High Court) Execution order against goods (Circuit Court) Judgment or decree (District Court)	Seizure of debtor's goods so they can be sold to raise the necessary amount of money owed, plus costs.
Garnishee order	Assigns to the creditor any debt owed to the debtor by a third party; creditor may intercept income and profits before they reach the debtor.
Instalment order	Creditor can apply to the District Court to have the debtor attend court in order to establish their means; the judge may then order payment in full or payment in instalments, taking account of the debtor's means.
Registration of the judgment	Creditor registers the judgment in the Central Office of the High Court; publicises the fact that there is a judgment against the debtor.
Judgment mortgage	Involves registering a judgment as a mortgage against the debtor's property; effectively, the judgment is converted into a mortgage and is registered in the Land Registry or Registry of Deeds; creditor may then decide to force a sale or to claim entitlement to the proceeds of a sale by the debtor.

The Enforcement of Court Orders Acts 1926 and 1940, as amended by the Courts (No 2) Act 1986, empowers the District Court to require a person in default of a court order to make payments in accordance with a schedule of payments arrived at by the court after an assessment of the defaulter's means. If the defaulter continues to default, he or she may be attached for contempt of court and may be imprisoned for that failure. Persons are not imprisoned for inability to pay a debt, only for wilful refusal to do so.

In *McCann v Judge of Monaghan District Court* [2009] IEHC 276, the plaintiff challenged the validity of an order for her arrest and imprisonment made by the District Court under the Enforcement of Court Orders Acts 1926 and 1940. It ordered that the plaintiff be committed to prison for one month for failure to comply with an instalment order which had been obtained by the creditor against her. Laffoy J held that the relevant provisions of the Enforcement of Court Orders Acts 1926 and 1940, which allowed for the plaintiff's imprisonment for failure to pay arrears on a debt without the need for her presence in court, were unconstitutional. The Oireachtas subsequently enacted the Enforcement of Court Orders (Amendment) Act 2009, which amended those provisions to require the debtor's presence before such orders could be made. The amendments include:

- Empowering a District Court judge to fix a new date for a hearing if there is no appearance by the debtor;
- Permitting the judge to request that the debtor and creditor attempt to resolve the matter by mediation;
- Providing for legal aid for debtors against whom instalment orders have been made.

The amendments introduced by the 2009 Act addressed the issues of concern identified in the *McCann* case. In December 2010, the Law Reform Commission published a report, *Personal Debt Management and Debt Enforcement* (LRC 100 – 2010), setting out proposals for much wider legislative reform to deal with debt, its enforcement, and the resolution of unsustainable personal debt.

Under the Family Law Act 1995, enforcement mechanisms such as attachment of earnings are available in respect of maintenance payments. Under such an order, the employer of a defaulting spouse would be required to deduct a specified sum and pay it directly to the spouse and children in whose to favour the maintenance order has been made. In addition, orders of foreign courts may be enforced in this jurisdiction under legislation giving effect to international agreements (see chapter 9, International Law).

B. Criminal Matters — Punishment and Enforcement

Punishment — General

A person convicted of a criminal offence by a criminal court may be subject to punishment. Depending on the offence, punishments could include a sentence of imprisonment, a money fine, an order to pay compensation, a community service order or a probation order. A sentence of imprisonment involves depriving persons of their liberty for a specified period of time. In general, such sentences of are considered to have a number of broad objectives: retribution, deterrence, protection of society, reparation and rehabilitation. Sentences are subject to the doctrine of proportionality in that they are required to be consistent with the circumstances of the offence, the relevant personal circumstances of the defendant, the likelihood of reoffending and the prospects for rehabilitation.

The impact of a crime on the victim is also a factor to be taken into account in determining sentence. Nevertheless, there are necessary limits to this because, as we have seen, the criminal law is an action between the State and the offender, not between the victim and the offender. A court is, however, required to take into account the effect of certain offences on the victim when formulating the sentence to be imposed. These are primarily sexual offences and offences involving violence, or the threat of violence, to the person (Criminal Justice Act 1993, s 5). The Criminal Procedure Act 2010 has amended the law in relation to victim impact statements in that it now allows family members of murder victims to address the court. Previously, only the victim of a crime was permitted to address the court following the verdict and prior to sentencing. An inference cannot be drawn where a victim does not wish to give a victim impact statement. Under the 2010 Act, the term "family member" does not include "civil partner" but it does include any other person who the court considers to have had a close connection with the person.

The court can find a person in contempt of court if he or she steps outside the agreed terms of the victim impact statement. The Criminal Procedure Act 2010, however, provides for an alternative approach. The legislation empowers the court, in the interests of justice, to order that information relating to evidence given by a victim should not be published or broadcast. This provides the court with a procedure to control information which it considers to be unfair to a party to the case. It effectively means editing a victim impact statement before it is published in the media, rather than doing it in advance of it being given in court. The person giving the statement will therefore not be subject to the fear of being punished for contempt.

Under s 100 of the Criminal Justice Act 2006, where a convicted person is liable to both a fine and a term of imprisonment, the court may impose a fine and make an order deferring the passing of the sentence whilst also specifying the term of imprisonment that it would impose should the offender fail to comply with the conditions set down in the order.

The courts have a number of mechanisms at their disposal to enforce the criminal law and punish those found guilty of a crime. The following are the main sanctions/punishments which can be handed down by a court in a criminal trial.

Figure 17.2 Criminal Sanctions

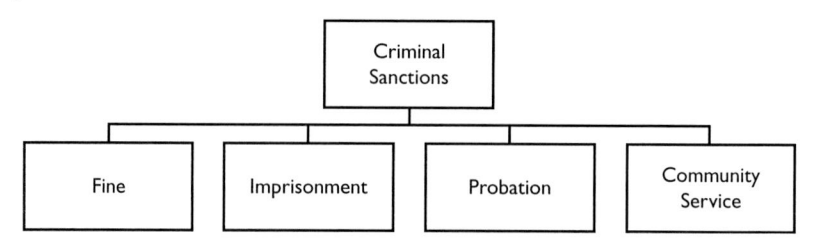

```
                    Criminal
                    Sanctions
         ┌─────────────┼─────────────┐
       Fine      Imprisonment    Probation    Community
                                              Service
```

Fines

A fine is a monetary penalty payable by a person upon conviction. Under the Fines Act 2010, there are five categories or classes of maximum fine applying to summary convictions. If a person is liable to pay a particular class of fine on summary conviction, the maximum fine is given in the table below which summarises the fine classes as set out in s 3 of the Fines Act 2010.

Fine Class	A	B	C	D	E
Maximum fine	€5,000	€4,000	€2,500	€1,000	€500

If the maximum fine on summary conviction for a particular offence was enacted or set before January 2011, the 2010 Act will now place that fine into one of the fine classes of A to E. The class the fine belongs to will depend on when the fine was set and the amount the maximum fine was originally set at. For example, if the relevant legislation set the maximum fine on summary conviction for a particular offence at €500 in 1992, a class D fine now applies. The table below summarises the fine parameters set out in s 4 (class A fines), s 5 (class B fines), s 6 (class C fines), s 7 (class D fines) and s 8 (class E fines) of the 2010 Act.

Fine Class	A	B	C	D	E
Fines Act 2010	s 4	s 5	s 6	s 7	s 8
Set in period	Fine (€)	Fine (€)	Fine (€)	Fine (€)	Fine (€)
1997 - 2010	4,001 - 5,000	2,501 - 4,000	1,001 - 2,500	501 – 1,000	1 - 500
1990 - 1996	2,770 - 5,000	1,732 - 2,769	693 - 1,731	347 - 692	1 - 346
1980 - 1989	2,329 - 5,000	1,456 - 2,328	583 - 1,455	292 - 582	1 - 291
1975 - 1979	971 - 5,000	607 - 970	243 - 606	122 - 242	1 - 121
1965 - 1974	492 - 5,000	308 - 491	124 - 307	62 - 123	1 - 61
1945 - 1964	235 - 5,000	148 - 234	60 - 147	30 - 59	1 - 29
1915 - 1944	128 - 5,000	80 - 127	33 – 79	17 - 32	1 - 16
Up to 1914	101 - 5,000	51 - 100	26 - 50	7 - 25	1 - 6

In a case where an indictable offence is tried summarily, the maximum fine that applies is a class A fine (s 10 of the 2010 Act). If the maximum fine for conviction on indictment for a particular offence was set in or after 1997, it is still the maximum fine for that offence. If the maximum fine was set before then, the value it was set at is multiplied by the appropriate multiplier. For example, if the maximum fine was set at €5,000 in 1984, one multiplies by two to obtain the current value of €10,000. The table below summarises the periods and relevant multipliers as set out in s 9 of the 2010 Act.

Set in period	Multiplier
1990 - 1996	1.75
1980 - 1989	2
1975 - 1979	5
1965 - 1974	10
1945 - 1964	21
1915 - 1944	39
Up to 1914	50

Section 15 of the 2010 Act provides for payment by instalments in circumstances where a requirement to pay the fine in full by the due date would cause undue financial hardship to the person or his or her dependants. Section 16 provides for non-payment of a fine to be enforced in a manner similar to that of a civil debt and the court can appoint a receiver where a fine imposed on indictment has not been paid by its due date. In addition, a convicted person may be subject to a term of imprisonment of up to 12 months if they fail to pay the fine by the due date.

Imprisonment
Incarceration through a sentence of imprisonment is a long-established device for the enforcement of law. Seeking to ensure that sentences are consistent throughout the court system is a concern. To assist in achieving this objective, the Irish Sentencing Information System (ISIS) was established in 2006. The Board of the Courts Service established it to plan for and provide information on sentencing decisions. The sentencing information system enables a judge, by entering relevant criteria into a database, to access information on the range of sentences and other penalties which have been imposed for particular types of offence in previous cases. Prior to the introduction of ISIS, there was limited information available to judges on sentencing practice in Ireland.

Once a sentence of imprisonment is imposed by the judiciary, enforcement of that sentence is a matter for the executive. The Minister for Justice is authorised by legislation to remit (reduce) sentences of imprisonment (Criminal Justice Act 1951). Ultimately, the executive determines the exact length of time a person serves under a sentence of imprisonment.

Probation

Under the Probation of Offenders Act 1907, an order for probation may be imposed upon an offender in certain circumstances. Such an order is a warning to the person that, if he or she does not keep the peace and adhere to conditions imposed by the court for a particular period, he or she will be liable to be brought before the court where punishment may be imposed. Under the 1907 Act, two types of order may be made: a conditional discharge and an absolute discharge.

A conditional discharge may be applied where a person has been convicted but the court considers it 'inexpedient', in all the circumstances of the particular case, to impose any punishment other than a nominal punishment. The convicted person may be required to enter into a recognisance to be of good behaviour for a period not exceeding three years. In the event of a breach of the recognisance, the convicted person may be brought before the court and sentenced. The person will be under the supervision of the Probation and Welfare Service during the relevant period.

An absolute discharge may only be applied in the District Court. In such circumstances, no conviction is recorded, notwithstanding the fact that the judge is satisfied that the offence has been proved. A compensation order may be made in favour of the victim (Criminal Justice Act 1993). The person subject to the absolute discharge may be required to make a payment into the court poor box.

Community Service

The Criminal Justice (Community Service) Act 1983 empowers the court to make a community service order in respect of any person over the age of 16 years convicted of an offence for which a sentence of imprisonment might otherwise be imposed. The convicted person must consent to the order. In addition, the court must be satisfied that the person is suitable to perform the work in question. Failure to perform the community service is itself an offence.

'Regulatory' Offences

A number of statutory bodies are conferred with enforcement powers in relation to regulatory offences. Legislation creating regulatory offences provides for penalties such as fines and imprisonment, but may also provide for other enforcement mechanisms such as 'improvement notices' and 'prohibition notices' under the Safety, Health and Welfare at Work Act 2005. Improvement notices may direct an employer to comply with statutory duties under the Act and may specify a date by which such directions should be fulfilled. Prohibition notices may require an employer immediately to stop carrying out a particular activity which may present a risk of personal injury to persons in a place of work.

Extra-Jurisdictional Criminal Enforcement

A number of statutes give effect to international agreements concerning enforcement of crimes committed outside the jurisdiction. Examples include the Criminal Justice Act 1994, which deals with international money-laundering operations in the context of drug trafficking, the International War Crimes Tribunal Act 1998, the Criminal Justice (United Nations Convention against Torture) Act 2000 and the International Criminal Court Act 2006, which deals with the crime of genocide.

C. Contempt of Court — Civil and Criminal

General

A person is held in contempt of court if he/she has disobeyed a court order (civil contempt) or has prejudiced the administration of justice or brought it into disrepute (criminal contempt).

Figure 17.3 Types of Contempt of Court

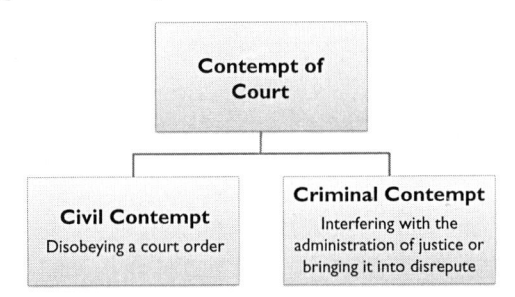

```
                    Contempt of
                       Court
                    ┌─────┴─────┐
        Civil Contempt      Criminal Contempt
        Disobeying a        Interfering with the
        court order         administration of justice or
                            bringing it into disrepute
```

Civil Contempt

Civil contempt of court involves the refusal to obey a court order. The person in whose favour the court order was made may bring to the attention of the court the fact that it has been disobeyed. The court may then order that the person in contempt be 'attached for contempt', i.e. that they be brought before the court. If the person gives an undertaking to obey the court order, that will normally be the end of the matter. If not, the court may lodge the person in prison until their contempt is purged, i.e. they agree to obey the order. The person may only be released by order of the court.

Criminal Contempt

Criminal contempt involves any action intended to prejudice the due course of justice or which brings the administration of justice into disrepute. This may include disrupting court proceedings (contempt *in facie curiae*); scandalising the court, e.g. making unfounded allegations or criticisms of judges and the courts; breaching the *sub judice* rule, e.g. engaging in conduct or making statements likely to prejudice pending court proceedings; or otherwise interfering with the administration of justice. Prosecutions for criminal contempt may be initiated by the DPP or a judge. A judge may try the case without a jury and impose sentence.

D. Judicial Review

The High Court has an inherent jurisdiction to supervise the acts of the inferior courts, tribunals and other public bodies. We have seen that the inferior courts, as public bodies, receive their powers from statute. Tribunals and public authorities (for example, local authorities) also receive their powers from statute. These statutes give such bodies the power to perform certain functions. These might include making grants of money, issuing licences or making bye-laws. In addition to statutory power, public bodies have what are sometimes referred to as 'common law powers': i.e. powers common to public bodies and natural persons. Such powers might include the right to sue and be sued, to borrow and spend money, to hold land and to enter into contracts.

Judicial review must be distinguished from appeal. 'Review' and 'appeal' are separate ideas. Judicial review is a creature of the common law. It is concerned with keeping public bodies within their 'proper' limits. Appeal, on the other hand, is a creature of statute. Different statutes set up different kinds of appeal. There can be appeals to courts or to individual officials. The grounds of appeal also depend on the statute in question. As we have seen, appeals range from a complete rehearing of the matter to appeals on a point of law. An appeal body may be empowered by statute to substitute its decision for the decision of the public body. In contrast, judicial review is concerned with the decision-making process, rather than the decision itself. In other words, the court is not concerned with the merits of the decisions of such bodies, only their legality. Judicial review seeks therefore to define the scope of public power, not substitute its views for those of the public body in question.

The law of judicial review has traditionally been based on the doctrine of *ultra vires* ('beyond the powers'). In essence, an *ultra vires* decision is one in which a public body does something not authorised by the language of the statute which confers the power upon it. The doctrine requires that such bodies, in exercising their power, do not go beyond the limits, or *vires*, explicitly or implicitly, conferred upon them by statute. Much depends upon the interpretation of the statute. The doctrine of *ultra vires* would treat ideas such as fairness and reasonableness as presumptions of statutory interpretation. An example of the application of the doctrine is the leading English case of *Bromley London Borough Council v Greater London Council* [1982] 2 WLR 62. In that case, statute required London Transport (as it then was) to run its affairs 'economically'. The House of Lords held that 'economically' did not mean merely 'not wastefully' but required London Transport *not* to run the London transport system at a loss. This meant that a decision by the Greater London Council to make a grant for the purpose of subsidising bus and rail fares in the interest of wider social benefits was *ultra vires* and therefore unlawful.

Public bodies may not abuse the discretion conferred upon them by statute. For example, public bodies may not fetter their discretion. This means that the decision-maker must keep an open mind and not follow a general policy by failing to take the circumstances of the individual into account. Also, the decision-maker must not take irrelevant factors into account or fail to take relevant factors into account when making decisions. Furthermore, the decision-maker must exercise discretion reasonably. A decision of a public body is said to be unreasonable if it is completely irrational or so absurd that no reasonable body could have made such a decision. This is sometimes referred to as 'Wednesbury unreasonableness' (see *Associated Provincial Picture Houses v Wednesbury Corporation* [1948] 1 KB 223; *State (Keegan) v Stardust Victims' Compensation Tribunal* [1986] IR 642; and *O'Keefe v An Bord Pleanála* [1993] 1 IR 39).

In relation to common law powers, public bodies may generally perform only acts that are necessary or reasonably incidental to their statutory purposes. Bodies that go beyond their powers are often described as "exceeding their jurisdiction".

The following remedies are available by way of judicial review:

- *Certiorari* — an order to quash a decision of a body which has been found to have acted outside its powers;
- *Mandamus* — an order requiring a body to carry out a lawful obligation;
- *Prohibition* — an order requiring a body not to exercise its powers, either completely or until certain conditions have been met;
- *Declaration* — a remedy answering the question as to the legality of a state of affairs or as to the rights of the parties, i.e. it affirms the legal position; it is a private, as well as public, law remedy;
- *Injunction* — an order of the court directing a party to an action to do, or to refrain from doing, a particular thing;
- *Damages* — the court, on an application for judicial review, is empowered to make an award of damages under Ord 84, r 24 (1) of the Rules of the Superior Courts (SI No 15 of 1986) if two conditions are met: (i) the applicant must have "included in the statement in support of his application for

leave... a claim for damages arising from any matter to which the application relates" and (ii) the court must also be "satisfied that, if the claim had been made in a civil action against any respondent or respondents begun by the applicant at the time of making his application, he would have been awarded damages".

- *Habeas corpus* — an order requiring the production of a person in court in order to determine whether their detention is legally valid; Article 40.4 of the Constitution is normally used for this purpose.

Judicial review actions are taken in the High Court. They may be taken on a number of grounds, the most common of which relate to an *ultra vires* act or a breach of natural justice. A breach of natural justice, or 'fairness' in the decision-making process, may relate to circumstances in which the applicant has been denied a fair hearing (*audi alteram partem*) or the decision has been made by a biased decision-maker (*nemo judex in causa sua*).

Judicial review procedure is governed by Order 84 of the Rules of the Superior Courts. It involves an application for leave followed by the substantive hearing of the matter if leave is granted. The application for leave involves an *ex parte* application to a High Court judge for leave to proceed. The application sets out the grounds on which relief is sought. If leave to proceed is granted, the applicant may then make the formal application for judicial review. The other party (the respondent) must be notified. Following a full hearing of the matter, the court determines whether the relief sought should be granted.

CHAPTER EIGHTEEN

REFORM OF THE COURT SYSTEM

A. Proposed Amendments to the Civil Justice System 325
B. Proposed Establishment of a Court of Appeal 325

Learning Outcomes

Upon completion of this chapter, the student should be able to:

- Identify the limitations in the jurisdiction of the existing court structure;
- Describe the nature of proposed reforms in respect of jurisdiction and appeals;
- Identify the proposed legislation introducing reforms;
- Appraise the likely impact of the proposed reforms.

A. Proposed Amendments to the Civil Justice System

The Courts and Civil Law (Miscellaneous Provision) Act 2013 was enacted on 24 July 2013. The 2013 Act will change the monetary jurisdiction limits of the District and Circuit Courts in civil proceedings. However, those changes have, at the time if writing, yet to be commenced by ministerial order. The limit of the District Court is to be increased from €6,384 to €15,000 and the Circuit Court from €38,092 to €75,000. In the case of personal injury litigation, the monetary jurisdiction of the Circuit Court will be limited to €60,000 The Minister for Justice has stated that that the purpose of the personal injury limit in the Circuit Court is to discourage possible inflation of awards and the attendant impact on insurance costs. The Government's expectation is that these changes will lead to a decrease in the costs of litigation. In particular, it is anticipated that the extension in the jurisdiction of the District and Circuit Courts will reduce the number of cases being dealt with by the High Court. This, in turn, is expected to lead to a decline in the number of appeals before the Supreme Court.

B. Proposed Establishment of a Court of Appeal

In July 2013 the Thirty-third Amendment of the Constitution (Court of Appeal) Bill 2013 was published. The Bill provides for the establishment of a Court of Appeal if the proposal is approved by the people in a referendum held in October 2013. The main features of the Bill are:

1. The Court of Appeal will have civil and criminal jurisdiction and will replace the Court of Criminal Appeal, for criminal cases;
2. There will be a right of appeal of all cases, including those involving constitutional issues, from the High Court to the Court of Appeal;
3. In exceptional circumstances, there will be a right of appeal from the High Court to the Supreme Court;
4. If the referendum is passed, the Oireachtas will bring forward legislation to provide for the establishment of the Court of Appeal. The Government will then make an order appointing a day on which the court will be established.

It is expected that the new court will be established by autumn 2014.

The need for a Court of Appeal is considered to arise mainly from the ongoing backlog of cases before the Supreme Court and the consequent long delays in cases being dealt with by it. The average delay for new non-priority cases in 2012 and 2013 was of the order of four years. Early in 2013, the Chief Justice announced her decision not to accept any new priority cases, given that there were over 70 cases on the priority list at that time. The Supreme Court in Ireland, unlike in many other common law jurisdictions, is the final appeal court in all cases. This means that, whereas in other countries the final appeal court mainly deals with cases involving substantial points of law or issues of major public importance, in Ireland, the Supreme Court is taken up with issues ranging from routine interlocutory orders through to major constitutional issues.

In 2009, the Report of the Working Group on a Court of Appeal chaired by now Chief Justice Susan Denham, recommended that a full-time Court of Appeal be established, ideally with a permanent panel of judges, to deal with both criminal and civil matters. The proposed court would function above the level of the High Court but below the Supreme Court. As well as dealing with civil appeals, it would be conferred with the existing jurisdiction of the Court of Criminal Appeal. The report noted that a large number of civil appeals coming before the Supreme Court did not involve any novel points of law or constitutional importance. They were in the nature of 'error correction'. The report concluded that appeals of this nature were not appropriate for the Supreme Court and were more suitable for an intermediate Court of Appeal. The establishment of a Court of Appeal would therefore allow the Supreme Court to deal primarily with cases of public importance, as is the case with the Supreme Court of the United Kingdom and the Supreme Court of the United States. This would reduce the workload of the Supreme Court and allow it to focus on developing the law. The Government's expectation is that after the establishment of the new appeal court, most appeals will be concluded at that court and only in exceptional circumstances, subject to the Supreme Court's own leave-to-appeal requirements, will cases proceed to be heard by the Supreme Court.

CHAPTER NINETEEN

Access to Justice

A. The Constitutional Right of Access to the Courts 329
B. Litigants in Person and 'McKenzie Friends' 330
C. Legal Aid 331
   Civil Legal Aid 331
   Criminal Legal Aid 332
D. Court Fees 332
E. Legal Costs 333

Learning Outcomes

Upon completion of this chapter, the student should be able to:

- Provide an account of the case law relating to the right to litigate;
- Explain the rights and entitlements of lay litigants before the court;
- Describe the main features of the legal aid schemes;
- Appreciate the circumstances in which the State meets the costs of legal representation.

A. The Constitutional Right of Access to the Courts

There is a constitutional right of access to the courts. This right was recognised for the first time by Kenny J in the High Court in *Macauley v Minister for Posts and Telegraphs* [1966] IR 345. In that case, the plaintiff sought a declaration from the High Court that the Ministers and Secretaries Act 1924, s 2 (1), was unconstitutional in that it required a litigant to secure the consent of the Attorney General before he could sue the minister. Kenny J held that the right to have recourse to the High Court to defend and vindicate a legal right was protected as a constitutional right under Article 40.3. In *State (Quinn) v Ryan* [1965] IR 70, the Supreme Court held that there was a right of access to the High Court to challenge the legality of one's detention. The Court further held that the courts had whatever powers were necessary to ensure that constitutional rights were vindicated. Finlay CJ, in *Tuohy v Courtney* [1994] 3 IR 1, held that the Statute of Limitations 1957 could not affect a person's right of access to the courts even though it may provide the defendant with a procedural defence to a claim on the basis that the plaintiff was statute-barred.

The courts have, however, held that unreasonably tight time limits, which have the effect of limiting access to the courts, may be unconstitutional. For example, in *White v Dublin City Council* [2004] 1 IR 545, the Supreme Court struck down a rigid time limit of two months for challenging certain planning decisions in circumstances where there was no possibility for extending that time. But, in *Re Article 26 and Section 5 and 10 of the Illegal Immigrants (Trafficking) Bill 1999* [2000] 2 IR 360, the Supreme Court upheld as constitutional a 14-day time limit for seeking judicial review of certain immigration decisions. In doing so, however, it emphasised that the legislation in question gave the Court power to extend the time limit for 'good and sufficient reason' (s 5(2)).

In *Tuohy v Courtney* the Court made a distinction between the constitutional right of access to the courts and the constitutional right to litigate. Finlay CJ defined the right to litigate as

> ... the right to achieve by action in the courts the appropriate remedy upon proof of an actionable wrong causing damage or loss as recognised by law...

This distinction was made in the context of the Statute of Limitations 1957 which placed statutory time limits on instituting proceedings. The Supreme Court took the view that such a time limit could not be said to undermine the constitutional right of access to the courts. Instead, it restricted the unenumerated right to litigate claims, because such time limits were not considered to limit the plaintiff's right to sue but to give the defendant the right to defeat the plaintiff's claim by pleading the statute. This does not, however, mean that time limits can never be challenged on the grounds that they undermine the constitutional right to litigate. In *O'Brien v Keogh* [1972] IR 144, the plaintiff challenged the constitutionality of s 49(2)(a)(ii) of the Statute of Limitations 1957. The provision created two different limitation periods for infants suing for damages for personal injuries. The Supreme Court held that the provision was invalid on the ground that it infringed the right to litigate in respect of those infants subject to the shorter of the two limitation periods.

B. Litigants in Person and 'McKenzie Friends'

Litigants are entitled to represent themselves before the court. They may choose to do so to avoid the attendant costs of engaging a solicitor and counsel. The courts tend to accommodate litigants in person as much as possible and not apply formal rules relating to pleadings and procedure as rigorously as would be the case with qualified lawyers. The appearance of litigants in person tends to be more common in family proceedings than other categories of civil proceedings. It would be unusual in criminal proceedings.

Litigants who are young persons or persons lacking capacity may be assisted by others, known as 'next friends', in both civil and criminal matters. A next friend may initiate proceedings. This would typically be a parent in cases involving minors. Also the court may appoint a guardian *ad litem* in child care and guardianship proceedings. Their function, as an independent person, is to represent the wishes and interests of a child in court proceedings. The court may also join a child to any child care and guardianship proceedings and appoint a solicitor to represent their interests (Child Care Act 1991, s 25 and s 26; Guardianship of Infants Act 1964, s 28, as amended by the Children Act 1997, s 11). If a minor is involved in a criminal matter, the presence of the minor's guardian is generally required during both police questioning and court hearings.

In addition, a lay litigant may receive assistance from a 'McKenzie friend'. The idea of a McKenzie friend originates in the decision of the Court of Appeal in England in *McKenzie v McKenzie* [1971] P 33; [1970] 3 WLR 472; [1970] 3 All ER 1034. In that case, Davies LJ quoted the following statement of Lord Tenterden CJ in *Collier v Hicks* (1831) 2 B & Ad 663:

> Any person, whether he be a professional man or not, may attend as a friend of either party, may take notes, may quietly make suggestions, and give advice; but no one can demand to take part in the proceedings as an advocate, contrary to the regulations of the court as settled by the discretion of the justices.

This statement has been accepted by the Irish courts as an accurate description of the role of a McKenzie friend today. The role of a McKenzie friend before the Irish courts was considered in the High Court by Macken J in *R D v McGuiness* [1999] 2 IR 411, which were family-law proceedings. Macken J said that

> a party who prosecutes proceedings in person is entitled to be accompanied in court by a friend who may take notes on his behalf and quietly make suggestions and assist him generally during the hearing, but… may not act as advocate.

Fennelly J, in *Re Applications for Orders in Relation to Costs in Intended Proceedings: Coffey & ors* [2013] IESC 11 at para 18 pointed out that a judge may, on occasion, as a matter of pure practicality and convenience, invite the McKenzie friend to explain some point of fact or law, where the party is unable to do so or do so clearly. That must always be a matter solely for the discretion of the judge. The McKenzie friend has no right to address the court unless invited to do so by the presiding judge.

C. Legal Aid

There are two legal aid schemes in operation in Ireland: civil legal aid and criminal legal aid.

Figure 19.1 Legal aid in Ireland

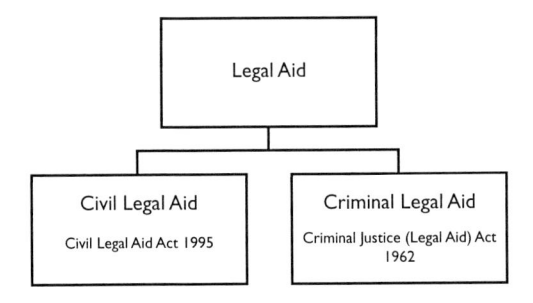

```
                    ┌─────────────┐
                    │  Legal Aid  │
                    └──────┬──────┘
              ┌────────────┴────────────┐
    ┌─────────┴─────────┐    ┌──────────┴──────────┐
    │  Civil Legal Aid  │    │  Criminal Legal Aid │
    │                   │    │                     │
    │ Civil Legal Aid   │    │ Criminal Justice    │
    │ Act 1995          │    │ (Legal Aid) Act 1962│
    └───────────────────┘    └─────────────────────┘
```

Civil Legal Aid

The State has enacted a scheme for providing for civil legal aid through the Civil Legal Aid Act 1995 and the Civil Legal Aid Regulations. In *O'Donoghue v Legal Aid Board* [2004] IEHC 413, Kelly J placed the right to civil legal aid on a constitutional basis. In that case, Kelly J ruled that a delay in granting a certificate for legal aid amounted to a breach of the constitutional entitlements of the plaintiff. In the earlier case of *Airey v Ireland* [1979] 2 EHRR, the State was held to have been in breach of the European Convention on Human Rights due to the non-availability of a State-funded legal aid system in matrimonial matters. In 1979, a non-statutory legal aid scheme was introduced and administered by the Legal Aid Board. Its function was to make the services of solicitors and, if necessary, barristers, available to persons of modest means at low cost.

The statutory scheme was introduced under the 1995 Act, administered by the Legal Aid Board. Under this scheme, legal aid and legal advice is provided to persons who satisfy the financial eligibility requirements and the merits test, and who make a contribution to the Board towards the cost.

Criminal Legal Aid

In *State (Healy) v Donohue* [1976] IR 325, the Supreme Court established the constitutional right of an accused person to be provided with a lawyer. The Criminal Justice (Legal Aid) Act 1962 provided an entitlement to criminal legal aid in certain circumstances. This entitlement arose where the means of the person charged with an offence and the gravity of that offence or exceptional circumstances surrounding the case, made it essential, in the interests of justice, that legal aid be granted.

A judge is required to inform an impecunious defendant following his conviction, or his guilty plea, where a sentence of imprisonment is likely, that he has a right to legal aid under the provisions of the 1962 Act. The failure of a judge, who proposes to impose a custodial sentence, to advise such a defendant appearing before him without representation of his constitutional right to legal aid, could amount to a denial of justice and render that conviction unsound (*McSorley v Governor of Mountjoy Prison* [1996] 2 ILRM 331).

D. Court Fees

Under s 9 of the Civil Law (Miscellaneous Provisions) Act 2008, the Minister for Justice is empowered to prescribe court fees. The court fees applicable to the High Court and Supreme Court are prescribed by SI No 239 of 2013, Circuit Court fees by SI No 240 of 2013 and District Court fees by SI No 241 of 2013. In *Murphy v Minister for Justice* [2001] 2 ILRM 144; 1 IR 95, the Supreme Court held that it was not unconstitutional that court fees should be charged, provided they were reasonable. In that case, the constitutional right under consideration was that of access to the courts. The responsibility for the collection of court fees was transferred to the Courts Service as of 23 January 2004 under the Courts Service Act 1998, Second Schedule, as amended. Court fees are charged for such matters as filing motions of notice, affidavits and notices of appeal; stamping of documents, making applications under the Licensing Acts, filing petitions of bankruptcy, etc. Court fees are normally not payable in family law matters.

E. Legal Costs

Fees payable to solicitors and barristers in both civil and criminal proceedings can represent a significant component of the overall costs of litigation. Generally, in civil cases, the losing party will bear the costs of both sides. In civil cases to which the Civil Legal Aid Act 1995 applies, the State may be subject to the costs of both the plaintiff's and defendant's legal representation. In criminal cases covered by the Criminal Justice (Legal Aid) Act 1962, the State will meet the costs of legal representation for both prosecution and defence. The court may award costs to either side in criminal cases to which the 1962 Act does not apply, though this would be rare. Where the defendant is found guilty, the State generally pays its own costs. The defendant will have to pay his own legal costs where the 1962 Act does not apply. Where the defendant is acquitted, the trial judge has discretion to award costs against the State. In *Dillane v Ireland* [1980] ILRM 167, it was held that a statutory provision that costs may not be awarded against a member of An Garda Síochána acting as prosecutor was not unconstitutional.

Section F

Alternative Dispute Resolution

CHAPTER TWENTY

ALTERNATIVE DISPUTE RESOLUTION

A. Introduction 340
B. Negotiation 340
C. Arbitration 341
   Introduction...341
   Advantages and Disadvantages of Arbitration 342
   The Arbitrator 343
   The Arbitration 344
   The Award and Enforcement 346
D. ADR: Mediation and Conciliation 347
   Introduction...347
   Mediation..347
   Conciliation 347
   Advantages and Disadvantages of Mediation/Conciliation.........................347
   Legal Framework and Reform..348
E. Tribunals 350
   Introduction...350
   Types of Tribunals..350
      A Rights Tribunal 350
         Appealing the Decision of a Rights Tribunal 352
      Tribunals of Inquiry 352
         Introduction..352
         Powers and Procedure..352
         Report of a Tribunal of Inquiry 353
   Reform...354
F. Ombudsmen 354
   Introduction...354
   Types of Ombudsmen 355
      The Ombudsman 355
         Introduction..355
         Powers of the Ombudsman 356
      Other Ombudsman 357
         Financial Services Ombudsman 357
         Ombudsman for Children's Office (OCO)..357

       Pensions Ombudsman 358
       Ombudsman for the Defence Forces 358
       Garda Síochána Ombudsman Commission 358
       The Legal Services Ombudsman...358
G. **The Injuries Board**..359
       Introduction...359
       Scope and Purpose 359
       Procedure..360
       Assessment of Damages 360
       Impact of the Injuries Board 361
H. **Coroner's Court**..362
       Introduction...362
       Inquest Functions and Procedure 363
       Findings of an Inquest 363
       Reform...364
I. **Regulators** 364

Alternative Dispute Resolution | 339

Learning Outcomes

Upon completion of this chapter, students should be able to:

- Discuss and distinguish between the alternatives to litigation when a civil dispute arises;
- Identify the advantages and disadvantages of negotiation, arbitration, mediation and conciliation;
- Differentiate between the types of tribunals and their respective functions;
- Explain the role and remit of the Injuries Board and comment on its impact on the Irish legal system to date;
- Identify disputes which may be referred to Ombudsmen and describe their key functions;
- Discuss the role of the Coroner's Court and other regulators in the Irish legal system.

A. Introduction

A party to a legal dispute has a number of options when it comes to resolving the dispute. One option is to litigate the matter before the courts. However, other options are available. Adjudicative bodies other than courts and processes other than litigation have been established to deal with specific types of legal dispute.

Article 37.1 of the Constitution states:

> Nothing in this Constitution shall operate to invalidate the exercise of limited functions and powers of a judicial nature, in matters other than criminal matters, by any person or body of persons duly authorised by law to exercise such functions and powers, notwithstanding that such person or such body of persons is not a judge or a court appointed or established as such under this Constitution.

This means that, in civil disputes, some limited and specified judicial functions can be exercised by persons other than judges and bodies other than courts, once authorised by law.

A number of adjudicative bodies have been so authorised and will be examined in this chapter.

Specialist quasi-judicial tribunals and tribunals of inquiry have emerged and, more recently, alternatives such as the Ombudsman model and the Injuries Board have had a significant impact on the legal system, often saving time and money and reducing the burden on the court system.

Other processes, such as mediation and conciliation, based on the voluntary agreement of the parties, have also become increasingly important.

B. Negotiation

Negotiation should be the first step in resolving any civil dispute. The parties to a dispute may negotiate a resolution themselves or may engage professionals such as solicitors or barristers to negotiate on their behalf. Many civil disputes are resolved through negotiation, obviating the need for a court hearing.

Negotiation has the following advantages over litigation:

- It is usually less expensive;
- The details of the dispute remain private;

- The parties to the dispute remain in control of the process;
- The parties remain in control of the final settlement.

However, it is not always possible to negotiate a settlement and, in such instances, other methods of dispute resolution, such as litigation or arbitration, may be utilised.

C. Arbitration

Introduction

Arbitration is the reference of a civil dispute to one or more impartial persons for a final and binding decision. The parties to a dispute agree, either before the dispute arises or after it has occurred, to submit the dispute to an independent third party, known as an arbitrator, for a decision.

Contracts may contain an arbitration clause, which is an agreement between the parties that any dispute arising out of that contract will be referred to arbitration for resolution. If there is no arbitration clause in a contract and a dispute arises, the parties may still refer the dispute to arbitration by entering into an arbitration agreement. A court may also stay any proceedings before it to allow arbitration to commence and must do so if an arbitration clause is contained in an agreement. An arbitration clause/agreement essentially means that the parties have agreed in advance that the decision of the arbitrator will be final and binding upon them.

In Ireland, arbitration is governed by the Arbitration Act 2010. The Act applies to all arbitrations, with the exception of some employment and consumer disputes. The Arbitration Act 2010 adopted the UNCITRAL (United Nations Commission on International Trade Law) Model Law 1985. The Act creates a 'default' position for the parties, containing a large number of provisions which apply unless otherwise agreed by the parties in their arbitration clause/agreement. It recognises the right of the parties to design the arbitral process to suit their needs and it minimises the possibility for court intervention, which is an important development in terms of minimising costs and ensuring the finality of the arbitration award.

The conduct of the arbitration is governed primarily by the arbitration agreement. This agreement establishes the method of appointment and powers of the arbitrator and how the arbitration is to be conducted. The Arbitration Act 2010 even allows for agreement in respect of the costs of arbitration between the parties. The parties themselves can determine the procedural rules which will apply to the resolution of the dispute. This is in contrast to a court action where the procedures are imposed on the parties.

The main purpose of arbitration is to resolve disputes outside the court system. Therefore the courts exercise very limited powers in relation to the arbitration process. Only in very limited circumstances will the court intervene.

Advantages and Disadvantages of Arbitration

There are a number of reasons why arbitration may be preferred over litigation:

Table on Advantages of Arbitration

Advantages of Arbitration	Explanation
Choice of arbitrator	Usually, one arbitrator is appointed by the parties. The parties may choose a specialist in the subject matter of the dispute. Where the dispute involves a highly technical problem, the parties may feel that a judge would not adequately understand the nature of the dispute and much of the evidence, in which event they may wish to have the matter resolved by an arbitrator, who is familiar with the topic in question. For example, the arbitrator may be an architect or a software developer, or someone with expertise in the relevant area. If the dispute involves parties who speak different languages, an arbitrator fluent in those languages may be chosen. A 'neutral' arbitrator from a country other than those of the parties to the dispute may be appointed in order to prevent the perception of bias.
Control over location, time and venue	The parties may choose the location, time and venue of the arbitration hearing. This is particularly useful for international commercial disputes, as a neutral venue may be chosen to prevent the perception of bias.
Privacy	Arbitration is in private whereas, in general, court actions are in public. If the dispute involves information of a confidential or commercially sensitive nature, the parties may prefer arbitration.
Speed	Arbitration should be quicker than litigation.
Cost	Arbitration should be cheaper than litigation, although this is not always the case.
Flexibility	Arbitration may be preferred because, with the arbitrator's consent, the parties can determine the procedures to be used at each stage of the arbitration.
Tailor-made remedies	The arbitrator may tailor the remedy to suit the situation and is not limited to the traditional remedies which may be awarded through the courts.

(Con't)

Advantages of Arbitration	Explanation
Enforceability	The arbitrator's decision and award is enforceable through the courts, if necessary.

However, there are also a number of disadvantages to arbitration and, depending upon the circumstances of the parties and the dispute, litigation or other dispute resolution mechanisms may be preferred.

Table on Disadvantages of Arbitration

Disadvantages of Arbitration	Explanation
No precedent/inconsistency of decisions	The traditional substantive law and common law rules of precedent do not apply to arbitrations. The arbitrator is not bound to follow previous decisions or any particular case law. Indeed, the parties can choose the law to apply to the arbitration and, in the absence of agreement, the arbitrator must apply the conflict of law rules.
No right of appeal	Under the Arbitration Act 2010, there are very limited grounds upon which a party may seek to have the award set aside.
Relaxed rules of evidence	Very relaxed rules of evidence may apply to arbitrations.

The Arbitrator

The Arbitration Act 2010 provides for the appointment of one arbitrator, unless otherwise agreed by the parties.

The arbitration agreement generally does not specify the name of the arbitrator, but rather provides for how the arbitrator is to be chosen. It will generally state that the arbitrator is to be appointed by agreement of the parties and, in default of agreement, provision is made for appointment by a third party. If necessary, the court can appoint an arbitrator under the Arbitration Act 2010. Either party can challenge the appointment of an arbitrator on the basis of impartiality or lack of appropriate qualifications.

An arbitrator's fees are a matter for agreement between him/her and those who appoint him/her. An arbitrator's only right is to the agreed or reasonable remuneration in the absence of agreement.

The main duties of the arbitrator are to proceed with the arbitration with reasonable speed, to exercise reasonable care and to act impartially and independently. An arbitrator must disclose any potential conflict of interest which exists when invited to accept the appointment and must also disclose any potential conflict of interest which may arise during the arbitration.

An arbitrator must not allow him/herself to be bribed, or to be in a position to show bias to one of the parties, for example if he/she has a relationship with one of the parties such that he/she would be likely to decide for or against that party. If so, he/she is in breach of the duty. The test is whether a reasonable person would regard the relationship as so close as to be objectionable. Impartiality is also jeopardised where the arbitrator is connected with the subject matter to the dispute in such a way that he is likely to lose or gain from the outcome. In such case, there would be a clear conflict of interest.

The arbitrator has a number of powers under the Arbitration Act 2010 and these apply unless the parties agree otherwise. The arbitrator may:

- Administer an oath and take evidence under oath;
- Award interest on the sum of the award, either simple or compound;
- Award security for costs;
- Order specific performance of a contract.

The Arbitration Act 2010 provides that the arbitrator is not liable for any acts or omissions during the arbitration. This reflects the long-accepted common law position that arbitrators are immune from liability for losses arising in consequence of their negligence.

An arbitrator may resign if allowed to do so by the terms of the arbitration agreement. An arbitrator may also be removed by agreement of the parties. Under the Arbitration Act 2010, the court can remove an arbitrator who fails to proceed without undue delay.

The Arbitration

The arbitration will begin either on the date agreed by the parties or, if no date is agreed, on the date when a written request to refer the matter to arbitration is received.

The arbitration agreement may require negotiations to take place to attempt to resolve the dispute before an arbitrator is appointed. If so, such negotiations must be held and the arbitrator may be prevented from commencing the arbitration until such negotiations have been held.

A party to arbitration may apply to the High Court under the Arbitration Act 2010 for interim measures, before the arbitration commences, if required.

One of the first things the arbitrator must do is examine the arbitration agreement to ensure he/she has jurisdiction i.e. that the dispute referred is in fact covered by the arbitration agreement and that he/she has the power to give the orders sought. For example, if the arbitration agreement provides for arbitration of a certain category of disputes only, then the arbitrator cannot deliberate on disputes which do not come within that category. Similarly, if the arbitration agreement restricts the findings which the arbitrator can make, then the arbitrator is limited to making findings allowed by the arbitration agreement. For example, if an arbitration agreement gives the arbitrator power to determine liability but not quantum (the amount which the party who is found liable must pay), then the arbitrator cannot decide on quantum.

Where there is a dispute about the validity of a contract containing an arbitration clause, the arbitration clause may be treated as an independent term of a contract so that an arbitrator will have authority to decide if the contract containing the clause is null and void due to illegality or some other vitiating factor. A party may challenge the arbitrator's jurisdiction and the arbitrator can rule on any such pleas. The party may then appeal the arbitrator's decision as to his/her jurisdiction, to court, within 30 days, during which time the arbitration process may proceed. Once the arbitration has commenced, the arbitrator may grant interim measures if satisfied that harm not adequately reparable by damages is likely to occur.

During the arbitration, the parties must be treated equally and given a full opportunity to present their case. The arbitrator can conduct the proceedings as he/she sees fit and can determine the admissibility of statements and the relevance, materiality and weight of evidence. The arbitrator can decide on the place and language of the arbitration, unless otherwise agreed by the parties. The arbitrator can also decide whether to hold an oral hearing or whether to conduct the arbitration on documents only. If one party requests an oral hearing, then that request must be granted, unless there is prior agreement by the parties to the contrary.

The arbitrator must decide the case on the basis of the law chosen by the parties and, in the absence of a choice, must apply the conflict of law rules. Whatever rules apply, both parties must get a fair hearing. Two common law principles, in particular, apply to arbitrations. These are:

- *Nemo judex in causa sua* — 'No man may be a judge in his own cause'. The arbitrator must be impartial;
- *Audi alteram partem* — 'Hear the other side'. Each party must be given an equal opportunity to present their case.

The arbitrator cannot simply make an award for one party where the other party fails to appear. However, provided adequate notice of the hearing is given, the arbitrator can proceed to hear the evidence of the party who appears and make an award on the basis of that evidence. This prevents one party from frustrating the arbitration by simply not appearing.

Arbitration proceedings may be terminated before an award is made if the parties agree to settle the dispute.

The Award and Enforcement

The arbitrator's award must be in writing and must be signed, dated and state the location in which it is made. The award must set out the reasons for the decision, unless the parties have agreed otherwise. The award is binding and enforceable between the parties. Subject to a contrary intention in the arbitration agreement, an arbitrator can also make an interim award, dealing with only part of the dispute.

A party to the arbitration has 30 days within which to request the arbitrator to correct an error or give an interpretation of part of an award. This may be done within those 30 days if the arbitrator agrees. A party also has 30 days to seek an additional award to deal with any claim omitted from the original award.

The only recourse to the High Court against the award is to have it set aside on the following limited grounds:

- Incapacity of the arbitrator;
- Invalidity of the arbitration agreement;
- Either party not given proper notice of the arbitration or was unable to present his case;
- The subject matter of the dispute is not within the scope of the submission to arbitration;
- The subject matter of the dispute is not capable of settlement by arbitration in the State, or is in conflict with public policy.

An application to have an arbitral award set aside must be made within three months of the date of the award. Where a court receives such an application, it may adjourn the application to allow the arbitrator to resume the arbitration or take other steps to eliminate the grounds for setting aside.

If one party refuses to comply with the award, the other party can apply to the High Court under the Arbitration Act to have the award enforced. The Act provides that an arbitrator's award shall be enforceable by the High Court in the same manner as a judgment or order of that Court with the same effect and, where leave is given, judgment may be entered in terms of the award.

D. ADR: Mediation and Conciliation

Introduction
Both mediation and conciliation provide alternatives to litigation and arbitration. Both are voluntary dispute resolution mechanisms, which are not binding on the parties. They have emerged in recent years as a popular method of resolving civil disputes, particularly in relation to large-scale commercial disputes, employment law and family law matters. A contract may contain a mediation or conciliation clause, in which case the dispute is referred to the stated method for resolution. Alternatively, in the absence of a mediation/conciliation clause, the parties may agree to refer a dispute to mediation or conciliation after a dispute has arisen.

Mediation
In mediation, the parties agree to refer the dispute to an independent third party (a mediator) who helps the parties reach a mutually agreeable settlement. The parties are under no obligation to reach a settlement and may leave the process at any stage, should they wish.

Conciliation
In conciliation, the parties to a dispute agree to refer the dispute to an independent third party (a conciliator) who brings the parties together to reach a settlement. If the parties cannot reach a settlement, the conciliator issues a recommendation as to how the dispute should be settled. The parties are free to accept or reject the conciliator's proposed settlement.

Advantages and Disadvantages of Mediation/Conciliation

Table on Advantages and Disadvantages of Mediation/Conciliation

Advantages of Mediation/Conciliation	Disadvantages of Mediation/Conciliation
It encourages reconciliation between the parties and helps maintain good relations between them.	It is sometimes described as 'soft justice' — nothing more than an additional layer of costs in the litigation stream and a process fundamentally at odds with the role of the court as decision-maker.
As the process is voluntary, it gives a greater degree of self-determination and sense of empowerment to the parties.	There are cases in which public interest dictates that a public hearing should take place and a public decision be made.

(Con't)

Advantages of Mediation/Conciliation	Disadvantages of Mediation/Conciliation
The parties control the process.	Some cases do not lend themselves well to mediation/conciliation, for example, disputes involving allegations of illegality, fraudulent conduct or impropriety. In such cases, the polarised positions that characterise these disputes inhibit discussion and settlement.
It may be less expensive than litigation (if a settlement is reached).	It may add an additional layer of expense (if a settlement is not reached).
It may be quicker than litigation (if a settlement is reached).	It may delay resolution of the dispute (if a settlement is not reached).
Useful if there is an absence of clear legal entitlement.	It may not be appropriate in cases where power imbalances put the parties on an unequal footing, allowing one party to place undue pressure on the other.
Confidentiality and privacy is assured.	There may be uncertainties in the law which need to be clarified, and only a court can do this.
It is useful if there is a need to avoid a win/lose situation.	Sometimes legal precedents need to be relied upon, or to be established for future cases.
The parties control the forum.	
Useful if the dispute has multiple parties and issues.	
It is useful where the monetary and non-monetary costs of litigation are disproportionately high in comparison to the issues in dispute.	
It is useful for claims where one or both parties are seeking remedies which are not available through the traditional court system, such as an apology, an explanation; flexibility in relation to financial repayments; changes in administrative procedures, etc.	

Legal Framework and Reform

There is currently no Irish legislative framework within which mediation and conciliation must operate. However, some legal initiatives have been introduced which actively encourage mediation and conciliation. For example, the Commercial Court list in the High Court, which was established in 2004 to deal with large commercial disputes, uses active judicial case management to improve the efficiency of the litigation process itself and also encourages the use of mediation and conciliation. Similarly, the Smalls Claims Court in the District Court is a mediation process for certain consumer disputes (which can be filed online and is available for a small handling fee), under which the first step is to seek informal resolution of the dispute using a document-only approach. The Family Mediation Service also provides an important alternative resolution facility.

In the UK, the use of conciliation and mediation is central to the civil litigation process, and the judiciary actively encourage the parties to engage in such ADR methods.

In 2008, the EU issued a directive on 'Certain Aspects on Mediation in Civil and Commercial Matters', which was designed to encourage the voluntary and amicable settlement of civil and commercial disputes by ensuring a balanced relationship between mediation and litigation. It requires all EU Member States to provide a suitable legislative framework to deal with mediation and civil process in cross-border disputes.

The Law Reform Commission, in its 2010 *Report on Alternative Dispute Resolution: Mediation and Conciliation* (LRC 98-2010), recommended an integrated approach to dispute resolution in which ADR plays an appropriate part and in which it complements the role of the courts in resolving disputes. It stated that such an approach would not prevent the court-based dispute resolution process from continuing to play a role in resolving disputes by agreement and that this could be achieved by the established practice of intervening at a critical moment in litigation to suggest resolution by agreement or though the structured innovations of, for example, the Commercial Court or the Small Claims Court.

It recommended that mediation and conciliation should be clearly delineated as quite different from litigation and could continue to be initiated by parties completely independently of litigation. It recommended that the courts postpone, or stay, proceedings if the parties have already made an agreement that includes an ADR clause, such as a mediation or conciliation clause. This mirrors the long-standing approach taken to arbitration clauses, now established on a statutory footing in the Arbitration Act 2010.

The Law Reform Commission also recommended the introduction of a statutory framework in the form of a 'Mediation and Conciliation Bill' to give effect to its recommendations. This Bill has not yet been introduced in the Oireachtas.

E. Tribunals

Introduction

Civil disputes may also be adjudicated upon by tribunals. The Constitution allows the Oireachtas to pass legislation to establish tribunals with limited powers to decide cases (rights tribunals) and investigate certain matters (tribunals of inquiry).

The legislation establishing a tribunal sets out the following:

- The purpose/function of the tribunal;
- The composition of the tribunal, including whether the members will be judges, barristers, solicitors, public servants or representatives of industry;
- The powers of the tribunal and the procedures to be applied;
- The duration of the tribunal. Some tribunals are set up to last indefinitely. Others are set up for a specific purpose only and, once that purpose is achieved, the tribunal ceases to exist.

The legislation also states whether the tribunal should be held in public or in private. Most tribunals are held in public. However, a tribunal dealing with sensitive issues, for example, the Refugee Appeals Tribunal, may be held in private.

Types of Tribunals

There are two main types of tribunals in the State, each with different functions

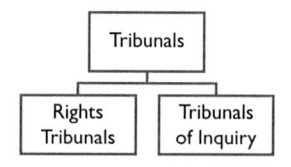

```
                    Tribunals
                   /         \
           Rights            Tribunals
           Tribunals         of Inquiry
```

A Rights Tribunal

Rights tribunals are usually permanent tribunals, established by specific legislation. Rights tribunals generally act like a court, interpreting and applying the law and making binding decisions on disputes between parties (although this is not always the case).

Rights tribunals aim to provide a quick, informal and inexpensive alternative to the court system in a specific area of law, for example, employment law. Rights tribunals deal with a wide range of disputes and the tribunal members are experts in the particular subject matter of the tribunal.

The legislation establishing the rights tribunal will specify the purpose, powers and composition of the tribunal and the procedures it must follow. Rights tribunals are funded by the State but parties appearing before a rights tribunal generally must pay for their own legal representation.

Table on Advantages of Rights Tribunals

Advantage of Rights Tribunals	Explanation
Cost	Rights tribunals do not charge fees and parties usually pay their own costs. Legal representation is not always necessary.
Specialisation	Tribunal members have in-depth knowledge and expertise in the subject matter of the dispute that judges in the ordinary courts could not build up.
Speed	Cases are usually heard more quickly and last for a shorter period of time.
Informality	Generally, wigs are not worn and the atmosphere is less intimidating than in a formal court setting.
Reduces burden on courts	Reduces the workload and congestion in the ordinary courts.

The following are the main rights tribunals in the Irish Legal System:

Table on Examples of Rights Tribunals

Rights Tribunal/Adjudicative Body	Function
The Employment Appeals Tribunal	This tribunal hears and decides cases in which an employee claims he or she has been unfairly dismissed.
The Refugee Appeals Tribunal	This tribunal hears appeals by asylum-seekers against decisions to refuse them refugee status.
An Bord Pleanála	This tribunal hears appeals against either the granting or the refusing of planning permission by a local planning authority.
The Equality Tribunal	The Equality Tribunal deals with complaints of discrimination under equality legislation. Its decisions and mediated settlements are legally binding.
Social Welfare Appeals Tribunal	The Social Welfare Tribunal deals with cases where entitlement to Unemployment Benefit or Assistance is refused due to an involvement in a trade dispute.
The Labour Court	This tribunal investigates disputes between employers and employees and makes recommendations for resolution.
Criminal Injuries Compensation Tribunal	This tribunal decides the level of compensation to be paid to persons who have suffered injuries in the course of a criminal act.

- Appealing the Decision of a Rights Tribunal

The terms of the legislation establishing the tribunal will state the extent to which a decision of the rights tribunal can be appealed to the courts. For example, a decision of the Employment Appeals Tribunal can be appealed in its entirety to the Circuit Court. However, the legislation may also provide that there is no appeal to the court except by way of judicial review in the High Court. This means that the court will not substitute its decision for the decision made by the tribunal, but will ensure that the decision was made fairly and in accordance with the principles of natural justice. If the decision of the tribunal was made without following fair procedures, it may be set aside by the High Court.

Tribunals of Inquiry

- Introduction

Tribunals of inquiry are usually temporary tribunals, established by legislation to investigate a specific matter of public importance.

- Powers and Procedure

In order to conduct its investigation, a tribunal of inquiry is vested with certain powers under the Tribunals of Inquiry (Evidence) Acts 1921 to 2004. A tribunal of inquiry is usually chaired by a judge or a senior barrister/solicitor. The tribunal can issue orders to force witnesses to attend and give evidence, and may apply to the High Court if a person refuses to give evidence or is in contempt of the tribunal. The High Court may then order a witness to give evidence. If an individual continues to fail to co-operate with the tribunal, the High Court may hold the witness in contempt of court and have the witness imprisoned until he or she has co-operated with the tribunal. Any statement or admission made at a tribunal cannot be used in evidence against a person in criminal proceedings. Strict procedures are usually applied, and witnesses called to give evidence before a tribunal of inquiry are usually cross-examined. It is a criminal offence to refuse to give evidence or to fail to co-operate with a tribunal of inquiry.

The State pays the running costs of a tribunal of inquiry, including the cost of legal representation for the parties appearing before it. This can involve a considerable expense on the State, with the costs of some tribunals of inquiry, for example the Mahon Tribunal, estimated to be between €250 million and €300 million. However, if a tribunal considers that there is sufficient reason to do so, it can order any person to pay the costs of another person appearing before the tribunal or the costs of the tribunal itself. This may happen if a person fails to co-operate with the tribunal or gives false or misleading evidence.

A tribunal of inquiry will usually conduct its inquiry in public although, if sensitive matters are involved, the investigation may be held in private.

- Report of a Tribunal of Inquiry

A tribunal of inquiry is charged with making findings of fact and, upon completion of its investigation, must submit a report to the Oireachtas setting out those findings. In some cases, the tribunal may also make recommendations for law reform/procedural changes to prevent the event which was the subject matter of the tribunal from recurring. It is important to note that a tribunal of inquiry is purely investigative and fact-finding — it does not make binding determinations on the rights or liabilities of parties involved. However, sometimes the findings of tribunals of inquiry can give rise to an investigation leading to independent criminal or civil proceedings.

The following are some of the most well-known tribunals of inquiry:

Table on Examples of Tribunals of Inquiry

Tribunal	Function
The Tribunal of Inquiry into the Beef Processing Industry, 1994	To investigate alleged irregularities in the beef industry in Ireland.
The Tribunal of Inquiry into the Blood Transfusion Service Board, 1997	To investigate the infection of large numbers of people in the 1970s and 1980s with contaminated blood products.
The Tribunal of Inquiry into Payments to Politicians (Dunnes Stores), 1997	To investigate the payment of money to politicians.
The Mahon Tribunal (formerly known as the 'Flood Tribunal')	To investigate payments to politicians in the context of planning decisions. This Tribunal ran from November 1997 to March 2012 and was the longest-running and most expensive public inquiry ever held in the Republic of Ireland, with costs forecast to reach between €250 million and €300 million.
The Moriarty Tribunal, 1997	To investigate payments to politicians, including former Taoiseach Charles Haughey.
The Lindsay Tribunal, 1999	To inquire into the infection with HIV and Hepatitis C of persons with haemophilia.
The Laffoy Commission, 1999	To investigate claims of child abuse within the State's industrial schools.
The Morris Tribunal, 2002	To investigate complaints concerning the conduct of some Gardaí in Donegal.
The Smithwick Tribunal, 2005	To investigate suggestions that members of An Garda Síochána or other employees of the State colluded in the fatal shootings of RUC Superintendents.

Reform

Tribunals of inquiry have imposed significant costs upon the Irish State and much criticism has been levied as a result.

In May 2005, the Law Reform Commission published a report on *Public Inquiries Including Tribunals of Inquiry*, in which it proposed reform of the selection process for an appropriate type of inquiry, drafting appropriate terms of reference, the rights of individuals and organisations to be heard and represented and the awarding of legal costs. It proposed the Tribunals of Inquiry Bill 2005, the aim of which is to consolidate and modernise the law regarding tribunals of inquiry.

The Bill contains the following proposals:

- The process for setting and amending terms of reference of a tribunal should be clarified;
- A tribunal of inquiry would be required, within three months of its establishment, to produce a statement of estimated costs and duration of the tribunal. This statement must be subsequently amended after significant developments;
- The Government be permitted, for stated reasons and following a resolution of both Houses of the Oireachtas, to dissolve a tribunal;
- Clarify the situation with regard to the granting of legal representation before a tribunal;
- Enable the responsible minister to request an interim report on the general progress or particular aspect of an inquiry, from the tribunal of inquiry;
- Allow tribunal reports to be admissible in civil cases, providing that the facts in a report or the opinions expressed therein are uncontested;
- Require the Minister for Justice and Equality, with the consent of the Minister for Finance, to make regulations which will set out maximum amounts of legal fees recoverable from the State;
- Require the Taxing Master of the High Court, when adjudicating on applications for costs in respect of third parties, not to exceed the amounts set out in the regulations.

F. Ombudsmen

Introduction

The term Ombudsmen is used to describe independent complaint-handling bodies which have been established by law. Referring a dispute to an Ombudsman is an alternative method of reviewing the decisions of public/ adjudicative bodies, but without incurring the considerable expenses associated with a judicial review application or other court proceedings.

In accordance with criteria developed by the British and Irish Ombudsman Association (BIOA), the term 'Ombudsman' should be used by a complaint handling body only if four key criteria are met:

- Independence of the Ombudsman from those whom he/she has power to investigate;
- Effectiveness;
- Fairness; and
- Public accountability.

Types of Ombudsmen

In Ireland, a number of different Ombudsmen exist.

Figure 20.1 Types of Ombudsmen

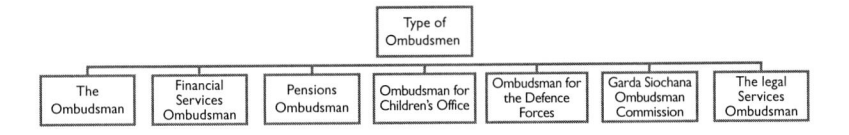

```
                        Type of Ombudsmen
    ┌──────┬──────────┬────────┬──────────┬──────────┬──────────┬──────────┐
    The    Financial  Pensions  Ombudsman  Ombudsman  Garda      The legal
    Ombuds- Services  Ombuds-   for        for the    Siochana   Services
    man    Ombudsman  man       Children's Defence    Ombudsman  Ombudsman
                                Office     Forces     Commission
```

The Ombudsman

■ Introduction

The office of the Ombudsman was established by the Ombudsman Act 1980. This was the first Ombudsman to be established in Ireland.

This Act has been subsequently been amended by the Ombudsman (Amendment) Act 1984 and by the Ombudsman (Amendment) Act 2012. The Disability Act, 2005 is also relevant to the Ombudsman's functions. The Office of the Ombudsman was established in 1984 and the service provided is free of charge.

The Ombudsman investigates complaints against Government departments and offices, local authorities, the Health Service Executive, An Post, the Irish Medical Council, An Bord Altranais, all publicly-funded third-level education institutions (including the universities and Institutes of Technology), Vocational Education Committees, the Central Applications Office, Solas, the Legal Aid Board, the National Treatment Purchase Fund, the QQI, the State Examinations

Commission, the Student Grant Appeals Board, the National Transport Authority, the Family Support Agency, Sustainable Energy Ireland and a range of other public bodies.

The list of public bodies whose actions the Ombudsman may investigate has been amended on a number of occasions but in particular by the Ombudsman (Amendment) Act 2012, which added an additional 180 public bodies to the remit of the Ombudsman with effect from 1 May 2013.

The following are typical examples of what people may complain about:

- Entitlement to old age and retirement pensions;
- Disputes about income tax credits granted by the Revenue Commissioners;
- Entitlement to higher education grants;
- Entitlement to livestock and other agricultural grants;
- Entitlement to local authority housing;
- Disputes about the medical card scheme.

Certain complaints are outside of the Ombudsman's remit. The Ombudsman cannot, for example, investigate:

- The actions of private companies or individuals, private practitioners, dentists, opticians, pharmacists, etc unless declared by the minister to be a reviewable agency;
- Actions taken in connection with clinical judgment by doctors;
- The "reserved functions of local authorities", i.e. certain functions exercised by elected representatives;
- Complaints relating to recruitment, pay and conditions of employment;
- Complaints in relation to the prisons and certain administrative actions in the area of asylum and immigration;
- Court decisions, matters which are already the subject of court proceedings, the actions of the Gardaí or actions taken in the running of the prisons;
- Where there is a right of appeal to an independent tribunal or appeal body such as An Bord Pleanála, for example.

■ Powers of the Ombudsman

The Ombudsman has extensive powers in law.

The Ombudsman can demand any information, document or file from a public body complained of and can require any official to give information about a complaint. If a person fails to comply with a request from the Ombudsman to provide any specified information, document or thing, the Ombudsman may apply to the Circuit Court for an order of compliance.

Once the Ombudsman has completed an investigation, he/she issues recommendations. The Ombudsman does not make a decision binding on the parties. The Ombudsman may refer any question of law arising from an investigation to the High Court for determination.

In most instances, the Ombudsman's recommendations are complied with but, if the body concerned fails to act on these recommendations, the Ombudsman may present a special report to the Houses of the Oireachtas on the matter. The adverse publicity for a Government department or other body if it became known that they failed to take account of any recommendation acts as an enforcement mechanism and, in the vast majority of cases, the Ombudsman's recommendations are implemented.

Other Ombudsman

- Financial Services Ombudsman

The Office of the Financial Services Ombudsman is a statutory body established under the Central Bank and Financial Services Authority, Ireland, Act 2004. The remit of the Financial Services Ombudsman is independently to investigate, mediate and adjudicate unresolved complaints of customers about their individual dealings with financial services providers.

- Ombudsman for Children's Office (OCO)

The Ombudsman for Children's Office was established by the Ombudsman for Children Act 2002. The role of the office is to safeguard and promote the rights and interests of children and young people under the age of eighteen. The Ombudsman for Children's Office can examine complaints about public bodies providing services or making decisions about children and families or organisations providing services on behalf of the State.

The Ombudsman for Children's Office also engages in research on behalf of children and contributes to Government policy. The office communicates on behalf of children and encourages the participation of children in society.

The Ombudsman for Children Act 2002 was extended on 30 April 2013, bringing a significant number of new public bodies and organisations providing a service to children on behalf of the State under the complaints and investigations remit of the Ombudsman for Children.

- Pensions Ombudsman

The Pensions Ombudsman Office was set up under Part XI of the Pensions Act 1990 (inserted by the Pensions (Amendment) Act 2002). The Pensions Ombudsman investigates and decides complaints and disputes involving occupational pension schemes, Personal Retirement Savings Accounts (PRSAs) and Trust RAC's where there is both maladministration and financial loss.

- Ombudsman for the Defence Forces

The Ombudsman for the Defence Forces was established by the Ombudsman (Defence Forces) Act 2004 and investigates complaints made by serving or former members of the Defence Forces about actions taken by serving or former members of the Defence Forces or civil servants.

Serving Members of the Defence Forces must first exhaust existing internal grievance procedures before the Ombudsman can review or examine the case.

- Garda Síochána Ombudsman Commission

The Garda Síochána Ombudsman Commission is an independent statutory agency, established by the Garda Síochána Act 2005, as amended by the Criminal Justice Act 2006 and the Criminal Justice Act 2007.

The Garda Síochána Ombudsman Commission is responsible for receiving and dealing with all complaints made by members of the public concerning the conduct of members of the Garda Síochána. It investigates the following:

- Complaints against members of the Garda Síochána;
- Any matter, even where no complaint has been made, where it appears that a Garda may have committed an offence or behaved in a way that would justify disciplinary proceedings;
- Any practice, policy or procedure of the Garda Síochána with a view to reducing the incidence of related complaints.

- The Legal Services Ombudsman

The Legal Services Ombudsman Act 2009, created an office of the Legal Services Ombudsman to oversee the handling by the Law Society of Ireland and the Bar Council of complaints by clients of solicitors and barristers.

The Act was signed by the President on 10 March 2009. However, the Legal Services Ombudsman has yet to be appointed and no commencement order has been signed for the Act.

When appointed, the Ombudsman will oversee the handling by the Law Society of Ireland and the Bar Council of complaints by clients of solicitors and barristers and may investigate complaints received by him/her in relation to the legal profession. The Ombudsman will also monitor and report annually to the Minister for Justice and the Oireachtas on the adequacy of the admissions policies of both professions.

G. The Injuries Board

Introduction

The Injuries Board, formerly known as the 'Personal Injuries Assessment Board', was established by the Personal Injuries Assessment Board Act 2003. This Act was subsequently amended by the Personal Injuries Assessment Board (Amendment) Act 2007. The Injuries Board is an independent body, funded by the State, which assesses the amount of compensation due to a person who has suffered a personal injury.

The Injuries Board provides assessment of personal injury claims for victims of the following accidents:

- Workplace;
- Motor;
- Public liability.

Assessment is provided by the Injuries Board without the need for the majority of current litigation costs, such as solicitors', barristers' and experts' fees, associated with such claims.

Scope and Purpose

The aims of the Injuries Board are as follows:

- To assess how much compensation is due to an injured party;
- To reduce costs and fees involved in the administration of personal injury claims;
- To reduce the amount of time it takes to finalise a claim for compensation;
- To relieve the courts of the burden of an increasingly large number of personal injures claims;
- To tackle increasing insurance premium rates arising from a costly adversarial approach to resolving personal injury claims.

Under the 2003 Act, anyone intending to seek compensation for a personal injury (other than a personal injury arising out of medical negligence) *must* make an application to the Injuries Board before any court action can progress.

The Injuries Board does not assess damages where:

- The respondent does not consent to an Injuries Board assessment being commenced (for example, if liability is in dispute);
- Because of the nature of the injury, the Board does not believe it can make an assessment within the nine-month timeframe required by the Act;
- The injury sustained is wholly or predominantly psychological;
- The type of liability is currently outside the remit of the Board, e.g. medical negligence;
- Matters of international law and treaties are involved, such as marine and aviation accidents.

Procedure

In order to make an application to the Injuries Board, the applicant must:

- Complete an application form, giving details of the accident;
- Pay the application fee (currently €45); and
- Supply a medical report from his/her treating doctor.

Many applicants engage a solicitor to make an application on their behalf, although this is not a requirement of the application.

Upon receipt of a claim, the Injuries Board informs the respondent about the claim. The respondent then has 90 days to consent to the Board assessing the claim and not dispute liability. If the respondent accepts liability and agrees to the assessment, he/she must pay an application fee (currently €650).

However, if the respondent does not accept liability or refuses to consent to the Injuries Board assessing the claim, the Injuries Board will issue the applicant with an authorisation. This authorisation then allows the applicant to pursue his/her claim through the courts.

Assessment of Damages

The Personal Injuries Assessment Board Act 2003 requires the Board to complete its assessment of damages within nine months of the respondent consenting to the claim, with some permitted exceptions. The Injuries Board assesses claims by reference to the medical evidence provided by the applicant and having regard to the level of compensation awarded for particular injuries. The process of assessment does not involve any oral hearings.

The level of compensation awarded for particular injuries is known as the book of quantum and the Injuries Board have some useful tools on their website, www.injuriesboard.ie, to help estimate the potential value of a claim.

According to the Injuries Board, in 2012, 10,136 awards were made with a total value of €217.94m. The average award was €21,502.

One limitation of the Injuries Board assessment is that it cannot award damages for future loss. If future loss is anticipated, a party will usually reject the assessment and proceed to court.

Also, the Injuries Board does not award legal or medical costs for/against either party. Any costs incurred must be paid by the parties to the claim.

Once the Injuries Board makes the assessment, both the claimant and respondent are notified. The assessment made by the Injuries Board is not binding upon the parties, unless both accept it. The claimant has 28 days to reject the assessment and the respondent has 21 days to reject. If either side rejects the award, the matter can then be referred to the courts.

The Personal Injuries Assessment Board (Amendment) Act 2007 provides that, where a claimant does not receive more than the amount of the original Injuries Board assessment in subsequent proceedings, he/she will not recover legal costs for those proceedings and may be held responsible for costs incurred by the respondent/defendant. The 2007 Act also provides that legal costs incurred in dealing with the Injuries Board process are not recoverable in the litigation process.

Impact of the Injuries Board

The number of claims being assessed by the Injuries Board has stabilised in recent years. In 2011, 9,833 claims were assessed.

The Injuries Board has made a positive impact in relation to the following (although there may be other causal factors):

- A reduction in motor insurance premiums;
- A reduction in claims processing costs;
- A reduction in the time taken to assess claims;
- The Courts have been freed to focus on more pressing matters as the number of personal injury litigation cases before the courts has decreased. In its first five years, the Injuries Board assessed over 50,000 claims. The number of awards made in the five years of 2006 to 2010 by the Injuries Board totalled nearly €1 billion overall. The amounts awarded by the courts throughout the country during the same period totalled approximately €320 million;

- Litigation costs associated with claims have been reduced;
- It provides a useful template for reform in other areas.

However, it should be noted that the Injuries Board is not without its critics. The courts still remain the main adjudicative body for personal injuries claims. The amounts of damages awarded by the courts are often larger, as the courts may make provision for future loss. Additionally, if a respondent does not consent to assessment or rejects the assessment, the requirement of having to go through the Injuries Board before being authorised to take the claim to court, can cause unnecessary delay and can actually increase legal costs for the parties involved.

H. Coroner's Court

Introduction

A coroner is an official charged with conducting public inquests into any violent, suspicious or otherwise unexplained death. The coroner is appointed by the local authority in whose area the coroner's district is situated. A coroner must be a barrister or a solicitor or a registered medical practitioner of at least five years' standing. The coroner acts on behalf of the State in the public interest. The Coroner's Court is regulated by the Coroners Act 1962 and the Coroners (Amendment) Act 2005.

In 1998, the Supreme Court, in the case of *Farrell (Dublin City Coroner) v Attorney General* [1998] 1 IR 203 listed the grounds upon which a coroner should exercise his or her discretion to conduct an inquest, as follows:

- To determine the medical cause of death;
- To allay rumours or suspicions;
- To draw attention to the existence of circumstances which, if not remedied, might lead to further deaths;
- To advance medical knowledge;
- To preserve the legal interests of the deceased person's family, heirs or other interested parties.

All sudden, unexplained, violent and unnatural deaths must by law be reported to a coroner. No doctor may certify a death which is due directly or indirectly to any unnatural cause. The coroner's inquiry is concerned with establishing whether or not the death was due to natural or unnatural causes.

If death is due to unnatural causes, then an inquest must be held by law. There is a legal duty on a registered medical practitioner, amongst others, to report such deaths to the coroner. The death may, however, be reported to a member of An Gárda Síochána not below the rank of sergeant, who will then notify the coroner. At common law, any person may notify the coroner of the circumstances of a particular death.

Inquest Functions and Procedure
The 1962 Act sets out the procedure under which inquests are held and the circumstances in which a coroner's jury must be summoned.

The purpose of an inquest is to:

- Establish the facts surrounding the death;
- Place those facts on the public record; and
- Make findings on:
    (a) the identification of the deceased;
    (b) the date and place of death; and
    (c) the cause of death.

An inquest has some similar aspects to ordinary courts: it is held in public; witnesses give evidence under oath; it is presided over by a professional person and there is often a jury. However, it is primarily an inquisitorial body, rather than an adversarial one. All witnesses who are called to give evidence at a coroner's inquest have the same duties, obligations and protections as a witness called before the High Court. The coroner conducts the inquest, determining which witnesses to call, the sequence in which they give evidence, etc.

A jury is required at an inquest if:

- The death was due to homicide, or occurred in prison, or resulted from an accident at work or a road traffic accident;
- A death occurred in circumstances, the continuance or possible recurrence of which might be prejudicial to the health or safety of any section of the public.

Findings of an Inquest
The findings that a coroner and jury may make are severely limited by the 1962 Act.

The coroner cannot give a verdict which would involve the implication of either civil or criminal liability on the part of the deceased. Therefore, inquests are generally stayed pending the conclusion of any criminal proceedings relating to the death. Where an inquest is opened and the Gardaí inform the coroner that criminal proceedings are contemplated, the inquest is adjourned. The inquest can only determine 'who, how, when and where'. The 1962 Act permits only the following verdicts:

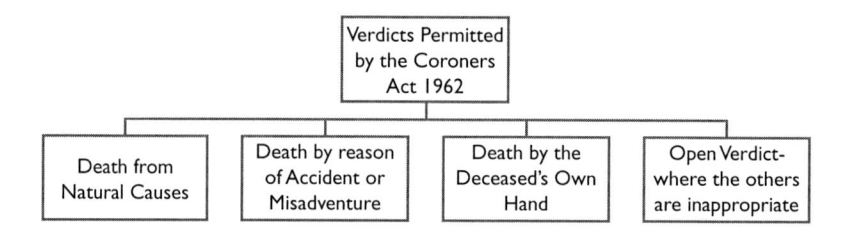

```
                    ┌─────────────────┐
                    │Verdicts Permitted│
                    │ by the Coroners │
                    │    Act 1962    │
                    └─────────────────┘
        ┌───────────────┬──────────────┬───────────────┐
┌───────────────┐ ┌───────────────┐ ┌───────────────┐ ┌───────────────┐
│  Death from   │ │ Death by reason│ │ Death by the  │ │ Open Verdict- │
│Natural Causes │ │ of Accident or │ │Deceased's Own │ │where the others│
│               │ │  Misadventure │ │     Hand      │ │are inappropriate│
└───────────────┘ └───────────────┘ └───────────────┘ └───────────────┘
```

These limitations have been heavily criticised in recent years, leading to pressure for reform.

Reform

In 2000, a working group established by the Minister for Justice and Equality reviewed the Coroner Service in Ireland. The group made more than 100 recommendations for reform. In 2003, following a recommendation of the working group, the report of the Coroner's Rules Committee was published. In 2005, the Coroners (Amendment) Act 2005 which amended the Coroners Act 1962 was passed. Further proposals for reform are contained in the Coroners Bill 2007, which has yet to be enacted.

I. Regulators

In recent years, a large number of regulatory bodies have emerged in Ireland.

A regulatory body can be defined as an independent body which has statutory recognition and powers/authority. These bodies typically exercise a regulatory function, either as a 'rule-maker' or 'rule-enforcer' and are usually established on a permanent basis.

Many of these regulatory bodies engage in the following activities:

- The setting of goals, rules and/or standards;
- Monitoring, information gathering and analysis, inspection, audit and evaluation;
- Enforcement, modifying behaviour, applying rewards and sanctions.

These regulatory bodies include the following, although this list is not exhaustive:

- The Bar Council of Ireland;
- The Competition Authority;
- The Data Protection Commissioner;
- The Environmental Protection Agency;
- The Commission for Communications Regulation (ComReg);

- The Equality Authority;
- The Health and Safety Authority;
- The Health Information and Quality Authority (HIQA);
- The Human Rights Commission;
- The Office of the Information Commissioner Ireland;
- The Law Society of Ireland;
- The National Disability Authority;
- The Standards in Public Office Commission;
- The Financial Regulator;
- The National Consumer Agency.

Section G

Law Reform

CHAPTER TWENTY ONE

LAW REFORM

A. Introduction 371
B. **Law Reform Mechanisms** 371
    Legislative Change — the Oireachtas...372
    Judicial Change — Courts..372
    Constitutional Change — Oireachtas and the Irish People..........373
    Change in EU Law 373

C. **Law Reform Agencies** 373
    The Law Reform Commission..373
    Others..375
    Limitations on Effectiveness of Law Reform Agencies 375

Learning Outcomes

Upon completion of this chapter, students should be able to:

- Discuss the law reform mechanisms in Irish law;
- Compare the role of the courts, Oireachtas, the Irish people and the EU in amending the law;
- Explain the role, composition and functions of the Law Reform Commission;
- Describe the limitations on law reform agencies.

A. Introduction

Law is never static and is constantly changing in line with the needs of society.

Pressure to reform the law comes from many sources:

- New legislation may be enacted and constitutional amendments put before the people in Ireland to give effect to Government parties' election manifestos, Programmes for Government or general public policy objectives;
- Various interest groups concerned with a particular subject may put pressure on the Government to enact new legislation to change the law;
- Public opinion and media pressure may also be brought to bear and contribute to law reform;
- The law may also be reformed in order to meet international obligations, whether created by the European Union, international treaties or the decisions of international courts, for instance, the European Court of Human Rights.

B. Law Reform Mechanisms

The Government, the Oireachtas, the judiciary and ultimately the Irish people, control the mechanisms by which the law can be reformed.

Figure 21.1

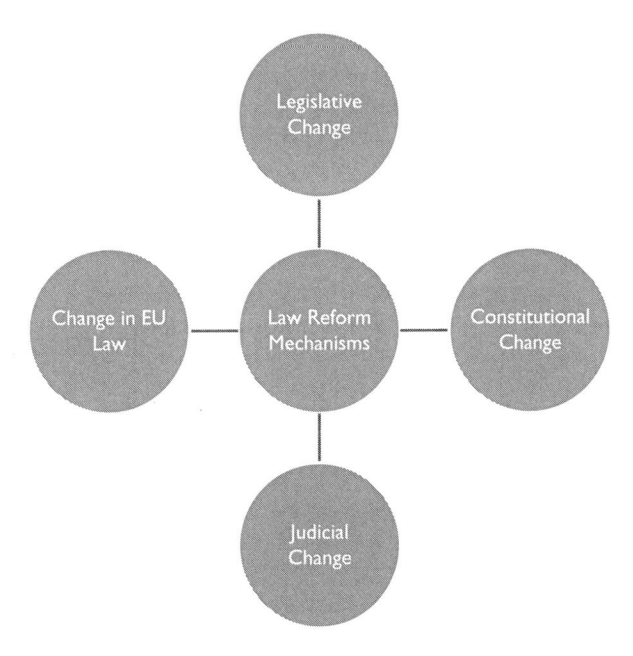

Legislative Change — the Oireachtas

This is the main mechanism by which Irish law is reformed. The Oireachtas may repeal old laws, consolidate or codify existing laws or enact new legislation. The procedure for enacting new legislation was examined earlier in the text. It is worth noting again that, although the Oireachtas is given legislative power in the Constitution, the Government essentially controls the process through the party system. Therefore, this method of law reform is commonly used to give effect to promises made in election manifestos and Programmes for Government. This method of law reform is also used to give effect to international treaties to which the Irish State may become a party, or to give effect to European directives. The ability to reform law through legislation is limited only to the extent that it must not conflict with the Constitution or our obligations under EU and international law.

Judicial Change — Courts

The courts play an important role in reforming the law, both in terms of the development and application of common law principles and in relation to the interpretation of legislation and the Constitution.

The judicial application of an existing principle of law in a new setting or the development of a new common law principle is equivalent to law reform.

Judicial interpretation of a piece of legislation may lead to a new or a clearer understanding of that provision. Additionally, judicial clarification may require amending legislation to remove a defect in existing statutory provisions or to remove an undesirable interpretation. If a statutory provision is deemed to be unconstitutional, new legislation is often required.

Also, judicial interpretation of the Constitution may lead to a situation where the Government may propose a constitutional referendum, in order to change an undesirable interpretation by the court.

However, there are limitations on the extent to which the courts can contribute to the process of reform. It is very much an ad hoc, rather than a planned, method of law reform. The courts can only decide upon cases which are brought before them and are, therefore, relying on the determination of the parties involved to bring the case through the courts. Additionally, judges are bound to follow the doctrine of precedent, which can serve to prevent radical judicial reform. Finally, as non-elected office holders, judges are hesitant about making decisions which change the law in areas of moral or social controversy or sensitivity. The courts will often suggest that such matters are for resolution by the Oireachtas, on which the power to make law is conferred under the Constitution.

Constitutional Change — Oireachtas and the Irish People
Finally, some proposed reforms of the law will require a constitutional amendment, therefore necessitating a referendum. This process was examined earlier in the text. It requires Oireachtas approval of the Bill containing the proposed amendment and a referendum, in which a majority of the people who cast a vote must vote in favour of the amendment. Any major changes in the structure of the Oireachtas, including the Dáil, Seanad and Office of the President, constitutional office holders, the courts, the trial of offences or the fundamental rights of citizens, will require a referendum. Therefore, it is ultimately the Irish people who have the final say when it comes to major changes in the law.

Change in EU Law
Changes to EU law can take the form of treaty change or the passing of secondary legislation (e.g. regulations, directives and decisions) by the EU institutions. Treaty change requires the approval of each Member State of the EU. In Ireland, this means ratification by the Oireachtas and normally, though not necessarily, by referendum to amend the Constitution to authorise ratification of the treaty change. Secondary legislation from the EU normally becomes part of Irish law automatically. All of these measures act to reform Irish law. Additionally, judgments handed down by the Court of Justice of the European Union may also have a significant impact on existing Irish legislation and/or case law.

C. Law Reform Agencies

The Law Reform Commission
Introduction
The Law Reform Commission is an independent statutory body established by the Law Reform Commission Act 1975. The State recognised the need for a new approach to law reform, enabling the law to respond to a rapidly-changing society.

The Law Reform Commission is the most significant law reform agency in Ireland. Its main functions are to keep the law under review and make recommendations for reform so that the law reflects the changing needs of Irish society.

The Law Reform Commission carries out its functions under the 1975 Act in two ways:

1. Pursuant to programmes of law reform which it draws up in consultation with the Attorney General and which have the approval of Government (the Commission is currently on its third programme of law reform); and
2. Pursuant to specific requests (or references) by the Attorney General to the Commission in relation to particular branches or matters of law.

Membership

The Law Reform Commission consists of a President, one full-time and three part-time Commissioners. The Commissioners are appointed by the Government for a term of up to five years and their appointment may be renewed. The Law Reform Commission Act 1975 provides that, in addition to members of the judiciary, members of the legal profession and academic lawyers, persons with qualifications other than those of a legal character who could contribute to the Commission may also be appointed to membership of the Commission. The Commissioners are supported by a Director of Research, two project managers, legal researchers and administrative staff.

Work of the Commission

The Law Reform Commission publishes reports and consultation papers on the subject matters in its programme for law reform. To date, there have been three programmes for law reform. Each proposed programme must be prepared by the Commission, agreed by the Government and laid before both Houses of the Oireachtas.

The Commission is currently working on its Third Programme for Law Reform 2007-2014 and preparations are under way on the proposed Fourth Programme.

Prior to this, the Second Programme of Law Reform (2000-2007) and First Programme of Law Reform (1977 and 2000) were completed. Details of all the reports, consultation papers and programmes for law reform can be found at www.lawreform.ie, the website of the Law Reform Commission.

When researching a subject area, the Commission considers both Irish and international case law, legislation, jurisprudence and academic writings, as well as the laws of comparable jurisdictions, and proposals put forward by law reform bodies in those jurisdictions.

The consultation process is of central importance to the Commission's work. Consultation may take several forms. In the initial stages of its research, the Commission may meet professionals working in a particular area, or representatives of interest groups. The Commission will then, in most cases, prepare a consultation paper, which will either be published or, if the subject is a specialised one, distributed to relevant experts. The Commission will seek written submissions from all interested parties, including members of the public and interest groups on the provisional recommendations made in the consultation paper. These submissions will be taken into account by the Commission in the drafting of the final report on the subject. In some cases, before the drafting of the final report, a seminar will be held to which the Commission may invite interested parties, or those who have made submissions.

Implementation of the Law Reform Commission's Reports

The Government has ultimate responsibility for implementing any recommendations for law reform from the Commission. The work of the Commission has resulted in a considerable body of reforming legislation being enacted, although this may often happen a number of years after the proposals were made. Also, proposals for reform may be overtaken by intervening events or political considerations.

Others

Other institutions/bodies have also contributed to law reform in Ireland. These include, for example:

- The Committee on Court Practice and Procedure;
- The Working Group on a Courts Commission;
- The Fair Trade Commission;
- The Constitution Review Group;
- The Constitutional Convention Group;
- The Competition Authority;
- Tribunals of Inquiry.

Limitations on Effectiveness of Law Reform Agencies

While the Law Reform Commission and other bodies can propose law reform, ultimately it will be up to the Government, through legislation or ultimately, the Irish people in the form of a constitutional referendum, to enact the change. Bodies such as the Law Reform Commission lack the power to give effect to their proposals and require the support of Government, particularly from the relevant minister, to enact the proposed change. Government may choose not to enact proposed reforms for a variety of reasons, some of which might be due to political pressure, or pressure from the media or public. Also, there is no requirement for government to consult the Law Reform Commission or any other body when proposing major law reform.

INDEX

A

Absurdity, in court 101, 103
Act of Union (1800) 39–40
'Administration of justice' *see* Ireland
Administrative law 30
All Party Oireachtas Group on the Constitution 77–8
An Garda Síochána 102
　functions 228–9
　Ombudsman Commission 358
An Iris Oifigiuil 10
Anglo-Irish Treaty (1921) 41
Anglo-Norman invasion (1169) 37
'Appearance', an 267
Aquinas, St Thomas
　on law 8
Arbitration law 30
　see also Disputes, resolving
Aristotle
　on law 8
Attorney General 84, 226
　appointment 227
　functions 227–8
　office structure 228
Austin, John 6
　Province of Jurisprudence Determined (1832) 7

B

Bail
　remands on 292–3
BAILII 117
Balance of probability 23, 301–2
Banking law 30
Bar Council of Ireland 212
　code of conduct 215–6
Barr, Justice 170, 171
Barristers 211
　see also Solicitors
　admission to profession 212–3
　discipline/conduct 215–6
　functions 212
　junior/senior counsel 214–5
　law library 213–4
　mode of dress 214
　necessary skills 214
Barristers' Professional Conduct Tribunal 216
Belfast Agreement ("Good Friday Agreement") 43–4, 280
Bentham, Jeremy 6–7
Bills
　abridged time 88
　amending Constitution 88
　consolidation 89
　money 87
　private 87
　private members' 89
　public 86–7
Blaney, Justice 99–100, 153
Book of Quantum 360
Brehon law 37
'Bretton Woods Conference' *see* United Nations Monetary and Financial Conference
British and Irish Ombudsman Association (BIOA) 355
British Empire 41

Bunreacht na hÉireann see
    Constitution (1937)
Burden of proof
    in civil cases 23

C

Canon Law 15, 30
Carroll, Justice 202–3
Catholic Church in Ireland
    under Penal laws 39
Central Criminal Court *see* High
    Court
Characteristics of law 5–6
Charter of Fundamental Rights 136
Chief State Solicitor's Office
    (CSSO) 228
Children's Court 277
Circuit Court
    civil cases originating in 260
    jurisdiction 265
        commercial/consumer
            protection 254
        criminal 287
        environmental matters 253
        family proceedings 253
        first instance 277
            transfer to High Court 277
        general/monetary 252–3
            reform of 325
        intoxicating liquor licenses
            253–4
        landlord/tenant 254
        local government elections/
            petitions 254
        malicious injuries 254
    payments into 269
    pleadings in 268–9
Circuit Criminal Court 21, 23

origins 42
first instance jurisdiction 275
Civil law
    aims 22
    cases 23–4
    criminal law versus 24–5
    provisions 23
    systems
        adversarial 16–7
        dis/advantages 15–6
        inquisitorial 17
        origins 15
        pluralist 16
Civil litigation
    payments into court 269–70
    pleadings 266
    reforming justice system 269–71
    settlement of cases 269
Commercial Court 256–7
Commercial law 30
Common law and equity 29
Common law system 115
    components 13–4
    conditions required 116
        binding/authoritative
            precedents 118–20
        non-binding 120
        hierarchical court system
            117–8
        locating/understanding case
            law 117
        rules regarding judgements
            117–8
    dis/advantages 15, 116
    liberal approach 123–4
    legal terms 121
    origins 13
    strict approach 123

Company law 30
Comparative law 30
Competition Authority
   Study of Competition in Legal Services (2006) 221–2
Competition law 30
Conciliation *see* Disputes, resolving
Connell, Archbishop Desmond 190
Constitution (1937) 49
  see also Constitutional rights; Irish State
  amending
    constitutional referendum 76
    ordinary referendum 75
    Referendum Commission 76–7
  distinguishing features 50–1
  interpretation of
    historical 74
    literal 72–3
    natural law 74–5
    purposive/harmonious 73–4
  main functions 49–50
  origins 42–3
  retrospective criminal law and 9
  reviewing 77
  separation of powers 63
    effectiveness of 65
    executive 64
    judicial 65
    legislative 64
Constitution Review Committee 50
Constitutional Convention 78
Constitutional law 29, 30
Constitutional Referendum 76
Constitution Review Group 77
Constitutional rights 66
  numerated 66–7
  education and children 68–9
  family 68
  property 69
  religious 69
  remedies for breach of 71
  unenumerated 69–71
Contempt of court *see* Court decisions
Contiguous zone 169
Contract law 28, 29, 30
Copenhagen criteria 138
Coroner's Court
  inquest function/powers 363–4
  reform 364
  remit of 362–3
Coroner's Rules Committee 364
Costello, Justice 110
Council of the European Union 141–2, 173–4
County Court 40
County Registrars 229, 312
Court clerks 229
Court decisions
  see also Judicial review
  civil matters
    contempt 319
    enforcing judgements 312
      court orders 312–4
    damages 309–10
    injunction 310
      Anton Piller 311
      Mareva 311
      quia timet 311
    remedies
      declaration 312
      specific performance 311
  contempt of court 319
  criminal matters

contempt 319–20
extra-jurisdictional
    enforcement 319
punishment 314–6
    community service 318
    fines 316–7
    imprisonment 317–8
    probation 318
    'regulatory offences' 318–9
Court of Appeal, proposed 325–6
Court of Assize 40
Court of Auditors (CoA) 135, 146
Court of Exchequer 40
Courts of Chancery 29, 38
Court of Criminal Appeal 42
    appeals from trials on
        indictment 281–2
    criminal jurisdiction 286
    miscarriage of justice 283
    stare decisis in 126
Courts of Equity 29, 38
Court of First Instance (CFI) 144
Court of Justice of the European
    Union (CJEU) 140, 144–6, 174,
    261–4
    case law 149
Court of Probate 40
Court Poor Box 318
Court procedures 297–8
    evidence, rules of
        direct 303
        hearsay 303–4
        law of 31
        opinion 304–5
        oral 302
        statutory intervention in 305
    locus standi 298–9
    limitation periods 299–301
    standards of proof 301

balance of probability 301–2
Court system
    reform of 325–6
Courts Service of Ireland 10, 117,
    230, 317
Costello, Justice 172
Criminal law 30
    civil law versus 24–5
    definition of 21
Criminal litigation
    indictment 293
        arraignment 293
        pleas 293–4
    prosecutorial system 288–9
    summary trials 21, 290
    trials on indictment 289–90
        appeals from 281
            against conviction 282
            against sentence 282–3
            by prosecution 283
        prosecution 290–2
        sending to trial 292
    victim's role in 294
Criminal offences 299
    in Ireland 21–2
    limitation periods 299
Curtin, Judge Brian 206–7
Customary international law 170–1
'Customary law' 168

D

Dáil Éireann
    Ceann Comhairle 59
        regarding Money Bills 87
    Constitution of 41
    State institute 58–9
        shared functions with the
            Seanad 60–1

Davies, Lord Justice 330
de Valera, Eamon 50
Declaration of incompatibility 181
Delegated (Secondary) legislation 82
　see also Legislation
　process 89–91
Democratic Unionist Party (DUC) 44
Denham, Chief Justice Susan 103, 326
Director of Public Prosecutions (DPP) 21
　appointment 225
　functions 225–6
　office structure 226
　to prosecute or not 289–92
Disputes, resolving
　alternative solutions 340
　　arbitration 341–2
　　　arbitrator 343–4
　　　　duties 345–6
　　　award/enforcement 346–7
　　　dis/advantages 342–3
　　Coroner's court *see* Coroner's Court
　　Injuries Board *see* Personal Injuries Board
　　mediation/conciliation 347
　　　dis/advantages 347–8
　　　legal framework/reform 348–9
　　negotiation 340–1
　　ombudsmen *see* Ombudsmen
　　regulators 364–5
　　tribunals, types of
　　　of inquiry 352–3
　　　　reforming 354
　　　rights 350–2

'Distinguish' 121
District Court 23
　appeals from criminal trials in 280–1
　civil cases originating in 259–60
　clerks 230
　criminal litigation 292
　de nova hearings 280
　jurisdiction 250, 266
　　commercial/consumer 251
　　criminal 288
　　environmental matters 251
　　family proceedings 251
　　first instance 275–6
　　　Children's Court 277
　　general/monetary 251
　　reform of 325
　　land/equity matters 252
　　renewal of intoxicating liquor licenses 252
　origins 41–2
　pleadings in 269
　Small Claims Courts 349
Doctrine of Direct Effect
　in EU law 153–6
Doctrine of Double Jeopardy 283–5
Doctrine of Indirect effect 106
Doctrine of Supremacy
　in EU law 151–3
Doctrine of ultra vires ('beyond the powers') 320
'Dualist theory' 170

E

Egan, Justice 107
Electronic Irish Statute Book
　website 83
Employment Appeals Tribunal 352

Employment law 31
Enforcement orders *see* Court decisions
English Common law 37
English Court of Appeal 155
Environmental and Planning law 31
Equity
　common law and 29
　in Ireland 38
　trusts and 30
EU (European Union)
　common agricultural policy (CAP) 161
　common fisheries policy (CFP) 161
　Directive 2008
　　'Certain Aspects on Mediation in Civil and Commercial Matters' 349
　history of 130–1
　　formation treaties 133–6
　institutions of 138
　　Commission 142–4
　　Council of the EU 141–2
　　Court of Auditors (CoA) 146
　　Court of Justice of the European Union (CJEU) 144–6, 149
　　European Central Bank 146
　　European Council (EC) 144
　　European Parliament 139–41
　membership 136–8
　　Copenhagen criteria 138
　withdrawal from 160–1
EU (European Union) Law 31
　Commission 142–3
　debt crisis in Eurozone 157–9
　development of 262

Doctrine of Indirect Effect 153–6
Doctrine of Supremacy in 151–3
Irish law and 150–1
principles, general of 150
private international law and 185
sources of 146
　primary 147
　secondary 148
　　case law of CJEU 149
　　decisions 148–9
　　directives 148
　　recommendations/opinions 149
　　regulations 148
state liability and 156–7
European Atomic Energy Community (Euratom) 132, 136
　with EEC 133
　treaties 133–6
European Central Bank (ECB) 135, 146
European Coal and Steel Community (ECSC) 131–2
European Commission 142–4
European Convention on Human Rights (ECHR) 44, 135, 173–4, 178
　into Irish law 179–81
　rights guaranteed by 179
European Convention for the Protection of Human Rights and Fundamental Freedoms (ECHR) 1950 179
European Council 144
European Court of Human Rights (ECHR) 173–4

European Court of Justice (ECJ) 144
European Economic Community (EEC) 43, 136
   with Euratom 132–3
   treaties 133–6
European Financial Stabilisation Mechanism (EFSM) 157
European Free Trade Association (EFTA) 161
European Monetary Union (EMU) 135
European Parliament 135, 139–41
Eurozone financial crisis 157–9
Evidence, rules of *see* Court procedures

F

Fair Trade Commission
   Report into the Restrictive Practices in the Legal Profession (1990) 214, 221, 224
Family law 29, 31
Family Mediation Service 349
Fennelly, Justice 331
Financial Services Ombudsman 357
Finlay, Chief Justice 94, 329
Francovich Principle 156–7
Functions of law 6

G

General Agreement on Tariffs and Trade (GATT) 177
Gidel, Gilbert Charles 169
Grattan, Henry 39

Grattan's Parliament 39–40
Green Paper 84
Greenland
   withdrawal from EU 160
Griffiths, Lord 103
Grotius
   on international law 169

H

Habeas corpus 322
Hamilton, Chief Justice Liam 206
Hart, Professor HLA 6
   The Concept of Law (Oxford University Press, 1961) 7, 25
Heads of Bill 84
Hearne, John 50
Henchy, Justice 73–4, 98, 106–7, 108, 126, 236
   on statutory interpretation 99
   schematic/teleological 100–3
Higgins, Chief Justice 259
High Court (Central Criminal Court) 21, 23, 241–2
   appeals to Supreme Court 281
   civil cases originating in 260–1
   "full original jurisdiction" 254–5, 265, 320
      company/personal insolvency matters 256
      Constitutional cases 255
      criminal 287
      equity/chancery matters 257
      family proceedings 256
      first instance 275, 278
         transfer from Circuit Court 277
      general monetary 255
      judicial review 255–6

Oireachtas Election/
    Referendum Petitions 257
  wardship 257
  judicial reviews 322
  origins 42
  payments into 269
  pleadings in 267–8
  stare decisis in 126
High Representative of the Union
    for Foreign Affairs and
    Security Police 143, 144
Higher Education and Training
    Awards Council (HETAC)
    217
Hobbes, Thomas
  Leviathan 5
Hoffmann, Lord 180
Honourable Society of King's
    Inn 212
House of Lords 321
Human Rights law 31

I

Injunctions 23
  see also Court decisions
Intellectual Property law 31
International Bank of
    Reconstruction and
    Development (IBRD) 176
International Court of Justice (ICJ)
    166, 176
International Criminal Court 182
International Development
    Association (IDA) 177
International law 31, 166
  agreements 172–3
  dualism/monism 170
  general principles 169
  Irish law and 170–2
  judicial decisions 169
  private 166–7
    codification/harmonisation
      185
    EU law and 185
    jurisdiction 184–5
  sources of 167
    customs 168–9
    treaties 168
  tribunals
    International Criminal Court
      (ICC) 182
    for Former Yugoslavia,
      Rhwanda, Sierra Leone
      182
  withdrawing from treaties
    183–4
  writings/teachings of publicists
    169
International Monetary Fund
    (IMF) 176–7
International Trade Organisation
    (ITO) 177
Ireland
  administration of justice in
    in public 236–7
    main features 235–6
  international organisations and
    173–8
Iris Oifiguil 87
Irish court system
  appeals
    de novo hearing 243–4
    findings of facts 244–5
    on a point of law 244
  appellate jurisdiction 243
  first instance jurisdiction
    243, 250

regulating business 243
McKenzie friend in 331
structure of 241
   courts of local/limited jurisdiction 242–3
   High/Supreme Court 241–2
Irish Declaration of Independence (1919) 41
Irish Famine (1845–50) 40
Irish Free State (*Saorstát Éireann*) 235
   Constitution (1922) of 41
Irish government *see* Irish State
Irish Institute of Legal Executives 220–1
Irish Jurists Reports 117
Irish Law Reports Monthly (ILRM) 117, 118
Irish Law Times 117
Irish legal system
   see also Constitution (1937); Irish court system
   equity 38
   EU law and 150–1
   impeaching a judge 206–7
   International law and 170–2
   origins 37
      Belfast Agreement 43–4
      EEC membership 43
      ECHR (European Convention on Human Rights) 44, 179–81
      Penal laws 39
      new system 41–2
      reform 40
         government 41
         land law 41
   statute (English) law 38
Irish Nation 51

Irish Parliament *see* Oireachtas
Irish President *see* Irish State
Irish Reports (IR) 117, 118
Irish Sentencing Information System (ISIS) 317
Irish State 51–2
   Council of 88
   Institutions of 52
      Council of State 56–7
      Dáil Éireann 58–9
      government 60
         composition 62
         executive power 64
         Green Paper 84
         Taoiseach/Tanaiste 62–3
      Oireachtas 57–8
      President 53
         functions of 53–5
         legislation 86–7
         removal of 55
      Presidential Commission 55
      Seanad Éireann 59–61
   nation 51
Irish Volunteers 39

J

Judgement creditors 313
Judicial Committee of the House of Lords 40
Judicial review
   definition of 320
   law of 320–1
   remedies available 321–2
Judiciary, the
   appointment 200–1
   hierarchy/composition 198–200
   immunities 204
   independence 202–3

judicial council/commission 204
qualifications 201–2
remuneration 203–4
termination 204
   impeachment 205–7
   resignation 205
   retirement 205
Judiciary Appointments Advisory Board 200–1
Jurisprudence 6, 31
Jury, the
   composition 207–8
   dis/advantages 209
   function 208
   reform 209–11
   verdict 208
Justices of the Peace 40
Justis 117

K

Keane, Chief Justice 71
Kearns, Justice 171, 180–1
Kelly, Justice Cyril 206, 331
Kenny, Justice 70, 126, 235, 329
King Edward VIII 42
King Henry 37
Kingsmill Moore, Justice 125

L

Laffoy, Justice 180, 237, 314
Land law 28, 29, 31
Latin maxims (Rules of language) 109
Law clerks 220
Law library 213–4
Law of Torts *see* Torts law
Law reform
   agencies 373–5
   limitations 375
   constitutional change 373
   EU law 373
   mechanisms 371
      courts 372
      Oireachtas 372, 373
Law Reform Commission 110, 349, 373–4
   membership 374
   Report on:
   Alternative Dispute Resolutions: Mediation and Conciliation 349
   Jury Service 2013 209–11
   Personal Debt Management and Debt Enforcement 314
   Public Inquiries Including Tribunals of Inquiries 354
   work of 374–5
Law School of King's Inn 212
Law Society of Ireland 216, 217, 218
Laws, retrospective 9
'Lawyer' 224
Legal Aid 331–2
Legal Aid Board 332
Legal personality 8–9
Legal positivism 6–8
Legal principle 5
Legal procedures 5
Legal profession 211
   fusion of 224
   law officers 224–8
   reform of 221–3
      new (proposed) regularity authority 223–4
Legal Services Ombudsman 358–9
Legal subjects, table of 30–1
Legislation

finding 83
interpreting 94
  aids to 104
    extrinsic/external
      commission reports 110
      historical setting 110
      parliamentary materials etc 110–1
      previous statues 110
  language rules 109
  presumptions 105–8
  principal approaches 96–8
    literal 98–100
    schematic/teleological 100–4
  traditional rules 95
    golden 95–6
    literal 95
    mischief 96
primary 82
  structure 83
process
  Bills *see* Bills
secondary 82
  control of 92
    by courts 92–3
    by Oireachtas 93
  introduction 89–90
  instruments 83, 91–2
LEXIS-NEXIS 117
"Lifting the corporate veil" 9
Locus standi (Standing)
  definition of 23
  requirement for 298–9

M

McCracken, Justice 103
'McKenzie friend' 330–1
Macken, Justice 331
Madrid European Council 138
Matthews, Justice 206
Media law 31
Mediation *see* Disputes, resolving
Medical law 31
Mens rea 21
Merger Treaty 1965 133–4
Minister for Justice, Equality and Law Reform 229
Money Bills *see* Legislation
'Monist theory' 170
Morality and law 6

N

Napoleonic Code 15
Natural law theory 8
Norman conquest 13
North Atlantic Treaty Organisation (NATO) 130

O

O'Donoghue, John (Minister for Justice) 206
O'Flaherty, Justice Hugh 206
O'Higgins, Chief Justice 73
O'Reilly, Emma 140
Obiter dictum 120
Oireachtas (Irish Parliament) 5
  acts of 83
    jurisdiction 108
  All Party, Group on the Constitution 77–8
  as State institution 57–8
  intervening in rules of evidence 305
  legislative powers 64

controlling secondary
  legislation 92–3
  reform 372, 373
Ombudsmen 354–5
  others 357–9
  power of 356–7
  remit of 355–6
Ombudsman for Children's Office
  (OCO) 357
Ombudsman for the Defence
  Forces 358
Ordinary Referendum 75–6
Organisation for Economic
  Co-Operation 130
Overrule 121

P

Paralegals *see* Registered legal
  executives
Penal Codes 15, 39
Pensions Ombudsman 358
Personal Injuries Assessment
  Board
  aims of 359
  compensations 360–1
  impact of 361–2
  procedure 360
Plato 8
'Poundage' 312
Poynings' Law 38
Per Incuriam 121
Presumption Against Extra-
  Territorial Effect 108
Presumption Against
  Retrospective Effect 108
Presumption Against Unclear
  Changes in the Law 107
Presumption of Compatibility with
  EU Law 106

Presumption of Compatibility with
  International law 106–7
Presumption of Constitutionality
  106
Presumption of Innocence 22
Presumption that a Statute Should
  be Given an Updated
  Meaning 107
Presumption that all Words Bear a
  Meaning 107
Presumption that Penal Statutes be
  Construed Strictly 107–8
Presumption that Revenue Statues
  should be Construed Strictly
  108
Private law
  subjects of 28
Probation Service 229
Procedural law 27
  definition of 26
Public law 28
  components 27

Q

Quinlan, Michael (Dublin County
  Registrar) 206

R

Ratio decidendi 119–20
Raz, Joseph 6–7
  The Concept of a Legal System
  (Oxford University Press,
  1980) 5
Registered legal executives
  (paralegals) 220–1
Regulators *see* Disputes, resolving
Remedies *see* Court decisions
Restitutio in integram 309

Retrials 285
Res Judicata 121
Revenue Commission 76–7, 312–3
Revenue debts 312–3
Revenue sheriffs 312
Reverse 121
Right of access 329–30
   court fees 332
   legal aid
     civil 331–2
     criminal 332
   legal costs 333
   litigants in person 330
   'McKenzie friend' 330–1
Right to litigate 329
Rights Tribunals 23
Rules of law
   definition of 9–10
   primary 7
   secondary 7

S

Scotland
   EU and 160
Seanad Éireann 59–60
   abolition question 61
   approving a Bill 86
   Cathaoirleach 60
   functions 60–1
     Money Bills 87–8
Second World War 182
Secondary sources of law
   commentaries/academic
     writing 191
   Canon law 190
   custom 189
Separation of powers 63
   see also Constitution (1937)
'Serious offence', definition of 293

Sharia Law 15
Shaw, Lord 96
"Sheedy Affair" 206
Single European Act 1986 134
Sixth of George I 39
Small Claims Courts 349
Solicitors
   see also Barristers
   admission to the profession
     217–9
   advertising 219–20
   discipline/conduct 219–20
   "no foal, no fee" 220
   role of 216–7
Solicitors' Disciplinary Tribunal
   219, 223
Special Criminal Court 21–22
   first instance jurisdiction
     278–9
St Andrews Agreement 1984 280
Stare decisis ('let the decision
   stand') 13, 115
   in Irish Courts 122–3
     Court of Criminal Appeal 126
     High Court 126
     Supreme Court 124–6
Statute law 38
Statute of Frauds 38
Statutory interpretation *see*
   Henchy, Justice; Legislation
Sub judice rule 320
Sub silento 121
Substantive law 27
   definition of 26
Succession law 31
Supreme Court of Judicature 40,
   241–2
   appeals by prosecution 283
   backlog of cases 325–6

criticised High Court 123
double jeopardy 284, 286
jurisdiction 265
   criminal 286
   incapacity of President 258
   reference of Bills by President 258–9
locus standi
   in constitutional cases 298–9
origins 42
literally interpreting Constitution 73–4
stare decisis in 124–6

T

Tanaiste 63
Tenterden, Chief Justice 329
Taoiseach 63
Tort law 28, 31
Treaty Establishing the European Community (TEC) 135, 147
Treaty of Amsterdam (ToA) 1997 135
Treaty of Lisbon 2007 136, 139–41, 160
Treaty of Nice (ToN) 135
Treaty of Rome 1957 136
Treaty on European Union 1992 134–5
Treaty on the Functioning of the European Union (TFEU) 136, 147
Trials on indictment *see* Criminal litigation

U

United Kingdom (UK)
   withdrawing from EU 160–1
United Nations (UN) 174
   General Assembly 174–5
   International Court of Justice (ICJ) 176
   Secretariat 175–6
   Security Council 175
      Economic and (ECOSOC) 175
United Nations Commission on International Trade Law (UNCITRAL) 185
United Nations Human Rights Committee 280
United Nations Monetary and Financial Conference 176
United Nations Charter 174–5

V

Van Gend criteria 153, 155

W

Walsh, Doctor Willie 190
Walsh, Justice 124–5, 264
Weber, Max 6
Westlaw 117
Woolf, Lord
   'The Woolf Report' 269–71
World Bank 176, 177
World Trade Organisation (WTO) 178